Bedford College

University of London

Memories of 150 Years

Edited by
J Mordaunt Crook

Royal Holloway and Bedford New College

2001

Published by
Royal Holloway and Bedford New College, Egham, Surrey TW20 0EX, UK

ISBN 0 902194 42 9

Contents

List of Illustrations iv
Outline Chronology ix
List of Contributors xi
Introduction 1
1. Marigold Pakenham-Walsh: Bedford College, 1849–1985 13
2. John Prebble: Biochemistry 47
3. Leslie J Audus: Botany 63
4. Margaret M Harris (née Jamison): Chemistry 81
5. Tatiana Wolff: English 95
6. Eva Jacobs: French 109
7. David Hilling: Geography 131
8. Grace Page & Alec J Smith: Geology 149
9. Patricia Howe: German 181
10. J Mordaunt Crook: History 201
11. Peter Armour: Italian 227
12. Paul M Cohn: Mathematics 243
13. Mark Sainsbury: Philosophy 253
14. Peter Rice-Evans: Physics 259
15. Maureen Young: Physiology 277
16. Elizabeth R Valentine: Psychology 295
17. Gavin Drewry & Jenny Brock: Social Studies & Social Science 313
18. Rodney Dales: Zoology 335
19. Dorothy Wedderburn: A New Beginning: The Merger of Bedford with Royal Holloway College, 1981–85 355
20. Marta Baker: Postscript: Sesquicentenary Celebrations Year 1999 377
Index of Names 383

List of Illustrations

Supplied by contributors, College Archives and photographers, and former and current staff and students.

Between pages 200 and 201

Biochemistry

1. Professor Dudley Cheesman, first Head of the Biochemistry Department.
2. Biochemists, 1963.

Botany

3. Dr Ethel Nancy Miles Thomas, first Head of the Botany Department.
4. The Müller House for unravelling the nutritional requirements of conifer seedlings.
5. The Siemans übermikroscop with which the Electron Microscopy Unit was started.

Geography

6. Geography Department teaching staff, 1920–85.
7. The Geography Department, 1951. Staff seated from left to right: Eleanor Vollans, Alan Mountjoy, Dora Smee, Gordon Manley, Eunice Timberlake and John Paterson.
8. Field class, Hadrian's Wall, 1959, Gordon Manley and Eleanor Vollans at back right.
9. Off to Egham, 1985.

Classics

10a. Dorothy Tarrant, Professor of Greek, 1936–50.

10b. Max Cary, Professor of Ancient History, 1908–46.

History

11. S R Gardiner: our greatest historian, Head of Ancient and Modern History 1862–81.
12. H W Nevinson: radical activist, Head of Ancient and Modern History 1885–91.
13. J W Allen: political theorist, Head of Medieval and Modern History 1891–1926.
14. Dame Lillian Penson: first woman Vice-Chancellor, Head of the History Department 1930–61.
15. From left, Ilse Crawford, Dorothy Wedderburn, Caroline Barron, Joe Mordaunt Crook, Nicola Sutherland and Karen Bull, St. John's Lodge, 16 January 1982.

Zoology

16. C L Boulanger, Head of the Zoology Department 1923–40, with glasses, facing the camera, in 1933.
17. H Munro Fox FRS, Head of Zoology Department 1941–54, in his Cambridge laboratory between 1941 and 1944.
18. Norman Millott, Head of the Zoology Department 1955 –69
19. Rodney Dales, Head of the Zoology Department 1971–85 (and RHBNC 1985–1992) c. 1971.
20. H W Marrett Tims, back left, Head of the Zoology Department 1898–1922 with Dr John Edkins (back right) Head of Physiology, Professor Harding (front left), Mathematics and Miss Ethel Hurlblatt, Principal.
21. Miss Ince, 1929–68.
22. Philippa Esdale 1915–19, probably taken on the occasion of her DSc in 1917.
23. C W Blaxland Benham, 1885–98.
24. Don Field 1951–85 (and at RHBNC 1985–98) in 1971. Chief technician to three departmental professors.
25. Zoology Department, 1957.

Between pages 312 and 313

Physics

26. Oliver Lodge on his honeymoon in 1877 in Heidelberg.
27. Frederick Womack: long-serving Head of the Physics Department. The spectrometer setting is curious.
28. The new Physics laboratory in Baker Street opened by Empress Frederick in 1891.
29. William Wilson: intellectual giant.
30. Kathleen Lonsdale: brilliant postgraduate.
31. William Wilson lecturing at Cambridge.
32. H T Flint: profound thinker.
33. Harold Richardson : ardent nuclear physicist.
34. Richardson's beta ray spectrometer.
35. Laboratory scene, 1970.
36. Physics staff and final year undergraduates in 1973. Standing, from left, 2nd Noel Stewart, 3rd Stuart Owen-Jones, 4th Michael Hoare, 5th Tom Taylor, 19th Robin Thomas. Sitting, from left, 2nd Nora Hill, 4th Dick Mansfield, 6th Harold Richardson, 7th Leo Pincherle.
37. A student snapshot of Peter Rice-Evans in Physics theatre, Acland.
38. Roland Dobbs with Her Majesty Queen Elizabeth The Queen Mother, Regent's Park 1984.

Psychology

39. Beatrice Edgell, 1871–1948.
40. Victoria Hazlitt, 1887–1932. Courtesy of British Psychological Association

A New Beginning

41. Signing the partnership agreement with Royal Holloway College, 1982. From left, Dr Roy Miller, Principal of Royal Holloway College 1982-85, Sir Owen Saunders, Chairman of the Royal Holloway College Council, Professor Dorothy Wedderburn, Principal of Bedford College 1981-85 and of RHBNC 1985-90, and Sir Cyril Clarke, Chairman of the Bedford College Council.

Postscript

42 The Fawcett Lecture 17 February 1999. Professor Dorothy Wedderburn, Principal BC 1981–85, RHBNC 1985–90; Baroness Warnock, College Visitor 1997–2000, and Professor Norman Gowar, Principal RHBNC 1990–99.

43 Honorary Fellows Awards Ceremony 5 May 1999. From left: Miss Patricia Brown, Member of Bedford and RHBNC Councils; Professor Janet Finch CBE, Vice-Chancellor of Keele University, and Mrs Sarah Tyacke CB, Keeper of Public Records and Chief Executive, Public Record Office.

44 Honorary Degrees Awards Ceremony 15 July 1999. Professor Alec Smith, Honorary Fellow and former Head of Geology Department is being presented to HRH The Princess Royal.

45 Winifred Procter (née Nash), who graduated in 1933, was the oldest attendee at the 'Down Memory Lane Reunion'.

46 'Down Memory Lane' Reunion at Regent's Park on 23 May 1999.

47 'Women and Brainpower' Conference 4–6 July 1999. Front row from left: Dr Lyndal Roper, History Department, RHBNC; Dr Amanda Vickery, History Department RHBNC; Professor Penelope Corfield (Conference Organiser), History Department, BC and RHBNC; Dr Yasodka Shanmugasundaram, Vice-Chancellor, Mother Theresa Women's University, India, and Professor Dorothy Wedderburn, Principal BC 1981–85, RHBNC 1985–90.

48 The plaque. Bedford Centre for the History of Women.

49 Opening of the Bedford Centre for the History of Women on 6 July 1999. Baroness Helena Kennedy QC (left) who delivered the Public Lecture 'Women & Brainpower' with Dr Amanda Vickery, History Department, RHBNC.

50 Honorary Degrees Awards Ceremony on 15 July 1999. Honorary Graduates seated with HRH The Princess Royal, left to right: Dame Pauline Neville-Jones DCMG, businesswoman and civil servant; The Hon Dame Mary Arden DBE, first woman Chair of the Law Commission of England and Wales; Professor Susan

Greenfield CBE, first woman Director of The Royal Institution of Great Britain, and Professor Patricia Easterling, first woman Regius Professor of Greek at Cambridge University.

51 'Down Memory Lane 2' Reunion at Regent's Park on 18 September 1999.

52 Bedford Gala Dinner on 1 October 1999. Former Presidents of the Bedford Students' Union with Elizabeth Kirk, Reid Student (first from left) and Josh Davis, President of the Students' Union, RHBNC 1999/2000 (second from right).

53 Bedford Gala Dinner on 1 October 1999. Mrs Marta Baker, Alumni Relations and Events Officer receives a bouquet from Dr Caroline Barron for masterminding the Sesquicentenary Celebrations.

Outline Chronology

1849 The College was founded by Elizabeth Jesser Reid for the higher education of women. It was originally called the Ladies' College, 47 Bedford Square.

1866 Death of Elizabeth Jesser Reid. She made provision in her will for the Reid Trust to be established to promote and fund women's education. The Trust was administered by Elizabeth Bostock, Jane Martineau and Eleanor Smith.

1874 The College moved to 8 and 9 York Place, Baker Street.

1878 The University of London admitted women to its degrees.

1900 The College was incorporated as a School of the newly created teaching University of London.

1913 The new College premises at Regent's Park, designed by Basil Champneys, were officially opened by HM Queen Mary who, with HM Queen Alexandra, was joint Patron of the College. In the same year, Caroline Spurgeon was appointed Professor of English Literature, at a time when Margaret Benson at Royal Holloway College was the only other woman University Professor in Britain.

1931 The Tuke Building named after Dame Margaret Tuke, Principal from 1907 to 1929, was opened by HM Queen Mary.

1941 On 10 May, the Regent's Park buildings were bombed. The students and most of the staff had been evacuated to Cambridge.

1946 The first ten male postgraduate students were admitted.

1948 Lillian Penson, Professor of Modern History, became Vice-Chancellor of the University, the first woman in any Commonwealth university to be appointed to this position.

1949 Centenary Celebrations included a visit by HM Queen Mary.

1965 Following the Robbins Report calling for an expansion in student numbers, the College admitted 50 male undergraduates.

1982 A partnership agreement was signed between Bedford College and Royal Holloway College, paving the way for the merger in 1985.

1984 HM Queen Elizabeth the Queen Mother, Patron of the College since 1953, paid a farewell visit to Regent's Park.

1985 Royal Holloway & Bedford New College Act became law on 1 August.

1999 Sesquicentenary Celebrations to mark the 150th anniversary of the founding of Bedford College included a visit by HRH The Princess Royal.

List of Contributors

Peter ARMOUR, BA (Manchester), PhD (Leicester), FRSA. Lecturer, Sheffield 1966–72; Lecturer, Leicester 1972–79; Lecturer, Bedford College 1979–1984; Lecturer, University College London 1984–89; Professor of Italian, RHBNC 1989–99; Head of Department 1989–96, Research Professor 1999–. Publications include: *The Door of Purgatory: A Study of Multiple Symbolism in Dante's 'Purgatorio'* (1983); *Dante's Griffin and the History of the World* (1989); articles on Dante, medieval Italian literature and culture and the art and poetry of Michelangelo.

Leslie John AUDUS, MA, PhD, ScD (Cantab), Hon FLS, FInst Biol. Lecturer University College, Cardiff 1935–40; FLt RAFVR (Radar) 1940–46; Japanese POW, Eastern Indonesia 1942–45; SSO ARC Unit of Soil Metabolism 1946–48; Hildred Carlile Professor of Botany, Bedford College, 1948–79 (Emeritus,1979–). Publications include: *Plant Growth Substances,* 4 edns. (1953, 54, 63, 72); *Physiology and Biochemistry of Herbicides*, 2 edns, (1964, 76); *Spice Island Slaves* (1996.)

Marta BAKER, MA (Lodz, Poland), AMIPR. PA to Professor Dorothy Wedderburn, Principal, Bedford College 1983–85. Administrative Assistant to Professor Dorothy Wedderburn, Principal RHBNC 1985–90; Administative Assistant to Professor Norman Gowar, Principal RHBNC 1990–92. Public Relations Administrator, RHBNC 1992–1996; Alumni Relations and Events Officer, RHBNC 1996–1999; Events Offiicer, RHBNC 1999–. Responsible for managing Sesquicentenary Celebrations 1999.

Jenny BROCK, BA, MPhil (London). Sociology Dept, Bedford College, Undergraduate student 1964–67; Postgraduate student 1967–69; Research Officer, Legal Research Unit 1969–72; Lecturer in Social Policy 1972–79. Currently Partnership Funding Manager, Tower

Hamlets Primary Care Trust. Co-author, with Gavin Drewry, of publications on the House of Lords.

Paul M COHN, MA, PhD (Cantab), FRS. Lecturer, Manchester University 1952–62; Reader, QMC 1962–67; Professor of Mathematics, Bedford College 1967–84; UCL 1984–86; Astor Professor of Mathematics, UCL 1986–89. Emeritus Professor of Mathematics, University of London and Honorary Research Fellow in Mathematics, UCL 1989–. Editor *London Maths Soc Monographs* 1968–77, 1986–93. Publications include: *Universal Algebra* (1965), 2nd edn (1981); *Algebra* vol 1 (1974), 2nd edn (1982), vol 2 (1977), 2nd edn (1989), vol 3 (1990); *Elements of Linear Algebra* (1994), and contributions to *Encyclopedia Britannica.*

Joseph Mordaunt CROOK, MA, DPhil (Oxon), FBA, FSA. Bedford College and RHBNC: Lecturer, Reader, Professor of Architectural History, Director of Victorian Studies 1965–1999. Slade Professor, University of Oxford 1979–80. Waynflete Lecturer, Magdalen College, Oxford 1985. Visiting Fellow, Gonville and Caius College, Cambridge 1986. Public Orator, University of London 1988–90. Emeritus Professor of Architectural History, University of London 1999–. Publications include: (ed) *Eastlake, A History of the Gothic Revival* (1970, 1978); *The Greek Revival: Neo-Classical Attitudes in British Architecture, 1760–1870* (1972, 1995); *The British Museum* (1972); (jointly), *The History of the King's Works, vols 5–6, 1660–1851* (1973, 1976); *William Burges and the High Victorian Dream* (1981); *The Dilemma of Style: Architectural Ideas from the Picturesque to the Post Modern* (1987, 1989); *The Rise of the Nouveaux Riches: Style and Status in Victorian and Edwardian Architecture* (1999, 2001).

Rodney DALES, BSc, PhD (London). Research Associate, University of California 1950–51; Lecturer in Zoology, Sir John Cass College, London 1951–55; Assistant Lecturer in Zoology, Bedford College, 1955, Lecturer 1956, Reader 1964, Professor and Head of Department 1970. Dean of Science 1974–76; Member of Council;

Secretary to the Board of Studies in Zoology 1965–1970, Chairman 1982–85; First Dean of Science, RHBNC. Emeritus Professor, University of London, 1992–. Publications include: *Annelids, Practical Invertebrates Zoology,* and over 80 scientific papers.

Gavin DREWRY, BSc (Southampton). Research Officer, Legal Research Unit, Bedford College, 1966–69; Lecturer in Government, 1969–84; Reader in Social Administration, 1984–89; Professor of Public Administration, RHBNC 1989–, Director of the Centre for Political Studies 1990–. Head of Department of Social and Political Science 1992–96. Publications include: books, chapters and articles on public sector reform, public law, the legislative process and parliamentary committees. Recent books: co-author *The Law and Parliament,* (1998); *Law and the Spirit of Inquiry* (1999).

Margaret Manderson HARRIS (née Jamison), BSc, PhD, DSc (London). Student of Chemistry, Bedford College 1932–35; Postgraduate Studentship at Bedford followed by posts as Demonstrator, Junior Lecturer, Lecturer, Senior Lecturer and Reader until retirement in 1979. Publications include: over 43 research papers mainly in the *Journal of the Chemical Society,* a textbook *Organic Chemistry* (with E E Turner, FRS 1952), contributed chapters to *Progress in Stereochemistry,* vol.2 (1956) and vol.4 (joint editor with B J Aylett 1969).

David HILLING, MSc (Wales), PhD (London). Lecturer in Geography, University of Ghana 1961–66; Lecturer in Geography, Bedford College 1966–78; Senior Lecturer, Bedford College and RHBNC 1978–96. Retired 1996. Honorary Research Fellow in Geography and Honorary Associate, RHBNC 1997. Publications include: *Barge Carrier Systems* (1978); *Africa–Geography and Development* (with A B Mountjoy 1984); *Transport and Developing Countries* (1996).

Patricia HOWE, BA, MA (London) from Bedford College. Bedford College: Assistant Lecturer in German 1966–69; Lecturer in German 1969–84; Member of Council; Westfield College and Queen

Mary and Westfield College: Lecturer in German 1984–88; Senior Lecturer 1988. Publications include: *Women's Writing 1830–1890* in *A History of Women's Writing in Germany, Austria and Switzerland* edited by M Catling (2000); *Die Wirklichkeit ist anders Ida Pfeifer's Visit to China 1847, German Life and Letters* (1999); *Grateful Astonishment and Faint Horror: Biographies of Fontane* (2000); *Theodor Fontane and the European Context: Literature, Culture and Society in Prussia and Europe,* edited with Helen Chambers (forthcoming).

Eva JACOBS, BA, MA (London), DUniv (Paris). Student at Bedford College 1951–56; Research Fellow, University of Nottingham 1957–60; Assistant Lecturer in French Language and Literature, Bedford College 1960–62; Lecturer, Bedford College 1962–78; Senior Lecturer, Bedford College 1978–84; Senior Lecturer, Queen Mary College 1984-1988. Publications include: *Voltaire and Tragedy* (1987) and a critical edition of Voltaire's *Zaïre* in *The Complete Works of Voltaire*, vol.8 (1988).

Grace M PAGE (née DUNLOP), BSc, PhD (Glasgow). Assistant in Geology, University of Edinburgh 1954–58; Assistant Lecturer in Geology, Bedford College 1958–59; Lecturer in Geology, Bedford College 1959–85; Lecturer in Geology 1985–91, RHBNC; Dean of Reid Hall 1962–71; Honorary Associate, RHBNC 1992.

Marigold PAKENHAM-WALSH, MA (Cantab). Assistant Secretary/Deputy Secretary & Registrar, Bedford College 1968–85. During the merger years, with Richard Hardy, Secretary of RHC, responsible for the drafting of the RHBNC Act which created the new College. During 1985–86 based at Regent's Park, helping with the move of the Academic Departments and of the Archive collection to Egham. Planning Officer, RHBNC 1986–90. Retired 1990. Honorary Associate, RHBNC 1991.

John PREBBLE, BSc, PhD (London). Lecturer/Senior Lecturer in Biochemistry, Bedford College 1960–85; Head of Department of

Biochemistry 1982–85; Dean of Science 1982–83; Vice-Principal, Bedford College 1983–85; Vice-Principal RHBNC 1985–97. Retired 1997. Honorary Fellow, RHBNC 2000. Publications include: *Mitochondria Chloroplasts and Bacterial Membranes* (1981); *Wandering in the Gardens of the Mind. A Biography of Peter Mitchell and Glynn* (to be published in 2002).

Peter RICE-EVANS, BSc, PhD, DSc (London), MBA (Columbia). Lecturer, Bedford College 1962–78, Reader in Experimental Physics, Bedford College 1978–88. Professor of Experimental Physics, RHBNC 1988–99. Retired 1999. Professor Emeritus, University of London and Leverhulme Fellow 2000–. Engaged in continuing research in positron physics, elucidating the formation of positronium.

Mark SAINSBURY, MA, DPhil (Oxford). Lecturer in Philosophy: Magdalen College, Oxford 1968–70; St Hilda's College, Oxford 1970–73; Brasenose College, Oxford 1973–75; University of Essex 1975–78; Bedford College 1978–84; King's College London: Lecturer in Philosophy 1984–87; Reader in Philosophy 1987–89; Stebbing Professor of Philosophy 1989–. *Editor Mind* 1990–2000. Publications include: *Russell* (1979); *Paradoxes* (1988), 2nd edn (1995); *Logical Forms* (1991).

Alec SMITH, BSc, PhD (University of Wales at Aberystwyth). Lecturer, UCL 1957–65; Reader, UCL 1965–77; Professor of Geology and Head of Department, Bedford College 1977–85; Foundation Professor of Geology and Head of Department, RHBNC 1985–92. Honorary Fellow, RHBNC 1998. Chairman NERC Geological Science Research Grant Committee, President of Geologists' Association and Founder of *Geology Today*. Medallist of Geological Society of London.

Elizabeth R VALENTINE, BA, PhD (London), FBPsS, CPsychol, Lecturer in Psychology, Bedford College and RHBNC 1972–92; Senior Lecturer in Psychology, RHBNC 1992–97; Reader in Psychology, RHBNC 1997–. Publications include: *Conceptual Issues in Psychology*, 2nd edition, (1997); *Psychology at Bedford College London 1849–1985*, RHBNC (1997); (with J Wilding) *Superior Memory* (1997); co-editor *Phenomenology and Cognitive Science: Handbook* (1996); editor *History and Philosophy of Psychology*.

Dorothy WEDDERBURN, MA (Cantab). Research Officer/ Senior Research Officer, Applied Economics, Cambridge 1950–65; Imperial College: Lecturer/Reader/Professor in Industrial Sociology, Director Industrial Sociology Unit 1965–81; Principal, Bedford College 1981–85; Principal, RHBNC 1985–90; Pro-Vice-Chancellor, University of London 1986–88. Retired 1990. Honorary Fellow, RHBNC 1991, Senior Research Fellow, Imperial College 1981–. Publications include: *White Collar Redundancy* (1964); *Redundancy and the Railwayman* (1964); *Enterprise Planning for Change* (with J E G Utting 1968); *Old Age in Three Industrial Societies* (with Rosemary Crompton 1968); editor *Poverty, Inequality and Class Structure* (1974).

Tatiana WOLFF, BA Hons, MA (London) from Bedford. Assistant Lecturer, English Department, Bedford College 1947–50; Teacher of English, Loughton County High School for Girls 1951–84. Publications include: an edition of Spenser *Fairie Queene*, book 6 (1959); Christopher Marlowe *Tamburlaine the Great,* Part 1 & 2 (1964); *Pushkin on Literature* (1971, 1986, 1999); *Lines on the Underground. An Anthology for London Travellers* (with Dorothy Meade 1994).

Maureen YOUNG, BSc Physiology (London) from Bedford College. Assistant SW London Blood Transfusion Unit 1939–41 (MRC and Ministry of Health War Emergency scheme). Demonstrator in Physiology, Bedford College 1941–46; Lecturer in Physiology, Sherrington School of Physiology, St Thomas's Hospital Medical School 1946–56; Senior Lecturer/Reader moving through department of Medicine to Gynaecology 1976–82; Personal Chair in Perinatal Physiology 1982. Publications include: works on foetal nutrition and growth; *What is Baby Expecting?* (in press).

Introduction

J Mordaunt Crook

"Oh I wish
That I were some great Princess, I would build
Far off from men a college like a Man's,
And I would teach them all that men are taught."

(Tennyson, *The Princess*, 1847)

When Bedford College celebrated its centenary on 19 May 1949, the thought that within thirty-five years the college itself might cease to exist, would surely have seemed preposterous. Of its eight science professors three were Fellows of the Royal Society; and among its arts professors–in the centenary procession that day, just a few steps behind Queen Mary herself–was Professor (later Dame Lillian) Penson, Vice-Chancellor that very year of the most powerful university in the world. As a thousand guests waltzed their way through the Centenary Ball, how many could possibly have guessed that Bedford would celebrate its 150th anniversary not as an independent college but as part of a most unlikely consortium with an even more unlikely name: Royal Holloway and Bedford New College?

And yet the signs were there for those with eyes to see. By 1962–when I arrived at Bedford as a Tutorial Research Fellow–the signals were becoming more insistent. Bedford's days as a college for women–albeit a college for women often taught by men–were already numbered. As early as 1956, the University Grants Committee–with an eye for expansion–had suggested that a college of higher education specifically set aside for women, might already be regarded as "an anachronism".[1] Four years later–with an eye to economy of scale–Senate House proposed that all three London women's colleges might at least consider admitting men.[2] It took three years to persuade Westfield and Royal Holloway. It took four to persuade Bedford.[3] By 1965–when I returned to Regent's Park as a Lecturer in History–the die was already cast. Henceforward, in an age of post-Robbins expansion, Bedford would welcome men as undergraduates–since 1946 they had been there as postgraduates–and on an equal footing with women. The implications of that change, however, took quite a while to sink in. In the first place, increasing numbers quickly ruled out residential accommodation on campus. Ancillary halls of residence would now be the rule. There had always been non-resident students at Bedford; but it had been the residents who set the tone of the place. That ethos would now change. In the second place, the admission of men presented a formidable challenge to our science departments. Integrated admissions had long been seen as the only possible solution to problems of recruitment; but more students brought more problems. We embarked upon expansion without first securing sufficient infrastructural resources. It was a curious paradox. The problem of insufficient science students had been solved, but only by creating an even trickier conundrum: how could we possibly balance increasing numbers–and accelerating costs–with fast diminishing resources? In the 1960s numbers expanded; in the 1970s funding contracted. By 1981 we were on the brink of bankruptcy. By 1983–when I delivered Bedford's last inaugural lecture, as Professor of Architectural History–the college had finally bowed to financial pressure. We agreed to merge with Royal Holloway.

But Bedford had never been academically autonomous. Teaching had always been shared on an intercollegiate basis. Even so, we had attempted to cover a very wide spectrum of subjects, in science as well as arts. After all, this was England's first institution for the higher education of women; proud of its ability to compete with men in any academic field. But we never in fact had a monopoly of women's higher education in London, or anything like it.[4] By the late 1870s–and right up to the turn of the century–there were more women studying at University College than at Bedford.[5] And nearly as many were studying–albeit with semi-detached status–at King's. Only at Bedford, however–and later at Westfield and Royal Holloway–was there an institution with a full range of teaching, specifically set apart for the higher education of women. That meant commitment to a body of corporate values tied up with the notion of separate development.[6] On 9 February 1911, when the Principal of Bedford, Margaret (later Dame Margaret) Tuke, and the Chairman of Council, Sir Arthur Dyke Acland, gave evidence to the Royal Commission on University Education in London–the Haldane Commission–their argument ran as follows:

Acland: [Bedford] College...comes, we think, third in rank....after University College and King's College... We are quite different...in our aims and work from, say, Newnham College at Cambridge or Somerville College at Oxford. We are not primarily, as they are, residential, with tutors added...[for] university teaching from outside is an essential part of their raison d'être. We are, to put it briefly, a kind of little University to ourselves...we have intercollegiate lectures, attended by both men and women, and we carry on our work just like one of the other colleges.

Haldane: As a complete University College?

Acland: Yes; and...we have just as much right to our position as a men's College would have.

Haldane: And you claim to do it on just as high a level as University or King's?

Acland: Yes... [unfortunately, they are Incorporated Colleges with a stronger financial base], we are without power in the University...

Mrs Creighton: Have you any endowment?

Acland: No, we have no endowment worth speaking of... The bigger we get the larger our expenses grow..."[7]

Plus ça change.

That notion of "a little University to ourselves" implied long-term investment on an ever-expanding scale. In effect, it involved the development of a parallel system within the University of London. In the long run, that commitment proved simply unsustainable. Bedford turned out to be the first and last University College for women in England. Even so, for over one hundred years the ideal was pursued with remarkable success. In the college's first 56 years some 4000 women attended lectures and classes.[8] And when Bedford opened its first laboratories in 1861, they provided women with the opportunity to study practical science, at higher level, for the very first time in England.[9] Purpose-built laboratories for Chemistry and Physics followed in 1890, and again in 1913, together with facilities for Biology, Botany, Physiology, Zoology and Geology. All very impressive. But those were the very decades when Oxford and Cambridge were in process of consolidating all their collegiate laboratories–women's as well as men's–into a single university system. By the time Bedford extended its laboratories in 1931, and rebuilt them in 1949, the very idea of segregated science–specifically for women–was beginning to look a little archaic. As late as the first world war, no doubt, separation did seem necessary. At King's, in the early 1860s, James Clerk Maxwell can hardly have been a welcoming figure: in the early 1870s, at Cambridge, he only allowed women into his physics laboratory during the vacations–when he himself was safely away in Scotland. At UCL, in 1874, women began by receiving instruction in a segregated physics laboratory; thirty years later, Sir William Ramsay "did not encourage women to research with him... [in] fact he rather discouraged women in his [chemistry] laboratory".[10] Such prejudices must have reinforced Bedford's wish to stay independent. Social attitudes, religious traditions and collegiate loyalties all contributed to the same centrifugal pressure. The constitution of the university, and the divergent origins of men's and women's colleges, encouraged continuing collegiate autonomy, and continuing duplication of resources.

Periodically, there were calls for specialisation; for smaller colleges in particular to concentrate their resources, and to make up deficiences by intercollegiate teaching. Lord Haldane proved to be a doughty supporter and fund-raiser for women's education. But in 1912 even he was beginning to have doubts.

Haldane: If we had not these separate institutions at the present moment in London, would it be better to concentrate upon a single central university?

Sir Walter Raleigh: It is the usual question: If you had a tabula rasa what would you do?...But you never have a tabula rasa in this world. We have places with a distinct history, and I should be very sorry to disregard the history entirely and to blot them out and to give them some other name, and so on. I think they have gone quite far enough in that direction by incorporating them in the University.[11]

Once again, *plus ça change*. The Haldane Commission came down in favour of Bedford becoming one of three Constituent Colleges of London University in Arts and Science, along with UCL and King's. But it also recognised that even as "a natural university centre for women students", Bedford could never match its larger, mixed-intake competitors.

In that same year, 1912, the Provost of UCL, Dr Gregory Foster–previously Lecturer in English at Bedford–tried to pour a little oil on these perennially troubled waters. "It [is] not a question of women's colleges", he explained to Haldane; "it is a question of small as compared with large".[12] Well, perhaps; but in practice the two arguments were inextricable: questions of gender were inevitably tied up with questions of scale. Had it not been for the concept of separate development–the notion of segregated tertiary education–intercollegiate rearrangement of departments would certainly have been a lot easier. Architecture, for example, once separately taught at both UCL and King's, had in fact been comfortably concentrated on a single site, in Bloomsbury, in 1913.[13] It could be done. But the argument for women's colleges and the argument for small-scale units proved, in effect, mutually reinforcing. And so, when the argument for separate women's colleges ran out of steam in the early 1960s, the argument for small-scale units was left exposed to counter-arguments of cost. Why maintain a full range of science laboratories once the ideal of segregated women's education had been abandoned? In any case, by that stage it was already clear that our endowments–apart from the princely gift of 100,000 guineas by Sir Hildred Carlile in 1913–had never really matched up to our ambitions.[14]

Between the 1920s and the 1940s, Bedford's problems were disguised: by the distinction of individual teachers; by the recruitment of high-calibre students; by steady–if not generous–public funding; and by–to modern eyes–an enviable absence of inflation. By the early 1960s, however, quite a few of our departments–languages as well as sciences–found themselves either under-subscribed and overstaffed, or else just chronically under-resourced. The prestige was still there; but, to use a sporting metaphor, the college was punching far above its natural weight. In the later 1960s, and throughout the 1970s, as costs rose higher and inflation eroded the bases of government funding, it became quite clear to successive official inquiries–notably Murray (1972) and Swinnerton-Dyer (1980–81)–that some sort of intercollegiate redistribution of resources was inevitable.

But how? The constitution of London University–a confederation of semi-autonomous units–made consensual redistribution fiendishly difficult. "How many brilliant energies have been squandered, how many sweet tempers have been soured in the gallant but forlorn attempt to solve the problem of the University of London!" That was H A L Fisher's view, and he was speaking in 1922.[15] If anything, the situation fifty years later was even trickier. We all knew there would have to be rationalisation; the problem was how to get there. Throughout the 1970s–sometimes in public, more often behind closed doors–Bedford debated its future. Informal approaches, at departmental level, were made to Westfield and UCL, notably by Physics, Geology and History. UCL had always been closer to our liberal, secular tradition; there had been cooperation in arts teaching from the beginning; and in 1903-5 there was even the possibility of an arms-length alliance, with Bedford re-sited in freehold premises in Tavistock Square.[16] But any form of union with UCL would always have been a manifestly unequal marriage. By the 1970s Westfield seemed to be the better bet. A united Bedford and Westfield College, concentrating on arts and social sciences–with science transferred to Egham or Mile End–was certainly a possibility.[17] That indeed was the preferred option of the Swinnerton-Dyer Committee on Academic Organisation in 1981.[18] In June of that year there was even the chance of an imaginative joint appointment: one Principal for Bedford and Westfield combined.[19] But there was little consensus in either college, and even less of a sense of urgency.

When negotiations with Westfield petered out in early summer 1981, Bedford was approached by King's College. Once again discussions–held between May and December that year–proved fruitless.[20] After the Christmas break the minuet began once more: our arts departments looked to Westfield; our scientists started to lust after the leafy acres of Englefield Green; and Royal Holloway itself continued to toy with the idea of a new University of Windsor, based on a union with Brunel. Each of these options was by no means impossible. But in the committee rooms of Bloomsbury the decision had already been made. The new Vice Chancellor, Professor Sir Randolph Quirk, came down firmly in favour of an alliance between Bedford and Holloway at Egham. That was the proposal, put for the first time on 26 January 1982, to a crowded Joint Faculties meeting in Regent's Park. And while

Bedford hesitated, the Senate House formulated its trump-card, the mechanism by which merger would be accomplished. On 31st March the University Court decreed that in future there would be only five government-funded centres for science in London University: University College, King's College, Imperial, Queen Mary and Royal Holloway. Westfield and Bedford were excluded, along with Chelsea and Queen Elizabeth. Bang went our twin-faculty structure; unless, of course, we moved to Egham. That draconian plan–sweetened with financial incentives–had in essence been the theme of three emergency meetings in a single day–the Joint Faculties; Academic Board; and Council of Bedford College–on 30 March 1982. Already widely, if unofficially, canvassed, the plan was presented on all three occasions as the only way to avoid redundancies at Bedford, particularly in science and social science. Thus was the deadlock broken. There were to be no more games of musical chairs: despite protests, despite demonstrations, the music stopped, and we found ourselves at Egham. It turned out in the end to be not at all a bad result; but we got there by accident rather than design.[21]

And not all of us went in the same direction. While talks of merger progressed at collegiate level, negotiations at departmental level–via Subject Area Review Committees–were already juggling with rationalised structures for teaching throughout the university. Bedford was pulled in several directions at once. In the event, Philosophy went to King's; most of Dutch and Italian to UCL; French was largely redistributed between QMC and King's; German between Westfield and QMC; Maths between UCL, QMC and King's.[22] The configuration of our departments was drastically re-ordered. One Professor of English left for Leeds, another for East Anglia via Leiden; the Professor of Aegean Archaeology departed for Gower Street; the Professor of Latin went to South Africa. And of course there were numbers of early retirements. Not a single arts department arrived at Egham intact.

Looking back–and hindsight is the historian's prerogative–one can see the wrong turnings clearly enough: those purpose-built laboratories in 1890 and 1913, 1931 and 1949; the seductions of a leafy leasehold in

1908;[23] the missed chances for intercollegiate rationalisation in the 1960s and 1970s; the rift with Westfield in 1981; the blundering choice of name in 1985. And there were broader mistakes as well. In the 1950s and early 1960s too much energy went into fighting only part of the battle for modernity: the fight for the admission of men. That unhappy episode obscured and delayed a much more fundamental challenge: the transformation of the college in keeping with a new world of big science and mass education. And there was one further distraction. Around 1970 student discontents diverted many of us from coherent forward planning: instead of restructuring our collegiate economy–pruning some departments and expanding others–we debated endlessly about novel systems of representation.

Ultimately, economic and educational trends on a much wider, national scale, conspired against us. The question of our leasehold site turned out in the end to be rather a red herring: Westfield's freehold in Hampstead failed to save it from the procrustean logic of big science. The smaller colleges had simply been overtaken by events. Towards the end–still snugly ensconced at St John's, and The Holme, and Hanover Lodge: the only college in the world with a royal park for a campus–some of us just shut our eyes to the hurricane blowing up outside. It takes a peculiarly solipsistic genius to keep a low profile in Regent's Park. But somehow we managed it. We were certainly not undistinguished: at the time of the merger we had two Fellows of the Royal Society and four Fellows of the British Academy. There were three FBAs in classics alone[24]. But we didn't shout about it. Bedford remained one of London's best-kept secrets. It was all very dignified; but as John Wesley reminded the Church of England, one can actually die of dignity. We learned too late the value of proactive PR.

But that's enough breastbeating. This book of essays celebrates the achievements of Bedford College over a period of 150 years. Its basis is departmental: it focuses on departmental loyalties, departmental memories. That means occasional duplication, and even occasional contradictions. Memory is a very selective instrument. Inevitably there are gaps. Dutch, Greek, Latin and Ancient History are not separately represented. There was no room for music and art, both of which–like teacher-training–played quite a part in the earlier life of the college. There was no room for Bedford's architectural history.[25] No room for student union activities. No room for the library. No room even for sport. These are significant limitations. Even so, there is more than enough to celebrate, and more than enough to remember. Endless tutorials on summer afternoons; the crunch of frost on winter mornings; wild geese and signets at The Holme; the scent of roses in the garden of St John's; the satisfying chunk of tennis balls in the park; a JCR with polished floors, and an SCR with stiff-backed chairs and bone-china tea cups; the sniff of leather bindings in the library; and when Finals were over at last, Summer Dances on the lawn, and the sound of steel bands echoing eerily through the trees. Too good to last.

References

1 *Report of the Council,* Bedford College (1956–57), 22.

2 *Ibid.* (1960–61), 22.

3 "The heroic age of women's education recedes one step further into the past... [Westfield's decision] is formal acknowledgement by an institution of impeccably feminist provenance that the process of assimilation has now gone far enough to make special preserves for women unnecessary...only Bedford College [remains]...to exemplify the principle of segregation" (*The Times* 29 May 1963, p11c).

4 N Harte, *The Admission of Women to University College, London* (1979).

5 F M L Thompson, ed, *The University of London and the World of Learning, 1836–1986* (1990), xix; J Howarth and N Courthays, 'The Political Economy of Women's Higher Education in late 19th and early 20th century Britain', *Historical Studies* cx (1987), 210. College Hall, for women at UCL, was founded in 1882, at 1 Byng Place (H Hale Bellot, *University College, London*, 1929, 373).

6 G Sutherland, in Thompson, *op cit*, 42, 49 and 'The Movement for the Higher Education of Women...c1840–80', in P J Waller, ed, *Politics and Social Change in Modern Britain* (Brighton, 1987), 91–116.

7 *Report and Minutes of Evidence of the Royal Commission on University Education in London* [Haldane Commission, *Parliamentary Papers* 1910, XXIII; 1911, XX; 1912–13, XXII; 1913, XI], qq 7176, 7195–6, 7198, 7282, 7322. Westfield mounted similar arguments, but lacked Bedford's broad spectrum of teaching (*ibid*, qq 8491 et seq) Conveniently, Haldane was also Visitor to Bedford College.

8 *The Times* 9 Nov. 1905, p13f.

9 *The Times* 20 May 1904, p5f.

10 Haldane Commission, q 7189; L Bennett, 'Women's Education: the Bedford Experience', in *Centenary Essays*, ed M Moore (RHBNC, 1988). Newnham established a chemistry laboratory in its college garden in 1875; Girton followed in the 1880s. In 1884 a disused Congregational Chapel in Downing Place, Cambridge, was converted into the Balfour biology laboratory, and used by women students until they were admitted into the university's Physiology and Chemistry laboratories in 1910–11. See A Gardner, *A Short History of Newnham College* (1921), 37–8; A Phillips, ed, *A Newnham Anthology* (1979), 77, 79; Sutherland, in Waller, *op cit*, 96, 112. For Maxwell as Cavendish Professor, 1871–79, see C N L Brooke, *A History of the University of Cambridge, iv, 1870-90* (1993), 182. For college laboratories at Oxford, see B Harrison, ed, *The History of the University of Oxford* viii (1994), 88. For UCL, see Bellot, *op cit*, 371.

11 Haldane Commission, q15, 351.

12 *Ibid*, qq 9571, 8495 and Final Report, pp 58, 61, 67. Haldane ruled out both Westfield and Royal Holloway as Constituent Colleges, on the grounds that they were essentially residential units rather than autonomous teaching institutions (*ibid*, Final Report, p67).

13 J Mordaunt Crook, 'Architecture and History', *Architectural History* xxvii (1984), 555–78.

14 Comparative figures for endowments, fee-income, university grants etc, in 1960–61, are given in N Harte, *The University of London, 1836–1986: an illustrated history* (1986), 256–7. Fund-raising for the Regent's Park site and new buildings in 1905-10 was, however, conducted with some panache (eg *The Times* 22 May 1905, p14; 30 June 1909, p13; 24 June 1910, p4).

15 Sir G Foster, *The University of London* (1922), 42.

16 M J Tuke, *A History of Bedford College for Women, 1849–1937* (1939), 206–7; *The Times* 2 June 1905, p3f; Haldane Commission, qq 9574–80, 9670–73.

17 In the Edwardian period, links between Bedford and Westfield had been "especially close" (Haldane Commission, q 8570); but until the 1960s Westfield remained primarily arts-based. When Haldane suggested that providing science teaching would be "prohibitively" expensive, Westfield replied that it had no wish to offer Honours teaching in science, except for Botany

(*ibid*, q 9728); it also regarded any major increase in numbers as "rather against the genius of the place". For records of the Bedford-Westfield Joint Consultative Committee, 1977–80, see Bedford College Archives, AL117 [meetings began in 1974–75, see *Report of Council*, 1974–75]; for minutes of the Joint Committee of Councils, 1979–82, see Bedford College Archives, GB176; for cooperation between the two colleges, 1972–81, see Bedford College Archives, 280/1/1-3.

18 Second Report, 28 May 1981; *The Times* 2 June 1981, p1; 14 Oct 1981, p24 and 16 Oct 1981, p6.

19 *Times Higher Education Supplement*, 15 May 1981, p3.

20 *The Times* 8 Jan 1982, p3. For details see Bedford College Archives, GB177 (Joint Planning Committee); also AR281/1/1 and 381/4/3. Physics was particularly involved in these negotiations.

21 The saga of merger was debated at length in *The Times Higher Education Supplement* for 1982–3.

22 These rearrangements followed recommendations from Subject Area Review Committees set up in the wake of the Swinnerton-Dyer Report (1980–81). For Bedford's own micro-restructuring working party (1982), see Bedford College Archives, AR283/4/3.

23 When the great appeal was in its early stages, in 1905, the necessity for a freehold site - "freehold ground of our own"–was invariably assumed, following the refusal of the Portman Estate to renew the York Place-Baker Street lease (eg *The Times* 4 April 1905, p8 and 22 May 1905, p14).

24 Professor J N Coldstream (Archaeology), Professor M L West (Greek) and Professor F R D Goodyear (Latin).

25 J Mordaunt Crook, 'The Villas in Regent's Park', *Country Life* cxliii (1968), 22–5, 84–7 (reprinted 1980) and 'The Architectural Image', in Thompson, *University of London, op cit*, 1–33. See also L Bentley, *Educating Women: a pictorial history of Bedford College* (1991).

Chapter 1

Bedford College 1849–1985

Marigold Pakenham-Walsh

Introduction

On 1 October 1849 a lecture given by the Rev C G Nicolay of King's College, London inaugurated The Ladies College in Bedford Square, London. On 31 July 1985 the Governors of Bedford College (University of London) surrendered the College's Royal Charter of Incorporation and on 1 August by means of the Royal Holloway and Bedford New College Act the College was joined with another former women's college to found a new school of the University of London on Egham Hill, Surrey.

Over the intervening 136 years the College had developed from a small privately funded centre for the higher education of women to a fully-fledged school of the University of London open to both men and women with about 1500 students in twenty academic departments–each containing Teachers appointed or recognised by the University–largely financed by public funds.

There is now some controversy about Bedford College's claim to be the first women's college, simply because in its early years it did not conform to the then recognised university pattern of full-time residential education adopted by the Cambridge women's Colleges and Oxford

Halls. In fact Bedford's priority is clear. The college's claim was set out in the first Bedford College calendar in 1888 by Miss Henrietta Busk (one of the first students of the College and pupil of its School, who was a life-long supporter of the College and who at her death in 1936 was commemorated by the imposing wrought-iron gates at the entrance to the Regent's Park buildings) "... we may congratulate ourselves that our attempt (at the Higher Education of Women) paved the way for the now successful women's colleges at Newnham (1871) and Girton (1869) and also the Somerville (1879) and Lady Margaret (1878) Halls".

Foundation 1849

The foundation of The Ladies' College in Bedford Square was part of a movement to open up higher education to those who were barred by various factors from the privileges of the exclusively Anglican universities of Oxford and Cambridge. In 1836 the University of London had been established by Royal Charter as an examining body in the Faculties of Arts, Laws and Medicine (but not Divinity). Its teaching was carried out by University College founded in Gower Street in 1836 as a 'God-less' breakaway from the established order, and by King's College in the Strand–founded in 1839 to counteract 'God-less-ness'–where Divinity was taught.

The Ladies' College was the product of Unitarian thought and planning. Its founder was Mrs Elizabeth Jesser Reid, a devout member of the Unitarian Church who was involved in the many progressive and philanthropic causes taken up by her Church at that time. Throughout her life she had held a dream of "a College for women or something like it". Her aim was not so much to fit women to earn their living and to aspire to high office as to save the daughters of the middle and professional classes from the "dreary futility of life" which was their experience in the early part of the 19th century. She believed that "the elevation of the moral and intellectual character of women (would lead) to an improved state of society".

In 1849 at the age of 60 after many years of consultation, encouraged by, and perhaps spurred on by the foundation in 1848 of

Queen's College in Harley Street, an Anglican establishment for the education of governesses, Mrs Reid fulfilled her dream. She provided £1,500 (expected to be returned to her from fee-income) for the lease of a house in Bedford Square–from which the College subsequently took its name–and for the setting up of a centre where instruction would be given largely by professors from University and King's Colleges in the following subjects:-

Biblical teaching from a strictly non-sectarian point of view, English Grammar and Literature, Latin, Moral Philosophy, Ancient and Modern History, Mathematics, Natural Science, Astronomy and Scientific Geography as well as the subjects normally taught to young ladies of Modern Languages, Elocution, Vocal Music and Harmony, Drawing.

Admission to the classes was open for a moderate fee to "Ladies above the age of 12 years", subject to references.

Early Years, 1849-1869

Mrs Reid had hoped that her new college might be managed by a committee of the enthusiastic ladies who had helped with the planning, with advice and help from the 'Professors' (the title given to all who taught at the College–largely teachers from University and King's Colleges). To her disappointment this proved impractical as the 'Ladies' had no notion of committee work or management and the Professors would not accept direction by amateurs. A form of governance was reluctantly agreed upon but never formally adopted whereby the original planning committee, including the three Trustees whom Mrs Reid had appointed to manage the loan of £1,500 which she had made available for 'pump-priming', formed the non-executive Board. The executive body was the Council elected from among the Board members and from two specially appointed Committees, one of the Ladies and Lady Visitors (the chaperones deemed necessary for classes taught by men) and one of the Professors. These two Committees were to be the "depositories of opinion which must in the long run decide any matters of principle", although the Ladies Committee was "to hold sway in all matters in which female propriety or comfort is concerned". Under this system the College operated uneasily until 1869. "Conflict between the Professors and the Ladies was a constant theme throughout these years."

Management was not the only problem. Contrary to Mrs Reid's hopes women students did not come flocking to the College. In the first term only 68 students registered and of these a high proportion were older married women who attended lectures out of general interest. This in turn caused the financial problems which were to haunt Bedford throughout its history since there was only one major endowment other than Mrs Reid's loan–soon to be converted into a gift–and apart from small sums obtained from supporters the College was dependent on fee-income. Mrs Reid was determined that fees should remain modest.

There were three reasons for this failure in recruitment. Young girls simply did not have sufficient grounding to enable them to cope with teaching at university level. There was still hostility to the idea of educating women. Finally in an era when religious differences were keenly felt there was strong suspicion of non-conformists and 'free-thinkers'. The 'non-sectarian' approach to Bible teaching caused difficulty especially for the Professors from King's College who were forced by their Principal to withdraw from Bedford. It was after one particularly bitter incident that the "one great principle of Education without Religious Test" was formulated by the Council–a principle which was upheld by successive Councils throughout the College's life.

Religious controversy was not the only reason why Professors were lost. The teaching of unprepared students was frustrating to fine scholars and the financial rewards were negligible. By 1850 seven of the thirteen Professors listed in the first prospectus had left and could not easily be replaced–which led to the cancellation of some courses to the chagrin of would-be students. A solution to the first problem was the establishment in 1853 of a Junior Department ('The School') for girls from nine years old, which was expected to increase fee income and serve as a 'feeder' to the College. The project was more successful in providing extra fee income than in introducing new students to the main college.

In 1856 the College was on the brink of financial ruin despite an appeal for funds mounted 1852 and the first hint of a 'merger' was heard. Queen's College, Harley Street, invited representatives to a conference "to agree on some united course of action concerning the ladies' colleges". Probably because of religious differences this was not followed up. Bedford struggled on but had the energy to tighten up its curriculum by introducing systemised courses of study in which Latin and Mathematics were compulsory to replace the existing haphazard choice of lecture courses. To help needy students Mrs Reid introduced the first ever scholarships for women.

Another difficulty came from the Bedford Estates, agents for the freeholders who threatened not to renew the lease of 47 Bedford Square on the grounds that the running of a school on the premises was not permitted under the terms of the lease. This was alarming but was eventually settled favourably to the College by personal appeal to the Duke of Bedford himself.

In 1860 Mrs Reid, now in her 70s, put in Trust the large sum of £16,400–the income (about £800 per annum) to be used for "such purposes connected with and in such manner for the promotion and improvement of female education as the Trustees in their absolute and uncontrolled discretion think fit". She nominated three unmarried women as Trustees with the direction that their successors should also be unmarried women. So Mrs Reid pursued her original intention that the power should be in the hands of women and expressed her doubts about the real support for the College coming from the male Professors.

Mrs Reid died in 1866 and, under the terms of her will, left the lease of 47 Bedford Square to the Trustees as well as the lease of No 48, which she had taken out in 1860 to provide residence for students, up to that time housed in her marital home in Greville Street nearby, and to allow the College (for a rent) to relieve the overcrowding caused by the school. The extra space also allowed the College to innovate by the introduction of practical science teaching.

The three Trustees as holders of the purse strings and landlords and Managers of the Residence were able to exercise a strong influence on developments over the next 25 years or more. All three were friends of Mrs Reid who had been involved in her many projects for social improvement over the years.

Miss Eliza Bostock was typical of the young women tied to family duties and without much formal education whom Bedford College was designed to help. Her influence came mostly through her support of her more confident co-Trustees, and she made many substantial donations to the College.

Miss Jane Martineau came from an influential Unitarian family. Her mother had been one of the 'founding Ladies'. She herself had been a student of the College. She acted as a much-respected Secretary of the Council from 1854 to 1896.

Miss Eleanor Elizabeth Smith was a comparatively new friend of Mrs Reid. She lived with her brother, the Savilian Professor of Geometry at Oxford, and was widely revered in the University for the strength of her intellect. She was able to supply stringent academic standards to the development of the College.

The Trustees shared Mrs Reid's dissatisfaction with the performance of the professors and in 1868 at the time of another financial crisis they staged what Miss Bostock later described as a *coup d'etat.* Before considering further injections of money from the Trust Fund they asked for assurances from the Council on three issues:

- That a high standard of teaching would be maintained;
- That the non-sectarian character of the teaching would be upheld;
- That a new constitution would be drawn up which would give the Council control over the academic affairs of the College.

With strong opposition from the Professors, some of whom resigned rather than submit to inspection, a report was commissioned from one of the Assistant Commissioners of the recent Royal Commission on Middle Class Education. As a result of this, under extreme pressure from the Trustees (they indicated that they would be prepared to issue Notice to Quit the properties) and, despite the objections from those who valued its financial input, the Council closed the Junior Department as inappropriate to an institution teaching at university level.

The Trustees went further in persuading the Council to stand down in favour of a temporary committee appointed by themselves whose office was to reorganise the College and manage its affairs until a permanent constitution was formed. This committee, chaired by the distinguished Rector of Lincoln College, Oxford, with the Chairman of the former College Council as his Vice and including the Trustees among its members, exercised autocratic rule from June 1868 to December 1869. There was a purge of the teaching staff, a 'lay' Education Committee was established to bring order to the hitherto chaotic teaching timetable, and a constitution drafted in a way to prevent the Professors from exercising undue influence over the affairs of the College. In July 1869 "Bedford College" (sic) was incorporated as an Association under Board of Trade Regulations for Companies not Trading for Profit. Under these Regulations persons employed by the College were excluded from Membership of the Governing Body (the former Board reconstituted as "The College") and from the executive Council elected from among the members. The new constitution also created a new office of Visitor or arbiter to which Erasmus Darwin, Chairman of Bedford College Council since 1851 and one of the Trustees of Mrs Reid's original loan, was immediately appointed. Under its power to set up sub-committees the Council invited the Professors to form a Board of Studies to advise the Council on academic matters.

The new Council under the Chairmanship of the Rector of Lincoln and containing a number of the distinguished and enlightened people who had served on the temporary committee as well as long-term supporters of the original College, was able to guide the College into a period of development and, if not prosperity, at least reasonable financial stability.

In York Place, 1870-1894

Three main factors aided the progress of the College in the 1870s and 1880s. The development of education for girls, exemplified by the foundation in 1873 of the Girls Public Day School Company (later Trust), ensured that there was a cohort of young women properly prepared for advanced work. In 1874 the College moved from Bedford Square to more spacious and conveniently sited accommodation at 8 and 9 York Place, Baker Street (now the Sherlock Holmes Hotel). The quaint arrangement for management established by Mrs Reid's will was retained–the Managers of the Residence (The Reid Trustees) took the lease on one house and the Council the other. The strict segregation, according to the level of fees paid, of resident from day students remained even to the extent of a dividing line drawn through the entrance hall dividing those parts of the hall funded by the residents from those open to all. Most importantly in 1878 the University of London (at that time an examining body only) opened its examinations to women. Bedford students were among those who matriculated in that year and in 1880 five Bedford students were awarded degrees. In 1880 the College also instituted a College Diploma or Certificate of Association awarded strictly on academic merit, to students who had followed a solid course of study but did not wish to sit University exams.

In 1884 the Art School (later renamed as the Bodichon Studio in memory of a distinguished former student and champion of the cause of education for women) was established "to provide a thorough training in Art". It was intended that the Art School should be self-financing but it continued to make calls on the general finances of the College until it was discontinued at the time of the move to Regent's Park.

The movement for university education in London accelerated during the 1870s and 80s. Westfield College opened in Hampstead in 1882 and Royal Holloway College in Surrey in 1886. University College admitted women to degree courses (though not in Medicine) in 1878. King's College had instituted 'Lectures for Ladies' as early as 1871 and in 1885 opened its Ladies Department (which finally received its Charter as Queen Elizabeth College in 1953) in Kensington. A residential hall for university women was opened in Bloomsbury in 1882. The London School of Medicine for Women (later the Royal Free Hospital School of Medicine) opened in 1874 and was for a long time the only medical school which admitted women students.

The requirements of the University BSc examination included practical work. Laboratory space in York Place was minimal and so in 1888 the Council mounted an appeal for funds to cover purchase of a lease of land to the rear of the College and the building of an additional wing in memory of William Shaen, one of the Trustees of Mrs Reid's original loan, Chairman of Council 1880–87, who as an officer of the University had been influential in gaining admission for women. With generous donations from well-wishers and from City of London Livery Companies the Shaen Wing was completed by 1891 at a cost of just under £6,000 and was formally opened by HIM The Empress Frederick of Germany (who was also Princess Royal of Great Britain). The new wing provided the first university-level Chemistry and Physics laboratories for women in London and allowed for a reorganisation of space in the main building to provide a laboratory for Botany, Geology and Animal Biology, as well as some additional rooms for residential staff and students.

Although Bedford was far from being an integrated college, some social developments which drew resident and day students together occurred during this time. A debating society (in which religious topics were banned) was formed and quickly became a member of the University Intercollegiate Debating Society. In 1888 a Sketching Club was formed and in 1888 the Musical Society–music was still part of the non-exam curriculum–embarked upon the "practice and performance of vocal and instrumental music under a professional conductor", the first conductor being the organist of St George's Chapel, Windsor. In 1887 the first of what was to become a series of Greek plays was performed, Euripides' *Iphigenaia in Tauris*. In 1891, a successful Boating Society was founded.

In May 1884 the first meeting was held of an Association of Former Students, one of whose earliest activities was the formation of a Library Committee to collect funds to buy books in memory of Mrs Reid.

In 1891 a Special Meeting of the Council considered a resolution that "the efficiency of the College would be promoted by the unification of the Education and Boarding Departments". This was not universally accepted, the Managers of the Boarding House in particular had objections. However the Council was able to put part of the proposal into effect in 1893 when the retirement of the much respected Lady Resident allowed them to look for a Principal who would fulfil the ideal of "exercising a strong personal influence among the students whilst possessing the high attainments that should qualify her for such a post as the educational head of the College". They were fortunate in being able to appoint Miss Emily Penrose, who was to become a legendary figure in the world of women's education, becoming successively Principal of Bedford, Royal Holloway College and Somerville College, Oxford, and being created Dame of the British Empire in 1927. Miss Penrose's qualifications were excellent. She had taken a first class in 'Literae Humaniores' (classical studies) from Somerville College, Oxford, and her lectures on Classical Antiquity at the British Museum were highly regarded. She was able to bring with her the ethos and mores of a fully integrated college. She took up her appointment in 1893 and by the end of her first term the Managers of the Residence offered the Council "the entire management of the Boarding House". This offer was eagerly accepted and at Easter 1894 Miss Penrose assumed the entire management of the two departments with a House Mistress to assist her in the Residence. This was not, however, the end of the involvement of the Reid Trustees in Bedford College. Until the award of a Treasury grant they continued to contribute to teaching costs. From the time of the move to Regent's Park until the merger with Royal Holloway College, the Trustees continued to have a presence in the College and made a regular award of a Reid Scholarship. From 1999 the Trustees are supporting a Reid

Studentship in The Bedford Centre for Women's History at Royal Holloway and Bedford New College.

Membership of the University of London, 1894–1900

It is difficult to overestimate the contribution of Emily Penrose to the development of Bedford College (for Women) as it became in 1895. She fully met the Council's ideal. Day students and boarders were fused into a single College, social events were arranged, clubs encouraged and a high level of pastoral care was arranged without encroaching on the precious freedom of the students. The teaching programme was brought to a standard where the Council was confidently able to apply for full membership of the new teaching university proposed at that time and to make the case for financial support from the Treasury. Miss Penrose was at the same time Educational Head, Manager of the Residence, Head of the Library and College Professor of Ancient History with a very small infrastructure to support her. She was required to remain resident in the College throughout the College term, yet her bed and board was not payable in the vacations. Despite her many responsibilities she had very little real authority and could only attend Council meetings by invitation. It was hardly surprising that in 1897 she accepted the invitation of the Council of Royal Holloway College to become that College's Principal. She is held in the corporate memory of both colleges with great affection and the new merged College adopted her name for the first building constructed in 1984, almost a century after her first arrival on the London university scene.

During the 1890s there were two academic initiatives. In 1891 the Teacher Training Department was set up, which included part-time courses offered in the evenings and on Saturdays to teachers already in service as well as a full-time training course. In 1895 a course in Scientific Hygiene was introduced which included work in the laboratories where Physiology had been taught since 1882 and was designed to qualify women as Lecturers in Hygiene, as 'Health Mistresses' in schools and as Government Sanitary and Factory Inspectors.

In 1894, after many submissions, the College was at last awarded an annual grant from the Treasury's five yearly (quinquennial) distribution. So began the administrative routine common to all British universities of quinquennial planning, ie the submission of a five year plan, a Government Visitation to discuss the plan and then announcement of a grant for the next five years. As a result of recognition by the Treasury the Technical Education Board of the London County Council (LCC) agreed to make annual grants (£500 pa in the first place) for the equipment and upkeep of the Science Laboratories in return for the right to nominate a fixed number of students to free places on appropriate courses. After an inspection in 1896 the Treasury increased its grant from £700 to £1,200 in recognition of "the appreciable amount of...university work" carried out. The Inspectors' general report was that "a good deal of the work judged by University standards is of an educational and preparatory rather than of an advanced or learned character, but it is distinctly good of its kind - liberal and scientific in spirit and treatment and of an academic type". This encouraged the Council to take on the lease of a third house–10 York Place–in order to bring the number of residence places to forty.

Miss Penrose was succeeded by Miss Ethel Hurlblatt, also an alumna of Somerville College. She came to Bedford from the University of Wales, where she was Warden of the pioneering Aberdare Women's Hall. Like many graduates of the women's colleges at Oxford and Cambridge at that time, she held the honorary degree of MA (Trinity College, Dublin). During her Principalship changes were made in the composition of the Council to allow representation of the Academic Staff meeting as of right. She was usually the elected representative of that meeting and was thus able to take part in policy making. During this time the infrastructure was increased by the addition of a resident Vice Principal and by a paid College Secretary.

In 1899 the College had the confidence to celebrate its (50 year) Jubilee in style, bringing together "all who had played an active part in providing university education for women". There was an afternoon meeting at the Headquarters of the University in South Kensington, to which an imposing number of universities and colleges admitting women were invited to send representatives. This was followed by a conversazione and exhibition of work at York Place. For former students there was a conference at the nearby Portman Hall and a garden party in the Botanic Gardens in Regent's Park.

To Miss Hurlblatt fell the task of pressing the College's case for inclusion in the teaching university now planned for London University's future. Bedford's case was strongly supported by Miss Penrose (while successfully pressing the later claim of Royal Holloway College) and by the College's most distinguished former student, Dr Sophie Bryant–the first woman to be awarded a Doctorate of Science by London University and by then Head Mistress of the North London Collegiate School–both of whom spoke out against a proposal for the creation of a separate Women's University. Happily the University of London Act which was entered in the Statute Book in 1900 cited Bedford College for Women (University of London) as one of its constituent schools.

Move to Regent's Park, 1900–1919

With the passing of the University of London Act, Bedford College, admitted to the University Faculties of Arts and Science, ended its isolated existence and became part of a federation with a right to call upon the facilities of the central University and take part in its intercollegiate activities. But it was not all plain sailing and there were additional expenses involved in for example the lease of yet another house in York Place to provide space for intercollegiate lectures.

Finance continued to be a problem despite the award of Treasury and London County Council grants, especially as the Reid Trustees had discontinued their substantial contribution to teaching salaries once the grants were in place. The additional houses could not provide the teaching space required for the expansion to 200 or more students deemed necessary to create a financially viable college. Nevertheless, the College Council bravely reported in 1900, when numbers stood at 180, that "It would be unwise to close departments or to discontinue to prepare students for the higher examinations at the present moment lest the College slip from the unique position it holds in the University and by a parsimonious policy forfeit its inheritance of half a century".

A committee was set up under the chairmanship of Sir Arthur Dyke Acland (who became Chairman of Council in 1903) to make a searching enquiry into the financial and general position.

One of the recommendations of this committee was for a new constitution. Since 1882 there had been unrest among the teaching staff at their exclusion by the 1869 Articles of Association from Membership of the College and of the Council. Various ameliorating measures had been taken through By-Laws, but in 1908 a petition was submitted to the Privy Council for a Royal Charter of Incorporation. This was granted on 11 January 1909 and set the constitution under which, with amendments to suit the times, the College operated until 1985. The Charter provided for a Board of Governors–the ultimate guardians of the constitution–and a Council of management composed of representatives of the University and the LCC, Staff Councillors–the Principal and members of teaching staff–whose numbers were not to exceed one quarter of the total number of Councillors and Elected Councillors, elected by and from the Governors, at least one third of whom were to be women. The Statutes included provision for the establishment of an Academic Board, whom the Council should consult before making decisions on academic matters and a Finance Committee. The office of Visitor was retained.

The other important recommendation was that the College should look for new premises. The lease of the York Place property was due to terminate in 1928 and the Portman Estate was not prepared to consider selling the freehold. In any case the premises were too small and crowded and affected by the increasing noise and dust of Baker Street. The cost of acquiring and equipping new premises was estimated at about £100,000 and the Council was adamant that they should be sited in central London. Once more an Appeal to friends and former students for funds was mounted and met with an encouraging response.

During this time of re-assessment Miss Hurlblatt offered her resignation on appointment in 1906 as Warden of the Royal Victoria College, McGill University, Montreal. On her retirement the Council acknowledged that "the College owes much to the unremitting zeal of its Principal in the initial years of the new order". Miss Hurlblatt herself wrote to her successor "I am glad and proud to think that I had a period of life and experience at Bedford in the days when pioneers were nearer and the old names so honoured in its history still associated with it."

After a short interregnum Miss Margaret Janner Tuke MA (TCD) took up appointment as Principal at Easter 1907. Miss Tuke had taken the Modern and Medieval Languages Tripos at Newnham College, Cambridge and at the time of her appointment was Tutor to Women Students and Lecturer in French at the University of Bristol. Her Principalship was to be a long one–till 1929–and covered, as one distinguished student of the 1920s put it, "a time when the right of women to be educated and contribute intellectually was on a firm basis at last and a great pool of intelligence was attracted to Bedford College".

In 1904 Her Majesty Queen Alexandra agreed to become the College's first Patron. She was joined in 1913 by Her Majesty Queen Mary, who in turn was succeeded by Her Majesty Queen Elizabeth, now Her Majesty the Queen Mother, who eventually came with Bedford to become Patron of Royal Holloway and Bedford New College. All three Royal Patrons have shown great interest in the College. The Arms granted to the College–and presented by Lady Cunard–include the emblems of the Danish Royal Family (sanctioned by HM Queen Alexandra) and of the Teck family (sanctioned by HM Queen Mary). The use of their family motto *Esse Quam Videri* was allowed by the relatives of Miss Bostock.

1908 brought an end to the anxious search for new premises when a legacy from Mr Robert J Turle allowed the College to negotiate a Crown Lease of South Villa, a Victorian house, and its eight acres of grounds in Regent's Park. New building began in 1911, and the College moved from York Place by degrees. The grounds and the villa itself were occupied as early as 1909. The architect appointed was Basil Champneys, already well known for his buildings at Newnham College,

Cambridge, and Lady Margaret Hall, Oxford. He designed a quadrangle with an Arts and Administration block to its east, flanked by two science buildings to the north and south, with the Villa itself (due to be demolished in 1916 under the terms of the lease) partially completing the square. A wing to the north provided dining and common rooms, some student rooms and a flat for the Principal with two 'pavilions'–linked by a 'Bridge of Sighs'–with rooms for staff and students. To the south was a separate library building, built at her own expense by Lady Tate and designed by her own architect Sydney Smith FRIBA, in memory of her husband Sir Henry Tate who had been a generous benefactor to the College at York Place. By 1913 the work was finished, the buildings opened by HM Queen Mary, the Royal Patron, on 4 July and the College was able to give its address as 'Regent's Park'. The arrival of Bedford College was not altogether popular with neighbouring residents, and the Crown Estates felt obliged to hand over some land to the west of the South Villa estate for public use. This became known to the protesters as 'The Paltry Sop'.

The cost of building and equipping the buildings was £130,000, entirely met out of contributions received, particularly from the LCC (£30,000), Sir Joseph Beecham (£30,000), Mrs Oliver (£10,000 for the dining and common rooms in memory of her husband the Hon Richard Oliver) and Amy Lady Tate (£10,000 for the Henry Tate Library).

> The academic conformation at that time is described in the Calendar for 1913–1914.
>
> "Courses of instruction–Students are prepared for all Examinations of the University of London in Arts, Science and Pedagogy, for the Cambridge Teachers' Diploma, the Bedford College Hygiene Diploma, the Sanitary Inspectors' Board Examinations. They may also enter the Art School (recognised as a School of Fine Art by the University of London) and the Horticultural Course (for would-be teachers). Single courses of lectures in any subject or subjects may be taken. There are extensive laboratories. Special facilities are

offered to those who wish to carry on research or more advanced work."

The Academic Departments were:-

In Arts–Greek, Latin, Ancient History, Modern History, Mathematics, Philosophy, English Language and Literature, French Language and Literature, German Language and Literature, Italian.

In Science–Botany (which included the teaching of Geology and later Geography), Chemistry, Physics, Physiology (including Hygiene and Bacteriology), Zoology and Psychology (taught in the Department of Philosophy).

This conformation was kept throughout the remainder of the College's history with the addition in 1916 of Social Studies, Geology and Geography and in 1919 of Dutch through the initiative of the University Board of Dutch Studies. The Art School was closed shortly after the transfer to Regent's Park and the Secondary Training Department regretfully closed 'for purely financial reasons' in 1922. In 1913–1914 there was 340 students, and postgraduates. The Tate Library held in the region of 22,000 volumes.

Although the Treasury Grant had been increased to £7,000 per annum in 1912 and the Technical Education Board of the LCC continued its annual grant of £800, the Income and Expenditure Account still ran at a loss and in 1913 the College once more went out to Appeal for an Endowment Fund. Its greatest success was a donation of a hundred thousand guineas from Sir Hildred Carlile MP in memory of his mother who had a lifelong interest in the welfare of girls and young women and had been a ready supporter of the movement for the higher education of women. The donation was applied to the funding of four Chairs–in Botany, English Literature, Latin and Physics. The College fell in with the University Scheme, adopted in 1908, whereby appointments to Chairs or Readerships or the conferment of those titles, are made by the University although the contract is with the

College, and Lecturers and Senior Lecturers are appointed by the College and recognised by the University after an appropriate period. The first University Chair held at Bedford was in Mathematics–the appointment made in 1912–followed in 1913 by English Literature (Bedford's first woman Professor) and French.

Apart from the introduction in 1916 of teaching in Economic History and Industrial Economics (leading to the foundation of the Department of Social Studies) as part of a training scheme for social workers in collaboration with the Charity Organisation Society, there were few major developments during the Great War. Bedford as a college for women did not suffer the fall in entry experienced in the university world as a whole. Student numbers held above 400 during the war years except in 1917 when they fell to 370. Stop-gap arrangements had to be made for staff away on active service. Five members of staff academic, technical and household, were killed or died of wounds received on active service. Their names are recorded in a memorial plaque still in the entrance hall at Regent's Park. Two Science Departments were involved in research for the Government. Otherwise staff and students engaged in all kinds of voluntary war work. Refugees from Belgium, France and Russia were admitted at reduced fees.

Post-War Expansion, 1919–1930

After the war the pressure for places increased sharply and by 1920 numbers in College had risen well above the 450 for which the buildings had been designed. The College was obliged to institute its own entrance exam and to insist that all applicants had either passed the University's Matriculation examination or obtained exemption from it. The students themselves expressed their understanding of the College's status as a University institution in 1923 by asking the Council to pass a regulation requiring all students who had matriculated to wear academic dress at lectures and at College functions.

To cope with the additional numbers, as a temporary measure, army huts were put up in the quadrangle and devoted mainly to Chemistry laboratories, for which there was a great demand. It was clear that a new permanent building was needed, especially as the loss of the South Villa was a constant threat. The clause in the lease requiring its immediate demolition had been waived during the War, but it was now reinstated, ameliorated by the concession that the Villa could stay until a new permanent building was in place. In the prevailing economic climate the Council and Principal did not feel that they should mount a direct appeal to the public, except to former students. A programme of fund-raising events was devised to raise Bedford College's profile as an intellectual and cultural centre. The success of this approach encouraged the planning of a new building in consultation with Maxwell Ayrton FRIBA who succeeded Basil Champneys as the College Architect.

Meanwhile funds raised from former students were applied to increasing the residence provision. By 1925 there were 200 residence places. In addition to the campus residence–Reid Hall and some rooms in the Oliver Building–six houses in Adamson Road and Buckland Crescent at Swiss Cottage formed College House for seventy-eight students. Two houses at 35/36 Dorset Square by Baker St Station, provided residence for twenty-nine students. They were named Notcutt House in memory of Rachel Notcutt (student 1868, Assistant in Latin 1880–91, Librarian 1883–95, member of Council and its committees 1891–21, and resident at the York Place Boarding house until 1894). Funds raised by former students were added to a gift from Mrs G T Pilcher (former student and Reid scholar) and her husband (member of Council 1893 to 1921) to equip the Pilcher Research Laboratory and to a bequest from Miss A C Sargant (student 1875–77 and member of Council 1901–1909) to provide a laboratory for plant physiology in the Botany Garden.

The Students' Union Society, with a loan from College funds, bought a sports ground in Northolt, Middlesex. This was later purchased by the War Office for its military airport and the sports pitches were moved to Headstone Lane, where the Union Society funded the construction of a pavilion and tea-room.

By 1927 sufficient funds had been collected to make possible a start on the new building. The foundation stone was laid by HRH Princess Mary on 9 June and building work began in December. In 1930 the South Villa was at last demolished and on 24 June 1931 the new building was formally opened and named Tuke Building by HM Queen Mary. The Tuke Building, costing £87,000 and consisting of a single storey central block with two-storey wings on either side, provided laboratories, teaching-staff rooms and lecture rooms as well as an assembly hall–the New Hall–for about 600 to which the former students, the Bedford College Old Students Association, had made a substantial contribution. On the roof of the north wing was an observatory, housing a telescope given by the Royal Artillery Institution which was ceremonially opened by the Astronomer Royal.

By the time Tuke Building was formally opened Miss Tuke herself had retired–in 1929. The College showed its appreciation and gratitude by appointing her as only the second Fellow of the College– Sir Hildred Carlile, the benefactor, had been the first appointment to this office, created in 1926. Bedford was gratified both for her sake and its own by Miss Tuke's creation as Dame Commander of the British Empire in 1931. In a tribute on her death in 1946 the College Council recorded that "the confidence which she inspired in others, her vision, determination and judgement made possible that great transformation of the College's place in the education world, which took place during her period of office...she was an educational force in the true sense of the term".

Peaceful Development, 1930-1938

Miss Geraldine E M (Gem) Jebb MA took up appointment as Principal at the beginning of 1930. She had taken the Cambridge Economics Tripos from Newnham College, where she had been Director of Studies and Lecturer on Economics after war service in the Employment Department of the Board of Trade. She came to Bedford from Armstrong College, Newcastle on Tyne, where she had been Lecturer in Economics since 1919.

The number of students at the time of Miss Jebb's appointment was 628 and of the teaching staff 73. At the end of the financial year 1931–32 the Accounts showed that there had been no overdraft for the first time since 1913 and a time of prosperity or at least freedom from financial anxiety could be expected. None the less the Council resolved to "keep always before them what they know to be three pressing needs of the College–funds for endowment, funds for repayment of debt (on the building) and funds for a new hall of residence".

During the decade student numbers rose to nearly 700. An inspection by the Court of the University produced the comment that "since the last inspection in 1924 the College has maintained its high reputation". The Council expected that "after years of struggle, overcrowding and financial difficulty the College would be embarking on a peaceful era of progress and development". This peaceful development was to be broken by the onset of the Second World War.

World War II, Cambridge 1939–44

In 1938 with the threat of war looming, the Vice Chancellor of the University announced that it was "the definite and considered opinion of the Lord Privy Seal that the University of London should in the event of war be evacuated from London and that its teaching should continue in university towns that were less vulnerable". Bedford accepted this advice and, having explored the possibilities of the University College of the South West (Exeter) and of Oxford, decided upon Cambridge as its refuge. The Principal, Miss Jebb, was exceptionally well placed to arrange this as her family was influential within the University and owned a large house in the city. So on the outbreak of war in September 1939 the evacuation took place and the College opened on 9 October with 465 students, most of whom were billeted with Cambridge families, with a small number lodged in two rented houses (later exchanged for one larger). The teaching in Science was carried on in the University Laboratories, in Arts in University lecture rooms, at Newnham College and in a rented house where the nucleus of the College Library (eventually about 10,000 volumes) was also housed. The more precious books were sent to a safe haven in the Midlands.

Through the generosity of the Jebb family the Principal's lodging and the administrative offices moved into Springfield, the Jebb family home. The Students' Union Society was offered hospitality including the use of playing fields by Newnham. At first it was confidently expected that the College would return to London in 1940. But this proved too dangerous and Bedford was forced to remain in Cambridge until 1944. During that time some adjustments were made to the accommodation, but the College remained scattered throughout the city, which "deprived the students of the full benefit of corporate life and provided many problems for the heroic teaching and administrative staff. Nonetheless the students remained cheerful and most of them took advantage of life in Cambridge". One former student has recounted how she and fellow students sacrificed precious clothing ration coupons on the fashionable scarves in College colours (white, purple and green) to preserve their Bedford identity. In the later years of exile the Principal arranged for a formal assembly to be held in the Cambridge Guildhall at the opening of each session. The College continued its practice of offering a programme of public lectures. Numbers fell slightly especially when the call-up of women for war service was introduced. Entrance exams were suspended.

A skeleton administrative staff remained in Regent's Park. The buildings were used for a number of war-time emergency offices, a children's nursery and as temporary residence for people who needed to work in London including for a time the Dutch Government in exile. In 1940 the BBC leased a large part of the buildings and remained there until August 1944. The two residences were closed. College House was taken over by various emergency services and Notcutt House remained unoccupied until it was irreversibly damaged by enemy action in 1941.

In February 1940 minor damage was done to the Regent's Park buildings by a run-away barrage balloon. But in a night-time air-raid in May 1941 a high explosive bomb demolished part of the North Science Building and incendiary bombs gutted the rest of the block, the whole of the Arts/Administrative block and the Oliver Dining Hall. The damage was kept to a minimum through the heroic action of the staff and tenants and there were no casualties. One member of the staff tells how a full breakfast, with sausages, was served the next morning from a make-shift kitchen in the Tuke Building.

A number of staff from all sections of the College were called up to active service or recruited into war work. There were two casualties among the Senior Staff. In 1940 Dr Gutkind, Head of the Department of Italian, who had been interned as an enemy alien was lost, presumed drowned, in the sinking of HMS Andorra Star. In 1941 Miss J Agnes Paterson was killed in an air-raid away from the College. She had been College Librarian since 1907 and had supervised the growth of the Library's collection from 13,000 to 62,000 volumes. She was commemorated in the Agnes Paterson Reading Room added to the Library in 1965.

During the years in Cambridge it was College policy to spend as little as possible on the upkeep of the Regent's Park buildings, to which the BBC as tenant made a considerable contribution, and to husband resources to provide for the return of the College to London. Immediately after the disastrous air-raid a Rebuilding Fund was established and a search for temporary accommodation begun.

Return from Cambridge, Rebuilding, Centenary Celebrations, 1944–51

During the summer vacation of 1944 the College was moved back to Regent's Park and opened on 26 October with 501 students in the "face of difficulties arising from the state of the premises, acute shortage of domestic staff, flying bombs and rockets".

A temporary lease was taken on Sussex Lodge in Regent's Park to house the Science Departments displaced from the North Science Building. Arts Departments shared space with the University's Institute of Archaeology in a Regency villa, St John's Lodge. Later in 1945 a lease was taken on another villa–The Holme. The administrative offices took over the ground floor of the campus residence, Reid Hall. To replace Notcutt House a lease was taken of a house in Broadhurst Gardens, Hampstead.

The return coincided with a sharp increase of applications for places partly resulting from the relaxation of the Ministry of Labour's War-time Regulations on the maximum age for full-time education and from the return of women from war service. In 1946 the Council recorded that "it is evident that for the next few years the College will find it impossible to meet all the demands on it from students who reach the normal admission standards", and pointed to the discrepancy between supply and demand for resident places in London. "There are too many women in lodgings." Despite this and the enormous difficulties and delays in obtaining licences for rebuilding and repair of damage, by 1946 the College had begun to assume a more normal appearance. The Library Reading Rooms (damaged by flying shrapnel) had been restored and all the books returned. Air-raid shelters had been removed and bomb craters in the North Drive filled in. The lawns and the Sargant Laboratory and greenhouse in the Botany Garden had been restored. A temporary hut had been erected on the hard tennis court for the Students' Union Society. Entrance Exams had been reinstated and the 'civilised' activities of Commemoration of the Founders (instituted at the students' request in 1936) and Presentation Days (dating from the admission of women to degrees of the University in 1878) and Public Lectures resumed. The academic teaching and research received an impetus from the creation by the University of Research Studentships and Fellowships. From this time onward the number of postgraduate students at Bedford increased. In 1949 the College was able to create three Research Fellowships of its own.

Immediately after the bombing in 1941 a start had been made on drawing up a rebuilding programme in consultation with the College Architect, Maxwell Ayrton FRIBA. By the end of 1942 the programme had been agreed upon as:-

Reconstruction of

- The North Science Block to be renamed Darwin (for Major Leonard Darwin DSc, Chairman of Council 1913 to 1920)
- The central Arts and Administration block to be named Herringham (Sir Wilmott Herringham KCMG, CB, MD,

FRCP, Chairman of Council 1920-1936, who left a collection of his wife's paintings, library and oriental artefacts to the College)
- The Oliver Dining Hall with the addition of a second storey for academic use.

At this time it was also agreed that the South Science Building should be renamed Acland (Rt Hon Sir Arthur Dyke Acland Bart, MA, LLD, Chairman of Council 1903–1913). The two sections of the Reid Hall residence were renamed Shaen and Bostock wings. Despite difficulties and delays all the new buildings were completed by the beginning of the session 1952–53 and formally opened by HRH the Princess Alice, Duchess of Athlone, accompanied by HRH The Duke of Athlone, Chancellor of the University.

Residence remained a problem. College House renamed Lindsell Hall for its first Warden, reopened in 1945, but at the end of the lease of Broadhurst Gardens in 1949 there was as yet no adequate replacement for Notcutt House. In 1947 a Crown Lease till 2008 was taken of another Regent's Park villa, Hanover Lodge, to provide immediate accommodation for 30 students and to form the nucleus of a hall for 150 to 180, but building restrictions and other complications prevented this from opening until 1965.

During this period of reconstruction the College celebrated the centenary of its foundation in 1849, once more in style, in a three-day festival. On 19 May a dinner was held in the newly completed Oliver Dining Hall at which 'all sections of the College' were represented as well as members of the University Senate and representatives of the Universities of Oxford and Cambridge. The College Visitor was host and the Guests of Honour were the Chancellor of the University and HRH Princess Alice. On Sunday morning there was a Service of Thanksgiving in the Parish Church of St Marylebone and in the afternoon an assembly in Tuke Hall was followed by a garden party attended by the Royal Patron, HM Queen Mary, to which representatives of British universities and of some North American women's colleges were invited. There were two performances of the specially written Centenary Play *No Spring Till Now* and exhibitions of work in the Departments. Monday was Present Students' (and their parents) Day at The Holme ending with a Centenary Ball in the Oliver Dining Hall. On Tuesday 21 May there was a reception in the floodlit Botany Garden for former students and members of staff–the former students presented a chiming clock to be mounted on the courtyard face of the Tuke Building. Finally those members of the domestic and technical staff who had been on duty throughout the festival were offered coach outings or an extra day's holiday. The total cost of the celebrations is recorded as £2,996 3s 1d.

Further Expansion, 1951-1965

Miss Jebb retired at the end of the 1950–51 session. The Council paid tribute to her work "in steering the College through a period of impressive growth in teaching and research in exceptionally difficult circumstances". Miss Norah L Penston BA, DPhil (Oxon), became Principal on 1 October 1951. Dr Penston came from the University of London's Wye College, where she had been Vice-Principal since 1945. Before that, she had been Lecturer in Botany at King's College, London. Her first task was to settle staff and students into the reconstructed buildings and to cope with the shortcomings of the older premises.

The Chancellor of the University, in opening the 'new' buildings had said "now that the restoration of your buildings has been completed, there is no doubt that Bedford is more decently housed than many other schools of the University…". However elsewhere in College, the standard of accommodation had not kept pace with post-war developments and the expansion of academic work–especially in the experimental sciences–and the College faced significant expense in updating services. The Library was running out of shelf-space for its collections, numbering 96,167 volumes in 1952 and increasing fast. Developments in teaching and research and the consequent revision by the University of degree courses called for additional staff and equipment.

Although Treasury grants (made through the University Grants

Committee) were not generous, with careful administration they enabled the college substantially to meet its needs in terms of staff and equipment in the 1952–57 quinquennium. To help meet the shortage of accommodation for teaching and research, the UGC grant-aided two building works–in Tuke Building the additions of a south wing and of a second storey to the original building, and in Acland the provision of mezzanine galleries to the lofty laboratories. The College was able to fund a small infill between the Oliver and Herringham Buildings, named Pilcher after the lost research laboratory. In response to a criticism by visitors from the UGC of the size and quality of facilities for students (805 in 1956–7), a further grant-aided project provided an infill between the two wings of the Reid residence for a Common Room and offices for the Union Society plus some additional study bedrooms. Yet another infill, between Acland and Herringham buildings, and incorporating the Werner Reading Room of 1913 named the Jebb Building, provided extra space for the Library and for the Departments of Physiology and Biochemistry, the latter established as a separate department in 1966. New properties were also acquired. A crown lease of 99 years was taken out on St John's Lodge in the Inner Circle of Regent's Park in 1961 on the departure of the Institute of Archaeology.

The Robbins Report and the Admission of Men, 1960–1971

The most momentous event of the 1960s was the admission of men as undergraduates–made possible by the granting of a Supplemental Royal Charter on 2 August 1965 altering the objectives of the College so as "to provide a liberal education for men and women". Men had been admitted as postgraduate students since 1946, but the proposal for them to be admitted as undergraduates had been the subject of discussion, some of it bitter, over many years. A serious concern of those who opposed the development was the retention of, if not increase in, the number of university places for women, and an important factor influencing the final decision was the Report in 1963 of the Robbins Committee which recognised that "courses of higher education should be available to all those who are qualified by ability and attainment to pursue them and who wish to do so", and called for a massive expansion in higher education. At the beginning of the session 1964–65, students numbered 978 and the College agreed to respond to the Report by increasing numbers by 20% by 1967–68 and by setting a long term target of 2,000 for the next quinquennium.

Once again, the problem arose of "how to accommodate additional numbers within the confines of the Regent's Park Site". This time, the constriction was not so much money–Government grants were available for additional buildings to meet the crash programme–as the limitations of the site, which the planning authorities regarded as saturated. Outline planning permission was given for a large building to the north of campus, but each time more detailed plans were put forward objections from planners, the landlord and the many Fine Art organisations were so many that the North Spur Building was never built. Instead, to accommodate research in Social Studies, Geography and Zoology, a lease was taken out on the former Diorama building in Peto Place, Park Square East, and the ingenious infilling between and within existing buildings was resumed. By 1968 all residents' rooms on the main campus, including the Principal's flat, had been handed over to academic departments. In the view of some of the former students, it was this expansion of numbers and the banishment of all residence from the main site, as much as the admission of men, which altered the character of the College and lost it its cohesive and collegiate character.

The extreme pressure on residence places was eased in 1965 by the opening of the new wing of Hanover Lodge. In 1967 a former hotel in Dorset Square was opened by Sir Charles Tennyson (Chairman of Council 1946–1963) as Tennyson Hall with places for 50 men. Freehold houses in Nottingham Place, Marylebone, acquired in 1961, became a women's' residence, later named Rachel Notcutt Hall and the lease of a small house at Wedderburn Road was acquired. Residence was to remain a problem throughout the rest of the College's life in London–not only because the number of places fell seriously short of requirement, but because of the demands made by the Halls on the finances of the College. Valiant attempts were made to keep the residences self-funding, but this was not always possible and later in the 1970s the College was forced to turn down the generous offer of an anonymous donation towards the building of another hall because of the demands its upkeep were likely to make on funds designed for teaching and research.

In 1963–64, during the discussions on expansion, Dr Penston finally retired. She had agreed to stay on beyond her normal retirement age because of staff shortages, exacerbated by the terminal illness of the College Secretary. The Council paid tribute to the hard work she had put in laying the foundations for an expanding School of the University as did her successor Mrs E M (Sally) Chilver, MA (Oxon), who took up appointment as Principal in January 1964. Mrs Chilver, a graduate of Somerville College, came to the College from the Institute of Commonwealth Studies after a career in journalism and in the Civil Service as well as in academic life (her research interests lay in anthropology). During the seven years of her Principalship she fulfilled her undertaking to build on the foundations laid by Dr Penston. She established Bedford as a co-educational college, brought management systems up to date with the help of the Registrar and the new College Secretary (herself a former student), encouraged scholarship and improved and expanded student amenities.

Men undergraduates were first admitted in October 1965 and fitted in well to the student body. However Bedford did not escape the 'student unrest' of the Sixties, and in 1969–70 endured a sit-in of the administrative offices. These troubles were on the whole amicably dealt with and discussions were initiated into how the student body might become involved in the management of the College. The junior academic, domestic and technical staffs were also anxious to have a say in management.

In 1969 membership of Council committees both executive and advisory was opened up to staff and students and a Staff/Student Joint Committee reporting to the Council created. In December 1970 the Governors agreed in principle that the Royal Charter should be amended to allow students to become fully participating members of the Council and to increase the range and number of Staff Councillors–

always retaining the lay majority of membership. A Supplemental Charter brought this into effect in 1971.

At this time 'pastoral care' of students was improved by the establishment through the local GP practice of a student Health Service and the appointment of Student Counsellors. In spite of the new Students' Union Society premises, recreational facilities were still inadequate, particularly in sport, though this did not prevent the development of an enthusiastic and successful football team.

In the University shake-up resulting from the Robbins report, Bedford recognised that the products of scholarship and research were crucial to teaching and that to play its full part in higher education Bedford should abandon its traditional, if implicit, policy of sacrificing individual research to teaching. There was encouragement to individuals by the introduction of an arrangement whereby a year's teaching could be concentrated into two terms, leaving the lecturer free to pursue research in the third term as well as the vacations. From 1965 Sabbatical Years were sparingly available. An indication of the increase in research activity is the increase in income from the Research Councils, Trusts and other bodies from £3,520 to £27,713 between 1960 and 1969. These grants were mainly for the Science subjects though the annual list of staff publications show that scholarship was being actively pursued in the Arts departments. The research base in Social Studies was enhanced by the establishment of the Legal and Social Research Units. With support from the Science Research Council a Scanning Electron Microscope Unit was set up for the Science Departments. A Data Link with the University computer was established–developing later in the 1970s into a full scale Computer Centre. The research facilities of the Botany Garden and Sargant Laboratories were improved.

There were new procedures for admitting students–through the Universities' Central Council for Admissions (the College entrance examination was reluctantly abandoned) and for examining them. From the session 1966–67 Bedford took part in London University's scheme for course-based Science Degrees whereby a student built up a degree by annual examination of course units.

In 1970 Mrs Chilver submitted her resignation on appointment to the Principalship of Lady Margaret Hall, Oxford. The question then arose as to the relevance to a college of mixed sexes of the requirement in the Royal Charter that "the Principal shall be a woman". Eventually yet another Supplemental Charter was granted deleting this qualification and the Council was able to appoint as Principal from October 1971 Dr John Nicholson Black MA, DPhil, DSc, FRSE, Professor of Forestry and Natural Resources at the University of Edinburgh. Dr Black had served in the Royal Air Force during the war and had wide experience in universities. He had graduated in Agronomy at Oxford and after gaining his research degree had moved to Australia to the University of Adelaide, returning to take up his Chair at Edinburgh in 1963.

The Final Years: the Foundation of Royal Holloway and Bedford New College, 1971–1985

Coming from one of the largest universities in the United Kingdom Dr Black was keenly aware that a college of only eleven hundred students with grant/fee income to match could not be expected to support as many as twenty academic departments in a wide spread of disciplines, especially at a time when public funding was seriously reduced. Under his guidance the College Council was beginning to work out a programme of rationalisation, building on academic strengths, when a Committee on the Governance of the University of London, chaired by Lord Murray of Newhaven, recommended that a solution to the financial problems of the smaller schools of the University "must be sought by some kind of amalgamation both physical and academic". However the immediate financial prospects did not appear so grave as to inspire concern within the College. Although talks on amalgamation with Westfield College were started without enthusiasm on either side, things remained much as they were until 1981 when further cuts in funding created a serious crisis throughout the UK university world.

Yet another committee on the academic organisation of London

University chaired by Sir Peter Swinnerton-Dyer recommended "a merger of small schools"–a recommendation strongly supported by both the outgoing and incoming Vice-Chancellors of the University and echoing the conclusions reached by an internal working party of the College. This was the situation facing Professor Dorothy Wedderburn, Professor of Industrial Sociology at Imperial College, London, when she took up office as Principal on the retirement of Dr Black at the beginning of the session 1981–82. Professor Wedderburn's own chapter in this volume (chapter 19) describes the pressures on the College resulting from tensions within the University arising from the changing climate of Higher Education and the solutions sought to the problems caused by these pressures. The final solution proved to be in the spirit of the advice given to small Schools of the University by the Murray and Swinnerton-Dyer Committees–the agreement to merge with Royal Holloway College to found in July 1985 a new institution at Egham.

As Professor Wedderburn relates in chapter 19, the years 1982 to 1985 were filled with anxiety and difficulty. Individuals were anxious and uncertain about the future. Time was taken up in endless meetings planning the new college in all its aspects. Teaching and research had to be carried out on two different sites while new premises were built and there was constant disruption as departments and residences packed up for removal to Egham, and in some cases to other schools of the University. The experiences of individual academic departments during this time are described in the departments' own chapters, but the scale of the evacuation exercise may be gauged by the estimate that about 250 removal pantechnicons left the Regent's Park and outlying properties during those years. Nevertheless, the College was able to cede its independent existence with style.

During the summer of 1985, though by now the Regent's Park site was shared with the incoming tenant, Regent's College, Bedford was able to hold a number of farewell celebrations. In June the Royal Patron, Queen Elizabeth the Queen Mother, came to say goodbye and to say how pleased she was that the College was moving to a place "just down the road" from her home in Windsor Great Park. On 15 July about

2,500 former staff and students attended a final Reunion. On 31 July the College flag, donated by Miss Norah McNaulty (student 1912-1915, member of the Registry Office from 1916, Registrar 1945-1962), flew all day over Tuke Building as it had for the Reunion. At dusk at the end of the last meeting of the Council it was hauled down and taken to Egham Hill, where the next day it flew over the Founder's Building together with the Royal Holloway flag, to mark the foundation of Royal Holloway and Bedford New College.

Acknowledgements

The information here is largely drawn from the formal records of the Council, though the sketch owes a great deal to

Dame Margaret Tuke's *A History of Bedford College for Women 1849 to 1937* (OUP 1939),

Dr Linna Bentley's *Educating Women–A Pictorial History of Bedford College University of London 1849 to 1985* (Alma Publishers 1991),

Professor Negley Harte's *The University of London 1836* (Athlone Press 1986),

Dr Gillian Sutherland's essay 'The Plainest Principles of Justice: the University of London and the Higher Education of Women' in *The University of London and the World of Learning*, ed F M L Thompson (Hambledon Press 1990), a paper by Elizabeth Bennett, then College Archivist, 'Womens' College Education–the Bedford Experience' published by RHBNC in the Royal Holloway College *Centenary Lectures 1886–1986*, and to a number of 'in-house' papers provided by the archivists of the new College.

Thanks are due to Miss Kathleen Spears (student 1932–35, on the staff of the Registrar's office 1937-39, College Secretary and Secretary of Council 1963–76), who read the draft of this chapter and proposed important amendments.

APPENDIX

Principals of Bedford College

1893–97:	Dame Emily Penrose (1858–1942).
1898–1906:	Ethel Hurlblatt (1866–1934).
1907–29:	Dame Margaret Tuke (1862–1947).
1930–51:	Geraldine E M Jebb (1886–1959).
1951–64:	Norah L Penston (1903–74).
1964–71:	Elizabeth M Chilver (1914–).
1971–81:	John N Black (1922–).
1981–85:	Dorothy E C Wedderburn (1925–).

Chapter 2

Biochemistry

John Prebble

Introduction

The Department of Biochemistry was only formally established by the College in 1966. It thus had a very short life in comparison with other departments considered in this volume. However Biochemistry as a discipline had been in existence for a considerable time as a part of the Physiology Department and from that base had played a full part in the development of Biochemistry in the University of London. It should also be noted that for many years, biochemical work was undertaken in the Botany department although this had little relationship to the formal development of the subject in the College.

Initiating Biochemistry in the Physiology Department

The initiation of biochemical studies came in 1925 with the appointment to a junior lectureship in Biological Chemistry of Margaret M Murray, a First Class Honours graduate from the department who had already started research in Biochemistry. She was described by Edward Mellanby as "one of the most promising women in Biochemistry in the country at present." At this time the department offered a general course in Biological Chemistry[1] and a further course in

Advanced Biological Chemistry for the Honours Physiology Students.[2]

In November 1925 the College Council resolved to apply to the Senate of the University for a recognised teacher post as Lecturer in Biological Chemistry for Margaret Murray. She is described as Junior Lecturer in Biochemistry here, although elsewhere she is described at this time as Junior Lecturer in Physiology.

The force behind these developments had been Professor J S Edkins, a mathematician who developed an intense interest in the application of physical and chemical principles to biological systems. Edkins was head of the department from 1896 to 1936. At the Promotion Committee in 1928, which converted Murray's junior lectureship in Biochemistry to a full lectureship in Biological Chemistry, Edkins spoke of "the increasing importance of the subject and of the necessity for having some specialised teacher in Biochemistry".[3] Murray continued her work in Biochemistry and for a while published in *The Biochemical Journal* as well as elsewhere.

In 1929 the University constituted a Board of Studies in Biochemistry to co-ordinate biochemical work in the University, most of which took place in the Medical Schools. Indeed the Board, as a matter of policy, felt that Biochemistry was not suitable as a subject for a first degree. Margaret Murray was appointed to the Board at the outset although she did not become a member of the Board of Studies in Physiology until about 1945, by which time she had become the Secretary of the Board of Studies in Biochemistry.[4]

In 1947 the Council applied for the conferment of the title of Reader in Biochemistry on Murray. However, this was overtaken by her appointment to the Chair of Physiology and Headship of the Department, a step that caused few raised eyebrows since biochemical teaching had become so important in the Department's activity. Such a move left vacant the lectureship to which Dudley F Cheesman was appointed in 1948. Cheesman had graduated in Chemistry from Imperial College in 1937 and, after obtaining his PhD, had gone to Sweden where he was a Research Associate at Stockholm University and a Swedish State scholar at Uppsala. Later, caught in Sweden because of the war, he had worked for the British Embassy in Stockholm. After the war he returned to England to work at the Royal Institution before taking up his lectureship at Bedford. Cheesman continued and developed the biochemical teaching and research in the Department.

An Honours degree in Biochemistry

Biochemistry as a degree subject in the University of London developed slightly later than at Oxford and Cambridge. Under the guidance of Sir Frederick Gowland Hopkins, Cambridge had started teaching Biochemistry as a Part II subject for the Tripos in 1924[5] while in Oxford, led by Sir Rudolph Peters, the first Part II papers in Biochemistry were sat in 1952. In a paper prepared by A (Sandy) G Ogston in 1944 at Oxford, it was noted "already courses exist in Cambridge and Liverpool. London and Leeds are known to be starting them". Indeed Peters kept in touch with the London Committee considering a Biochemistry degree.[6]

These discussions started in London in 1944. The Board of Studies in Biochemistry records its view that "the University of London should institute BSc courses in Biochemistry. Detailed recommendations will be submitted at a later date". A Sub-Committee, which included Dr Margaret Murray, was appointed to consider the problem of degree courses in Biochemistry[7]. The principal recommendation was a three-year course in Biochemistry for the Special degree,[8] but the Sub-Committee rejected the idea of a joint Honours degree.[9] The Board itself now felt it could "reverse its former decision of some years standing that Biochemistry is a postgraduate subject[10] and approved the proposal.[11]

Despite this propitious start, the first students were not admitted to courses for the degree until University College acted in 1954. The reason for such an extensive delay was the continuance of a long drawn out battle with the Board of Studies in Chemistry who were uneasy about such a development. Indeed even in 1954, ten years after the Board had initiated proposals for a Single Honours degree, arguments were still continuing with the Chemists who in Cheesman's view "failed to understand the uniqueness of the biochemical discipline".[12] Three students began the second year of the Biochemistry programme in 1954 even though the regulations had not been finally approved.[13]

At Bedford College, Murray asked Dudley Cheesman whether he would like to offer the course as a single-handed enterprise on the understanding that he would continue to offer courses to students in Physiology. He recalled "with distinct foreboding, I agreed. My teaching load increased to some 25 hours a week!" The College Council recorded in its report for 1954–55 that "The College now offers facilities for three new degree courses instituted recently by the University–viz in Biochemistry…next session two students have already been accepted in Biochemistry."[14] In fact the first student to graduate in Biochemistry, Daphne Norden in 1957, was already in her first year as a student in Chemistry when these decisions were taken. Norden went on to an appointment as Demonstrator and then Assistant Lecturer in Biochemistry.

Student numbers registered for the Biochemistry Special degree were very small by the standards of the late twentieth century but were very respectable for Bedford at the time. While in the first year of operation, 1955–56, only two students were registered, this number rose to 6 by 1959–60 which equalled the number registered for the BSc Special degree in Physiology for that year.

The degree programme involved biochemical courses only in the second and third years, the first year being dominated by Chemistry and included Physiology. Students took some lectures at University College during this period since Bedford had but one senior teacher. The Part I examination, taken after two years, and Part II taken after three years, were University examinations sat solely by the students of University and Bedford Colleges. First Class Honours was not achieved by the early students in Biochemistry but the first student to receive such an award was a Bedford student, Eileen Temperley in 1960.

At the very end of the 1950s, a number of changes occurred which influenced the future development of Biochemistry. Margaret Murray decided to retire from the department in 1959. Before leaving she wrote to the Principal to clarify the position of Biochemistry in the department: "I hope that in any steps taken as a result of my resignation that the interests of biochemistry and physiology are borne equally in mind."[15] Concurrently the University appointed Cheesman to a personal Readership in Biochemistry. Cheesman then became acting Head of Department until the arrival of Professor Wilfred Widdas in 1960 and took the decision to transfer most of the biochemical activities to new accommodation being made available to the department in the Tuke extension.

The Joint Honours degree

The first steps in setting up a Joint Honours degree in Biochemistry in the University were taken by Cheesman. In an extensive memorandum dated 21 January 1960, he wrote to the Chairman of the Board of Studies in Biochemistry proposing such a degree based primarily on the need to widen access to the discipline for undergraduates:

> "The only means whereby a prospective student may hope to acquire an undergraduate training in Biochemistry is to secure admission to the BSc Special course at University College or Bedford College. The entrance qualification for this course is a General Certificate of Education with Chemistry, Mathematics (Pure or Pure and Applied) and Physics (or Botany or Biology or Zoology) at Advanced Level. If Physics had been passed at Ordinary Level, an appropriate examination must be passed during the first term of the course. It follows that candidates who have passed only in Chemistry and two biological subjects at Advanced Level cannot be admitted to a course in Biochemistry, a subject in which their biological training, sometimes excellent, has stimulated their interest."[16]

Referring to papers published in *The Biochemical Journal*, Cheesman concluded that "many major contributions to our subject are made by workers who show no evidence of more than a rudimentary knowledge of Mathematics and Physics". Cheesman noted that Biochemistry would only be offered for Part II with either Chemistry, Physiology, Botany or Zoology as the other subject. He recognised the high standard in both subjects that would be required for a student to gain high Honours.[17]

The Board agreed the proposals although there was argument for a time about the possibility of overlap between subjects if the degree were in Biochemistry and Chemistry, or Biochemistry and Physiology. The Senate approved Biochemistry as a subject for Part II of the Joint Honours degree in July 1961.[18]

Creating a Department of Biochemistry

In the early days of biochemical teaching, the accommodation provided was in the Physiology Department housed on the first floor of Acland Building. The larger of the two teaching laboratories was appropriate for chemical work, with its dark polished teak benches with racks of reagents at the back of each place. However in the autumn of 1959, the College was able to provide extra science accommodation with a wing at the east end of the Tuke building coupled with an extra floor on top of the building. The top floor of this wing was devoted to the Physiology Department and was used for an animal house and for specialised biochemical accommodation. Cheesman moved to an office in the new space and the main laboratory, of very modest size, was also allocated to Biochemistry. Here research students and third year students could be taught. For the first time there was a cold room. Daphne Norden, the assistant lecturer, also had a small office opposite the laboratory. There was now an identifiable locus for Biochemistry in the College although the space was not sufficient to accommodate second year students who continued to be taught in the Acland building. Biochemistry was still not taught to first year students.

It was during the period of occupation of the Tuke extension that an incident occurred which demonstrated the tension that always exists in academe between the administrative and academic sides of institutions. The College's fire alarm siren was installed in the Biochemistry laboratory window. The siren was powerful and literally deafening to anyone unfortunate enough to be in the laboratory when it was activated. Cheesman complained with characteristic force to the authorities who were as usual sympathetic but no action was taken. At a fire drill, a student standing close to the window was so terrified when the siren sounded that she dropped the biochemical preparation on which she had been working for three days. Cheesman was incensed and immediately went to the administration who were, as usual, sympathetic, but unmoved. Cheesman returned to the laboratory and removed the brushes from the siren motor! The problem did not recur.

The following year saw further strengthening of Biochemistry. Eileen Temperley started work as a research student of Dudley Cheesman working on aspects of muscle biochemistry. John Prebble was appointed to an Assistant Lectureship, having been recruited from the Botany Department where he had been working on biophysical problems. Dr Norden completed her term as Assistant Lecturer in 1961 and took up an appointment at Chelsea College. Prebble, now resuming his interests in the study of bacterial carotenoids, was appointed as Lecturer. Peter Zagalsky from Cambridge took up a one year demonstratorship in Biochemistry. Zagalsky initially worked on biochemical issues of blood glucose permeation with Professor Widdas but later, with Cheesman, on carotenoproteins from lobster.

In 1962 Zagalsky was promoted to Assistant Lecturer and John Lagnado, from the Medical Research Council, was appointed to a lectureship in Biochemistry. Initially Lagnado, who had obtained his qualifications in McGill University, Canada, worked on muscle with Cheesman but later became interested in and an authority on microtubules. The Biochemistry section of the Department now consisted of a Reader, Cheesman, two Lecturers (Lagnado and Prebble) and an Assistant Lecturer, Zagalsky, who was promoted to Lecturer in 1965. Around this time Mr Ted Hawkes was appointed the Chief Technician (Laboratory Superintendent) and together with a team of some four technicians gave unstinting support to the Department's activities.

Biochemistry was now a coherent group of staff composing almost half of the Department of Physiology and, arguably, an adequate nucleus for a viable department in the College at that time. Inevitably such a group sought such an identity within the College comparable to that of other disciplines, a goal which was reached by small steps. The Council report for 1961–62 describes the department as "Physiology (including Biochemistry)". In 1962–63 the title is "Physiology and Biochemistry" while in 1965 a separate Biochemistry Department is listed. Such a progression could be justified on the basis of increasing undergraduate numbers reading for the BSc Special degrees. In 1963–64 for example, there were 14 biochemists, the same number of psychologists, 16 zoologists, 20 botanists but only 10 physiologists. Postgraduate students were now becoming a significant part of the department's activities, although even later they rarely numbered more than 6 at any one time.

In 1963–64, the College put in hand a complete refurbishment of the first floor of Acland for the biochemical section of the department which would occupy this accommodation following the move of the Physiology section into the new Jebb building. The two teaching laboratories were refurnished with new benching and fume cupboards, the old darkroom was converted to a cold room, and research laboratories were created for the members of staff. Two of these laboratories were provided by a grant to the department from the Wellcome Trust, one laboratory being formed by partitioning the lecture theatre. This work was completed in the spring of 1965. The Biochemistry section recommenced work in its new accommodation in the autumn of 1965 with a quantity of new equipment purchased with a grant that came with the refurbishment. The College created the new Department of Biochemistry on 1 January 1966 with Dr D F Cheesman, Reader in Biochemistry, as its Head of Department. On the 1 October 1966 the title of Professor of Biochemistry was conferred on Dr Cheesman. Thus with 19 students registered for the BSc Special degree, Biochemistry at Bedford College had come of age with its own department, the second oldest Biochemistry Department (outside the Medical Schools) in the University of London. Other departments soon followed in Queen Elizabeth College, Royal Holloway College, Chelsea College and elsewhere.

Halcyon days

The achievement of departmental status, after what seemed somewhat of a struggle to the biochemists, brought with it a fresh enthusiasm for both teaching and research. It is true that in terms of its diversity the teaching load associated with providing a full coverage for the Special degree was taxing for the staff. There was, however, an enthusiasm among the younger members for a subject which itself was now blossoming with new discoveries illuminating the core of what was taught. Thus, over the years 1965 to 1975 there was an explosion in basic biochemical knowledge which led to real insights being gained on fundamental questions of protein structure, how proteins, lipids and carbohydrates were synthesised and how the cell conserved its energy from oxidations. All this new knowledge, together with the beginnings of the application of genetic concepts, needed to be fed directly into the teaching syllabus at the third year level while also modifying the second year syllabus. For a while there was still no first year course in Biochemistry. A major factor dictating the success of the group at this stage was the encyclopaedic knowledge of the group's leader, Professor Dudley Cheesman. Cheesman had the capacity to encompass in considerable detail the developments across the whole field and, because of this, to inspire and inform his younger colleagues.

In the 1960s during the cold war, links were created, initially by Lagnado, between the department and universities in East Germany, particularly Leipzig. Lagnado had been invited to run a workshop on isoenzymes arising out of his earlier research interests but this link was developed so that several members of the department visited Leipzig. In view of the political sensitivity of such a relationship, it should be noted that these visits were for purely for scientific purposes.

Despite the substantial teaching load, the research of the group continued to develop. Cheesman, who became Dean of the Faculty of Science in 1967, worked primarily on the chemistry of muscular contraction being funded by the Muscular Dystrophy Group. However earlier he had worked on aspects of proteins. A review of surface properties of proteins published in the early fifties was particularly influential on the field.[19] Professor Munro Fox of the Zoology Department had interested Cheesman in the protein in eggs of a tropical South American snail. Cheesman published on this and other similar proteins. The snails (each having a name!) laid bright pink eggs and were a familiar sight (and smell) in Cheesman's laboratory. One star performer, Lizzie, was capable of laying eggs equivalent to 20% of her body weight each evening. However, because of prolonged in-breeding by the mid-60s, new animals were required. These duly arrived from South America in a rather large box which unexpectedly also contained several snakes (included as a gift from the dealer). Not knowing whether they were poisonous or not Cheesman instantly presented them as a gift to the Zoo.

Lagnado now developed with the support of the Medical Research Council studies on brain biochemistry eventually focusing on the microtubular proteins of this tissue. This activity occupied him for some years until the field became congested with research workers supported by better facilities than could be mustered in a small department. During secondment as a Professor to the University of Zambia at Harare, Lagnado transferred his interest to the study of microtubules in *Trypansomes*, protozoans responsible for sleeping sickness. The objective was to seek sites for drug attack in this organism, the work being supported from the World Health Organisation and the Wellcome Trust. Zagalsky took up studies on the blue carotenoprotein in the lobster shell, *crustacyanin*, but also examined a variety of other related proteins. Later he became involved in the European Space programme's work on crystallising proteins at zero gravity. Prebble's interests were in bacterial carotenoids and were focused primarily on the photoprotective function of these pigments in microorganisms. The research interests attracted a number of research students, many from overseas. All members of staff supervised candidates for the PhD degree, some two or so students on average gaining the degree annually.

Undergraduate numbers continued to rise from 14 students reading for the Special degree at the department's foundation to 42 ten years later. In the early years, such was the shortage of graduates in Biochemistry that students never needed to apply for jobs but were offered them through the Head of Department. Students admitted to the department to read Biochemistry were distinctly disappointed by not being able to start work on their chosen field until the second year of their programme. Eventually in response to student pressure, the department initiated a half course unit in the early 1970s. The remainder of the first year was devoted to Chemistry (Physical and Organic), Physiology and Mathematics. The second year was devoted initially to Biochemistry, Organic and Physical Chemistry although later the proportion of Chemistry (just over 60%) was reduced in order to accommodate more Biochemistry.

The increasing student numbers, coupled with the development of the discipline, caused the department to seek a fifth member of staff. Initially the College agreed to a Special lectureship for 1967-8 for Dr Gertrude Glock, who had a long association with the Physiology Department. In 1968, a temporary assistant lectureship was made available by the College and Rhoda Quarmby, a research student of Peter Zagalsky, was appointed. In due course the lectureship lapsed and the department continued with four staff until, in 1973, a lectureship was established and Dr John Clarke from St Mary's Hospital Medical School was appointed. Dr Clarke's area of expertise was enzymology, a field which the Department was finding difficult to cover.

This period was not without its problems. The growth of the subject led to large numbers of new periodicals and many new books, mostly very expensively priced. The department's library budget did not cover such expansion and difficult choices had to be made. One member of staff was thrown out of a well-known London bookshop for reading part of a certain expensive text each morning on the way to work and taking notes! The department subsequently bought the book for the library.

The gathering storm

The rapid development of biochemical knowledge, which had been such a stimulus to the group in the 1960s and early 1970s, now began to be a burden in the late 1970s. The discipline was racing ahead. Other biochemical departments which had started later had now increased in size well beyond that of the Bedford Department. Each member of staff had to cover at an advanced level a number of diverse topics and were required to keep abreast of the developments in such topics. New areas of the discipline, such as immunology, endocrinology etc, once regarded as subjects of interest only to specialists, were now becoming parts of mainstream biochemical education. While the staff were conscious of the strains of teaching with so few staff, the College was aware that two of its departments, Physiology and Biochemistry, were below what was seen as viable size. While Botany and Zoology had eight staff each, Biochemistry (and Physiology) had only five members each. For the College, the issue came to a head with the impending retirements of both the Professor of Physiology and the Professor of Biochemistry.

The College's Academic Board in 1980 decided to set up a Working Party to consider the future of the Departments of Biochemistry and Physiology. The Working Party, which regarded its remit as concerned with academic matters but not questions of cost effectiveness, consisted of the Dean of the Faculty of Science, the Heads of Botany, Geology and Zoology together with the Head of the Department of English. In addition to collecting advice internally, it sought the views of external experts from Cambridge, Cardiff and two London Medical Schools. The Working Party noted the growth in undergraduate numbers in the department and the relatively high proportion of high Honours graduates. There was some criticism of final year papers although the department pointed out that they had all been approved by external examiners. The postgraduate numbers were constant, but relatively low compared with other departments, and external funding in later years had dropped to a low level. Both the space available to the department and the facilities were said to be inadequate. It was recommended that an established chair in Biochemistry should be created and supported by five lecturers. Substantial funds would be required for equipment. Failing this it was reluctantly concluded that the department should cease to teach the single Honours degree. The report noted however that

> "it would be difficult to justify the closure of a Department with a large intake of successful undergraduates...and considered that such a closure would be liable to misunderstanding and would threaten the viability of other departments in the Faculty of Science and perhaps the College as a whole".

Such a complex series of conclusions were not easy for the Academic Board to digest. The recommendations of the Committee were however overtaken by the increasingly serious problems facing the entire College. A further committee, set up in the summer of 1981 to consider the College's future, recommended that the College seek a merger. King's College, London, was seen as a suitable partner. While the College management started formal discussions, the department made early approaches to the King's Biochemistry Department led by Professor Henry Arnstein. Arnstein was sympathetic, indeed enthusiastic, about a merger and several happy meetings took place between the two departments. However the successful discussions between the biochemists were not mirrored by talks at the higher level. By Christmas 1981 the negotiations had collapsed.

The seriousness of the College's problems led to the proposal for a 'stand alone' plan which envisaged the closure of six departments, three in each Faculty. In Science, Biochemistry, Chemistry and Physiology were identified for closure. All three departments protested strongly to the College and three College Senate representatives (including one in Biochemistry and one in Chemistry) saw the Vice-Chancellor personally about the matter. The Vice-Chancellor felt the College should seek another merger. By Easter serious discussions were underway with Royal Holloway College which had a thriving Biochemistry department under the leadership of Professor Jack

Pridham. Both departments were enthusiastic about the possibilities for the merger although both sides later, inevitably, had reservations, some major, as the problems of merger became apparent.

End game

In the summer of 1982, Professor Dudley Cheesman, Bedford's only Professor of Biochemistry retired. In the early days Cheesman had almost single-handedly built up degree teaching in Biochemistry at the College and was responsible for initiating the Joint Honours degree in Biochemistry in the University of London. He had created a department from a group which he had formed in the Physiology Department and above all he had been a strong academic inspiration to his colleagues. The administration had known the full force of his anger if he became aware that another member of staff or a student was being unfairly treated. His sympathies had stretched to a wide range of people, particularly those with unusual backgrounds, special difficulties or those from overseas. Throughout his academic life he had always found the time to give students personal attention. Such an approach was probably the reason for his nickname among physiology students in the 1960s, "Cuddly Dudley".

John Prebble (who was also simultaneously elected Dean of the Faculty and later appointed Vice-Principal) became Head of Department (initially acting Head) in 1982. The problems facing the department (now consisting of only four academic staff) were basically three-fold. Firstly there was a large number (greater than in earlier years) of high calibre students who needed to be provided with at least the same quality of courses as previously. Drawing on their cordial relations with King's College, help was given to the department by Dr Mike Canon in teaching some aspects of molecular biology. Otherwise, the teaching load of the staff was increased temporarily. Secondly, the department needed to plan for its future in the merged situation at Egham, and also for the painful process of closure at Regent's Park and removal. Thirdly, there was a need to maintain during this disruptive phase, the general life and morale of the department particularly for the sake of the students. It is noticeable that research plans did not feature in this list. The staff endeavoured to maintain their research activity but time and energy were now seriously eroded by all the problems of a small department.

The final graduates in Biochemistry at the College were a particular cause of satisfaction for the staff. In all 22 students obtained degrees in Biochemistry, 17 of them in the single Honours programme, the highest number in the department's life. Of these more than half obtained First or Second Class honours. On the day of the final viva, the department, anxious to conclude its life on a high note, entertained the external examiner, a leading British biochemist, to an excellent lunch. In the second viva after lunch, the examiner asked a question of the candidate and promptly fell asleep. The candidate's answer was nevertheless satisfactory and she gained a good degree!

The Department of Biochemistry at Bedford College had a short life but, nevertheless, it had a major role in the shaping of teaching of non-medical Biochemistry in the University. Several of its students had subsequently made significant contributions to the subject. Its Professor believed that small was beautiful, a belief which may in part have been influenced by the fact that sadly, the Regent's Park site beautiful as it was, had not the space to sustain scientific work in the late twentieth century. However the high standard of its graduates contributed to the College's reputation in science teaching. Despite its small size, limited equipment and cramped space, it also contributed in its research to the fields in which its staff were interested.

Acknowledgements

I wish to acknowledge the use of a manuscript note on the history of the department by the late Professor D F Cheesman. I wish to express my appreciation to John Lagnado and Peter Zagalsky for their valuable comments on the manuscript and to Dr Ann Whitehead for her recollections of the department.

References

1 The terms Biological Chemistry and Biochemistry (also Physiological Chemistry) are in practice virtually synonymous and use of the former has now largely ceased although early in the century it was the usual description of work on the chemical aspects of living things.

2 *Bedford College Calendar* 1927–28.

3 Report of the Promotion Committee to the Council meeting, 22 March 1928.

4 *Curriculum vitae* for Murray, Bedford College Archives D730.

5 M Weatherall & H Kamminga *Dynamic Science Biochemistry in Cambridge, 1898–1949.* Wellcome Unit for the History of Medicine, 1992.

6 M G Ord & L A Stocken *The Oxford biochemistry Department, Its History and Activities 1920–1985.* The Department of Biochemistry, Oxford 1990.

7 Minutes of the Board of Studies in Biochemistry, 24 March 1944.

8 Informal record of discussion of a meeting of the Sub-Committee, 21 June 1944.

9 Informal record of discussion of meeting of Sub-Committee, 5 May 1944.

10 Informal record of discussion of meeting of Sub-Committee, 31 March 1944.

11 Minutes of the Board of Studies in Biochemistry, 21 July 1944.

12 Notes on the History of the Department left by Professor D F Cheesman.

13 Reported to the Meeting of the Board of Studies in Biochemistry, 22 October 1954.

14 Report of the College Council for 1954–55, p27.

15 Letter, Murray to the Principal, 13 January 1959.

16 Minutes of the Meeting of the Board of Studies in Biochemistry, 21 January 1960.

17 Minutes of BSc Sub-Committee of Board of Studies in Biochemistry, 1 February 1960.

18 Report to Board of Studies Meeting, 28 February 1962.

19 D F Cheesman & J T Davies (1954) *Physicochemical and biological aspects of proteins at interfaces.* Adv. Protein Chem. 9, 439–501.

Chapter 3

Botany

Leslie J Audus

The first fifty years in the life of the College saw the birth of modern botany. In 1859 Darwin published *The Origin of Species* which drew heavily on data from the plant kingdom. Later his pioneering studies on plant growth led ultimately to the isolation of plant hormones. In microscopy the substage condenser and apochromatic lens revealed the intricacies of nuclear division. Hydroponics launched precise studies on the mineral requirements of plants. One can only guess the impact such major advances had on Bedford students at that time. However biology of a sort was taught from the beginning with W B Carpenter MD, FRS, Professor of Physiology at the Royal Institution and of Forensic Medicine at University College giving a short course on 'Natural History' which must have included information an plant structure and functioning. Botany emerged as a subject in its own right in 1872 when Alfred William Bennett MA, BSc, FLS was appointed to teach it and was given the courtesy title of professor. He was assisted by a geologist, Catherine A Raisin BSc (London). The move from Bedford Square to York Place in 1874 and the opening of the degree examinations of London University to women in 1878 brought great changes. The improved accommodation promoted lectures for degree students although formal departmental structures were not yet set up. Instruction in Botany and Geology took place in a communal lecture room and in smaller rooms for informal coaching and the investigation of specimens.

In 1892 Catherine Raisin, then the only member of the College staff to hold a DSc, took over the teaching of both Botany and Geology. Later In 1900, when the College became a School of the University, she was the first member of the College staff to serve on the University Faculty of Science. She had one part-time assistant and occasionally an untutored 'boy' to produce material for practical investigation. Botanical study at that time was of types from the main Classes of the Plant Kingdom, their morphology, anatomy and reproductive systems together with a smattering of basic ecology and descriptive physiology. Facilities for experimental work were minuscule. That year (1892) marked the appearance of the first Botany graduate, Mary Easterbrook Hicks, listed in Div 11, with Third Class Honours.

A discrete Botany unit began to emerge with the appointment of Ethel Nancy Miles Thomas BSc (London) as Assistant Lecturer for the Michaelmas term in 1900. A graduate of University College, she had been a postgraduate protegée of Ethel Sargant, a distinguished Cambridge botanist who had guided her research on double fertilisation in *Caltha* and on developmental seedling anatomy. In 1908 she was appointed Head of an independent Botany Department. Ann C Halket BSc was also appointed full-time Demonstrator. A department was then taking on a modern shape. A description of that fledgling unit has been provided by Miss A S Davey, BSc (London), who graduated from there in 1912. She wrote, "There was a total of 12 to 14 students of which 2 to 3 were taking honours.(....) The whole of the course was taught by the Head of Department assisted by one demonstrator". Ethel Thomas promptly made her students *au courant* with contemporary trends in Botany and invited senior botanists to give short courses of lectures on their specialities. They included Agnes Arber (née Robertson) DSc–on the phylogeny of the ferns–and Marie Stopes, palaeobotanist and pioneering advocate of birth control.

Ethel Thomas was an inveterate go-getter. In the 1911–12 session, as soon as the decision was made to move on to the Regent's Park site and the house, South Villa, was officially leased, she quickly appropriated space in its grounds and staked out a Botany garden. Her efforts were directed predominantly to promoting Physiological Botany and so cajoled the College Council to fit out the conservatory of South Villa as an experimental greenhouse. Thus while new laboratories for Botany, Geology and Zoology were being built as the North Science block, experiments in Botany were conducted in that conservatory while lectures continued in York Place. Unversed in experimental matters, she recruited part-time lecturers, as for example in the same session Mr D Thoday MA (Cantab), later Professor of Botany at University College, Bangor, gave six lectures and associated practicals on 'Metabolism', presumably the first 'modern' Physiology course to be given in the department. The practical work was difficult since students had to transport the available apparatus from York Place to South Villa, a distance of well over half a mile, set it up and, afterwards, take it back. They had also to make up their own standard reagents.

In the 1913–14 session the new Botany Department was occupied; it was palatial in comparison with the cramped rooms of York Place. Based an a continental design, the main laboratory was tiered up from the north-facing windows to provide uniform illumination for microscope work on all benches. A further luxury was a separate Physiology laboratory with chemistry-type benches. Surrounded by acres of ground suitable for cultivation, Ethel Thonas began to prepare students for the Royal Horticultural Society examinations and the new University Degree in Horticulture. For this expansion of the curriculum William Neilson Jones MA (Cantab) was appointed Assistant Lecturer to provide horticultural as well as physiological teaching. Two demonstrators, Miss T L Frankerd BSc (London) and Miss A J Davey BSc (London) and a 'skilled horticultural assistant', J V Hart DipHort (Oxford & Reading) were also appointed. Consequently student numbers rose to 60 in 1916: the Botany Department had become the largest in the College.

There was very little postgraduate research for higher degrees in science in the College at that time. Thus between 1886 and 1919 there were only eight such degrees of which Botany produced two. According to Miss Davey "Miss Thomas really started (....) research in the face of great opposition". Miss Halket and Miss Frankerd were active investigating the physiology of salt marsh plants and the mechanisms of plant responses to gravity respectively. In the 1914–15 session Ethel Thomas was awarded a DSc for her work on developmental seedling anatomy and was made a Reader by the University.

There were, during that period, two major College events promoting Botany and stemming largely from Ethel Thomas's contacts. One was the death in 1909 of Alice Caroline Sargant, aunt to the Cambridge botanist Ethel Sargant, Ethel Thomas's mentor. She left £1000 to the College "to be applied to buildings, equipment, endowments or otherwise in connection with the Botanical Laboratory". Ethel Thomas proposed that the bulk of the money be used for a greenhouse/laboratory in her Botany garden, but, because of persistent wrangling over sites and plans, such a construction was not to be realised until 1925, long after Ethel Thomas had left the College.

The other event was the raising of a fund to provide research facilities in London for woman botanists. With the increasing flow of female graduates, women had difficulty in finding suitable accommodation, men being given priority for the relatively few places available in university departments. In the suffragette spirit of the age, a group of women botanists and their friends set up such a fund and Bedford College was selected as the obvious establishment to approach. Ethel Thomas, a subscriber to and negotiator for the fund, offered £500 to Council to defray the cost of building extra research rooms for such senior botanists' use in the new department. In the 1914–15 session the money was used to build a suite of laboratory rooms along the east wall of the corridor connecting the Oliver Dining Hall and North Science. But the project had been dogged by difficulties; who for example would allocate the research places, the Donors' trustees, viz Ethel Thomas and Ethel Sargant, or the Council? Unfortunately the fund was insufficient to meet all the Donors' requirements and so the Council finally decided to reimburse them with money provided by a councillor, Giles

Theodare Pilcher, in commemoration of his wife's year as President of the Old Students' Association. Thence the research rooms became 'The Pilcher Wing', an unhappy title neglecting all reference to the pioneering spirit of the Women Botanists. However the rooms continued to be used for botanical research for a number of subsequent years and as late as 1950 long-established staff were still aware of the rooms' botanical connection although they had long been occupied by staff of the Arts Faculty.

The growth of that botanical 'empire' of Ethel Thomas aroused jealousy and resentment in other science departments culminating at the beginning of 1916 in a furore which split the College down the middle. It had come to the notice of some members of the Academic Board that Ethel Thomas had twice taken courses for the 2nd MB Part 1 in Organic and Applied Chemistry and passed the examination on the second occasion. This was the trigger which fired a Council inquisition accusing Ethel Thomas of thereby neglecting her teaching. Her defence, that she had to improve her knowledge of Chemistry to stand in for William Neilson Jones away on war work, and her convincing demonstration that student performance had not suffered, fell on deaf ears and on June 28th, 1916 the Council resolved (perfectly legally) not to renew her 3-year appointment. This draconian treatment raised vigorous written protests from other College staff and from a country-wide group of senior British botanists. All three demonstrators in the department tendered their resignations. But the Council remained adamant and eventually Ethel Thomas accepted £1000 in compensation and shook the dust of Bedford from her feet.

Her academic enemies had had their way, leaving a large well-established department floundering leaderless. William Neilson Jones, still away on war work, was offered the headship but declined it. In his absence some lectures were given by his wife, Mabel Chevely Rayner, a pioneering authority on mycorrhizas. Although Ann Halket withdrew her resignation, research had virtually stopped. Then James Small BSc, DSc (London) was appointed Lecturer and ran the Department with only Ann Halket to help him. He revivified research somewhat with a series of studies on the floral biology of the *Compositae* and the nature of gravitropic response.

In the summer of 1919 William Neilson Jones returned from war service, accepting the headship, and in May 1920 the Senate appointed him to a University Chair, the first in science in the College. At the same time James Small resigned to go to a chair in the Queen's University, Belfast and Mr S Garside MSc (Manchester) replaced him. Miss M S Rivett BSc (London) as Demonstrator also managed the Botany garden. The department was thus much depleted with student numbers small and only four members of staff. A similar situation was to persist during most of the inter-war period so that final-year advanced teaching for Honours relied heavily on intercollegiate courses.

At the end of the 1923–24 session the Sargant bequest was used to build the glasshouse/laboratory for which Ethel Thomas had agitated so vigorously. Erected on the Botany garden site it was opened officially in July 1925 by Lord Justice Sargant, a member of the donor's family. In addition to a well-lit laboratory there was a large hot-house in which ferns, cycads and other exotic plants could be grown for teaching purposes.

After the turmoil of the Thomas regime the department settled into a long tranquil period of teaching, characterised by an increased cover of physiology and genetics. There was little staff research but a trickle of graduates stayed on to study for higher degrees. There were three DSc degrees awarded, namely to Miss K B Blackburn in 1924 for the cytology of sex determination in *Lychnis*, to the Misses M H Carré and Helen K Archbold for biochemical studies on apples in storage, both the latter working partly at Imperial College. Helen Porter (née Archbold) eventually became Professor of Plant Physiology at Imperial College, was elected to the Royal Society and became a Fellow of Bedford College a few years before its final demise.

In the 1924–25 session William Neilson Jones became the first Hildred Carlile Professor of Botany. He was very catholic in his botanical tastes and his studies ranged over wide territory. Early interest in genetics and sexual expression in dioecious species moved to other aspects of plant behaviour including epinasty, leaf tropisms, intrinsic polarity in organs and plant chimaeras. He was also, in the best sense of the word, a gadgeteer, being particularly concerned with providing undergraduates with experimental tools which could be simply made and operated. One very strange phenomenon discovered in the department at that time was the promotion of starch grain hydrolysis by polarised light. Over the period 1924–26 the phenomenon was explored by Miss E S Semmens, Miss E C C Baly and William Neilson Jones in colaboration with the physicist the Rt Hon Lord Rayleigh. The possible biological significance of the phenomenon invoked much speculation at the time but the mechanism and import still remain obscure.

From the mid-twenties onwards research interests were directed more and more to tree nutrition and the role of mycorrhizas. Just before World War II William Neilson Jones and Mabel Rayner were given an Agricultural Research Council grant to investigate the Bagshot Sands on Wareham Heath in relation to their infertility for the growth of nursery conifer seedlings. At that time it was expected that special composts would provide magical nutrients for the recalcitrant seedlings. Many and varied composts were prepared on the Sargant Laboratory site and two assistants worked on the project there, namely Alan G. Morton MSc (Liverpool), PhD (Cantab) and later Miss Ida Levisohn, an experienced mycologist and refugee from Nazi Germany. The Forestry Commission supplied a 'Muller House' for the cultivation of conifer seedlings. It was an open-sided building with glass-louvred sides, allowing free through-flow of air but ensuring that the root environment was under strict experimental control. That work sounded the death knell of the compost-nutrient theory and established specific mycorrhizal fungi as the particular requirement of the seedlings.

In 1937 Garside emigrated to South Africa and E F Warburg MA, PhD (Cantab) was appointed to replace him. At that time Ann Halket was awarded her DSc for wide-ranging studies of plant development. Then came World War II and the department migrated to the Botany School at Cambridge, taking with it only a basic minimum of books and equipment. Teaching was reasonably unaffected with mutual pooling of staff and students of the two botany departments. In the 1940–41 session an air raid destroyed the North Science building and everything in it although the Sargant Laboratory was not damaged and research on tree nutrition continued although somewhat restricted. In the 1942–43 session Ann Halket retired after 35 years of continuous service to the Department and Robert Brown BSc, PhD (London) replaced her.

Because North Science was in ruins on the return to London, the three science departments of Botany, Zoology and Geology started the 1944–45 session in temporary accommodation in Sussex Lodge, a Georgian villa outside the Park at the top of Sussex Place. That ramshackle old house, riddled with dry rot, stood in about half an acre of delapidated gardens where once were tennis courts on which pre-Wimbledon tournaments were staged. The old dining room became the main laboratory shared between Botany and Zoology, giving rise to serious time-tabling problems. The communal lecture room was the old coach house. Seminars were held in the small 'Cow Room', so named because it had once housed a collection of rare ceramic cows. Congestion there was excessive, incubating an educative intimacy for both students and staff. Botany's small preparation room and research laboratory were in the old semi-basement kitchens. The ancient electric wiring demanded a power-rationing routine for the use of energy-consuming gear like autoclaves. Nothing substantial could be left on overnight. Furthermore courses were much simplified because of the lack of skilled laboratory technicians and equipment.

As part of war reparations Dorothy Harrison-Church BSc (Wales) was appointed 'Museum Assistant' and commissioned to reconstitute the library, herbarium and museum, all destroyed during the blitz. Over the five years of her employment she was remarkably successful, trawling an extensive range of sources for books, back-runs of periodicals, spare museum specimens etc. Much of the comprehensive herbarium of British flowering plants was built up on her own collecting excursions.

In 1945, after two years in the department, Robert Brown resigned. His subsequent career took him to the Regius Chair of Botany in

Edinburgh. William T Williams ARCS, PhD (London) replaced him. In the early post-war euphoria there was a marked upsurge in research activity. Bill Williams extended his work on stomatal mechanisms. Philip F Wareing BSc (London), replacing Demonstrator Ann Conolly BA (Cantab) in an Assistant Lectureship, started research on the responses of seedling trees to day-length in relation to their seasonal dormancy, pioneering work which led him later at Manchester to identify abscisic acid, a natural growth regulator in plants and to his fellowship of the Royal Society. William Neilson Jones retired at the end of the 1947–48 session after thirty years in the chair and Leslie J Audus MA, PhD (Cantab) was appointed to succeed him. E F Warburg moved to the Curatorship of the Oxford University Herbarium and Yolande Massey PhD (Durham) was appointed in his place. Dorothy Harrison-Church, her task completed at the end of 1950, was replaced by Francis Rose BSc (London) in a Demonstratership. His Easter field course in Langdale in 1949 launched one student, Jean Paton (née Comyn) to eventual prominence as the country's leading liverwort expert.

Before that move into the new Darwin Building, Bill Williams went to the Chair of Botany at Southampton University where he was to pioneer the computer mapping of plant communities. With his going the College lost an exceptionally versatile academic. He was a brilliant pianist who wrote sparkling Noel Coward-type reviews for student performances. He was replaced by Bernard Sharman PhD (Leeds), a plant developmental morphologist. Phil Wareing left for Manchester and was followed by Barbara Menzies BSc (New Zealand), PhD (Cantab).

The change of headship did not affect research for the Forestry Commission, despite the death of Mabel Rayner soon after the change, since Ida Levisohn continued to work on mycorrhizas and other root-inhabiting fungi. In fact microbiology was to be a continuing research theme throughout the life of the Department; topics were rust fungi (Barbara Menzies, 1950–57), the genus *Auricularia* (Eric Duncan, 1957–61), fungal enzymes (Alan Bull, 1961–65), fungal genetics (Barry Faulkner, 1961–65), mycorrhizas, lichens and pollution (Brian Ferry, 1965–84), bacterial flagella structure (Malcolm McDonough, 1965–84) and the interaction of herbicides with the soil microflora (Leslie Audus, 1948–79), including the first isolation of an organism *Bacterium globiforme* adapted to degrade 2,4-D, a selective herbicide (Kathleen Symonds, 1958).

The additional facilities for Botany in the new Darwin (North Science) Building included an illuminated constant environment room for growth studies and a sterile room for microbiological procedures. Occupation in the autumn of 1952 brought staff additions. Linna E Bentley BSc (Manchester), PhD (London) was appointed specifically to teach Plant Biochemistry. Norah L Penston BA, DPhil (Oxon), FLS, a botanist from Wye College staff, was appointed College Principal. Since, as such, she had by statute to be an academic, she was thus included on the teaching staff of the department and gave occasional lectures.

The Sussex Lodge privations had highlighted the need for a central workshop to construct apparatus designed in departments for specific research projects. At that time only Physics possessed such facilities. Leslie Audus therefore launched the idea with the relevent committee and soon after the Sussex-Lodgers moved into their reconstructed laboratories on the main site the Science Workshop was set up in the basement of the Herringham Building. Eventually it was to take on board the running of the College motor transport pool, used mainly for field work in the Botany, Geology and Zoology Departments.

Another College development stemming directly from the Botany Department was the College Shop. At that time, because Botany students found it impossible to locate flat-ground 'cut-throat' razors for sectioning plant material for microscopic examination, the department kept a small stock for sale. The notion that a College Shop could function better as an intermediary retailer, was suggested to and approved by the Principal and eventually a stall run by the Bursar's Department appeared in the Herringham entrance hall. In a very short tine a proper shop catered for most of the needs of all students. Another development in which the Botany Department was essentially involved was the establishment of an Assistant Lectureship in Statistics.

Previously Botany staff had taught their own statistical analysis methods but had campaigned for a College lecturer to teach a basic course and give advice to research workers in Botany. They supported a similar drive by the Psychology Department. In due course Miss M A Creasy BSc (London), with experience in agricultural yield problems at Rothamsted Experimental Station, was appointed to the Psychology Department.

The year 1953 saw staffing developments in relation to the new accommodation. It included a Professorial Research Assistant, a Departmental Assistant, ie a graduate for practical-class preparation beyond the scope of the technical staff, and a full-time Departmental Secretary. Up to that tine the immediate post-war phase had continued with one secretary shared between the three Darwin departments. Leslie P Turnbull BSc (New Zealand) was appointed to a new Assistant Lectureship. The session was to mark an unusual performance by an undergraduate, Sheila Morissey. In a third-year special study for her BSc she showed, for the first tine, that the insectivorous pitcher plant *Nepenthes* resembles the mammalian stomach in secreting hydrochloric acid in its digestive exudate.

During the 1955–56 session a Readership was established with particular reference to the teaching of Plant Biophysics and Douglas G Spanner ARCS, PhD (London), DIC was duly appointed. Barbara Menzies retired at the end of 1957 and left for the University of Sydney, Australia. Eric Duncan BSc (St Andrews) replaced her.

During 1953 Leslie Audus's book *Plant Growth Substances* was published. It went through two more expanded editions (1959 and 1972) and was the standard text on the subject for many years. In 1964 he edited a comprehensive treatise *The Biochemistry and Physiology of Herbicides* which was also greatly enlarged in a 1976 two-volune edition. It was still the main reference book on the subject when he retired. Other books published by staff over a similar period were *A Pocket Guide to Wild Flowers* (1956) by Francis Rose and colleagues, *Plants that Eat Animals* (1967) by Linna Bentley, *Air Pollution and Lichens* (1973) by Brian Ferry, Sue Baddeley and colleagues, and *Introduction to*

Thermodynamics (1964) by Douglas Spanner. The latter was to be praised as the clearest treatment of the subject ever written for biologists.

Douglas Spanner's theories an the mechanism of solute transport in the phloem of vascular plants called for the study of the fine structure of sieve tubes using electron microscopy. With characteristic enterprise he located at Cambridge an old Siemans 'übermikroscop', previously removed from Germany as part of war reparations and one of the first commercial instruments. It was then available for £300. In November the Academic Board approved its purchase for the department. During the 1958–59 session it was installed in a small cubicle partitioned off from the chief technician's office. It was far from operational and many components needed repair or replacement with up-to-date equivalents under Douglas Spanner's DIY expertise. This venture generated so much interest in the Zoology Department that, early in the sixties, a successful joint Botany/Zoology application was made to the SERC for a new Metro-Vickers EM6B microscope. During the 1963–64 session there was extensive site testing and the 'Bothy' (originally servants' quarters at The Holme) was found to be almost perfect for an EM Unit since it was remote from both the earth vibrations caused by the tube trains and from mains power surges. Installation was completed there in a number of converted rooms at the end of 1964 and Douglas Spanner moved in and took charge. Raynor Jones, a highly skilled technician, was appointed to maintain and service the microscope. The old Siemens übermikroscop found its way into the National Museum of Scotland in Edinburgh. Later a second small transmission microscope was acquired for teaching purposes and in 1970 the unit took on board the University Board of Studies in Zoology Stereoscan facilities.

Radioactive tracer chemicals were also being used at that time by Douglas Spanner to follow solute movement in the phloem. John Prebble BSc, PhD (London) was appointed to assist him. Francis Rose was very active at that time on the Field Studies Council and the Society for the Promotion of Nature Reserves.

At the end of the fifties the growing pressure for teaching and research space made it necessary to ask the Forestry Commission to find other accommodation for Ida Levisohn's work and thus free the Sargant Laboratory. After her departure in the 1961–62 session Linna Bentley and Leslie Turnbull drew up plans for its extension and modernisation into a Botany Garden Unit. This marked the end of an era since, in the autumn of 1960, George Butler retired as head botany gardener after 38 years of service; he had had much to do with the design of the original greenhouse and lay-out of the site.

The spatially scattered London Colleges had long since meant that contact between the staffs of botany departments for informal seminars on teaching and research was minimal. Consequently Professor Thomas G Bennet-Clark (King's) and Leslie Audus founded the Hales Club (after the famous eighteenth century London botanist Stephen Hales) to promote such interchange between plant physiologists and to entertain guest speakers.

Leslie Audus's advent had introduced research on the nature and action of hormones in roots and, after a thirty year lapse, reinstated an active interest in plant responses to gravity. Work on the latter was largely concerned with identifying the gravity sensors. In one such probe a new phenomenon, plant organ growth curvatures in strong magnetic gradients, was uncovered and christened magnetotropism. The mechanism behind that serendipitous response still remains obscure. However, delicate microsurgery of the root tip, a technique pioneered by Dr Barry Juniper of Oxford University, finally confirmed sedimenting starch grains as the gravity sensors there. What cell changes such sensors induced were first elucidated by Hilary Rose (née Griffiths), the postgraduate first to coax the recalcitrant übermikroscop to perform. In 1959 David Bellamy BSc (London) entered the department to work on bog ecology with Francis Rose. An energetic and charismatic student, he organised 'Kronika Botanika', a postgraduate seminar stimulating staff and student alike. His later popularity as television personality and outspoken advocate of conservation led to a fellowship of RHBNC in 1996. The Departmental Assistant in 1959 was Max Hooper, a pioneering worker on the relationship between species number and age in British hedgerows.

During the 1963-64 session Bernard Sharman was appointed Reader. His research on morphogenesis in apical meristems was based an his pioneering development of flash photography under high-magnification, such inventiveness extending to his teaching techniques in plant anatomy. Linna Bentley spent half the session studying ion exchange in oat at the Macaulay Research Institute in Aberdeen. Brian Ferry BSc (London) replaced Alan Bull PhD (Notts) who went to Queen Elizabeth College and ultimately to a chair at Canterbury. Two visitors during the session were Professor D S Fensom, from Mount Allison University, Canada, working with Douglas Spanner on bio-electric potentials associated with solute transport, and Professor Paul-Emile Pilet from the University of Lausanne working with Leslie Audus on hormone transport in roots. At the end of the session Norah Penston retired as Principal and thereby the Department lost a friend and part-time member of staff.

The new Botany Garden Unit was completed in the mid-sixties and involved the partial demolition of the Sargant Laboratory. Only the 'tropical' greenhouse was retained. New features included high-intensity lighting for growing uniform experimental plants and two specialised rooms for work with radioactive tracers. Later (circa 1970) the 12 original composting and potting shed housed two controlled environment cabinets for the study of photomorphogenesis of seedlings (Donald Brett).

During the 1965–66 session Leslie Audus took over the editorship of the *Journal of Experimental Botany* and continued in that office until August 1974. For many years up to and after his retirement he was a member of the Annals of Botany Company. He also served on the editorial board of *Phytochemistry*. At the beginning of the 1966–67 session he was awarded the ScD of his alma mata, the University of Canbridge. During the 1967–68 session he was President of Section K (Botany) of the British Association for the Advancement of Science.

Leslie Audus's reputation in plant growth regulator and herbicide studies took him far afield. He was Visiting Professor for two separate semesters presenting advanced courses in the University of California at

Berkeley (1958) and the University of Minnesota at Minneapolis (1966) respectively. In 1963 he visited the USA Academic Year Institute, an organisation set up to update mature graduate schoolteachers. He gave short lecture courses and seminars in fifteen major universities there. There were extensive research tours abroad. In 1959 he was guest of the Nicholas Copernicus University, Torun, Poland, inaugurating the Polish Plant Growth Regulator Group. In the spring of 1967 he visited Russia to lecture and consult with scientists in Moscow and Leningrad on the use of plant growth-regulating chemicals in agriculture and horticulture.

After the Robbins Report and the admission of men undergraduates, pressure for more space intensified. The Geology and the new Biochemistry departments were particularly in need. The result was the Tuke-Darwin Infill Building whereby Botany and Biochemistry acquired an additional shared laboratory, equipped specifically for microbiological work. It included a refrigerated room for culture storage. Sharing led, as in Sussex Lodge immediately after the war, to time-tabling problems and understandable tension between those technicians preparing for practical classes.

In 1966 Linna Bentley spent some time in Southern Africa running the Department of Botany in the University of Basutoland, Bechuanaland and Swaziland. Bernard Sharman resigned in 1967 to take up a Professorship in the University of Calgary, Canada, and Donald Brett BSc (London) replaced him to teach morphology, anatomy and some developmental physiology. Leslie Turnbull resigned at the end of the session to become College Registrar. Douglas Spanner spent four months at Mount Allison University in Canada, teaching and extending his collaborative research with Professor Fensom (see previous). During the 1971–72 session he was awarded a DSc (London) and had conferred upon him the title of Professor of Plant Biophysics. Linna Bentley was promoted to Senior Lecturer.

With the establishment of the Computer Unit in the College and the rapid expansion of its use, Leslie Audus joined the College Computer Committee in 1972, to look after biological interests, and the University Computing Resources Committee to represent the smaller colleges. In 1973 he joined the Advisory Board to the Director of the ARC's Letcombe Laboratories concerned with problems of plant/soil relations in agriculture, an Institution almost unique in its remit. Donald Brett, whose interests had extended to dendrochronology, published a number of analyses of timber from medieval sites in London.

Leslie Audus retired at the end of the 1978–79 session after thirty-one years in the chair. William G Chaloner PhD (Reading), FRS, from the chair of Botany at Birkbeck College, succeeded him. Anthony D Stead BSc, PhD (Bangor) was appointed to a Lectureship to teach growth physiology previously covered by Leslie Audus.

The advent of Bill Chaloner, as a leading palaeobotanist an the international scene, brought a shift in research emphasis in the department. He made Bedford College the base for an intercollegiate course in Palaeobotany, which had been running for some years and taken by Geology and Botany students from several London Colleges. Facilities were extended by the addition of a scanning electron microscope and in the 1980–81 session a new course on Electronmicroscopy and Ultrastructure was started. A succession of research fellows visited the department to profit from his advice and guidance. Other research activities concerned growth regulators with particular reference to flowering (Tony Stead), thermophilic algal biochemistry (Tom Ford), dendrochronology and climate (Donald Brett). and the status and development of shingle beach vegetation at Dungeness (Brian Ferry and Stephen Waters).

Bill Chaloner's eminence brought honours as well as responsibilities. In his research field he was Chairman of the Organising Committee of the Ist International Palaeobotanical Conference at Reading. He was elected President of the International Organisation of Palaeobotany. Just before the move to Egham he was awarded the International Medal of the Palaeabotanical Society. He gave generously of his time to the University and to science in general. He served as chairman of both the Scientific Publications Board of the Royal Society and the Science, Medicine and Engineering Sub-Committee of the

Central Research Fund. During the 1982–83 session he was elected to the University Senate and appointed a trustee of the Royal Botanic Gardens, Kew.

In those last few years the department contributed much to the restructuring of biology teaching. Bill Chaloner presented a teaching module on evolution to the Open University. Linna Bentley and Brian Ferry served on committees revising the London University A-level syllabus in Biology and writing the new General Science Modular Syllabus for the East Anglian and London Region Examining Boards respectively.

In the dying days of the department during the move to Egham, Linna Bentley, although having taken early retirement, continued to teach part-time Botany courses for geologists and geographers. And thus the wheel came full circle. The dubious politics of academe, which so cruelly interrupted the career of Ethel Thomas, that vigorous, progressive midwife of the infant department, had, after nearly seventy years, also brought about its demise.

APPENDIX

Heads of Botany Department, 1849–1985

1849–	W B Carpenter FRS
1872–91	A W Bennett
1886–1908	Catherine Alice Raisin DSc
1908–16	Ethel Nancy Miles Thomas DSc
(1916–19)	James Small DSc and Ann Halket DSc
1919–48	William Neilson Jones
1948–79	Leslie J Audus ScD
1979–85	William G Chaloner FRS

Chapter 4

Chemistry

Margaret M Harris (née Jamison)

Chemistry at the College might be said to have begun when Sir Oliver Lodge, and later Dr S U Pickering, gave some talks to the girls in Bedford Square. But the seed that grew and flourished was planted by Holland Crompton, who took over in 1888. The College was by then in York Place, now Baker Street, and London University had admitted women to its degree examinations ten years before. The stage was set for a new Chemistry Department to develop, and Mr Crompton rose magnificently to the challenge.

He was the child of a north country industrial family; his mother was a Scot and much of his childhood education was gained in Germany. On his return to England he set his sights on the Central Technical College, and the study of Chemistry. He was a man of all-round culture, related to the Potters (of Beatrix fame); he played the cello, and was an early member of the Fabian Society. Aware that Chemistry was a subject to be studied and practised in tandem, he set up a small laboratory in the College lecture rooms in Baker Street. He later collaborated with the architect to design laboratories for the new buildings in Regent's Park. The Regent's Park site held the whole Department's practical facilities, but when in 1930 expansion allowed division into inorganic and organic branches, the older area became the organic section and the new lab the inorganic.

Meanwhile, during the 1914–1918 war, Crompton took on a research programme, under the auspices of the Royal Society, and carried it out at the same time as his teaching, working all hours of the day and night.

When the Department was sub-divided, Holland Crompton became Head of Organic Chemistry and Director of the Laboratories while Dr J F Spencer became his partner as Head of the Inorganic and Physical section.

The growth in university places for girls drew attention to the shortage of 6th form teaching; some of this was partly catered for by local grammar schools and some by the vision of the Girls' Public Day School Trust. It was a two-way movement; Nancy Irons, who taught me Chemistry at Putney High School, had graduated at Bedford College in 1922, under the eye of "that nice Mr Crompton".

When I came as a fresher to the College in 1932 at the age of 18 these were my first impressions:

> From the front door you turn left, and then right towards the Physics Department, and immediately set off up the little wooden stairs. Passing the Physiology floor, the second flight leads to a door into Chemistry. The first door on the immediate left is open. It emits the sounds and smells of a laboratory, and there is Dr Mary Lesslie, in a fresh white coat, tending a bubbling flask. The door opposite leads to a small laboratory with an inner office, which is the suite of Dr E E Turner, the present Head of Organic Chemistry, more frequently found working with Dr Lesslie in her larger room. Next along the passage is a darkroom which houses a polarimeter, and then an organic research laboratory, big enough for two workers, with fume cupboards, benches, a table, and a commodious Belfast sink. On the right-hand side is the tiered lecture theatre. Its fine demonstration bench and ample blackboards are well lit by large windows overlooking the quadrangle.

The corridor opens on to a landing where the South Science central staircase arrives. On the left is a well-fitted chemical and equipment store, efficiently run by two girls in green overalls, Ellen and Ivy. Next on the left is the large organic teaching laboratory, and opposite is the Chemistry library containing Beilstein, and the journals of the Chemical Society, the American Chemical Society, Berichte and Liebig's Annalen, among others. Through the next door is the organic research laboratory, which accommodates about 12 postgraduates. Through the opposite door is the head of Tuke staircase; on the left of the landing a balance room houses rows of shining brass swing balances, each with its little box of brass weights.

On the right is the inorganic store and, beyond this, the inorganic teaching laboratory, a large room with good light and an old-fashioned high ceiling providing a healthy environment. Past the technicians' workshop, on the other side of the corridor, is a row of laboratory/studies suitable for inorganic or physical chemists.

On our first morning in 1932 we assembled in the inorganic laboratory, each to be allocated a cupboard (personal territory) and given, by Dr V C G Trew, a tube containing a powdered mixture whose composition we had to identify. We set about a regular series of tests; qualitative investigations such as fusion on a charcoal block using a blowpipe to get maximum heat, or bending platinum wire and forming a borax bead whose colour, after fusing with our mystery mixture, could (with other diagnostic tricks) lead to the identification of four or five components. Quantitative methods, such as titration and gravimetric processes, were also required.

This class of 1932 encountered no suggestion of triumphant feminism, although present-day students might find this improbable; our start at Bedford seemed the most natural educational consequence, and this is mainly attributable to our teachers. Dr Trew had been an undergraduate at Bedford, its first internal PhD in Chemistry, and the first woman to hold a teaching and research post in the whole of the University. Her speciality was magnetochemistry, and with Dr J F Spencer she investigated the effect of strong magnetic fields upon the apparent weight of specimens. She was one of the earliest women to win a DSc, and she was our guide to discipline in that laboratory.

On the organic side we came under another truly remarkable woman, Dr Mary S Lesslie. She had benefited from a Scottish education, working equally with men students, was appointed a Demonstrator in 1927, and came south from Dundee with a trunk containing not only her personal effects and books but a vacuum desiccator, the first seen in the Department. As Holland Crompton's health was failing, she shouldered a large proportion of the organic teaching until, in 1928, Dr E E Turner was appointed Reader in Organic Chemistry in a sideways move from East London (later Queen Mary) College. He was a man of wide experience and practical enthusiasm. He and his friend G M Bennett had carried out and published research even as undergraduates; during the 1914–18 war he became research assistant to Sir William Pope in Cambridge and investigated the synthesis of arsenicals, presumably with military potential. While a lecturer at Goldsmiths' he had begun to think about the structure of optically active molecules, and this combined with the interest in arsenicals led to the preparation of an optically active arsenium salt during a period at the University of Sydney.

Before Turner came to Bedford, he had pondered on Kauffler's formula for biphenyl. Biphenyl was made up of two benzene rings joined together; according to Kauffler, the benzene rings were parallel to each other. Turner accumulated evidence that they were co-axial and, in the absence of blocking groups, rotated freely relative to one another. Unsymmetrically placed groups caused mirror-image isomerism and hence optical activity. The optical stability (rate of racemisation) of a specimen should be related to the size of the block(s). When, after the war, Linus Pauling was finding that all atoms have characteristic size, the relationship between size and racemisation rate could be made more precise by measuring energies of activation for racemisation.

At Bedford, Turner soon saw the advantage of collaboration with Mary Lesslie, herself a fully competent stereochemist who had trained and published work under Professor Alexander McKenzie at Dundee. This collaboration set a direction for the organic section which is still followed fruitfully over the world today (1999).

The undergraduate practical organic course of 1932 was based on J B Cohen's book, and we made compounds, including Wöhler's 1828 synthesis of urea from inorganic materials: potassium cyanide, red lead oxide, and ammonium sulphate. This synthesis had proved an important philosophical maxim–that organic chemicals were not intrinsically different from inorganic chemicals, and did not owe their existence to a 'vital force'. This was thrilling–we didn't just read about it, we repeated it! Standing at what was soon to be regarded as an inadequate fume cupboard, one heated potassium cyanide in an iron dish. When the cyanide had melted, the red lead oxide was slowly stirred into the hot mass. After the violent reaction, the cooled melt was treated with ammonium sulphate and extracted with water. The filtered solution was evaporated on the waterbath, and crystals of urea, identical with the natural product, were obtained from alcohol. One wonders what the reaction of a safety officer would be to this exercise today if he watched us, unprotected by goggles or masks, stirring the molten cyanide, and noting the smell of bitter almonds.

For practical physical chemistry we used Dr J F Spencer's book. Ten or twelve experiments were permanently set up in the physical lab to be worked through on Saturday mornings under Dr Trew's supervision and guidance; it was pioneering teaching within the university, and possibly within the country. Dr Trew had another interest which proved pastorally helpful later. She was an early member of the Theosophical Society (she even inherited Annie Besant's typewriter). When cults began to capture the minds of innocent students who were diverted from their work, Miss Trew was able to produce a useful folder full of relevant information.

When, in 1945, the Royal Society opened its fellowship list to women, no fewer than three of that first distinguished intake–Rosalind

Henley (later Pitt-Rivers), Kathleen Yardley (later Lonsdale) and E M Stephenson–had received at least part of their early scientific education in that little Chemistry Department between 1921 and 1931. (Bedford had also nurtured Sophie Bryant–the first woman DSc, a mathematician, and a great headmistress of North London Collegiate School.)

One memorable feature of daily life was a large (4′6″ x 2′6″) heavy wooden box which stood on the landing outside the organic store. This was the ice box, filled regularly by an iceman who brought an enormous block of ice up the stairs on his shoulders. It nearly filled the box, and the research worker would use an ice-pick to chip the required amount from this block. The ice-box offered a certain communal element, as with women at a well. Ice was essential for many preparations; if the supply ran out there was no alternative but to take a bucket down to Baker Street and to beg an obliging fishmonger to let you have what was needed.

Dr Turner gave the first two years of fundamental organic chemistry lectures; Drs Spencer and Trew gave the inorganic and physical chemistry courses. In the final year specialist courses were given on topics which varied from year to year. Dr Spencer gave a course on the history of chemistry which consisted largely of biographies of chemists, illustrated by slides, as well as his physical chemistry lectures.

After graduation, some students stayed to take higher degrees (MSc, MPhil or PhD). The problem of maintenance arose, and was not readily solved. The temporary post of Demonstrator was ideal, but very few such posts were available at any one time. With hardly any College scholarships for Bedford graduates, and only the Holland Crompton (£30 per year) exclusively for scientists (not only chemists!), it was necessary to look elsewhere. The University offered a few scholarships, and when the DSIR began to support students, Bedford was among the first to profit by it. Later, grants from the Agricultural Research Council and the Medical Research Council, and the Fulbright Fellowships (USA) became available to a small number. However, in 1937 there were three PhDs and 2 MScs from the organic sub-department.

Ishbel Grace MacNaughten Campbell came as a Demonstrator in 1936; she had her PhD from St Andrews, and had been to Cornell where she held one of the first Commonwealth Fellowships awarded to a woman. To our regret she left us for a post at the college in Southampton in 1938 and we lost a remarkable experimenter and teacher, full of good sense and harmless fun. She eventually became a Reader at the University of Southampton, and educated a following who were proud to refer to themselves, even when professors, as "Ishbel's boys".

Her main research interest was the organometallics of Groups 5 and 6. Some of these smelled really disgusting, and there was one memorable day in Bedford when Ishbel left her tellurium compounds and went to have lunch, taking her place next to a young lecturer from the Greek department. After a minute or two, and without comment, he set down his knife and fork, got up, and walked away. The young aesthete was Louis MacNeice.

The threat of war became clearer during the 1938-39 session; to bring students back to the metropolis in wartime could be foolhardy. A shortage of scientists was expected nationally, so the departmental teachers were instructed to continue teaching the normal three-year course but to condense it to two years. The College evacuated to Cambridge, and began the autumn term of 1939 there only one week late. Queen Mary and Bedford College Chemistry Departments were offered the hospitality of the Pembroke Street laboratories for teaching; how fortunate we were! Cambridge householders provided accommodation; they were often academic, cultured, mildly left-wing people, and had already received evacuees and made every effort to integrate them into their home lives. But the first wave of evacuees (from bombed industrial areas) had already decided to return to their devastated cities, leaving their hosts vulnerable to the billeting officer. The Bedford undergraduates were readily welcomed. Our stalwart Matron, Mrs Beatrice Craggs, answered calls for help on her bicycle, with a little pharmacy and first-aid treatment in her basket in front. Our Principal, Miss G E M Jebb, lived in Springfield, Sidgwick Avenue, and office accommodation was offered at Newnham just down the road. The Chemists, however, had their own territory for the duration of the war in Pembroke Street.

The teaching laboratory was large, with five long benches, two of which were allotted to Bedford. The fittings were in some ways antiquated by Regent's Park standards–for example, some of the ceiling lights were gas-burners so reflux condensers had to be set up with especial care lest 'bumping' led to a fire. At one end was a smaller laboratory in which Dr Turner, Dr Lesslie and I could work and watch over the undergraduates as well. Apart from teaching, our major assignment was to prepare pure samples of hydrocarbons–mainly heptanes, octanes, and nonanes. Because these hydrocarbons could not, at that time, be separated from mixtures, the only way to get a pure specimen was to synthesise it by a reliable method from pure starting materials. Dr G B B M Sutherland was developing the new technique of infra-red spectroscopy, to relate the IR spectrum of a hydrocarbon to its chemical structure. Delia Simpson (Agar), who worked with him, held a demonstratorship in physical chemistry at Bedford. A scheme for identifying the hydrocarbons in a specimen of petrol from an enemy aircraft might, for example, lead to finding its source. We had an open-ended assignment to make as many pure (largely aliphatic) hydrocarbons as we could: by the end of the war we had made 6 heptanes, 13 octanes, 20 nonanes, 6 methylhydrindanes and about half a dozen others.

For some Bedford postgraduates life was more complex. E E J Marler was caught in Holland at the start of the war and was interned until the liberation. Dr Jessie Mole, the Holland Crompton Scholar of 1937, was employed by ICI (first at Widnes and then in the Technical Services department in Liverpool) when, at the start of the war, they hastily reversed their policy of never employing women. She returned to London in 1950 with the Ministry of Supply, Atomic Energy Division, and hence to the Atomic Research Establishment at Harwell (1955–1975) where she was assistant to the Director for the rest of her professional life. Just before I retired, she brought in an old suitcase, hastily packed with her research chemicals when war broke out–it had not been opened. We put it in a good draught and opened it. Sure enough, the old bottles contained arsenicals whose preparation she had not had time to publish. Some of them had been made later by Dr Valerie Goldberg, one of the 'married women returners' supported by the Salters' Company.

At Cambridge a distinguished refugee, Dr Max Perutz, had obtained crystals of the blood protein, haemoglobin, and an X-ray diffraction pattern from which he hoped to deduce its complex structure. To do this it was necessary to read not only the location but also the intensity of each spot. Such tedious work would now be done by computers, but in their absence it fell to two women assistants, one of whom, Dr E M Davidson (later Beyts), was a Bedford Chemistry postgraduate. Such work was very boring and demanded high accuracy–but the eventual outcome was a triumph.

On 10 May 1941 we heard that the College had been seriously damaged by bombing. Three of us ran to the station to catch the first London train. When, after a miserable journey in an icy train, we reached Regent's Park we found that the North side (Botany, Zoology and Geology) had suffered worst while Chemistry had escaped. Beside the path up from the Little Gate there was a medium-sized bomb crater. Dr Turner immediately saw a use for it, and we threw a lot of dangerous chemicals into its depths–where they probably remain, under the turf.

A year before the exodus to Cambridge an event took place whose significance to Chemistry at Bedford could not have been predicted. A girl from Essex, Muriel Hall, arrived as a new undergraduate. She was to stay as postgraduate, Demonstrator, Assistant Lecturer, Lecturer and Reader, and finally to assist in the move to Egham before she retired. Her whole professional life was as a member of the College, on which she brought distinction in every way. She published papers, and was awarded the PhD and the DSc; she guided research students through their higher degrees; she gave delightful and enlightening lectures; she was a University examiner and contributed to the Board of Studies in Chemistry (including chairing the Higher Degrees Sub-Committee); and she advised the architect when the research laboratories were extended. During the war she tackled the synthesis of antimalarials; her main interests lay with the optically labile compounds for which she devised ingenious syntheses and, more recently, this expanded to include a variety of topics, including liquid crystalline compounds which enabled her to advance her interest in spectroscopy, especially NMR.

Her door was always open to students seeking advice and help. It was as a result of their acquaintance with Dr Hall that the Salters' Company set up financial arrangements to help 'married women returners'. After her retirement she visited old colleagues in New Zealand, Thailand, Hong Kong, Princeton and Hungary, to name a few, and welcomed countless foreign students and their families back to stay with her in her home in this country. When she hosted the Royal Society of Chemistry's meeting of the Liquid Crystals group in 1984, it was attended by delegates from a wide area including Asia, North America and Europe.

The 1941 bombs dispelled any thoughts we had of an early return to London. But by January 1944 the decision was made to take the risk and preparations were put in train to open in Regent's Park in October. Undeterred by the untimely arrival of the V2 bombs we did indeed start in October. Chemistry was again fortunate to be in its old familiar premises. Being an Air Raid Warden in Marylebone was not all that different from in Cambridge, although transport to and from home was sometimes disrupted. But the future was bright.

Professor Spencer retired, and Professor E E Turner FRS took over the headship of a unified department. Dr Barrer came for 2 years. Drs Lesslie and Trew were lecturers, I was a part-time lecturer, and Drs Hall, Grove and Taylor were demonstrators. In 1946 men were accepted equally with women as postgraduates but not yet as undergraduates. The session opened with a record number of 685 students in the College. There were 10 postgraduates in Chemistry, 6 of them men. The Royal Society and ICI gave grants for equipment and the DSIR funded two research students under Professor Turner. Bedford was the first women's college to attract a UGC grant.

It was not long after we settled back in Regent's Park before we had an interesting influx of postgraduate students from abroad, many of them women from countries where higher education for women was something new–Fatima Minhaj, Sardar Mahboob, and Shaki Ahmed, and Yasmeen Badar from Pakistan. Teresa Poole (Todtleben) from Poland had spent some of her teenage years in Ravensbruck and a labour camp in Germany–she went on to establish educational links with Strasbourg and Saarbrucken, and a flourishing interaction with various Polish universities at the University of Surrey, where Renate Koenigsberger established and organised a substantial chromatography and analytical laboratory while in academic posts there. After Margaret Oblitas (Wilden-Hart) went to teach in St Stephen's Girls' School in Hong Kong, Cheung King Ling and Wong Ka Wing came to Bedford; S P Bakshi from Lahore became Head of the Government College, Jammu; Richard Mazengo came, financed by the Rockefeller Foundation, and returned to a post at Makerere College, Uganda; and Birawan Prakobsantasukh, who was sent by the Government of Thailand, returned there to administer education for women there. W L F Armarego from Malta started his higher education in Alexandria; he left Bedford (with his wife Pauline) for a post in the John Curtin Foundation in Australia. Victor Sanchez del Olmo from Madrid later took Chairs at Vigo and Barcelona before returning to Madrid; Osman Dusouqui taught at Kuwait and, during the troubles, in Vienna; cheerful Herb Siegel went back to the States; Henry Shine, financed by the Institute of Petroleum, worked in Texas; P K Patel came from Gujurat via Kenya–he won an Amy Lady Tate scholarship; Shyam Singh was helped by the British Council; and there were many others.

Naturally some of our own graduates stayed on to take research degrees and proceeded to do very interesting things. Caroline Pearce (Mason) went to Los Alamos via Buffalo; Lily Baxendale was a founder member of the pharmaceutical firm, Biorex Laboratories; Norvela Forster (Jones) became an MEP; B L Wedzicha became Professor and Head of Food Chemistry at Leeds; and Derek Bryce-Smith Professor at Reading University, applied himself to a study of zinc deficiency and lead toxicity. A very gratifying proportion took up teaching, whether at school, college, polytechnic or university level. Ann Cooke (née Mellor) was one of these. She carried out much interesting research, first at Bedford, then at the University of Malta and again in Bedford, subsequently becoming a schoolmistress.

Staff came and went. Dr J W Smith, an expert on dipole moment studies, followed R M Barrer; Dr K E Howlett, who gradually shouldered much of the administrative work, arrived as an Assistant Lecturer and in 1953 was awarded an ICI Fellowship for 3 years, progressing to Lecturer and Senior Lecturer. Dr Hall and I gradually went on to Readerships. A refreshing new discipline came with Dr M E Farago (née Baldwin) who developed an interest in the uptake of metals by plants, often as coordination compounds–these research lines blossomed at Bedford and over 30 years she carried them globally, publishing countless papers and bringing many people to the department either as researchers or as visitors. Dr F E Prichard brought in infra-red spectroscopy.

A major change in 1958 was the retirement of Professor Turner and his replacement by Professor P B D de la Mare. He was a New Zealander who came to work with Ingold and Hughes and became a Reader at University College. Under his leadership the research schools flourished, and with his international contacts more research workers, both junior and senior, were attracted to the department. His field of study was organic reaction mechanisms, particularly the reaction of chlorine with aromatic compounds where addition was frequently found to accompany substitution. He relished the intellectual challenge of investigating reaction pathways and detecting minor intermediate products which shed light on them. Seven years later he was offered the Chair of Chemistry at the University of Auckland which, to the regret of the whole department, he accepted. He was succeeded by Professor G H Williams, a free-radical man.

Roger Bolton's interests were also in reaction mechanisms, and he worked with Professor de la Mare; John Tillett investigated organic sulphites with success; John Sandall was a physical organic chemist particularly interested in dipole moments and NMR; Professor Arthur James studied the physical chemistry of biological systems; and Dr David Murphy was interested in the oxidation of phenols and collaborated with Dr W T Dixon until the latter's shocking early death.

We were very fortunate in our infrastructure. No laboratory ever had better chief technicians than Fred Robinson, George Watts-Liquorish and Ron Mitchell. Fred and George were excellent organisers–their stores were always in perfect order–while Ron was a craftsman of genius. He could work in wood, in metal and in glass, and he could invent. Thanks to him we had ball-and-stick models, made to scale with authentic bond angles before such things came on the market. He made apparatus which thermostatted a polarimeter tube and adapted it so that two solutions could be separately brought to temperature, mixed, and run into the polarimeter tube for immediate reading; these were perfect circumstances for studying atropisomerism as well as racemisation rates. And nobody who saw it would forget Professor Turner's annual 'Liquid Air Lecture' at which he was helped by Ron.

May Sherwell and Gladys Brooks stand out among cleaners. Mrs Brooks, who lived in Marylebone, held keys which enabled her to open up the College at about 6.30 in the morning; any of us who worked all night could have an early cup of tea with Mrs B.

Two departmental secretaries, Isobel Bereton and Doris Storey (née Greaves), covered many years. They were both very efficient, and Doris outstanding. One could take her a much worked-over manuscript and ask her to type it in the style favoured by the journal one hoped would accept it for publication, and it would reappear in a form to delight the most critical referee.

Fifty years after I entered the Department, Professor Williams had the sad task of leading it (a year early) into the process which was to end in annihilation.

In 1965 male undergraduates were accepted, and in 1966 we had a very lively group (many of them to take Firsts in 1969) who were a pleasure to teach. One of them was Kyriacos Constantinou Nicolaou. He went to the States, and is now one of the world's most famous organic chemists. His particular skill is in devising syntheses of enormous naturally occurring molecules. Take Taxol, the highly effective anti-cancer agent obtained from the yew, which unfortunately has the drawback of unpleasant side-effects. Related to it are equally complex drugs, which are naturally occurring and can be scraped off coral reefs, but are available in only very small quantities. As Nicolaou says, unless the organic chemists can come up with syntheses of these compounds the world's coral reefs are at risk. He and his groups at the Scripps Research Institute, La Jolla, and at the University of California at San Diego, have just synthesised vancomycin, separating out atropisomers along the way–it contains a 2,2'-dihydroxybiphenyl unit and can be synthesised from (+)-carvone in many stages, often with very high yields. He quotes R B Woodward: "There is an excitement, adventure and challenge, and there can be great art, in organic synthesis." May he long continue. Bedford Chemistry may be lost to Regent's Park, but it has its creative sons and daughters scattered out over the world.

Acknowledgements

In composing this essay I have had encouragement and practical help from old friends and colleagues–notably from Keith Howlett, Muriel Hall (Hargreaves), Henry Shine and Roger Bolton. While thanking them heartily let me make it clear that any errors of fact or judgement are mine, and mine alone.

Chapter 5

English

Tatiana Wolff

When Mrs Elizabeth Jesse Reid pioneered higher education for women by founding the Ladies' College in Bedford Square in 1849, of the first four Professors appointed, the Reverend A J Scott became Professor of English Literature and Moral Philosophy, a chair he held concurrently with the Chair of English Language and Literature at University College, London.

He was only to stay for one year, moving in 1851 to Manchester to become Principal of Owen's College. Dame Margaret Tuke records him as being a brilliant lecturer, drawing in a large number of students to his lectures on Moral Science and English Literature. In fact English Literature was the most popular subject with the first intake of Ladies - who, according to the prospectus, could enter the Preparatory School from the age of twelve upwards. All classes were chaperoned by Lady Visitors.

In spite of his short stay the Reverend Scott managed, presumably because of his non-conformist views on religion (confirmed by his post at University College), to cause two of the other Professors, who in their turn were associated, with the Anglican King's College, London, to resign on the orders of their Principal. This was symptomatic of the difficulty experienced by the new College in uniting on the one hand staff members associated with University College, and on the other those affiliated to King's.

The tenure of the second Professor of English at Bedford, the Reverend Thomas Wilson, proved even shorter. He survived for only one term. Previous to his appointment to Bedford College he had resigned a curacy and left the Church of England, his publications being theological rather than literary. His heterodox views had not been discovered when he was appointed and he was asked to resign, which he did at once. Francis Newman, the Professor of History and Mental and Moral Science, resigned at the same time since he shared Thomas Wilson's heterodox views.

Short term tenures for Professors of English at Bedford remained the order of the day for several more years: Professor Leopold Smart stayed one year, as did Professor Andrew Findlater, who then transferred to taking charge of the Preparatory School which had been opened in 1853 in association with the College, which now took in pupils from the age of nine. Professor Thomas Blackburne and Professor John Jephson (who assisted in an edition of Chaucer's Works and later edited Shakespeare's) only survived a term each and they were followed by R D Hoblyn and Thomas Spencer Baynes, again for a year each. Baynes, however, then stayed on at the College for a further year as Professor of History. At last, in 1859, a Professor was appointed who settled in for eight years: George Macdonald.

It was during this time–in 1851–that George Eliot, listed as Mary Ann Evans, spent one Lent term at Bedford College studying mathematics; and–in 1852–one of Dickens' daughters, Catherine, was also listed as a student.

George MacDonald was both a poet and a novelist. A graduate of Aberdeen University, he had settled for a time in Manchester and it was while he was there, in 1855, that he published his narrative poem *Within and Without*, which won the admiration of both Lord Tennyson and Lady Byron. When he became Professor of English at Bedford College, he moved to London for life and numbered among his friends:

Browning, Ruskin, Carlyle and Tennyson.

During George MacDonald's term as Professor, an Assistant–J Lewis Kinton–was listed in the Department for the first time. After his retirement, MacDonald settled to much more writing, both of poetry and prose, including stories for children.

George MacDonald was succeeded as Professor of English by John Wesley Hales, who managed to combine the post with that of Professor of English Language and Literature at King's College, London. His "withering sarcasm" finds a mention in Margaret Tuke's *History of Bedford College*, but she also quotes A W Pollard, later Keeper of Printed Books at the British Museum, as saying that he was the "best teacher of English I have known", and adds that during the twenty-three years that he held office he won the admiration of his students for the insight he provided into literature and for training them in logical precision of expression. From London, he moved on to Trinity College, Cambridge.

John Wesley Hales was followed in 1890 by Dr Henry Frank Heath, who is noted by Margaret Tuke as giving the first course of public lectures at the College on 'Modern Masters of Fiction'. All these early teachers of English had held the courtesy title of Professor; thereafter titles were more specific. Heath was followed in 1897 by Thomas Gregory Foster, who is listed more precisely as Lecturer in English rather than Professor, and as having two assistants in the department: a Deputy Lecturer, Miss Howell, and an Assistant, Miss A B Covernton. From 1900 he combined his work at Bedford College with that of Assistant Professor of English Language and Literature at University College, of which he later became Provost; and in 1905 he joined the Council of Bedford College.

Miss Covernton deserves special mention as she stayed in the Department right up to the start of the Second World War, rising to the rank of Lecturer. In 1910 she published an edition of *The Lay of the Last Minstrel*.

An interesting letter survives from A W Pollard in 1901 in which he writes:

"Do you think it would be possible, without the special leave of the Council, to add to the particulars of the English Professorship the following precautionary note: 'The Council desires to obtain the services of a teacher equally competent on the side of Language and of that of Literature. Should this be found impossible, the right is reserved of making a separate appointment for each subject. It is absolutely necessary for our University Status that the Language teaching should be in the hands of a sound philologist. It is very important that the Literature should be taught by a sympathetic professor, likely to attract outside students. It is becoming increasingly difficult to find any one man (or woman) able to combine the gift of literary exposition with the very high knowledge of philology now insisted on.'"

As it happened, several future English Professors at Bedford College moved comfortably between the teaching of Medieval and Modern Language and Literature.

Foster was followed as Lecturer in English Language and Literature in 1910 by Percy Goronwy Thomas. In the same year, Thomas was joined by Miss Caroline Spurgeon as Lecturer in Literature and Miss E M Spearing as Assistant.

Percy Goronwy Thomas remained Professor of English Language and Medieval Literature at Bedford College till 1940. His first published work was a glossary of the Mercian Hymns, published in 1903. He then went on to write on Alfred and the Prose of his Reign in the *Cambridge History of English Literature*, vol 1 (1907), edited Greene's *Pandosto* also in 1907, published an *Introduction to the History of the English Language* in 1920 and a work on *English Literature before Chaucer* in 1924, among other articles and editions.

Caroline Spurgeon was appointed as Lecturer in Literature in 1910. Three years later, in 1913, a new University Chair was created for the English Department so that there was now to be a Professor of English Language and Medieval Literature and a Professor of English Language and Literature. The Department was now the biggest in the College: in

1912 there were 153 registered students. Miss Caroline Spurgeon was appointed to the new Chair.

Up to 1912–13 no woman had been elected to a Professorial Chair in any British University. The year was therefore a turning point in the history of women's higher education. This is how Caroline Spurgeon described her interview and appointment in a letter to her aunt, her mother's sister, who acted as her surrogate mother, her mother having died in childbirth:

> "I can't believe it **yet**. I came home from my interview with the Board absol. in the depths–1 felt 1 hadn't the ghost of a chance. It was the most ghastly ordeal–a 1000 times worse than Paris–one of the men nearly fainted beforehand and quite lost his nerve and I had to take him in hand and buck him up! We were all shut up together waiting–4 men & myself–for an hour & a half.
> Tukey tells me I was the only candidate who had their self-possession and nerves–that the men looked ghastly–with their teeth chattering! & that I appeared perfectly debonair & happy, exactly like my usual self–except that I looked so young–not a day more than 30!
> Wasn't it lucky? I had on my little light grey suit with the white collar...and a new little black hat, & I know I looked nice & clean. It interests me that women have more control over themselves at a nervous crisis of that kind than men...
> So I am to be in the red brick building in trees..."[1]

On July 4th 1913, Bedford College's new brick buildings in Regent's Park had been opened by Her Majesty Queen Mary, the Patroness of the College, and in the same year the College had received a magnificent benefaction from Sir Hildred Carlile in memory of his mother, Maria Louisa Carlile. One of the Chairs created from this endowment was the Hildred Carlile Chair of English Literature. It had all come together for Caroline Spurgeon–she was to remain for fourteen years the only woman to hold a Chair at Bedford. Her name became

1 Bedford College Archives (Caroline Spurgeon's correspondence).

synonymous with the study of Shakespeare's Imagery, because of the works she published in 1930 *(Leading Motives in the Imagery of Shakespeare's Tragedies),* 1931 *(Shakespeare's Iterative Imagery)* and 1935 *(Shakespeare's Imagery and what it tells us);* but her first publications were on Chaucer: an edition with an introduction of the Miller's and the Wife of Bath's Tales in 1901, a work in French on Chaucer–*Chaucer devant la critique en Angleterre et en France depuis son temps jusqu'a nos jours,* dedicated to Emile Legouis, in 1913–and *Five Hundred Years of Chaucer Criticism and Allusion, 1357–1900,* in eight parts between 1914 and 1925.

In retrospect it is amusing to read a letter Caroline Spurgeon wrote in 1910 in which she says: "...at the age of 4 & 20 1 did not know what lit. was and had not read a single play of Shakespeare's–and, what was more, did not want to!"

In her history of the College, Dame Margaret Tuke drew attention to the fact that during the years of Caroline Spurgeon's professorship, many distinguished people lectured to the English Department, including Walter de la Mare and C F Tucker Brooke, Emile Legouis and William Garrod.

In 1919 Caroline Spurgeon asked that a Reader should be appointed in English Literature as the work load was becoming too heavy. The Reader appointed was H V Routh. He was to remain Reader till 1930.

In the previous year Una Ellis-Fermor's name had first appeared among the staff. In 1920 she was listed as Assistant Lecturer and the following year as Lecturer. She was soon to start publishing many important works on drama, the first being on Christopher Marlowe in 1926. The title of one of her many books–*The Frontiers of Drama*–epitomises her long and influential career at Bedford College. She never stopped expanding them.

In contrast to Una Ellis-Fermor's long stay at Bedford, Helen Waddell's was very short: she was Junior Lecturer for one year, 1922–23, but it is interesting that someone who was to be so well known for her books on the Desert Fathers, on Peter Abelard and the Wandering Scholars should have spent a year teaching English at Bedford, her first published work having been *Lyrics from the Chinese* in 1913.

Another brief sojourn was that of Oliver Elton, who was visiting Professor of English at Bedford College from 1927–29. He published works on a wide range of English Literature, but later became especially well known for his translation from the Russian of Pushkin's *Evgeny Onegin.*

In 1929, as Reader in the Department, Routh sent invitations to several distinguished English scholars to lecture at Bedford College. In January, John Dover Wilson read three lectures on Shakespeare; in March, Helen Darbishire lectured on Milton and Herbert Grierson on Humanism and the Churches in the XVII Century; and in May and June H W Garrod lectured on 'The English Ode'. The fees for these lectures were £8 per lecture, inclusive of travelling expenses; but Professor Grierson having checked the fare from Edinburgh managed to get his fee changed to £8 plus travelling expenses!

In the same year, in February 1929, Professor Caroline Spurgeon had lectured on the 'Leading motives in the imagery of Shakespeare's Tragedies'. That seems to have been her swansong. She retired that year and was replaced as Hildred Carlile Professor by Lascelles Abercrombie.

Lascelles Abercrombie had been publishing poetry and studies on poetry since 1908 and it is as a poet that he is chiefly remembered. He had originally embarked on an Honours course in Chemistry at Owen's College, Manchester; but he gave up the study of science without a degree when he was invited to lecture on poetry at Liverpool University. However, as Oliver Elton writing on him for the British Academy after his death noted, images from chemistry and physics were scattered throughout his poetry; and he described him as a 'metaphysical' poet. In 1922, he had been appointed to the Chair of English Literature at Leeds and in 1923 he had given the Clark Lectures at Cambridge.

Throughout his time at Bedford College, he continued to publish poetry–a collected edition came out in 1930 in the Oxford Poets series; and he was in great demand as a lecturer on poetry. Oliver Elton wrote that he talked eagerly of the craft and theory of poetry and said of his delivery: "His skill as a reader was conspicuous... minutely expressive, never missing a shade…" Although he had never taken a degree, he was to receive many honorary ones and was elected Fellow of the British Academy.

He left Bedford College at Christmas 1935, to become Goldsmiths' Reader in Oxford and Fellow of Merton. He wrote at the time: "It was a wrench, making up my mind to leave Bedford, but the balance seemed to go down on the Oxford side." He died three years later.

While Lascelles Abercrombie was still Professor, John Butt was appointed as Lecturer in Literature in 1930. One of his students, Margot Hope, who subsequently became his wife, never forgot his musical reading of Pope. He was to become the General Editor of the Twickenham edition of Pope's works.

In 1931 Una Ellis-Fermor was appointed as Reader. Two years later there was another very significant appointment to the English Department. Kathleen Constable–soon to be Kathleen Tillotson–joined the Department as part-time Assistant teaching Anglo-Saxon and Middle English (appointed at the time for a maximum of four years!). She was to remain a key figure in the Department for nearly forty years.

In 1936 Frank Percy Wilson was appointed to the Hildred Carlile Chair of English Literature. F P Wilson had served in the army in the First World War and had been severely wounded–he was to limp for the rest of his life. After the war he first returned to his own University at Birmingham and began to lecture there, but in 1921 he moved to Oxford where he was appointed Lecturer in English and then Reader and began to publish works on Elizabethan and Jacobean life and literature. In 1929 he became Professor of English at the University of Leeds and it was from there that he moved to Bedford. In 1943 he was elected Fellow of the British Academy.

Louis MacNeice was teaching Greek at Bedford College at that time (1936–39) and used to participate in meetings of the English Department's Reid Society. Margot Butt remembers that the students reading English liked to regard him as one of their own staff.

When the Second World War broke out in 1939, F P Wilson, Una

Ellis-Fermor, Kathleen Tillotson and John Butt were all teaching in the English Department. In the same year they were joined by Agnes Latham, who in 1929 had published the standard text of the poems of Sir Walter Raleigh.

The College, together with Queen Mary College and the London School of Economics, was evacuated to Cambridge. John Butt joined the Civil Service and left the Department but his contact with it was not broken and he was later to publish with Kathleen Tillotson an important work on Dickens: *Dickens at Work* (1968).

Being a student of English at Bedford College in Cambridge during the war, one felt extremely privileged: all lectures by members of the London and Cambridge English Faculties were open to us. What riches! Elizabethan and Jacobean literature with F P Wilson and E M W Tillyard; an ever expanding area of drama–Marlowe, Shakespeare, Ibsen and the Irish dramatists–with Una Ellis-Fermor; Chaucer and Langland with Kathleen Tillotson and H S Bennett; the Metaphysical poets, George Eliot and Virginia Woolf with Joan Bennett–one could go on and on.

To interpolate a personal note: my own contact with Bedford College had started curiously. The girls' school in Hampstead I attended had as one of its Principals L Susan Stebbing, the distinguished Professor of Philosophy at Bedford College. As one of the other Principals of the school was devoted to the works of Gilbert and Sullivan, every year the school performed one of their operas on the Bedford College stage, so that my own first contact with Bedford College was as a fairy in *Iolanthe*: "tripping hither, tripping thither, nobody knows why or whither"! Not surprisingly, when the time came to trip to University I went to Bedford College in Cambridge. Among my earliest and most enduring memories are of constantly laughing out loud at Kathleen Tillotson's lectures on Chaucer, to whose work I became devoted for life; and reading out essays in tutorial classes to Professor Wilson as he walked round us, always kind and humorous in his response, emphasising his points with the stem of his pipe. So aware were we of his devotion to his pipe that when he moved to Oxford to the Merton Chair of English in 1947 we spent a long time searching out a particularly fine Meerschaum pipe to give him as a leaving present.

Several other people had now joined the Bedford English Department, which was no longer divided between Language and Literature. This had been decided at the the retirement in March 1942 of Professor Thomas, who had been Professor of English Language and Medieval Literature since 1910. In 1940, while Una Ellis-Fermor was on sick leave, Muriel St Clare Byrne was appointed as a temporary Lecturer, and in 1942 Phyllis Hodgson was appointed first as Junior Lecturer and the following year as Lecturer in English Language and Medieval Literature. A year later she was joined by Pamela Gradon; initially appointed as a temporary assistant, she was to become Lecturer in 1949.

At the end of the war in 1945, Bedford College returned to Regent's Park and the English Department soon found itself beautifully housed in Decimus Burton's villa, The Holme, with a garden going down to the lake. When F P Wilson came under pressure to move back to Oxford he wrote of it with glowing appreciation: "my rooms in the new Regency house the College has acquired have the most magnificent view over lake and lawn".

During the war MA studies had been suspended but in 1945 an MA group in English was recruited. It consisted of Joan Grundy, who had graduated at Bedford College in 1943, myself, who had graduated in 1944, Margery Morgan, who had graduated in 1945 and Katherine Lorimer (later Worth), who had graduated at Newcastle-on-Tyne also in 1945. Our research subjects ranged from Medieval literature to Elizabethan literature and from the plays of Eugene O'Neill to the influence of English literature on the Russian Romantics. Subsequently three of us were given temporary appointments as Assistants in the Department.

In 1947 F P Wilson did return to Oxford to become the Merton Professor of English Literature and Una Ellis-Fermor became the Hildred Carlile Professor of English Literature with Kathleen Tillotson as Reader. In the previous year Norman Lacey had joined the Department as Assistant and in 1948 M R Ridley joined as part-time

Lecturer. It was rumoured when he came that he was the prototype for Dorothy Sayers' Lord Peter Wimsey. In fact she had created the character before she met Roy Ridley, but when she met him she felt he was just how she had pictured her hero. In 1949 there was another cheerful addition when Graham Midgely was appointed Assistant Lecturer. In 1951 he returned to Oxford and subsequently took Orders and became Dean of St Edmund Hall. He died in 1999 but his warm, entertaining character will not be forgotten by his colleagues and students both at Bedford College and in Oxford.

It was at this time, between 1947 and 1950, that I had the privilege of being asked to work as Temporary Assistant in the English Department during the absences of Norman Lacey and Roy Ridley: an experience I will never forget. It was then that I started work on my edition of Alexander Pushkin's critical writing, *Pushkin on Literature,* which finally was published in 1971.

In 1950, Pamela Gradon having moved to Oxford, to St Hugh's College, a new member joined the department: Geoffrey Britton, and he was soon joined among others by Mrs Vivien Salmon. The next major change came in 1969 when, on the retirement of Professor Ellis-Fermor, Kathleen Tillotson became the Hildred Carlile Professor of English Literature and Phyllis Hodgson the Professor of English Language and Medieval Literature, Agnes Latham became Reader and Geoffrey Britton Senior Lecturer. Among the new members appointed was Jacqueline Bratton as Lecturer.

In 1965 Kathleen Tillotson was elected Fellow of the British Academy and the next few years saw several publications by her and by other members of the staff of the English Department. *Dickens at Work* by Kathleen Tillotson and John Butt, which came out in 1968, has already been mentioned, and in 1969 Kathleen Tillotson also published Introductions to editions of *Dr Thorne* and *The Woman in White*, while Phyllis Hodgson, who in 1958 had published a definitive version of her edition of *The Cloud of Unknowing*, published an edition of the *Prologue to the Canterbury Tales*.

In 1970 Richard Cave joined the Department as a lecturer and in the following year both Kathleen Tillotson and Phyllis Hodgson retired and Agnes Latham became acting Head of Department. The Hildred Carlile Professorship remained vacant till the following year when Mrs Anne Barton was appointed with Inga-Stina Ewbank as Reader. She in her turn became the Hildred Carlile Professor in 1974 and in the following year John Dixon Hunt joined the Department as Reader and published his work on the *English Landscape Garden:The Genius of the Place*, which was shortly to be followed by *The Figure in the Landscape* and by *Andrew Marvell.*

In 1975 Jacqueline Bratton's book *The Victorian Popular Ballad* came out and the following year Richard Cave's edition of George Moore's *Hail and Farewell.* In view of later developments it is interesting to note that in 1977 the students of the Department had participated in the NUS drama festival in Edinburgh in a production of Beckett's *End Came.*

In 1978 John Dixon Hunt was appointed to a personal Chair of English Literature and lectured widely on English landscape gardening design. In the same year Katherine Worth's book *The Irish Drama of Europe from Yeats to Beckett* was published. Richard Cave was extending his studies of Irish writers, writing on both Yeats and Beckett, while Geoffrey Britton together with Rosalind Field ran a popular course on 'Medieval English and related French Literature'.These activities continued throughout 1979–80, and included a production of plays by Yeats and Strindberg, the latter in a translation by Inga-Stina Ewbank.

At the beginning of 1979 Katherine Worth was appointed to a personal University of London Chair in Drama at the newly opened Department of Drama and Theatre Studies at Royal Holloway College. This was the first Chair in Drama in the University, something that would have pleased Professor Ellis-Fermor, whose pupil Katherine Worth was. This was later to become an established Chair. A few years later she was to be joined in that Department by Richard Cave and Jacqueline Bratton.

In 1980–81 Professor Hunt had organised an exhibition at The Holme on the theme of Villas in Regent's Park and had become the

Editor of a new international quarterly: *The Journal of Garden History.* The following year he published a life of Ruskin *The Wider Sea,* while Jacqueline Bratton published *The Impact of Victorian Children's Fiction.*

In September 1982 the English Department left its beautiful premises in The Holme in preparation for the move of the whole College to Egham, to be merged with Royal Holloway College. This took place in September 1983, though some third year students were still taught that year at Regent's Park.

Throughout its history Bedford College English Department had engendered many definitive studies in English Language and Literature, the names of the Professors and Readers becoming synonymous with their subjects, for example Caroline Spurgeon on Imagery; F P Wilson on Elizabethan and Jacobean Literature and as Editor, together with Bonamy Dobrée, of *The Oxford History of English Literature* and then of *The Oxford Dictionary of English Proverbs*; Una Ellis-Fermor on the Frontiers of Drama in the widest sense, taking in Marlowe, Shakespeare, the Jacobeans, the Irish Dramatists, Ibsen–the list is endless; Kathleen Tillotson on Michael Drayton and then as the great Dickensian of the age–culminating in 1962 when she became joint Editor of the Clarendon edition of his complete letters (which has now reached Volume XI); Agnes Latham on Sir Walter Raleigh; John Dixon Hunt on the English Landscape Garden; Katherine Worth on Samuel Beckett. One should also mention that among its former students there have been successful writers, for example the novelist Jane Gardam. It is impossible to mention everyone but the message is clear: English Studies flourished at Bedford College and continues to do so at Royal Holloway College, which now incorporates it and its proud tradition.

APPENDIX

Professors of English, 1913–85

1913–42	Percy Goronwy Thomas
1913–29	Caroline Frances Eleonor Spurgeon
1929–35	Lascelles Abercrombie, FBA
1936–47	Frank Percy Wilson, FBA
1947–69	Una Ellis-Fermor
1969–71	Kathleen Tillotson FBA
1972–74	Phyllis Hodgson
1972–74	Anne Barton, FBA
1974–85	Inga-Stina Ewbank
1978–82	John Dixon Hunt

Chapter 6

French*

Eva Jacobs

A great friend of Elisabeth Jesser Reid, writing of her in 1843, mentioned that he had an impression she was not strong in French.[1] Inadequate though the founder's own accomplishments may have been, French was to become one of the leading subjects at Bedford College. It was already well established in girls' boarding schools, and young women of good family were usually taught at least the rudiments.[2] This gave French a potentially central place in the curriculum of the new college as an appropriate and respectable subject. No one could have foreseen, however, the development of French in the College as a major academic subject, and the growth of the Department of French into one of the most distinguished in the University of London.

As an academic subject in the newly-founded college, French did not get off to a particularly auspicious start. The College did indeed include a Professor of French, Raymond de Véricour, among the first teachers appointed in 1849, but he left after one term.[3] His successor,

* I should like to record my gratitude for the help given to me in writing this chapter by my friend and former colleague Dr Jean Bloch. She provided me with written-up material from the departmental archives, and made invaluable suggestions for improving the first draft.

Adolphe Ragon, remained in post for almost twenty years, but he does not appear to have left any mark.[4] All heads of department at the College were accorded the title of professor, regardless of their academic standing or of the level at which they taught. While some were eminent teachers at University and King's Colleges, and offered their services to Bedford either for extra income or philanthropically in the interests of the education of women, others were, to say the least, obscure. The suspicion lingers that Ragon was little more than a native speaker, employed to teach the young ladies to speak, read and perhaps even write the language. The minimum entrance age to the College was only twelve, and for some years it hovered in the uncertain space between a school and an institution for higher education–a place where French as a non-academic subject had a natural role.

Moreover, when in 1853, the College opened its own Junior School, in order that girls might be better prepared by their preliminary education for the more advanced studies offered by the College, French was among the subjects taught to the nine-year-olds admitted to the School. Rivalry between the School and the College ensued, with the School threatening to be more successful than the College. This ran counter to all the founder's aspirations, and in 1868[5] a crisis arose during which the decision was made to close the School, and a new Constitution for the College was formulated. A Committee was made responsible for running the College, and one of its first acts was to dismiss two foreign professors, who taught modern languages at both the School and the College. One of these was Professor Ragon, whose long-standing services were almost certainly deemed to be of too low a standard for an institution aspiring to offer genuine higher education to women.

A couple of short-term incumbents, Charles Cassal[6] and Mons. Bocquet[7] followed, after which A Roulier held the professorship until 1881. Meanwhile the University of London, which at that time was purely an examining body, had in 1878 at last opened its degrees to women, and it is astonishing to discover that as early as 1881 the first three women from Bedford College to obtain a degree (all in the Faculty of Arts) were each placed in the First Division. Among them was Mary Rickett, who was awarded the University Prize in French. She had presumably been taught by Roulier, but she may have had other teachers as well, or perhaps had lived in France. In any case, the study of French would have formed only a relatively small part of her degree. The original London Bachelor of Arts degree, established in 1837, had consisted of a wide range of compulsory subjects, including mathematics, astronomy, mechanics, physiology, botany, classics and history, to name but a selection, together with translation from either French or German. Only medicine and law were excluded from the Arts, being classed as professional studies.[8] By the time Mary Rickett obtained her prize, a separate Science Faculty with a Bachelor of Science degree had been created, so the BA was no doubt confined to what we would now consider the Humanities, with the addition of mathematics. But the range of subjects was still very broad, and although Mary Rickett won the prize in French, it does not seem to have been her major interest, for she went on to take both the Classical and Mathematical Tripos at Newnham College, and became a lecturer in mathematics there.[9]

An expatriate Frenchman like all his predecessors, A Roulier published a small number of 'teaching' books: a French grammar and textbooks of French composition, that is to say, materials such as extracts, notes and discussions, for teaching students translation from English into French. His publications are surprisingly interesting, however, for the history of the teaching of French in England. For instance, *The Second Book of French Composition for Advanced Classes* (Hachette 1881), on whose title page he is described as 'French master at Charterhouse, Professor of the French Language and Literature at Bedford College, London, and Assistant-Examiner in the University of London' includes examples of English texts used for a variety of recent examinations: 'For Appointments as Student Interpreter at Constantinople' (1879); 'For the Home Civil Service Examinations' (1879); 'For Sandhurst' (1879 and 1880), among others. In particular, his book reprints various examination papers of the University of London, including ones for the Examination of (sic) Women for Certificates of Higher Proficiency (1870) and the General Examination for Women (1876). These must be the kind of papers that were sat by Bedford College students before 1878, and they reveal that the level at which women were offered examinations by the university before it opened degrees to them was already very high. Even more fascinating are the examples of texts for translation into French for the BA Pass and BA Honours degrees for 1879. They are extremely difficult literary texts, which clearly follow the model of texts chosen for translation into Latin and Greek. The emphasis today in the universities on the 'modern' language means that the translation of demanding literary texts from a student's mother tongue into a foreign language no longer takes pride of place, but Roulier's texts remind us what an impressive intellectual exercise for undergraduates this could be. Perhaps those French professors, all native speakers, who taught at Bedford College and the various other London colleges, did not quite grasp how ambitious the goals were that they set their students. One wonders how Mary Rickett managed to reach the required standard in French along with all the other subjects she had to master for her degree examinations.

What is certain is that by the 1870s, the study of French as a preparation for the University of London examinations could not be viewed merely as a leisure activity for young ladies of good family. Roulier's successor at Bedford College, B Buisson, makes the point forcibly: "Un second trait caractéristique des examens de l'Université de Londres, c'est qu'ils sont plus que chez nous la récompense du travail et de la préparation assidue…Ces examens se composent, surtout pour les langues, de passages à traduire, de versions accompagnées de nombreuses questions philologiques, archéologiques et historiques".[10] Not only did London pioneer the study of modern languages in the universities of England, but it prided itself on rigorous and exacting standards, which it contrasted in all its disciplines with the amateurish laxity sometimes prevailing at Oxford and Cambridge.

Buisson was Head of French at Bedford only during 1881, probably for less than a full academic year, but he does seem to have been particularly interested in the education of women. In 1883, he published in France a short account of the provisions for the higher education of women in England, Scotland and Ireland,[11] which gives a lot of detail about the courses, costs and administration of various institutions, including Bedford College. He makes the point that most teachers at Bedford were still at that time attached to other establishments, and that many were also examiners for the University of London.[12] He also describes the Bedford syllabus for various subjects, including that for French. Under the heading 'Language' comes the study of the language, the laws which governed the formation of French words, notions of etymology, prose and translation, and the study of the great authors of the seventeenth century (rather oddly under the language heading). The heading 'Literature' covers only nineteenth-century French literature, with three named authors, Victor Hugo, Lamartine and Alfred de Musset, and the rest summed up as 'etc'. It is incidentally rather galling to discover that his descriptions of Girton and Newnham, where he seems to have been royally received, sound a note of admiration that is singularly lacking from his extended, but very dull account of Bedford. The glamour of the younger Cambridge women's colleges was already outshining the worthy practicality of the more venerable Bedford.

In 1881 the College appointed A Esclangon as Head of French. He remained until 1889 and, like many of his predecessors, wrote 'teaching' books. The title pages of his *Second French Course* (1886) and his *Third French Course* (1888) list an astonishing variety of posts which he appears to have held concurrently.[13] He is the first Head of the French Department to be described as 'Lecturer in French Literature, Bedford College, London'. The reason for this must be that the title of Professor, given casually to all and sundry in the early years of Bedford College, had gradually acquired in the university as a whole, a prestigious academic connotation which had to be earned and deserved.

Esclangon's *Courses* are very detailed and very thorough, and anyone working through them would have a very sound knowledge of the French language–at any rate of the language as it was as the nineteenth century drew to a close.

His successor, Augustin Gasne, is notable only for his obscurity. He appears to have published nothing at all, and may well have relied on his predecessors' excellent French courses, grammars and editions of French texts for teaching purposes. He was Head of the French Department from 1889–1892. During these years, the College was in serious financial difficulties, partly owing to the demands for laboratories and equipment made by the science departments, and partly because student applications were falling. Rival institutions at Oxford, Cambridge and London vied for the small number of women who sought higher education, and in particular the opening of University College to women students in 1878 had adversely affected Bedford College. Numbers at Bedford in 1890-91 sank to a ten-year low, standing at ninety-five in the Michaelmas Term, and fee income was correspondingly reduced.[14] Presumably Gasne, like those before him, was offered only a part-time post, and paid a pittance based on student numbers and the amount of teaching required. It is not surprising that with few students, and finances in a parlous state, the College was unable to attract a French teacher of distinction.

The College's fortunes began to change in 1894. Under the double impetus of an energetic new Principal, Emily Penrose, and the receipt of the first grants of public money from the Treasury and London County Council, both in 1894, student numbers rose quickly. The students' fees were lowered, and their teachers were marginally better rewarded.

Meanwhile, in 1892, Gasne had been replaced by Victor Oger. He left a post as Lecturer in French Language and Literature at University College, Liverpool, and Victoria University, Manchester, to come to Bedford College as Head of Department. One rather wonders why, for he can hardly have been attracted by the salary, which was £101 in 1894-95, rising to £168 in 1899–1900, and falling back to £150 in 1906-07.[15] His post must have been part-time, with a salary based, as always, on student numbers and teaching hours, Nevertheless, unlike many of his predecessors, on the title page of the various publications where he mentions his post at Bedford College, he makes no claim to other positions held concurrently. There are hints in his introduction to his edition of Erckmann-Chatrian's *Madame Thérèse* that he may originally have been an exile (voluntary or involuntary, we do not know) from France, for he states that his French translations of some of Gladstone's writings were banned by M Buffet under the Presidency of the late Marshall MacMahon "because, said the ministerial decision, 'il n'est question dans ces livres que de liberté'".[16] Maurice de MacMahon was the second President of the Third Republic from 1873–79, and Buffet was President of the National Assembly at that time. They were both resolutely conservative, repressing the republican and anticlerical press. Gladstone's anti-papal pamphlet, *The Vatican Decrees in their Bearing on Civil Allegiance: a political expostulation* was published in 1874. In it, he asserted that adherence to the Church of Rome, with its doctrine of papal infallibility, was incompatible with loyalty to one's own country. Oger's translation was published in Brussels in 1875, with Gladstone's own authorisation, or so he claims. By 1882 Oger was working in Edinburgh as 'Professor of the French language and literature in the Merchant Company's Ladies' College, but it is perhaps a romantic fantasy to extrapolate from all this that he was an exile, for in truth little is known about him. Nevertheless, a number of the texts he edited for English students[17] have a 'leftish' flavour, and this suggests that he may have found Bedford's tradition as a deliberately non-sectarian institution particularly congenial.

Oger remained at Bedford until 1909. During his years as Head of the French Department, momentous events were taking place at the College and within the University. In 1900, after much cogitation and controversy, the University of London became a teaching university, and Bedford became one of its constituent schools. This meant that the College had to accept standards for its teachers imposed by the University. For instance, the University would not give the status of 'Recognised Teacher' to anyone who had no published work; the use of the titles Professor and Reader was discouraged, unless authorised by the university; and minimum salaries were laid down for the various categories of teacher. In 1907 Professors had to receive £600 per annum, Readers £300, and Recognised Teachers £150.[18] Bedford struggled to meet these requirements, but improvements to salaries were made, and in 1906 a fixed minimum of £425 had already been established for Heads of Departments holding full-time appointments.[19] Since we know that Oger earned only £150 in 1906–07, we have proof of our earlier surmise that he worked part-time. This suggests that French was not considered a major department of the College. In contrast, and rather surprisingly, as early as 1903, the German Department at the College gained as its Head the distinguished scholar J G Robertson under arrangements by the University for Chairs to be assigned to its various constituent schools. French, as an academic subject, seems to have been left behind.

The decline in the French Department was reflected in fluctuating and falling numbers, which caused the College some concern, and in June 1904 the College Sub-Committee in French looked at various remedies, including giving one session's notice to Oger. Nevertheless nothing much happened for the time being, partly, no doubt, because the College could not afford to pay Oger a pension. His successor was eventually appointed in 1909, and the choice of the new incumbent marked a radical departure from precedent.

As we have seen, all holders of the post of Head of French up until 1909 had been native speakers. None of these could have claimed great academic distinction, though between them they had produced a significant number of textbooks, such as grammars, annotated passages for translation both ways, and editions of literary texts for the use of students. These men were mostly rooted in school-teaching, and either had taught or, more often, were teaching concurrently at various schools. Most were also examiners for the universities, London especially, but sometimes Oxford and Cambridge and others. They worked hard, no doubt, eking out a modest living, with little time or incentive for scholarship. But Oger's successor broke the mould in all sorts of ways. First of all, she was a woman, Fanny Cecilia Johnson. Secondly, she was English, and thus provides evidence that Bedford

College at last recognised that to be an academic specialising in French demanded something rather different from being an educated native speaker. Thirdly, she was home-grown, having entered Bedford as an undergraduate in 1894. So she had been Oger's student, and had remained at the College as an Assistant Lecturer, Lecturer, Senior Lecturer and Head of the Department, all in the space of 15 years.[20]

Fanny Johnson was a specialist in Old French language and literature, but she had to undertake most of the teaching in the Department across all areas, with a little help from part-timers, including Oger himself, who seems to have continued to give the odd hour's teaching here and there. Bedford students also attended lectures at University College, and visiting academics occasionally gave a series of lectures at the College. Among these was the highly respected Emile Legouis, who gave four lectures in the Lent term of 1911.

Whether as a result of her own efforts, or because the College generally was becoming more popular, Fanny Johnson presided over a dramatic increase in student numbers. By 1912 she was seeking to expand the department on the grounds that in addition to students taking Pass degrees, there were now twenty candidates for Honours, compared to only one in 1907, and three of these were preparing for the MA. The Honours students were held to require twelve lectures a week, plus those they attended at University College. Miss Johnson argued that the preparation and marking of Honours and Pass degree students would be more adequately catered for if there were further assistance available for the more elementary work of the department. It is interesting to find that in the annual statement of costs that had to be submitted to the Principal of the University of London, dated 21 January 1911, the grand total of expenditure for the Department of French was £653.17s.0d. Of this, £400 was paid to the Head of Department, and £50 to M Legouis for his special lectures, while the rest was spent on a lecturer providing two courses, a part-time assistant and the cost of Bedford students attending intercollegiate lectures. But Miss Johnson did not get her extra assistant until 1915.

Two years later, apparently still dissatisfied with the teaching arrangements in the department, she proposed a fundamental change for French. English had already in 1913 been divided into two departments: English Language and Medieval Literature, and English Literature. Fanny Johnson suggested a similar model for French. This would enable her to devote herself to teaching linguistics and Medieval French literature, in which she had specialised in Paris, but on which she had been unable to spend much time since the increase in size of the department. She had an available candidate for the headship of the proposed Department of Modern French Literature, Gustave Rudler. For once, events moved quickly, and on 6 August 1918 the Secretary of the College Council wrote to the Academic Registrar of the University to confirm that arrangements for the division of French had been made and that Professor Rudler had agreed to be Head of the Modern Department. Fanny Johnson and Gustave Rudler were each to have full control and direction of their own departments. Johnson's department was to teach history of the language, Romance philology, historical and modern grammar, translation from French into English and English into French, conversation and Medieval literature. Rudler's department was to teach free composition in French, dissertation (ie essays on literature written in French), *exposés* (ie seminar papers given in French) and French literature after 1500 AD. It was stipulated that the sole assistant in French should divide her time equally between both departments, but that as the departments expanded further, lecturers would be assigned to one or the other according to their subject. It was also laid down that students would not be able to exceed ten hours of tuition per week in both departments together in the case of Honours, with three hours for a Pass degree, three for Intermediate and two for matriculation.

Gustave Rudler had not come from nowhere. When Fanny Johnson suggested sharing French with him, he already held a University Chair in Modern French Literature, created in 1913 with funding from London County Council and assigned to Bedford College. It is not entirely clear what that meant in practical terms. Did he do any teaching in the department apart from giving intercollegiate lectures? Was Fanny Johnson in some sense his 'boss' before the department was divided? At all events, his tenure of the Chair was interrupted during the First World War, for he served in the French army. It is presumably on his return that he took up the headship of the Department of Modern French Literature, but he obtained the newly established Marshal Foch Chair at Oxford shortly afterwards, and left Bedford in 1920.[21]

Rudler is the first of the Bedford professors to have been an academic scholar in the modern sense of the word. The long list of his publications dating form 1898 to 1947 shows that he had wide-ranging interests, with a lifelong enthusiasm for Benjamin Constant.[22] His distinguished career at Oxford lasted until his retirement in 1949, but it would be difficult to claim that he had a great influence on Bedford, or vice versa. Indeed, when his *Festschrift* was published in 1952, the Bedford Library did not figure on the list of subscribers.

Fanny Johnson remained at Bedford until 1933. She did not obtain a Chair, and her only publication appearing in the British Library Catalogue is a scholarly edition of an Old French text, dated 1942.[23] She seems to be the first of a long line of women who devoted their lives to the College, committed themselves mainly to teaching and administration, struggled to keep the department going with often inadequate resources, and allowed their male colleagues to reap the rewards of greater public recognition.

Meanwhile, the two departments were evidently successful, for they were soon granted a full-time assistant each: during 1919 a Miss Page was appointed to the Department of Modern French Literature, and on 19 August 1919 René Legros was chosen from among sixteen applicants to be Assistant Lecturer in French Language and Medieval Literature. He was to remain at Bedford until 1955, and the author of this chapter was his student–the direct link therefore stretching eighty years across the century!

Rudler's successor as Head of Modern French was Francis Yvon Eccles, who, like Rudler, held the University Chair in Modern French Literature assigned to Bedford. He remained until 1934, and one cannot help wondering how well he fitted into the College with its secular tradition and ethos. Educated at Westminster and Christchurch, Oxford, he converted to catholicism at the age of 31. Even before his appointment to the Chair, he had in August 1917 given a series of three lectures at Bedford College to a summer school for the Secondary Teachers' Guild. Published in 1919 by Oxford University Press, under the title *La Liquidation du Romantisme et les Directions actuelles de la littérature française*, these lectures castigate the spiritual decline of France under the influence of the Romantic movement, and praise the regeneration of the true French (Catholic) soul as expressed by writers such as Maurice Barrès, Jean Moréas and Charles Maurras–all Catholic writers of the extreme right. Of course, these lectures were given during the war, and a certain excessive patriotism (Romanticism having generally been considered a 'Germanic' phenomenon, the influence of Rousseau notwithstanding) is perhaps comprehensible. But we also find that in 1938 Eccles wrote the preface to his own translation of Hilaire Belloc's *An Essay on the Nature of Contemporary England* (1937). In this long, mainly biographical piece, he describes his long-standing friendship with Belloc, with whom he claims to have been inseparable at Oxford. Stressing his friend's militant Catholicism, he describes with approval Belloc's anti-semitic views on the Dreyfus Affair, and in particular Belloc's horror at the influence he believed that Jewish and Masonic propaganda had on the English. As a result of this propaganda, the English, he claims, were naïvely deceived into accepting that Dreyfus was an innocent victim of the anti-semitism of the French military establishment. It is astonishing to find Eccles defending and agreeing with Belloc's position on the Dreyfus Affair as late as 1938, for Belloc's own text shows neither recognition nor repentance at the injustice that led to Dreyfus's imprisonment. In the same preface Eccles also heaps fulsome praise on the perfect impartiality of Belloc's *The Jews*, a book which serves as a classically anti-semitic text.

Given that in his published writings Eccles made no secret of views that would today be described as racist and fascist, his appointment to a Chair in the University of London, an institution founded with articulated liberal intentions, is a token in itself of that liberalism, and of the University's dedication to freedom of thought and speech. Eccles published little during his tenure of the Chair, but he was invited to give the Taylorian lecture at Oxford in 1922. Otherwise it is difficult to see that he added much to the lustre of the department.

René Legros has only one publication listed in the British Library Catalogue, and that is a collection of passages for translation into French, dated 1922. He is therefore in the earlier line of educated native speakers, rather than the modern conception of academic scholars. But he did have an outsize personality, and for more than thirty years stimulated and terrified his young female students in equal measure. During his formal lectures on French literature, given to all three undergraduate years together, he would strut about on the rostrum with his gown flapping, looking like a small eagle. Then he would suddenly stop, having spotted some hapless girl wearing a sparkling new engagement ring. Pointing an accusing finger at her, he would pronounce 'Amor furor brevis est'–love is a brief fury–and utter a cynical laugh, before moving back to Racine or Molière. His eccentricities made him an object of endless speculation among his students, but he remained obdurately silent about his private life. Nevertheless, his students were not wrong to attribute all kinds of romantic or suspect aspects to his life, for he had in fact been the subject of a very public scandal.

The story is told by Margaret Drabble in her biography of Arnold Bennett.[24] In July 1907, Arnold Bennett, already a famous writer, and just turned forty, married Marguerite Soulié, a thirty-three year-old Frenchwoman. He came from a poor background and had had a hard life, but was on the way to being very rich. He also had ingrained bachelor habits and was a workaholic. She had artistic pretensions and soon developed an extravagant lifestyle. They slowly drifted apart. In 1920, when she was forty-six, she met René Legros, who was only thirty, through the newly set up Anglo-French Poetry Society, of which Bennett was president. Marguerite was on the committee, as was Edith Sitwell. Marguerite had nurtured ambitions to be an actress, but had to content herself with giving French poetry recitals, including one at Bedford College. Her affair with Legros soon became public knowledge. She visited him alone in his flat, and went off on holiday with him, using her husband's money to pay the bill. Everyone knew that she lavished her husband's wealth on the penniless lecturer, who was accused of gold-digging.

When the Bennetts obtained a legal separation in November 1921, Mrs Bennett received an absurdly generous settlement, but she had lost her status as the wife of a famous man. Margaret Drabble concludes this dramatic episode by saying, "Legros was never to appear on the scene again, and nobody knows what happened to him".[25] It is true that we do not know how long his liaison with Marguerite lasted, nor how much money he managed to extract from his infatuated middle-aged mistress. But we do know that he kept his post at Bedford until his retirement at 65. Rather interestingly, another of his recurring eccentricities during lectures was to break off suddenly and ask his audience, "Do you know how much I'm getting for this lecture?" A rhetorical question to which he immediately shouted the answer, "Twenty pounds." Twenty pounds an hour in 1954–it seemed a fortune! The students were correspondingly impressed. At that time, a whole day's moonlighting at the Zoo or at Lord's–the common resource of Bedford students–earned £1 precisely. It was perhaps his taste of wealth as a young man that made Legros want to pretend that he was still rich.

Gladys Turquet, who published as Gladys Turquet-Milnes, Milnes being her maiden name, succeeded Eccles as Head of the department in 1934. She was already Head of French at Westfield College, having been appointed to that post in 1916 as a young woman; she died only in 1977.[26] In 1921 she had obtained a University Readership, presumably on the basis of two books she published in 1916 and 1921 respectively, *Some Modern Belgian Writers* and *Some Modern French Writers*. These publications were followed in the 1920s and 30s by further books, still mainly on early twentieth-century authors. She also published original essays and poetry in French. Her husband, a Frenchman whom she had married in 1912, was himself a poet. Her particular interest lay in the thought of the philosopher, Henri Bergson (1859–1941), and his impact on French culture and literature. Bergson was the central figure in the reaction against materialism and determinism, believing that these led to a reductionist interpretation of human life. Instead, he emphasised the reality of psychical or spiritual life, with freedom and spontaneity manifested in action. Turquet traced his influence on numerous writers, and her works show that she had a wide-ranging and deep knowledge of English, American, French and Belgian literature. Her method was one of exposition and interpretation, rather than of scholarship and close analysis. This spilled over into her lecturing style. She lectured at Bedford to all three Honours years together. In the front of the lecture hall were the finalists, behind them, the second-year students, and at the back, ignored and bewildered, the freshers. At the end of a formal lecture, she would ask the finalists which writer they wanted her to lecture on the following week, for she spoke as fluently and discursively as she wrote. Among the many suggestions proffered, she would choose: Sainte-Beuve, Verhaeren, Molière, Maeterlinck. And she lectured in French. To a first-year student, straight from school French and school texts, she might almost as well been lecturing in Chinese on Chinese literature. But lectures in those days were considered less as a method of comprehensive teaching, than as a stimulus to private study. The onus was on the student to follow the paths that satisfied her intellect or stimulated her imagination, and she could only hope that by some miracle the writers she had chosen to study would appear on the examination paper in general French literature. For the whole of seventeenth-, eighteenth-, nineteenth- and early twentieth-century literature was examined in a single three-hour paper, written in French, set by the University and not by the college department. Consequently, almost any subject might or might not turn up, and students lived in trepidation as they awaited the day of judgment.

Professor Turquet's DLit speaks of her distinction and the respect in which she was held by her colleagues, but it is doubtful whether she would have met the criteria that obtain today for academic research or teaching. When she retired in 1952, she already seemed to belong to another age, and her successor was awaited with eager anticipation by the students.

John Stephenson Spink was already Professor of French in the University College of Southampton when he was appointed to the Chair of French at Bedford College. He was not happy with the situation he found in his new post, and immediately made representations about the unsatisfactory staffing position. The department had been reunited in 1934, and on his arrival it consisted of two Readers, Legros and Dr Jessie Murray, who held the established Readership in Romance Philology, Dr Eileen Le Breton, the only Lecturer, and Mrs Blanche Laycock, a part-time Assistant Lecturer, who was an educated French speaker in the older tradition. The fact that both Legros and Dr Murray were due to retire in 1955 and 1956 respectively allowed Spink to propose some radical changes for the department.

In particular, apart from requesting additional academic staff, he insisted that the courses offered to students had to be restructured to meet the needs of the University syllabus. Teaching in the department was still based on a two-year post-intermediate course, but the Honours degree now always took three full years, and new arrangements were required for an introductory course in all areas to be taught separately to first-year students. Moreover, courses had to be taught by specialists. Dr Le Breton, who was a specialist in nineteenth-century literature, was teaching mainly sixteenth-century literature, and in addition was seriously overburdened with marking. No one was covering twentieth-century literature adequately.

Professor Spink received a sympathetic hearing from the departmental staffing committee meeting held on 12 May 1953, but in fact was granted only an additional assistant lecturer for the following session.

How detrimental to the students was the admittedly appalling staffing situation in the early fifties? If examination results are anything to go by, it would be difficult to argue that the students were disadvantaged in any way. The cohort that graduated in 1954, for instance, obtained five out of the nine first-class Honours degrees in

French awarded by the University of London–an outstanding and perhaps not entirely typical achievement, although Bedford results in French tended to be at the top end of the scale. The amount, if not the quality, of teaching was obviously still only a relatively minor element in the whole business of studying at that time, and personal involvement and effort on the part of the student were paramount. If anyone suffered, it was the staff, overworked, especially with marking, forced to teach over too wide a range of subjects, and quite unable to find any time at all for research.

Gradually, in the course of the twenty-one years during which Spink was Head of French, the Department was able to expand. Dr Le Breton was eventually able to teach her speciality, and to pursue significant research in her own subject, because a distinguished scholar, Claude Adrien Mayer, came to teach sixteenth-century literature. Colin Duckworth came as a young lecturer to teach twentieth-century literature. Both went on to Chairs in other universities, Mayer to Liverpool, and Duckworth to Auckland and, later, Melbourne. Faith Lyons succeeded Jessie Murray as Reader in Medieval French. Nicol Spence came as Reader, and introduced modern linguistics in addition to historical philology. Eva Jacobs and Jean Bloch, both of them Spink's own research students, were appointed to teach seventeenth- and eighteenth-century literature, and later Pauline McLynn joined the Department to teach the modern period.

Professor Spink himself was an inspiring teacher, who devised a comprehensive programme of undergraduate literature courses, which were taught by genre, but with a strong sense of chronological development. He undertook to lecture on a wide range of writers, though his focus was the literature and ideas of the seventeenth and eighteenth centuries, and, as such, consonant with the major areas of his research. That research gained him an international reputation, and he was honoured by the French with nomination as an Officier de l'Ordre National du Mérite. The long bibliography of his writings printed in the *Festschrift* published in his honour in 1979[27] is evidence of his main interests: the history and development of French free-thought, and the writings of Jean-Jacques Rousseau. His influence spread across a wide range of institutions of higher education, for a significant number of his research students obtained, and many still occupy, posts in universities in Britain and abroad.

Under Spink's leadership, the Bedford French Department became one of the most eminent in the country and attracted undergraduate and postgraduate students of the highest quality. He was a determined believer in the intellectual equality of women, and after male undergraduates were admitted to the college in 1965, he never attempted to achieve an artificial balance of the sexes in his own department. The result was that women remained in a large majority, owing both to the College's history as a women's institution, and to the attractions of modern languages as a subject for women. He thus contributed significantly to the higher education of women, a fact of which he was rightly particularly proud.

When he retired in 1973, the French Department was strong and and successful, and the College appointed an eminent scholar, Felix Leakey, already a Professor in the University of Reading, to be the new Head. It was a time of change, and universities were forced to adapt to new demands. Combined Honours, perhaps more geared in modern languages towards potential careers than the single subject degree, had already been introduced into the syllabus. This radically altered the nature of French studies, allowing students to opt for the more 'modern' elements, a choice which tended to be popular at a time when the notion of 'relevance' was gaining currency. Professor Leakey was enthusiastic about students spending a year in France–or six months in each country in the case of combined modern languages–and thus it was soon made compulsory for students to spend the third year abroad, creating a four-year Honours degree. Only in the rarest cases was exemption granted on compassionate grounds. This was in accord with his own emphasis on practical language skills, for he was himself a bilingual speaker and believed that his students should approach as closely as possible to bilingualism, or indeed trilingualism. Nevertheless, he was far from accepting, as some university departments have latterly tended to do, that the primary object of university language studies was to teach fluency in the modern language. Acknowledged as a world authority on Baudelaire,[28] to whom he devoted virtually all his research, he kept academic goals firmly in mind, and shared with his students his passion for the analysis and appreciation of French poetry.[29]

Leakey was able to increase staff numbers during his tenure by appointing Malcolm Smith, a young and already outstanding Renaissance scholar, Elizabeth Gardner, a former student of the Department, and Claire Isoz, who replaced Faith Lyons. But although he was a committed and able administrator, his interests lay elsewhere, and in 1979, under new arrangements for rotating headships, he ceded the Headship of the Department to Nicol Spence, who had already obtained a personal Chair. In July 1982, Spence handed it back to Leakey on taking early retirement. Dr Le Breton retired at the same time, having served the College for thirty-four years.

The department, like the College, at that time was under considerable strain. The University had decided to cut costs by merging the smaller colleges one way or another. The French Department, like most other Arts departments, was dismayed that it was a merger with Royal Holloway College that was being supported by the University and by the College administration. On 17 June 1982, the Departmental Board in French expressed its strong opposition to a merger with Royal Holloway College and voted unanimously to stay on the Regent's Park site, or, failing that, to stay in central London, as part of a merger with another central London college.

It was not to be. The merger took place, and the Bedford French Department, which had already lost staff in anticipation of the merger, lost more staff to early retirement, resignation and transfer to other colleges. Within very few years, only Jean Bloch was still in post at the new college.[30]

What remains is a history: the history of a department which from small beginnings and modest achievements developed into one of the principal Arts departments in the University of London, with a galaxy of eminent scholars, committed teachers, and a large number of students who were, and still are successful in many walks of life. The sadness that accompanies what so many perceive as the unjustified destruction of Bedford College as an independent entity, must be tempered by the knowledge that for 135 years the College played a vital role in higher education–and particularly in the education of women. In this, the Department of French had a central part, and its history, although the end was abrupt, does leave something to celebrate.

References

1 Margaret J Tuke, *A History of Bedford College for Women 1849–1937* (1939), 4.

2 As the daughter of a wealthy Unitarian ironmonger, Elisabeth Reid might be expected to have gained some knowledge of French during her education. Indeed, Tuke uses the 1843 comment to surmise that she did not attend a boarding school, since 'French usually took a leading place in boarding schools at the beginning of the nineteenth century'. (Tuke, 3–4).

3 Louis Raymond de Véricour apparently left Bedford to take up a post as professor of Modern Languages at Queen's College, Cork. He remained there from August 1849 until his death in 1879. A number of books by him are listed in the British Library Catalogue under the name Raymond de Véricour, and he had already published *Modern French Literature* (1842) and *Principles of History* (1845) before he took up his post at the newly-founded college for women. See Frederic Boase, *Modern English Biography*, vol V (1965).

4 In 1843 Adolphe Ragon was already a teacher at the London Mechanics Institute, which was to become Birkbeck College. See C Delisle Burns, *A Short History of Birkbeck College* (1924), 67-68. The British Library Catalogue lists a number of books by A E Ragon, and on some of the title pages he is described as Professor of the French language at the City of London College and at the Birkbeck Institute. The dates of his listed publications range from 1879 till 1897, which suggests that if this is indeed Adolphe Ragon, he must have been very young when he took up his post at Birkbeck in 1843, and, moreover, that he published nothing until some thirty-five years after then. I am more inclined to think that A E Ragon may have been Adolphe's son, and that he succeeded him at Birkbeck, though not at Bedford. All A E Ragon's books appear to be 'school' texts grammars and simple editions of literary works.

5 Mrs Reid had in fact died in 1866, but her work was carried on by dedicated friends.

6 Hugues Charles Stanislas Cassal (1818–1885), who published as Charles Cassal. His short stay at Bedford during 1868–69 as Head of the Department of French was in addition to his two principal posts, for he taught French at University College School from 1856 until his death

and was Professor of French at University College from 1860 until his death. The extensive list of his publications in the British Library Catalogue indicates that, like his predecessors, he wrote mainly 'teaching' texts: grammars, readers, editions and translations. See Boase, and H Hale Bellot, *University College London* (1929), 326–7.

7 I have been unable to find any trace of Bocquet, apart from his surname, listed by Tuke, 340.

8 F M L Thompson, 'The Humanities', in *The University of London and the World of Learning 1836–1986*, ed F M L Thompson (1990) 61.

9 Tuke, 311.

10 'A second characteristic of the examinations of the University of London is that they are more than in our case (ie France) the reward for hard work and assiduous preparation… These examinations consist, above all for languages, of texts for composition and of translations into the mother tongue with numerous philological, archeological and historical questions.' B Buisson, *Université de Londres*, Paris (1879) 18.

11 B Buisson, *De l'Enseiqnement Supérieur des Femmes en Angleterre, en Ecosse et en Irelande*, Paris (1883).

12 *Ibid* 28.

13 There must have been a 'First Course', but I have not seen a copy. The posts listed include Examiner in French to the University of London, Lecturer in French Literature King's College Ladies Department, Lecturer to Ladies, Higher Education for Women, Oxford, Professor of French in the City of London Middle Class School, Finsbury, etc.

14 Tuke, 139.

15 Tuke, 181.

16 Erckmann-Chatrian, *Madame Thérèse*, ed Victor Oger, London (1900) vii.

17 Editions of French literary texts and collections of French passages for translation into English.

18 Tuke, 197.

19 Tuke, 208.

20 Tuke, 297.

21 *The French Mind. Studies in honour of Gustave Rudler*, ed Will Moore *et al*, Oxford (1952), iii.

22 *Ibid*, 347-351.

23 *La Grant Ystoire de Monsignor Tristan "Li Bret"*, Edinburgh (1942).

24 Margaret Drabble, *Arnold Bennett*, London (1975). I am indebted for the lead on the

connection between Legros and the Bennetts to Averil Cohen, a student in the Department of French at Bedford from 1952–1955.

25 *Ibid*, 261.

26 I have not been able to discover the date of Professor Turquet's birth.

27 *Woman and Society in Eighteenth-Century France*, ed Eva Jacobs *et al*, London (1979).

28 A complete list of Felix Leakey's publications up to 1990 is to be found in his *Baudelaire, Collected Essays*, 1953–1988, ed Eva Jacobs, Cambridge (1990), pp303–305.

29 Professor Leakey founded a popular and successful annual French poetry-speaking competition for the students, which continued for a number of years after the department moved to Egham.

30 Only four members of the Bedford French staff went to the merged college. Of these, Elizabeth Gardner and Pauline McLynn left in 1987 and 1991 respectively, and Malcolm Smith became Head of the Joint Department from 1985 until his untimely death in 1994. As the merger took place, Felix Leakey took early retirement, Claire Isoz transferred to King's College, and Eva Jacobs transferred to Queen Mary College.

Chapter 7

Geography

David Hilling

The early days

In the beginning was Geography. The Rev James Booth, actively involved on the committee which had developed the working arrangements for the new Bedford College, was himself appointed in 1849, the opening year, to teach Astronomy and Scientific Geography. He was followed at the end of the first year by the Rev Thomas Wilson who, having taught English in Germany for some years, arrived at Bedford to teach English, Astronomy and Geography. He failed to attract students to his courses, perhaps because of his unorthodox religious views rather than the quality of his teaching, and, having made no mark on Geography–a distinction he shared with a number of those teaching the subject in the 19th century–he was rapidly succeeded from 1851 to 1854 by Alexander Bain, an evening-class educated weaver, whose main interest was in the link between Physiology and Psychology.

In having non-specialist teachers of this kind Bedford was no different from other universities–as an academic discipline at this level geography was slow to develop and was often taught as an adjunct to wider Moral or Natural Philosophy courses or in association with Mathematics, Astronomy or Geology. Indeed, it was not until 1917, at

Liverpool and Aberystwyth, that full Honours degrees in Geography became available at British universities. During the 19th century, Bedford provided general education rather than degrees and much of the teaching was 'scarcely of a university character'(Tuke, 1939, 26). Geography was seen as a desirable element in this and was taught by a succession of 'professors', few of whom could be described as geographers in any real sense of the term, and most of whom combined its teaching with some other discipline. An Austrian, Gottfried Kinkel, 'among the most popular professors' (Tuke, 230), taught Geography between 1854 and 1866 being at the same time Professor of the History of Fine Art.

A few were better known as geographers. Between 1869 and 1874 Professor William Hughes of King's College also taught at Bedford and was a prolific writer of school manuals of Geography, produced an atlas of classical history and also wrote on the nature of geography (Freeman, 1969, 39). In a lecture at Bedford in 1870 he expounded on the relationship between geography and physical science–although arguing for the unity of the subject it was for him essentially physical, being based on astronomy and geology. He argued for the use of the term 'social' in place of 'political' geography and for him 'every page of history bears evidence... of surrounding locality (geography)' (Freeman, 39).

German-born E G Ravenstein came to London in 1852 and after early retirement from a career in the Intelligence Department at the War Office taught at Bedford from 1882 to 1885. He was recognised at the time as a cartographer and historian of exploration and in 1902 received the Victoria medal of the Royal Geographical Society for his studies of population distribution based on the censuses of 1871 and 1881. He introduced ideas such as push/pull influences on migration, selectivity in migration processes and step-by-step migration, which 'remain a starting point for work on migration theory' (Grigg, 1974, 247).

For several decades after Ravenstein Geography at Bedford was marginalised: the College was increasingly preparing students for degrees of London University, but there was no degree in Geography.

Geography continued to appear in the prospectus under the newly formed Geology Department but for a number of years no course was provided. However, change was in the air. With the appointment in 1884 of J Scott Keltie as Inspector of Geographical Education there was a national crusade for the improvement and better recognition of the subject at all levels. It may not be without significance that this coincided with the expansion of Empire: the potential and problems of overseas territories being based on an understanding of their geography, there was, not surprisingly, an upsurge of interest in commercial geography. After 1905, time was allocated in schools for the teaching of Geography so that there was an increased demand for specialised teachers. During the First World War geographical knowledge was critical in the production of intelligence handbooks–Miss M Heath, appointed to teach economic geography at Bedford in 1916, was for example released to work in the Admiralty–and after the war such knowledge was seen as a contributory factor in maintaining peace.

Interestingly, at Bedford the pressure for an enhanced status for Geography came primarily from the Geology Department and in particular from Dr C A Raisin, who was on the University's Board of Studies in Geography. Miss Heath's salary had been guaranteed for three years by an anonymous donor and negotiated by Dr Raisin. Miss Heath's teaching–she did not return to Bedford–was taken on by Professor Lyde of UC and Miss Blanche Hosgood, and a formal programme was initiated, first for the University's Diploma in Geography, after 1919 for a BA General degree, and then in 1924 for BA Honours and BSc Special degrees.

A Geography Department

Geography courses were provided under the umbrella of the Geology Department until the retirement of Dr Raisin in 1920 when a separate Geography Department was created with Miss Hosgood as Head of Department, a position she held until her retirement 27 years later. She was appointed University Reader in 1923.

Seen from the 1990s, Miss Hosgood is a shadowy figure. However, by the mid-1930s she had built up a Department of about 50 students, mostly reading for Honours degrees, and with some going on to PhDs. Miss Hosgood did not write for publication and her views, however they may have been expressed, are now lost. She is remembered by her students as "remote", "strange", even "forbidding" and her lectures are recalled not for their academic content but for the chalk boards, ready-prepared by Mr Tichner, the technician, with which they were illustrated. She lectured on economic geography (the physical geography having been taken over from Dr Raisin by Dr Hawkes in Geology), France and a range of other world regions. She held weekly tutorials and took a field class every other year. Interestingly, on Dr Raisin's death in 1944 she left £100 for the creation of a prize in memory of Miss Hosgood to be awarded to a second year student for the purchase of field-work equipment. The Hosgood Prize is still awarded annually.

During the 1920s, a succession of assistant staff were appointed to Geography, each moving on after a short stay to make a name elsewhere, as for example J N L Baker and E W Gilbert at Oxford. But when in 1930 Geography moved into new accommodation in Tuke Building, there was a change in style and a new continuity with the appointment of Dr Dora Smee, a Bedford graduate of 1925 who had then done an MA and PhD. Her main interest was historical geography but she travelled widely and was able to teach a wide range of regional courses from first-hand knowledge.

Dora Smee was a forceful character who did not suffer fools lightly, but as an inspiring teacher and demanding tutor she was respected and rewarded with great loyalty by her students. Her chain smoking, disposable cigarette holders, insistence on skirts for all field work and what she called closed knickers for a visit to a steel works (where there might be open-tread steps!) are the stuff of legends. She undoubtedly provided a firm academic basis, and as an enthusiastic and energetic field worker (Timberlake, 1982) she was instrumental in making field work (numerous day visits and longer field classes) an essential and memorable part of the student experience for those who accompanied her to Ireland, the Lake District, Scotland or the Midlands. Her recipe for good field work was to go, observe, record, and tap local knowledge –still sound advice. Through Dora Smee numerous students became involved in data collection for Dudley Stamp's first national Land Use Survey of the 1930s and also in Smee's personal ridge and furrow and soil surveys in the vicinity of Haselbech, her Nothamptonshire home. The 75,000 hand-auger soil samples involved many students over several decades and must be something of a record for a small area survey of this type. The results were deposited with the Northants County Records Office.

In 1931 Eunice M Timberlake ('Tim' to colleagues and students alike) joined the staff, being the College's first Special graduate in Geography. Tim taught basic physical geography but her main expertise was in survey and map projections, in which she provided an intercollegiate course, and later, in cooperation with the UC Department of Photogrammetry and Surveying, an advanced survey course with professional accreditation. The Bedford geographers remember her for her clarity of explanation, cheerfulness and infinite patience in dealing with their allergies to things mathematical–the height of the Abbey National Building in Baker Street, measured by generations of students, showed unbelievable variations. Tim was, with Dora Smee, a founding member of the Institute of British Geographers. They were great friends and over a period of 34 years collaborated closely, especially with respect to field work.

The average class size in the 1930s was about 15 but the geography staff, rarely more than three, were expected to cover the bulk of the nine-paper London syllabus–not for them the luxury of specialisation that lecturers now expect. Basic work in physical geography and cartography was covered, and social and economic geography was linked with regional courses, of which Bedford staff taught at least three. The range of options was increased by students going to other colleges–a practice that was to continue with declining numbers, and certainly decreasing need, into the 1980s.

Cambridge interlude

During the summer of 1939, Bedford students were alerted to arrangements made for an evacuation to Cambridge should war be declared. October saw them in Cambridge, the geographers sharing a room with Queen Mary College in the Cambridge School of Geography, Downing Place. The LSE geographers were also there, but with a room of their own.

Individual students were billeted in private homes around Cambridge and the bicycle became their main means of transport. Several geographers were temporarily in the crowded house of Professor Frank Debenham, Cambridge geographer and member of the Scott polar expedition, and this undoubtedly served to create a special relationship between the two departments–Debenham was to visit the Park after the war as a guest of Geog Soc and presented the Department with a globe/sundial–still to be seen in the 1970s. Some students were housed with Lady Maud Darwin, daughter-in-law of Charles Darwin, where they had to use the back gate, took breakfast in the dining room and were allowed to entertain in the library–with young men to be introduced to Lady Maud or her companion! Those with Louis Clarke, Curator of the Fitzwilliam Museum, took dinner formally with him every evening and had a special door-bell code so that the liveried footman did not feel obliged to don his uniform jacket to open the door for the girls. A dinner guest, in fact Clarke's wine merchant, impressed by the ladies sharing the table commented, "Gad, Louis, you can pick 'em", only to be told, "these ladies are my guests". Undoubtedly, not all the geographers had such digs.

Some of the geographers still look back with great nostalgia to war days in Cambridge. Certainly, there was no real collegiate or departmental life and some felt that they were not full members of anything. However, Cambridge allowed the evacuees to participate in some student society activities and the influx of so many women in a university with a high proportion of men meant that there were many parties, invitations and a fuller social life than in London. Some geographers clearly made the most of this–the coffee shops did well, dancing was popular with partners plentiful and tea parties frequent–although some missed Bedford teas with delicious, creamy, fattening cakes to which names such as strata, magma and pothole had been given. But even Bedford could not have produced these during the war. Those who had to return in vacations to the London of the blitz even appreciated the relative peace of Cambridge.

There is nothing new in students seeking extra-curricular employment but with the war in progress it assumed patriotic overtones. Geographers became involved in serving tea to troops on trains at the station, serving and washing up at the British Restaurant, making camouflage netting, doing night shifts at the Pye radio factory, vacation work on farms and even serving as guinea pigs for medical research into TNT poisoning–and there was always fire watching. Pay for this was three shillings for a night shift from 7.00pm to 7.00am with an extra one shilling and six pence for working on until 8.30am. One student was thought to be too young to operate a stirrup pump but the street warden thought that she could be useful, "standing up and passing water"!

And academic work continued. The hospitality of Professor Debenham and the Cambridge geographers still evokes the highest praise, and with their room, part of the Bedford geography library and access to the Cambridge facilities, students were able to carry on working. The only male member of the Bedford staff, Dr A H Matthews, being a climatologist, had volunteered for the RAF Meteorological Service and sadly lost his life in action later in the war. However, Hosgood, Smee and Timberlake went up to Cambridge and while students attended occasional Cambridge lectures, for the most part they followed their own lecture programme but with increasing need for joint arrangements with QMC and LSE.

While initially there was some field work–Breckland and Denver Sluice are particularly remembered–this became more difficult as time went on. As part of surveys related to the 'plough-up' campaign, Dr Smee supervised field work in Huntingdonshire and Fenland and there were occasional problems with over-zealous police and military not convinced by student credentials–hardly surprising in the case of a group with a student with a German name and background. While at Cambridge, Miss Timberlake widened the scope of her teaching to astro-navigation for Navy and Air Force cadets. With Professor Debenham she was involved in cartographic work for the preparation of models of different theatres of war, and with G E Benest she produced a definitive set of astro-navigation tables (Benest G & Timberlake E, 1945) and did work on a new map projection for a chart to be used by air navigators engaged in air rescue work with sea convoys.

One of the department's students at Cambridge, remembered as 'difficult' by one of her peers, was Monica Cole who graduated with a First in 1943. She was then awarded the Busk-Howell postgraduate scholarship and in the following year a University postgraduate studentship. She became a research assistant in the Ministry of Town and Country Planning and in 1947 completed her PhD on the factors influencing the production and use of building materials in Britain. After academic appointments in South Africa and at the University of Keele, she returned to her alma mater in 1964 as Professor of Geography and Head of Department.

Back to the Park

It was decided to take the College back to Regent's Park for the 1944–45 session but, with continued bombing and further damage to the buildings, start of term was delayed by several weeks. The geographers were fortunate in being able to move back into their first floor Tuke rooms but in the words of one student this was "a dour time" with a view of the damage, work in progress on demolition, and severe shortages of books and equipment.

Dr A E F Moodie, an historical and political geographer with special interest in the Balkans, joined the staff in 1944 in place of Dr Matthews. He is remembered for being "proud of his working class background" and being "the reddest of the bunch"–not too difficult one suspects–and for his stimulating and jovial lecturing style. Dr O H K Spate, with research interests in Asia that were later to make him an authority on that region, taught briefly at Bedford in 1945–46 before moving to a Senior Lectureship at LSE, and was replaced by Alan B Mountjoy.

Alan Mountjoy, invariably known either as The Major or just ABM, had a distinguished war record, earned an MC and had gained first-hand experience in North Africa and Italy which stimulated his special interest in problems of population geography and development. These themes were to become the focus of his teaching, research and prolific publication record during 39 years at Bedford. His war experience as an infantry and mortar officer gave him a real appreciation of the significance of physical geography in influencing human activity. ABM taught the main economic geography course and also regional courses on the Mediterranean and Africa, with increasing emphasis on problems of development. His book on *Industrialisation and Underdeveloped Countries* (Hutchinson 1963) was a pioneering work and an early example of the growing concern of geographers with development issues: it was to earn him world-wide recognition. He was later to establish a Masters course in development which opened the department to overseas students.

That the department still has a strong interest in development studies and in Africa is eloquent testimony to the firmness of the foundation established by Alan Mountjoy (Hilling, 1989). Always immaculately dressed, often with a button hole, he is remembered for his "military bearing carried without affectation", for his "warm, kindly, open nature" and famously for terminating one field class (he did many and always with military precision) with the words "must get home to prune the roses before tea". Falmouth and Pembrokeshire were his favoured field areas but there can surely be no truth in the story that ignominious retreat was the outcome of a confrontation with a gun-toting Welsh farmer during one field class.

An important milestone in the development of Geography at Bedford was undoubtedly the appointment–on the retirement in 1948 of Miss Hosgood–of the first Professor, Gordon Manley. Following degrees from Manchester and Cambridge and a short period working at the Meteorological Office, Gordon Manley held lecturing posts at

Birmingham, Durham and Cambridge, where he must have come into contact with the Bedford evacuees. He came to the Headship of the Department with a well established academic reputation as an authority on climatic trends (in rather different form, still a part of the department's academic portfolio) and much sought after commentator on exceptional climatic events–his *Manchester Guardian* articles were to give him a wide audience. Much of his own research was based on detailed field observations and not surprisingly he was to enhance the role of field work already developed by Smee and Timberlake.

His lectures were "entertaining", "anecdotal", "haphazard as a patchwork quilt" and "challenging" while outside the lecture room he was "friendly" and "charming" and took a genuine interest in each and every student–they certainly remember his coffee sessions in the department, sherry parties at his home and the chocolates handed to them as they went into the examination hall. His arrival each morning, with or without umbrella, provided the local weather forecast and when asked at a meeting of girls' school heads what was required of students, he supposedly replied, "red hair and a well turned ankle". He would not have got away with it now.

The first ever Royal Geographical Society grant for an expedition organised by women students was to the joint Bedford/Newnham Lake Masvatn (northern Iceland) Expedition of 1952 (a full report of which is now in the Bedford Centre archives); and a 1956 expedition to Greenland is still commemorated on the Romney's Kendal Mint Cake wrapper. In the same year, also in Greenland, the Department's Tutorial Research Fellow, Michael Holland, tragically lost his life in a blizzard while engaged on research in connection with the International Geophysical Year–Gordon Manley being on the British National Committee for this event.

Manley, wisely in retrospect, was cautious in adopting the 'new' quantitative geography that was becoming the vogue, but his scope for innovation was restricted by the University's rigid syllabus with its heavy emphasis on regional geography, and also by limited opportunity to make additional appointments. However, he did manage to boost the average staff number to six or seven from the three of the 1930s. In 1948, Eleanor Vollans joined the staff, initially to teach biogeography, but eventually to concentrate on the historical geography that was her main research interest. One of her interviewers said of her, "Miss Vollans is a scholar"–and who would disagree? Students found her "meticulous, ordered lectures" a delight for note taking. In 1954, Clifford Embleton, a geomorphologist, joined the staff and in 1957 Michael Chisholm strengthened the economic geography. Manley made judicious use of short-term appointments (Margaret Harris, John Paterson, Jean Clark, Cecilia Buckley) to boost staffing and, being a firm believer in the Cambridge tutorial system, established the post of Tutorial Research Fellow–successively held by Michael Holland, Jane Soons, Joan Kenworthy, Margaret Storrie, Brenda Turner and J L Tamblin. Manley also appointed the department's first externally-funded research assistant–Elizabeth Shaw.

There can be no doubt that under Manley the department had a much raised profile in terms of research, publications and external linkages; and he created an atmosphere of academic enquiry and discussion for which he may not have received sufficient credit. Yet the department remained relatively small. From an average annual intake of 24 students early post-war, intake actually dropped to about 18 before rising again in the late 1950s to 22–still a year-group size giving cohesion. The overwhelming impression of the students of the time was that the department was a most friendly and happy place to be–and much of the credit for this must surely go to Manley for the social climate he created. For him, the Bedford days were "perhaps his happiest" (Steers, 1980, 513).

Expansion and diversification

Manley's departure in 1964 to head the new Department of Environmental Studies at the University of Lancaster and the appointment of former Bedford student Monica Cole as Professor and Head of Department was to bring significant changes of style and substance. Where Manley's management was informal and homely, that of Monica Cole tended to be confrontational and she was far less accessible to staff and student. She had a force of character which gained her few friends but did much for the department as it expanded and diversified. The latter half of the 1960s was, of course, a period of general university expansion and at Bedford it also saw the arrival of the first male undergraduates; Geography admitting them ahead of most departments in October 1965. A geographer William Maxted, in 1967 became the first male President of the Student's Union and in the next four years was followed by two others–Monty Grigg and Hywel Griffiths. The male geographers were making their mark.

From the cosy-group size of the Manley era, the intake doubled to 42–45 and the staff number increased from 6–7 to 10–12. Perhaps the Manley style would not have been appropriate for the larger department; perhaps the department would not have expanded under him. However, for the majority of the students, the social life was relatively unchanged and the academic opportunities were greatly enhanced.

Most students had traditionally read for the BA degree and officially the department's base was in the Faculty of Arts. In 1966 Geography became a science although students could still register for either BA or BSc degrees and could switch, almost at will, between the two. Monica Cole was herself a BSc graduate, her research was science-based and an increasing range of courses were laboratory based with associated claims on space, funding and technical resources. By the mid-1970s the department could rightly claim to have extensive laboratories for biogeographical and geomorphological work together with an herbarium. This was a substantial change from the Manley times.

Also in 1966, the University of London Faculty of Science introduced its new course-unit degree scheme with year-by-year examination. Geography was immediately able to adopt this in place of the traditional nine papers, all examined in the final year, which one student described as "stultifying"–but charitably blaming the University and not the department. Where previously large parts of the set syllabus had to be taught by whoever happened to be available, the department could now introduce new courses more closely related to staff research expertise and teaching interests; and it could emphasise particular academic areas. Student choice was greatly enhanced and they could adopt either broad-based or more specialised and possibly vocationally-oriented programmes. The new flexibility called for a more complex advising system which was smoothly introduced by Miss Timberlake and later taken on by Michael Eden, David Hilling and Duncan McGregor.

The appointment in 1964 of Michael Eden with interests in tropical ecological systems especially in Latin America (he was leader of the Royal Geographical Society's 1968 Amazon hovercraft expedition), and also remote sensing was clearly a strengthening of Monica Cole's research in these same areas and the appointment of Peter Cazalet (1968) and Robert Brown (1972) were steps in the same direction. Michael Eden sadly died in 1997. Also in 1964, Ivan Jolliffe, a coastal geomorphologist, joined the staff from the Hydraulics Research Station, Wallingford, and he was joined in 1968 by Colin Patman, originally to teach economic geography and Iberia but with growing interest in coastal zone planning and management. The Department became the home for a new international journal, the *Journal of Shoreline Management*, and so another distinctive area of teaching and research came into being. Jolliffe and Patman initiated Spanish field classes with a coastal bias for second year students; with changes of location, and now for first year students, these are still a popular part of the programme.

In the more traditional teaching areas, Christopher Green (1964), first as Tutorial Research Fellow and then as Lecturer, assumed responsibility for the geomorphology which had previously been covered by Clifford Embleton; and David Hilling, appointed in 1966 after five years in West Africa, joined Alan Mountjoy to broaden the economic geography, Africa and development courses and later went on to develop a less conventional Geography of Maritime Transport course. George Worrall joined the Department in 1967 to teach the basic geology which had for long been taught by the Geology Department.

On the retirement of Miss Timberlake in 1969, the survey teaching was briefly taken over by Ian Dowman and then by Duncan McGregor. The location of the field class changed from Hastoe to Rogate but student memories of both, suitably censored, would fill a book! In the 1970s, with Christopher Green, Duncan McGregor, a glacial geomorphologist by origin, laid the foundations for the department's emerging interest in quaternary science, but he later developed research and teaching interests in tropical geomorphology and land use, thus strengthening the development studies group.

In 1974, Rob Potter, a graduate of the Department, was appointed to teach urban geography. For long a part of the University syllabus, this had not previously been taught as an option at Bedford. He was to go on to develop this in a Third World context and with particular reference to the Caribbean–a further expansion of the development studies group. Interestingly, Rob Potter would in 1994 become the second Bedford geography graduate to become its Head of Geography.

From a traditional home on first floor Tuke Building, in the late 1960s the Department expanded into premises in Peto Place, on the east side of the Park, and in 1972 into space in the new Tuke-Darwin infill; the human geographers were relocated to the top floor of Oliver Building. On the termination of the Peto Place lease in 1975, the Tuke space was modified to accommodate laboratories.

Mounting concern over Monica Cole's management style led in 1975 to the appointment, as Professor of Physical Geography and Head of Department, of Ron Cooke, Reader elect at UCL with Monica Cole remaining as Professor of Geography and becoming Director of Research in Geobotany, Terrain Analysis and Related Resource Use. Ron Cooke brought the human geographers back into Tuke and initiated courses in arid zone geomorphology. In 1981 he returned to UC and later became Vice Chancellor of the University of York. He was replaced by John Thornes who, with merger arrangements well advanced, moved in 1985 to Bristol. In 1976, Geoffrey Fisher joined the staff to develop courses in soils and soil management but was sadly to die in 1988 after the move toEgham. On the retirement of Eleanor Vollans in 1981 the staff was joined by Tim Unwin who infused fresh energy into historical courses and later developed an intereristing new course on viticulture. Just prior to the move to Egham the coastal group was further strengthened by the appointment of Jack Hardisty with research interests in the theoretical aspects of near-shore processes, and Don Thompson became the Department's first Computer Analyst.

There was jocular speculation on the reasons for the ever-shorter time that Geography was able to keep its Departmental Head. Yet it has to be said that both Cooke and Thornes developed excellent relations with other departments and also with the College administration, successfully promoted the department's interests, stimulated a widening range of external contacts at home and overseas and provided the vibrancy and growing academic credibility which was to be the foundation of the department's success once at Egham.

Merger mania

Frustration at the inability to expand the College on the Regent's Park site led to joint discussions with Westfield, which had no geography, and with King's College, which did. Geography immediately set up four joint working parties with KC geographers, a vast amount of time was expended and plans for the full integration of the two departments were well advanced when, at the end of 1981, it became clear that this merger was not to proceed. Arrangements then moved ahead rapidly for a merger with Royal Holloway where Geography was unmatched and fortunately the department was of a size and strength which meant that it would still be able to flourish.

For the first time in its history the department was able to plan coherent use of space in what was to become the Queen's Building; this it was to share with Geology, and the main responsibility for this fell to Geoff Fisher and Rob Potter. John Thornes left the department in March 1985; David Hilling was Acting Head for its last few months in the Park and for the move to Egham in the summer of 1985–he has no other claim to be the driver of the 'holiday car' which conveyed exuberant Geographers to their new kingdom.

The spirit of geography survives

It was apparent from the enthusiastic response to my request for recollections from former students that they looked back with great fondness to their years in the department. They sensed social cohesion, a great spirit of camaraderie and pleasant, helpful staff-student relations. In all this, field work clearly played a part. From the early 1930s it was a significant component in the department's teaching, either as one-day or longer classes in a variety of locations, and after 1970 was a fully examined, but no less enjoyable, part of the syllabus. It provided, and thankfully still provides, unmatched opportunity for students to get to know one another and also the staff. Also back in the 1930s, Geog Soc was one of the most active societies at Bedford; it continued to flourish at Cambridge and is still contributing to the life of the department. In 1968, one consequence of the 'year of revolution' was the mandatory establishment of department staff-student committees; but in Geography, this has always been more than something that had to be endured–it has been an effective forum and a real initiator of change.

Since being at Egham the department has gone from strength to strength. Physical facilities and equipment beyond the dreams of those at Bedford provide for a yearly intake of nearer 100 students and a staff of over 20, and in 1996 the department gained the coveted Grade 5 in the Research Assessment Exercise. With all these changes, the spirit of conviviality and caring rooted in Bedford days lives on. And for most of the students, like their predecessors, this will be remembered when much of the geography has been forgotten. That is as it should be.

Acknowledgements

In the preparation of this chapter I am particularly indebted to over 80 former students who responded, sometimes in great detail, to my request for recollections; with their permission this material has now been placed in the Bedford Centre Archives. I am grateful to the staff of the Bedford Centre, to Warwick Jacobs for permission to use his cartoon picture, and to Chris Green, Duncan McGregor, Alan Mountjoy, Rob

Potter, Tim Unwin and Eleanor Vollans for time they spent in discussion or commenting on a first draft. Errors remain mine.

References

Benest, G E & Timberlake, E M (1945), *Astro-navigation tables for the common tangent method*, Cambridge, Heffer.

Freeman T W (1969), *A Hundred Years of Geography*, London, Duckworth.

Grigg, D B (1974), 'A first English new geographer', *Geographical Magazine*, 46, 246–7.

Hilling, D (1989), 'Alan B Mountjoy: an appreciation' in R B Potter & Tim Unwin (eds), *The Geography of Rural Urban Interaction in Developing Countries*, London, Routledge, 1–10.

Steers, J A (1980), 'Obituary: Gordon Manley', *Trans. Inst. Brit. Geog.*, 5(4), 513–7.

Timberlake, E M (1983), 'Obituary: Dora K Smee' *Trans. Inst. Brit. Geog*, 5(8), 120–1.

Tuke, Margaret J (1939), *A History of Bedford College for Women*, 1849–1937, London, Oxford University Press.

APPENDIX

Heads of Geography Department, 1920–85

1920–48	Blanche Elsie May Hosgood
1948–64	Gordon Manley
1964–75	Monica Cole
1975–81	Ron Cooke
1981–85	John Thornes
(1985–)	David Hilling

Chapter 8

Geology

Grace Page and Alec J Smith

The development of Geology at Bedford College can be divided into four phases, corresponding to the influences of the four main Heads of Department. Catherine Raisin (1890–1920), the first full-time Head, established teaching and research in Geology and was instrumental in the formation of a separate Geography department. Leonard Hawkes (1921–1956) introduced annual excursions to France and Scotland to let students observe geology in the field. During the depression and war years, however, very few students were attracted to the subject and there was little growth of the department. Basil King (1956–1977) brought with him a new analytical approach to both geochemistry and structural geology. Student numbers, undergraduate and postgraduate, increased dramatically, especially following the admission of men. King appreciated the need for Geology departments to be large enough to support the sophisticated and expensive research equipment required for modern rock analysis but was unable to achieve the consolidation he envisaged. He was ahead of his time. Alec Smith (1977–1985) persuaded the University that, to be viable, Geology departments had to be larger and the only way to achieve this was for them to merge. At the end of the 100 years the Bedford geologists found themselves in an enlarged, strengthened new department–a realisation of King's dream.

The First Graduates–the 1880s

In 1884, Bedford College decided to offer preparation in most of the subjects of the BSc examination of the University of London. Thus, it was that, in 1885, Mary Forster was appointed College Professor of Geology and teaching in Geology began. She was followed, in 1886, by Grenville A J Cole. He was 27, and was a Demonstrator at the Royal School of Mines where he had studied under J W Judd. He continued as a Demonstrator at RSM whilst being Head of Geology at Bedford College.

The following extract from the Report of Council (1888–89) gives some indication of the classes he was teaching. He was preparing students for the College's examinations, not University examinations.

> "I must say, considering the extent of the subject, that I am pleased with the result of the Examination. Both students must have worked with real interest. Miss Simpson's paper in many points is really excellent. Of course for BSc papers a good deal of stratigraphical reading would be required, and the few serious mistakes in both papers would be avoided."

Amongst the Bedford students entering for the University's BSc examinations, the following successes in Geology are recorded:-

1884	A C S Zimmern	2nd Class Honours Geology
1888	A R M Smith	3rd Class Honours Geology
1889	E A Aston	1st Class Honours Geology
1890	J C Glenn Bott	2nd Class Honours Geology
1891	E J Lewis	3rd Class Honours Geology

I: Catherine Alice Raisin 1890–1920

The Making of a Teaching and Research Department

Catherine Raisin became Head of Geology in 1890 when Grenville

Cole left to be Professor of Geology in Dublin. She had applied for the post in 1886 and for a Demonstratorship in Botany to which she had been appointed. By early 1891, she was also appointed Head of the Department of Botany. The arrangement was convenient since Geology and Botany were sharing a classroom in the College building at 8 York Place, Baker Street. Provision for practical geology here was extremely basic.

In the year when she was appointed in Geology, Miss Raisin observes, "by the Students of Geology the lack of a petrological microscope is much felt". Council was offered specimens for addition to the Geological Collection. Miss Raisin observes, "... until a Geological Cabinet or a chest of shallow drawers can be provided for their reception this offer cannot be definitely accepted".

She built up the geological collections. 118 mineral specimens were presented by the Trustees of the British Museum (Natural History). In 1898, further specimens were presented by Mrs Morton Sumner, a benefactor of the Department. 1100 fossils came from the Natural History Museum. In 1896, the extension of College into 10 York Place gave accommodation for science laboratories. Geology and Botany now had a shared laboratory. The Technical Education Board of the London County Council gave a special grant of £500 for the laboratories. By 1898, Miss Raisin could report, "the fittings of the Botanical and Geological laboratories and the research room have been completed". A teaching and research department had been achieved.

Catherine Raisin "So distinguished..."

Catherine Alice Raisin was 23 when, in 1878, the University of London opened its examinations to women. By 1879, she had taken the BSc Intermediate Examination in Science. She studied both Geology and Botany at University College, under Professors Bonney and Bowen, and in 1884 graduated BSc with Honours in Geology, being placed first in the list. She also studied Biology under Professor Huxley "to get knowledge of present life to be able to understand fossil remains".

She was clearly accepted by the geological world in London. From

1891 to 1894, she was Vice-President of the Geologists' Association. In 1893, she was awarded a grant from the Lyell Fund of the Geological Society. Her list of publications is considerable. Many are on metamorphic and igneous rocks from Wales, but also on rocks from abroad–the Vosges, the Karakoram, Abyssinia, Egypt. Some are joint with Professor Bonney. She gained her DSc from London in 1898. By 1900, Bedford College was established as a School of the University of London and Dr Raisin represented the College on the Faculty of Science.

When the Geological Society celebrated its Centenary in 1907 she was a delegate. She reported, "The Gathering was in all ways a great success. It was attended by representatives of...our country, our colonies and from all civilised countries. It was a magnificent gathering of men famous in science from all parts of the world", and she added, "Except for a representative of a Belfast College, I was the only woman among the delegates; and many would have regretted it if they had not included some representative of women geologists". In his turn, Archibald Geikie, the President of the Geological Society, graciously wrote, "We have also to express our sense of the honour conferred upon the Society by the fact that the College was represented by so distinguished a delegate as Miss C A Raisin".

The Move to Regent's Park–Research Encouraged

The College outgrew its accommodation in York Place, and in 1913 moved into purpose-built buildings in Regent's Park. Geology was in the North Science Block and had a suite of rooms, including labs, map room, museum and research rooms. From 1910 the assistant staff included Demonstrators and a Lab Assistant Mr S H Morris, "a capable man". Dr Raisin had encouraged research in the Department–now there was room to pursue it and higher degrees could be achieved.

During Catherine Raisin's time as Head of Department, the number of students taking Honours in Geology gradually increased. Her best students–three who achieved First Class degrees–all came at the end: Miss L M Devonshire and Miss H M Wood in 1919, Miss D L

Reynolds in 1920. At the same time, students also started to work for higher degrees. Miss I H Lowe who had graduated in 1913, and was employed as a Demonstrator throughout the war years, gained her MSc in 1920.

Miss Raisin's Research Students

Helen Marguerite Muir-Wood gained a research award from the Committee for Scientific and Industrial Research which enabled her to stay on at College and receive training in research methods with Dr Raisin and in 1920 gained an MSc. She went on to work in the Natural History Museum, becoming the first woman Deputy Keeper and in 1935 she gained her DSc in Palaeontology. In 1958 she was awarded the Lyell Medal of the Geological Society for her 'fundamental contributions to the knowledge of *Brachiopoda*' and became OBE in 1960. At the museum she was very firm, meticulous in the care of her collections, fierce with any researcher who might venture to disagree with her opinion of a specimen, and demanding of her assistants. But, she was kindness itself to women research students.

Doris Livesey Reynolds also had a successful geological career. She became Assistant in Queen's University, Belfast, returned to Bedford College as Demonstrator, then to University College London, and on to a Lectureship at Durham. She gained her MSc in 1924 and DSc in 1937. She married Professor Arthur Holmes in 1939. They moved to Edinburgh where she was awarded a Leverhulme Research Fellowship. On returning to London, in 1962, she was made an Honorary Research Fellow by the College.

Dr Reynolds was a controversial figure in geology, holding views, especially on the origin of granite, which were not accepted by all petrologists. For many years her theories were dismissed. It was therefore with great pleasure that she learned, in 1960, that the Geological Society had awarded her the Lyell Medal for her researches in petrology. "...her investigations in the field and in the laboratory and the stimulation given to workers in geology by the meditations of an original mind, unawed by the prestige of the 'Establishment'". In accepting the medal

Dr Reynolds paid this tribute to Dr Raisin, "It was Catherine Raisin who first interested me in geology, and from whom I inherited my love for petrology; I owe very much to her long memory and unbiased teaching".

Geography Begins

From 1849 when the College opened, Physical Geography was offered as a subject. From 1885 the College Professor of Geology undertook the teaching. Mr Grenville Cole had been taught by Professor Judd to pay special attention to "viewing earth features in the field". Dr Raisin also believed in observing scenery and travelled widely to do so. By 1916 she had come to feel that Geography should be taught "as a definite subject" believing that it was "beginning quite successfully", and pressing for the appointment of an Assistant Lecturer in Geography to give courses in Political Geography. An Academic Diploma in Geography was introduced. It is clear however that Dr Raisin felt that the study of Geology was an essential basis for Geographical studies:

> "For those who enter on school teaching (and they form the majority) I know no better subject for general training in science and widened thought than geology–precise in its methods, and yet giving broad interests in its bearing on earth features and geographical methods".

The University instituted an Honours Degree in Geography in 1919. In 1920, when Dr Raisin retired, the decision was taken to separate the two departments. Dr Raisin also had a view about what might be called Applied Geology. She felt that men were inclined "to drive all interest in science towards practical applications"–engineering for instance. "Most important as are these developments, it would be dangerous if they were the objective of all intellectual effort".

Catherine Raisin–a Testimony

In the 1890s there were only two women holding College

professorships–Catherine Raisin and Beatrice Edgell. When Catherine Raisin died in 1945, at the age of 90, it was Beatrice Edgell who wrote her obituary in the Bedford College Old Students Association (BCOSA) Journal and gave this picture of her:

> "Above average height, with a striking profile, she looked what she was, a strong personality. Neither colleagues, nor students, could lightly disregard her opinions on College matters. Her earnestness and sincerity were always beyond question, even when one disagreed with her point of view".

In the Report of Council we read:

> "Dr Raisin's complete devotion of her time and energy was outstanding. Her attention to details of departmental organisation and her interest in the work and careers of students in the Geology Department were unsurpassed while the firmness of her convictions and her outspoken expression of them made her throughout the many years of her connection with Bedford College a great force in College affairs".

II: Leonard Hawkes 1921–1956

Little Growth–Quiescence and Frustration

When Dr Raisin retired the Head of Department post was advertised as a Readership, but no appointment was made at that point, Dr Stanley Smith acting as Head for one year. In 1921 Dr Leonard Hawkes was appointed. The Department was then small with only 28 students in all years. There was a full programme of undergraduate courses:- Intermediate, Physical Geography, BSc Pass, BSc Honours in Mineralogy and Petrology as well as postgraduate courses for MSc and PhD Field courses, both day excursions on Saturdays in term and a ten day excursion at Easter, appear in the Calendar for the first time. Dr Hawkes had only one full-time and one half-time Demonstrator to assist him with all this teaching.

Dr Hawkes came from Armstrong College, Newcastle-upon-Tyne,

part of the federal University of Durham where he had graduated BSc in 1912, MSc in 1916 and been a lecturer from 1919. His research at this time had been much influenced by Goldschmidt and other great Scandinavian geologists when he spent a year at Kristiania University and later when he worked as a field assistant in the Norwegian Geological Survey. His other interest, the Tertiary Volcanism of Iceland, had already been fuelled by four summers there and was to continue through the 1920s and 30s.

Research under Hawkes

Some of Dr Hawke's students in the 1920s caught his enthusiasm for Icelandic rocks. J A Ledeboer, H C Cargill and E M Guppy all published joint papers with him on Icelandic intrusive rocks; Ledeboer and Cargill also gaining an MSc. There were, however, few research students in the 20s and none at all in the 30s and 40s. The Demonstrators in the Department did do research. I E Knaggs in 1924 and A I McDonald in 1925 were awarded PhD. F W Cope published on the Carboniferous of Derbyshire in 1933 and B C King on intrusives in Kircudbrightshire in 1937. King went on to gain his PhD in 1945 and W D Evans, another Demonstrator, in 1940.

A Lectureship–but no Professorship yet!

In 1927 the full-time Demonstratorship was replaced by a Lectureship which was held by Miss E W Gardner until 1929. She was a palaeontologist but she also had an interest in the Recent Geology and landforms of the Fayum Desert, Egypt. She was succeeded by Miss Emily Dix, an expert on the flora and invertebrates of the Coal Measures and other Carboniferous strata of South Wales and the English Midlands. In recognition of this work she was given an award from the Murchison Fund of the Geological Society in 1936. Dr Dix lectured at Bedford College until 1947 when ill health forced her to retire.

When Dr Hawkes was appointed Reader and Head of Department in 1921 the Principal, Miss Tuke, assured the Academic Registrar of the

University that "when funds permit, it is the desire of the College Council to create a Professorship of Geology". When, in 1932, Dr Hawkes made application for a professorship it was rejected because "Bedford College could not afford the luxury of a professor" on the grounds that "firstly, only a small number of students are taking geology, though there have been more honours students in the last year or two, and secondly, there are few professional openings for women." He had to wait until 1948 for the title to be conferred.

Careers for Women in the 1930s

Miss Tuke in her *History of Bedford College* remarks that "Geology is a subject which–since it does not lead to school posts–secures only a small number of students. The few who are able to follow inclination rather than the demands of a career find special pleasure in it". A search of the BCOSA Journals of the late 20s and 30s does reveal 10 of the 30 General Degree students who had taken Geology becoming assistant mistresses in schools. In contrast, only 2 of the 9 Geology students became teachers. Some did find employment in geology. J A Ledeboer and A P Hetherington became Demonstrators. E M Guppy became a Senior Experimental Officer in the Institute of Geological Sciences, assistant to the Chief Petrologist and later personal assistant to the Director of the Geological Survey and Museum. She was awarded the MBE in 1967. F W M Garratt became an Indexer in the Mineral Resources Department of the Imperial Institute. Nancy Parkinson became Honorary Hospitality Secretary at the National Union of Students, serving there until 1939. She later joined the staff of the British Council, rising to be Head of the Home Division, becoming CBE in 1946 and DCMG in 1965. On retirement, she returned to Bedford College, joining the Sociology Department as Leverhulme Research Fellow. She liked to remind geologists in College that though she was now a sociologist she too was a scientist and had a degree in Geology. Many of the geology graduates married and did not pursue a career in the subject. Doris Reynolds was a notable exception.

Geography grows–Geology declines

While the numbers of students entering for Geology degrees dwindled, the numbers of Geography Ancillary students increased. They made up 50% of those attending the Easter field courses. There were also Botany, Zoology, Chemistry and Maths students. The Intermediate Class increased too at this time. There were students to teach, but no Honours Class.

The Blitz and its aftermath

Dr Hawkes and Dr Dix kept the department going when the College was evacuated to Cambridge during the War. The department suffered extensive damage in the blitz and many of the collections, including much of Dr Hawkes' Iceland material were lost. There were no Geology Honours graduates in this time. When College returned from Cambridge in the summer of 1944, Geology had to be housed at Sussex Lodge until the North Science block–Darwin Building–was rebuilt in the early 50s. A full-time Demonstrator was appointed to see to the badly damaged collection.

Honours for Hawkes–a Chair at last!

For Dr Hawkes this was a time of recognition. In 1946 the Geological Society awarded him the Murchison Medal for researches into igneous rocks, especially the Tertiary Volcanics of Iceland. In 1948, he was at last appointed University Professor. The supreme recognition came in 1952 when he was elected to the Royal Society. The University of London conferred the emeritus title on him when he retired in 1956 and in 1962 the Geological Society gave him their premier award, the Wollaston Medal, for his services to the Society and in acknowledgment of "his breadth of vision and detached critical perception" in geological matters, including the field of international geology.

More Students–More Staff

Gradually the numbers in the Department increased. The first Honours student for 18 years, Awdry Naylor, graduated in 1951. More were to follow. The Demonstratorship, held by E Jones, was converted to an Assistant Lectureship. There was more teaching to be done and more staff were needed. In 1947 Dr Emily Dix was succeeded by Norman Hughes, also a palaeobotanist. He in turn was succeeded in 1953 by Charles Holland, stratigrapher-palaeontologist with special interest in the Ludlovian strata of the Silurian. A second Assistant Lecturer was appointed–the first year class was increasing in size and more help was required. There were more ancillary students. Also, Special students were now required to do a piece of independent field work and each had to be visited. A J Moss, J T Temple, A A Wilson and Robin Nicholson were Assistant Lecturers at this time.

Hawkes Remembered

Leonard Hawkes was Head of Department for 35 years. He died in 1981 aged 90. In an obituary Basil King remarks on Hawkes' "critical, even iconoclastic attitude" which, as a young man, King had admired. He notes, "pretence to Leonard was unacceptable, but with his innate courtesy and charm he could and did express opinions which in another would have appeared outrageous". Hawkes himself claimed that his extravagant statements were a device to persuade the women in the College to enter into debate, to argue a point, to discuss. He was one of those who fought for the admission of male undergraduates to Bedford College, to create a normal academic community. He found it frustrating that the Council and Governors refused for so long to admit men as students. Charles Holland described him as "in some ways a most gregarious man but in others he was very much alone". Brian Sturt found him "an absolutely delightful person" who "did everything possible to help a young man in his first post to feel part of an academic community". He was austere, yet charming, and despite his outspoken views, kind, considerate and sensitive to the feelings of others. Especially he was careful not to criticise the changes which a new Head was making in a Department which had been his for 35 years. After he retired he continued to visit the Senior Common Room to have coffee, read *The Times*, have a nap perhaps, before going on to committee meetings at the Royal Society.

III: Basil Charles King 1956–1977

King returns–Geology becomes analytical and the Department expands

Basil King was appointed Professor and Head of Department in 1956. He had been a Demonstrator in 1936–38, leaving on his appointment as Chemist-Petrologist to the Geological Survey of Uganda. He was to remain in the Colonial Geological Survey in Africa until 1948 when he was appointed to a Lectureship in the University of Glasgow. He gained his PhD (London) in 1945 and DSc (Glasgow) in 1950. His research was particularly on the volcanic and other igneous rocks in Uganda and into the nature and petrogenesis of Tertiary igneous rocks in Skye and Arran in Scotland. In 1950 he was elected Fellow of the Royal Society of Edinburgh and in 1959 was awarded the Bigsby Medal of the Geological Society for this work. Once again, a petrologist–an igneous petrologist–was Head of Department.

Expansion–enter the men!

The department was to flourish under King's Headship. In Hawkes' last ten years, from 1948 to 1957, there had been only 8 Honours graduates in total, 5 Special and 3 General. In the next ten years there were 38, 25 Special and 13 General, and in the following decade, 1967–77, after the admission of male undergraduates in 1965 there were 175, 134 Special and 41 in Combined Subjects. There was at this time a national increase in demand for geology places; even so the growth of the undergraduate population of the department was spectacular.

Postgraduate Research gets under way

The development of research was perhaps even more dramatic. By October 1956, Professor King requested provision in the Departmental Grant for three research students. Research Studentships and

Fellowships were obtained from the Department of Scientific and Industrial Research (DSIR)–later becoming the Natural Environment Research Council (NERC)–the University of London, the British Council, NATO and the Science Research Council (SRC). Research Assistants swelled the numbers of research workers, these being funded by research grants as well as by a College appointment.

The technical staff too increased gradually. Mr S H Morris retired in 1955 after more than 40 years service. The position of Chief Technician was taken by J W (Jack) Keith who had two or three juniors to assist.

Geochemistry Begins

The Department had to be re-equipped to handle the increased research demands. Professor King had himself been a chemist in the Colonial Survey. He knew the need for geochemical analysis of rocks, as well as the optical determination of minerals, in petrological research. The department needed a geochemical lab and, by 1958, he had equipped one and persuaded College Council to appoint a Research Assistant to man it. Mirror stereoscopes were also required for the analysis of land surfaces in aerial photographs–an invaluable technique for the geological map maker which, coincidentally, Dr Hawkes had been asked to evaluate in Northern Rhodesia in 1930.

All-round Growth

By 1967–68, ten years after King's appointment, a snapshot survey shows ten full-time PhD students in the Department. The undergraduate total of 85 comprised of 29 BSc Special Geology students, 15 BSc General students, 19 Two-year Ancillary Geography students and 22 others taking Geology courses for one year only. Male undergraduates had just been admitted. The staff had increased to seven–one professor and six lecturers. Their research interests show the increasing diversity of the subject. No longer is there a simple division into petrologists and palaeo-stratigraphers. Structural Geology, especially, is introduced.

Peter H Banham, appointed in 1962, had research interests both in the tectonics of Basement rocks in Norway and in the glacial tills of Norfolk. He also served as consultant in Geology and Physiography to the Nature Conservancy and on the Advisory Council for England.

W W (Bill) Bishop, joined the Department in 1965. He had been an officer of the Geological Survey of Uganda. His main field of study was the Cainozoic sedimentary environments of the East African Rift and their associated mammalian fauna, including hominids. He was also interested in Pleistocene chronology in Scotland and the Midlands. In 1969 he was appointed Reader at Bedford College, then in 1973 he was appointed Professor at Queen Mary College. Shortly before his untimely death in 1977, aged only 45, he had been appointed to the Directorship of the Peabody Museum in the University of Yale, with a Chair in the Department of Geology.

Grace M Dunlop, appointed in 1958, had research interests in the Brachiopoda and in Carboniferous stratigraphy in County Mayo and Arran.

Derek Powell, appointed in 1965, researched into the Moine rocks of NW Scotland–heir composition, structure, age and history–choosing to live there when he retired.

Edward P F Rose, appointed in 1966, is a palaeontologist-stratigrapher. He succeeded C H Holland on his appointment to the Chair of Geology at Trinity College, Dublin. Rose's research is on the Echinodermata, especially echinoids, and the Tertiary rocks of the Mediterranean area. He also writes on engineeering and military geology from experience gained when he held a commission in the Territorial Army.

Brian A Sturt, appointed in 1958, led a research group–in collaboration with the University of Dundee–studying the structure and petrogenesis of the Caledonian metamorphic and igneous rocks of North Norway. He became Professor and Head of Department of Geology in the University of Bergen in 1970. From there he collaborated with Professor King in a project, funded by NERC, investigating the basement and cover relationships of the Caledonides of West Norway.

King's major research project, mainly funded by NERC, was the structural and volcanic evolution of the northern part of the Kenya Rift Valley. In this he collaborated with research workers from the University of Leicester. W W Bishop's work in the Rift was complementary to King's, providing an understanding of the environments in which the volcanism occurred and giving a timescale. Together they administered the group known as EAGRU–the East Africa Geological Research Unit. In the course of eight years 15 research students worked on the projects. Their field mapping formed the basis of six geological maps (1:125,000) of the area, produced for the Government of Kenya. The geological editing was undertaken by Dr Greg Chapman and Dr Peter Truckle. Norman Sinclair Jones was the draughtsman. The Ministry of Overseas Development contributed to the cost of editing and printing.

More Geochemistry equipment please

Further geochemical analytical equipment was required for the petrological investigations involved in the various projects. X-ray diffraction equipment had been provided by 1968 through a NERC grant, but there was no funding for the X-ray fluorescence spectrometer which was also needed. This was a problem besetting Geology Departments across the country. Analytical equipment had become sophisticated, expensive to buy, run and maintain, and often required more space than was available. The University's Board of Studies in Geology urged a "coherent programme in the acquiring of additional much-needed resources". For larger equipment Colleges should seek to attract funds for research equipment to be sponsored by the Board of Studies for all.

Collaboration or Amalgamation?

In March 1968 King approached Professor Donovan of University College with a suggestion of collaboration. Would UCL support Bedford in an application for funding for the XRF to be housed at Bedford, in the new laboratories, but for the joint use of both departments? In April 1968 the Interim Joint Standing Committee of the Academic and Collegiate Councils set aside a small reserve to encourage schemes of rationalisation. By the end of May a joint application had been made to this Special Equipment Needs Fund for the funding for the XRF. It was successful.

There were problems on the staff side too. In March 1969, King writes "the subject has diversified into many new fields requiring specialised staff in research and teaching". The new BSc degree structure introduced in 1965 allowing students to select from a number of Course Units, had called for the provision of a selection of specialist courses especially in final year. The Board of Studies had called for collaboration also in teaching between Colleges. When they met in March 1968 King and Donovan had agreed to cooperate on advanced courses such as Micropalaeontology and Applied Geology but they also looked ahead to possible amalgamation.

A joint committee of the Geology Departments in the two Colleges was established in July 1969 to consider the problems of amalgamation. There were difficulties–practical difficulties. Firstly, the space available was on two sites, and could only be united at one place if another department could also be involved. Secondly, the students were not only single honours geology candidates, there were geographers and joint-degree students at Bedford and engineers at UCL. Thirdly, the finances were different, in particular at least half of Bedford Geology's funding came from external sources. No amalgamation scheme was forthcoming.

"A Mini-Centre of Excellence"

In June 1970, King made an even more radical suggestion–the African Geology research led by himself and Bishop should go, complete with technical backup, equipment and research workers to Leeds where there was already a centre for African Geology leaving the rump to go to University College and teach the Bedford undergraduates from there. The Principal, Mrs Chilver, referred the proposal to Lord Annan, the Provost of University College. She had come to the conclusion that Geology rationalisation was 'a non-starter'. But, of the African research at Bedford she said, "it is a mini-centre of excellence with no future in a small school and should go elsewhere". Such a proposal has "never been done before. Genuine rationalisation involves a financial settlement. Who does it? Jobs must be guaranteed. Court and College officers need to face pertinent financial questions". It was not to be. For one thing, Bedford College's Academic Board did not want to lose its Geology Department.

Appointments in Geochemistry and Structural Geology

There were to be no more dramatic moves. Staff numbers remained constant at seven until King retired in 1977. Two appointments were made in this period. In 1970, when Brian Sturt left to become Professor at Bergen, Ian L Gibson was appointed in his place. He was a geochemist, whose research interests were in the volcanic rocks of the Ethiopian Rift and the plateau basalts of Iceland. When Bill Bishop left in 1973 to become Professor of Geology at Queen Mary College, Alan D Gibbs was appointed. He was a structural geologist who had worked on the Basement rocks in Greenland. He also had an interest in the problems of radioactive waste disposal and theories of North Sea tectonics. He collaborated with Peter Banham on tectonic studies in the Jotunheimen area of the Norwegian Caledonides.

Undergraduate numbers continued to increase, reaching a peak of 54 Honours students in total in the department in 1977. Research student numbers remained steady–two to four awards being achieved each year and seventeen PhDs being awarded in the period 1970–77, making a total of 27 during King's headship. Five of these were Bedford undergraduates.

King–Retrospective

Recognition of King's researches came with the award of the Murchison Medal of the Geological Society in 1971. On his retirement he was granted the title Emeritus and was elected a Fellow of the Royal Society of Arts. In 1978 the Edinbugh Geological Society awarded him the Clough Medal for his contributions to Scottish Geology.

King's contribution to the College was first and foremost as a teacher. He loved his subject and wanted to impart it to all. In the old tradition he gave the full course of first year lectures, believing that the Professor should give a comprehensive, rounded series of lectures to the whole class–geologists, geographers, biologists, chemists and physicists. To final year students he discoursed on the Solar System, Classical Geochemistry in the style of Goldschmidt and Geophysics of the Earth. Postgraduates particularly benefited from his teaching in the field–how to observe, how to record, how to interpret. His map-making technique was superb. By his service as External Examiner he tried to uphold educational standards in Uganda, Ghana and the West Indies.

In College he was known for his obstinate determination to achieve recognition for Geology. The department had been small during Hawkes' time. King wanted more space, more staff and more equipment and was prepared to fight for it. He joined those who, like Hawkes, were striving for the admission of male undergraduates. When, in 1966, that happened, the numbers in the department increased dramatically. Later, his energy was directed towards the merger of the University's geology departments. Again, he demonstrated his tenacity, indefatigable drive and persistence. The merger of departments did not come until August 1985, only six weeks before his death in September 1985 at the age of 70. He knew of the move to Egham, and the departmental mergers, and was well pleased, seeing it as a realisation of the dreams he had had twenty years before.

To his many research students and staff he was, in turn, a demanding taskmaster, an autocratic head, an inspiring teacher, a convivial companion and a kind and generous friend. He is remembered with affection.

First Class Honours

Under King's Headship there were six First Class Honours graduates. Diana Sutherland (BSc 1958) was the first First Class Geology graduate since Doris Reynolds in 1920. She undertook a PhD research project (PhD 1966) and continued in academic work; Audrey Haywood (BSc General 1958) took the more usual course of teaching, becoming a headmistress; Jane McQueen (BSc 1972) and Alastair Baird (BSc 1975) both went on to do research in structural geology in the NW Highlands under Derek Powell, gaining their PhDs in 1976 and 1985 respectively, Baird taking up an academic post at the University of Kingston; Richard Reed (BSc 1973) entered marine civil engineering, becoming director of a company which operates world-wide; Nick Rogers (BSc Geology/Chemistry 1974) went on to geochemistry research and so to a lectureship at Goldsmith's College and thence to the Open University.

Career Openings in the 50s, 60s and 70s

The paucity of career opportunities for women in Geology, noted by Miss Tuke in the 1930s, persisted into the 1950s. As in the past, they went into school teaching (Naylor 1951, Morris 1952, Bloomer 1959, Chick 1959, M Aquinas 1961, Lea 1963, Sr M Adrian); museum work (Samuel 1959, Mansfield 1970); experimental officers with the Geological Survey (Davies 1955, Sadler 1956) and librarianship (O'Hare 1964). Unusually, Margaret Marsh (BSc 1952) found commercial employment in a petroleum technology consultancy. None of these posts involved field work. Research projects, however, did offer this possibility: Sutherland (1958, PhD 1966) in Uganda; Turner (1959, PhD 1963) in the French Alps; Pocock (1961, PhD 1965) in Saskatchewan and Hubbard (1962, PhD 1966) in the West of Ireland. This was also a route into academic posts.

Women also found employment as geochemical analysts in universities (Tyler 1959, Bartle 1961, Marriner 1970) also undertaking their own research projects. BGS employed women geochemists (Flannagan 1971) permitting them to do field collecting abroad. The British Antarctic Survey employed women as research assistants in the UK eventually allowing visits to Antarctica (Brown 1964).

When the first men graduated most went into mining, often prospecting in Africa or Australia (Rhemtulla 1967, Fowler 1968, Garlick 1969, McGarry 1969, Watkins 1969, White 1969, Jones 1970, Kennedy

1971), but as the North Sea Oil industry opened up they became well-loggers and geophysicists in the UK, Middle East and Far East (Hopkins 1971, Kyriacou 1973, Edwards 1975, Ross 1975, Gollop 1976). Women too entered the oil industry, office-based at first in seismic interpretation work (Smart 1977), but gradually undertaking well site visits (Dilks 1975), Rosemary Johnson (1973) even becoming Exploration Manager for a major oil company.

Others went on to academic research (Sanzen-Baker 1969) and usually to lecturing (Beck 1967, Gardner 1968, Moorhouse 1969, Lazell 1970, Scurry 1970, Truckle 1971, Boldy 1976). Andrew Scott (1971) undertook research in Palaeobotany with Professor Bill Chaloner, was appointed to a lectureship at Chelsea and then at RHBNC, gaining a personal chair at Royal Holloway in 1997.

IV: Alec J Smith 1977–1985

The Department's future is sssured–leadership and negotiation

Alec Smith was appointed Professor in 1977. His interests were in sedimentary rocks, marine geology–especially ocean margin sedimentation. He investigated the sediments of the English Channel, studied active marine sedimentation off Japan, coastal sedimentation in Brazil and took part in an ocean-drilling programme in the Pacific. For the first time a 'soft-rock' geologist was Head of Department. He served on many committees dealing with maritime matters:- the Greenwich Forum on Maritime Affairs, the Watt Committee on Energy Resources, the Department of Trade and Industry Advisory Committee on Resources from the Sea. He had therefore an interest in the application of geology to economic matters. He was awarded the Coke Medal of the Geological Society in recognition of 'his work on the regional geology of the Continental Shelf and marine sedimentology'.

Undergraduates and Postgraduates–the record

During Smith's Headship the number of undergraduates in the Geology Department remained high, peaking at 57 in 1982/83 even though total numbers in the College were declining at this time. Men now outnumbered women by 2 or 3 to 1 rather than the 7:1 average of King's time. Postgraduate scholarships remained at a steady two per year. Sixteen PhDs were awarded in the 8-year period. A proportion of graduates went on to do research, most now going to other universities, Hodgson (1978), Roberts (1979), Freeman (1979) and Collier (1984). Some stayed, such as Neil Tilston (BSc 1979, PhD 1983) and Gillian Rex (BSc 1980, PhD 1983).

Careers in and out of Geology

Women were now quite frequently employed as geologists. Jane Evans (BSc 1978) geochemist with BGS, Karen Bass (BSc Environmental Earth Science 1981) media work including environmental topics, Regan Walters (BSc 1981) site investigation work in civil engineering consultancy, Nicola Vink (BSc 1985) seismic interpretation.

Men still went into oil and mining. Some became teachers. Others however pursued very different careers unrelated to geology–for instance, art design, stockbroking, business consultancy. Clearly, at this stage, a degree in Geology was more than just a vocational qualification.

There were two First Class Honours graduates in Smith's time, both in 1980. Alan Roberts, after research in structural geology, joined a company creating structural products for the oil industry. Kim Daulton (Geology/Maths) went into accountancy.

Staff changes during Smith's Headship.

When Ian Gibson went to the University of Guelph, Canada, in 1979, Andrew D Saunders was appointed in his place. He also was a geochemist, a young man who in 1980 gained the President's Award of the Geological Society given for distinguished work by a person still under 30 years of age. His research concerned the nature, composition and genesis of ocean crust; subduction zones, especially the Antarctic Peninsular. He participated in the Deep Sea Drilling Project in the Gulf of California.

While Saunders was in post a new X-ray fluorescence spectrometer was acquired. The Intercollegiate Analytical Facility, which had been set up in 1968, was upgraded. With the support of the intercollegiate users, a successful grant application was made to NERC and to the University. The automatic sample changer was a boon allowing 24-hour operation to continue without anyone working a night-shift.

In 1984 Andrew Saunders left to go the University of Leicester and in his place Matthew F Thirlwall was appointed under the UGC's 'new blood' scheme. He also had been awarded the President's Medal of the Geological Society. His research involved volcanic rocks in several settings including the West Indies, the Karakoram and Palaeozoic volcanics in Scotland. With Dr Marriner he wrote new software for rapid processing of XRF analytical data. His expertise in rock analysis was to be invaluable to the department in establishing geochemistry in the new building at Egham.

In another stroke of fortune, Martin A Menzies agreed in 1985 to join the new venture. His interests are in mantle enrichment processes; lithospheric peridodtites and pyroxenites, ultramafic xenolites. With Matthew Thirlwall he participated in the negotiations which led to the acquisition of a multi-collector thermal ionisation mass spectrometer for the new department. But this anticipates the future. The story of how it happened, the story of the Geology Department from 1977 to 1985 is one of the drive, energy, devotion, relentless effort and wiliness of Professor Smith in his ambition to see the department, staff and students, transplanted in an environment where it could continue to flourish. These are his recollections of the events.

I considered myself most fortunate to be given the Chair of Geology at Bedford College. It was with intense pleasure that I arrived from University College London, into a well balanced, harmonious department in what was, without doubt, the best situated College in the University of London. A College with a great tradition and two very active Faculties. The Geology Department was well equipped and had spacious apartments. I succeeded Basil King, who had a great reputation and who, on retirement, had gone to live in Arran, and Leonard Hawkes, his eminent predecessor, who still frequented the Common

Room. It had been suggested to me by the Provost of University College, that I should, on my arrival in Regent's Park, immediately develop some form of close association between the Geology Department of UCL and my new department, but only a few hours in my new College had made me a Bedford man!

At that time, the geologists of the University of London, through its very active Board of Studies, were remarkably collaborative–sharing equipment, supporting teaching programmes–and, therefore, something of a model for the rest of the University. This was to be important later.

Even by contemporary standards, the Geology Department at Bedford was small, though because of its successes many academic and industrial visitors had gained the impression that it was much larger than it actually was. This happy, indeed halcyon, circumstance was within a short time of my arrival to be under threat. Throughout the nation, university departments were under threat of closure–subjects such as Russian and Music had already been 'rationalised' in some universities. The national provision for the teaching of geology was under scrutiny and the Oxburgh Report suggested that the nation was producing too many geology graduates for national needs and that research funding was spread too thinly: there were, in fact, too many geology departments. Concurrently, the national financial provision for university education was threatened with reduction. The University of London, because of its proliferation of Colleges and Schools, considered itself to be particularly vulnerable and the first attempts were being made to reorganise its many medical schools.

At this critical time a meeting of the geologists of Westfield, Chelsea and Bedford Colleges was held at Bedford College–these departments were already collaborating closely. They proposed, by telegram to the Vice-Chancellor, that the three departments should be amalgamated into one to be sited at either Chelsea or Bedford College. That telegram was to give geology a special place in the proposals for reorganisation within the University.

Bedford College, under the leadership of its Principal, Dorothy Wedderburn, had, about this time, begun to explore the possibility of amalgamation with another college of the University because the College's home in Regent's Park was on lease from the Crown Commissioners and that lease did not have long to run before it had to be renewed and at a higher cost to the College. Plans for an amalgamation with Westfield College, not the most ideal solution, were to falter and, while University College London favoured a complete take-over, King's College entered with a plan for a two-site development.

With talks beginning with King's College, it was natural to draw the geologists of that College into the embryonic plans for the amalgamation of the geology departments. When the geologists of Westfield College withdrew, talks between the geologists of King's, Chelsea and Bedford took a more urgent turn, each group believing that, should an amalgamation be achieved, the joint department should be located in their college! A home at any of the colleges seemed sensible, but Bedford's geologists held the weakest position unless the lease on the Regent's Park site could be extended. The Chelsea geologists, under the able leadership of Derek Blundell, came to prefer a move to King's College–a move which found favour with the Principal of King's College and which was accepted, with some reluctance, by the Principal of Chelsea College.

By this time the Geology Board of Studies was taking an interest in developments but rejected a radical proposal from Bedford College geologists that all the geologists of the University should seek to amalgamate into a University of London Geological Institute on the Regent's Park site, funding from outside earnings the cost of the lease: perhaps an outrageous suggestion at the time but one which, with hindsight, could have had far reaching consequences.

In a short time the Academic Board of Bedford College became less favourably disposed towards a two-site amalgamation with King's, partly because King's College had severe constraints on the space immediately available, though it had plans to use part of the adjacent Somerset House and had sights on property across the Thames near Waterloo Station. Thoughts, instead, turned to an amalgamation with Royal Holloway College. The latter had a large site in the 'green belt', had similar traditions to those of Bedford, a magnificent Founder's Building and several new science laboratories. The 'down-side' included, in the view of many, remoteness from the academic 'centre of gravity' in central London and a somewhat restricted, two faculty structure similar to that of Bedford College.

Early in the discussions concerned with the amalgamation of Royal Holloway and Bedford Colleges, I asked to be allowed, and was granted permission, to speak at a meeting of the Joint Academic Boards. At that meeting

I proposed that an amalgamated (King's, Chelsea, Bedford) Geology Department should be located on the Royal Holloway site. The response from the Boards was heartwarmingly enthusiastic and I was encouraged to promote the idea.

The response from the geologists of King's and Chelsea departments was, to say the least 'chilly', indeed, from some quarters, hostile, in spite of the prospect of the creation of a new, purpose built facility. The Principal of King's College redoubled his efforts to locate the amalgamated department on a King's site and many of the geologists who would be involved counted the prospects of personal losses if we went to Egham–of facilities in central London, the 'distant' location and the costs of relocating families. The Board of Studies took a neutral view and seemed to regard the location of a new Department of Geology at Egham with a degree of incredulity and not a little amusement, though it did favour the concept of the amalgamation of the three departments.

Throughout the ensuing period there was an overwhelming desire that the amalgamating department should be strong wherever it was located and should match the established strengths of the UCL and Imperial geology departments. The 'amalgamators' dearly wished that our friends at Queen Mary College should be party to our plans; but sadly this did not occur. The geologists of Birkbeck College, wedded to their traditions of adult education also remained aloof.

Matters at this stage moved to a higher plane; the Principal of King's, Ian Cameron, and Dorothy Wedderburn, Principal-Designate of Royal Holloway and Bedford New College, as the new institution at Egham was to be called, entered into serious debate about the location of the amalgamating department. At this stage the geologists to be affected were by no means unanimous in their views concerning their future.

The Vice-Chancellor of the University, Randolph Quirk, called in an independent adjudicator–Professor Alwyn Williams, Principal of Glasgow University and himself a geologist–to weigh up the merits of siting the amalgamating department at King's or at RHBNC. He favoured the Royal Holloway site. What I think is most noteworthy about this outcome was the readiness of most of the geologists affected to accept this decision. Sadly, others, with distinguished contributions to research and teaching at King's and Chelsea took the decision not to join the new enterprise though by this time there had been new recruits to the staff of Bedford who had joined in the full knowledge that a move was imminent and saw it as a challenge and an opportunity. The outcome was a well-balanced staff of about the right size to match our aspirations. Derek Blundell, who had favoured a move to King's College, immediately threw his energies, with great effect, into the creation of the new department at Egham. The geographers of Bedford College also saw that the move, with Geology, to Egham would offer them new opportunities.

What followed is history: a move to portakabins and the relocated 'temporary' Departure Lounge of post-war Heathrow Airport relieved, through the mud and snow, by the sight growing before our eyes of what was to become Queen's Building, later to be declared open by Her Majesty Queen Elizabeth, and funded by part of the proceeds of the sale of our Regent's Park assets. For me it was a particular pleasure: it was almost exactly in the position, landslip phenomenon notwithstanding, where I had once stood, when the future had been far from clear, and said to a visiting Japanese professor "If we are to come here, this is the place I would like our new department to be!"

Immense credit must go to Peter Banham, of Geology, and Rob Potter of Geography, for the way in which they liaised with the architect in transforming the wishes of the incoming staff into the finished building. No words can give full credit to the efforts of everyone involved–particularly Keith Stephens and the technicians in all the amalgamating departments, and the secretarial staff, especially Julie Brown. All the staff, in spite of family relocations and previous doubts, created a new department with a tremendous esprit de corps. All this would have been of little value had not the incoming students from the three old departments seen the significance of what was afoot–they had their troubles too, but rose to the occasion. I would like to think that no-one suffered unduly, but I know that was not the case. The traditions of the old departments, however, came together well, led by Bob Howie from King's, Derek Blundell from Chelsea and myself from Bedford; and while the Geology Department at RHBNC, later to become Royal Holloway–University of London, was new, its roots led back to Lyell, Fleet, Hawkes, Taylor, King, Gregory, Will Smith and many others. Each old department brought strengths and in the years which followed, when other established geology departments with long histories and great achievements, were swept away. King's, Chelsea and Bedford geologists put down roots which, shallow at first like the Ginko trees we planted outside Queen's, have grown to maturity on the ground of Thomas Holloway's dream. Now the Geology Department of Royal Holloway is established and highly regarded, both nationally and internationally, and its future is assured. By any account it has proved to be an asset to the College and has rewarded the faith of the members of that Joint Academic Board in the early debates about the amalgamation of Bedford and Royal Holloway Colleges who favoured the creation of a Geology Department at RHBNC.

There can be no doubt that, in spite of much pain at the time, it was all worth while. For those deeply attached to the traditions of Bedford College there should be intense pleasure in what the geologists of Bedford College–a hundred years in the making–have achieved.

100 Years of Geology at Bedford–Bibliography

Architects Plans–Science Block B, 1910 (Royal Holloway, University of London, Archives, AR511/1/68).

Bedford College Annual Reports of the Council.

Bedford College Calendars.

Bedford College Old Students Association *Journals*, 1927–1982.

Council Minutes, Bedford College London.

Dunham, K (1982) 'Leonard Hawkes' in *Biographical Memoirs of Fellows of the Royal Society*,Vol 28. 125–139.

Papers in Geology Department Correspondence File 1900–1977 (Royal Holloway, University of London, Archives, AR336/1/1-5).

Papers in Geography Department Correspondence File 1878–1927 (Royal Holloway, University of London, Archives, AR336/5/1–2).

Papers on Geology Rationalisation File–Quinquennium 1967–1972 (Royal Holloway, University of London, Archives, AR341/17/12).

Papers in Geology Research Grants File 1962–1985 (Royal Holloway, University of London, Archives, AR350/6/1–16).

Personal files for Catherine Raisin (D168), Leonard Hawkes (D645), Doris Reyolds (D171), Helen Marguerite Wood (Student file 1711) (Royal Holloway, University of London, Archives).

Photographs of geology field excursions 1922–1962 (Royal Holloway, University of London, Archives, PH4/1).

Press cuttings 1887–1980 (Royal Holloway, University of London Archives, RF129/1/1–20).

Proceedings of the Geological Society of London

Tuke, M (1939) *A History of Bedford College for Women, 1849–1937.* Oxford: Oxford University Press.

Higher Degrees Awarded to Students in the Department of Geology, Bedford College

1920	I H Lowe	MSc Geology	BSc 1913
1920	H M Wood	MSc Geology	BSc 1919
1934	H M Muir-Wood	DSc Palaeontology	
1922	F J Relf	MSc Geology	BSc 1906
1924	D L Reynolds	MSc Geology	BSc 1920
1937	D L Reynolds	DSc Geology	
1925	A I McDonald	PhD	(staff)
1926	H K Cargill	MSc Geology	BSc 1925
1926	J A Ledeboer	MSc Geology	BSc 1925
1929	M E Odell	MSc Geology	BSc 1921
1940	W D Evans	PhD Geology	(staff)
1945	B C King	PhD Geology	(staff)
1956	C H Holland	PhD Geology	(staff)
1960	A Naylor	MSc Geology	BSc 1951
1963	J A Turner	PhD Geology (external)	BSc 1959
1963	R C Tyler	MSc Geology	BSc 1959
1965	D Roberts	PhD Geology	
1965	A R Woolley	PhD Geology	
1965	Y P Pocock	PhD Geology	BSc 1961
1966	J A E B Hubbard	PhD Geology	BSc 1962
1966	D S Sutherland (Milne)	PhD Geology	BSc 1958
1966	F C Cox	PhD Geology	
1968	D L Speedyman	PhD Geology	
1970	J E Martyn	PhD Geology	

1970	J W Oldham	PhD Geology	
1971	M P McClenaghan	PhD Geology	
1971	P K Webb	PhD Geology	
1971	M A Worthing	PhD Geology	
1971	B Collins	PhD Petrology	
1972	G R Chapman	PhD Geology	
1973	S J Lippard	PhD Field Geology	
1973	J N Carney	PhD Geology	
1974	S D Weaver	PhD Geology	
1975	M H L Pickford	PhD Geology	
1975	J S Sceal	PhD Geology	
1975	P A Madgett	PhD Quaternary Geology	
1976	A P Hill	PhD Geology	
1976	W B Jones	PhD Geology	
1976	R M Knight	PhD Geology	
1977	N R Charnley	PhD Geology	
1977	J A MacQueen (James)	PhD Geology	BSc 1972
1977	O Tittirananda	PhD Geology	
1979	M Golden	PhD Geology	
1979	D G A Scurry	PhD Geology	BSc 1970
1980	S M Bennett	PhD Geology	
1980	G R Challis	PhD Geology	
1980	F W M Hopper	PhD Geology	
1981	H Y Chun	PhD Geology	
1981	J J Forster	PhD Geology	
1981	C C Johns	PhD Geology	
1981	D R Mattey	PhD Geology	
1983	A H I Mahdi	MPhil	
1983	Y K Hong	PhD Geology	
1984	G M Rex	PhD Botany	BSc 1980
1984	N C Tilston	PhD Geology	BSc. 1979
1985	M J Hole	PhD Geology	
1985	M F Emre	PhD Geology	
1985	S P Kelley	PhD Geology	

1985	A B Moyes	PhD Geology	
1985	A Baird	PhD Geology	BSc 1975

Geology Department Staff 1885–1985

Heads of Department

1885–1886	Mary Forster
1886–1890	Grenville A J Cole, FGS
1890–1920	Catherine A Raisin BSc, DSc London
1920–1921	Stanley Smith, MA Cantab, DSc Dunelm (Acting Head)
1921–1956	Leonard Hawkes, MSc, DSc Dunelm, FGS, FRS (1952) [Professor from 1948]
1956–1977	Basil C King, MSc Dunelm, PhD London, DSc Glasgow, FGS, FRSE
1977–1985	Alec J Smith, BSc, PhD Wales, FIMM, FGS, CEng (1978) [RHBNC 1985–92]

Demonstrators in Geology

1910–1915	Miss P Bowen-Colthurst, Final Geol Hons Oxon
1910–1914	Miss Ida Slater, BA Dublin, Nat Hist Tripos Cantab [became Mrs Lees]
1914–1920	Miss I Lowe, BSc London (Bedford 1913)
1915–1917	Miss M Munro, BSc London
1920–1922	Miss L M Devonshire, BSc London (Bedford 1919)
1922–1926	Miss A I McDonald, MSc Wales, PhD London (Bedford 1925)
1922–1925	Miss I E Knaggs, Nat Sci. Tripos Cantab, PhD London
1925–1927	Miss J A Ledeboer, BSc London (Bedford 1925), MSc (1926)
1927–1931	Miss D L Reynolds, BSc, MSc London (Bedford 1920,1924), DSc (1937)
1932–1933	J W Harris, BSc, PhD St Andrews
1933–1934	F W Cope, MSc Manchester
1934–1936	A P Hetherington BSc London (Bedford 1933)
1936–1938	B C King, MSc Dunelm, PhD London (1945)
1938–1939	W D Evans, MSc Wales, PhD London (1940)

1946–1948	G Theokritoff, BSc London
1948–1949	Miss O Robins, BSc London [became Mrs Bradley]
1949–1951	E Jones, BSc Wales [became Assistant Lecturer 1951-1953]

Assistant Lecturers in Geology

1951–1953	E Jones, BSc Wales
1953–1956	A J Moss, BSc Reading
1954–1956	J T Temple, MA, PhD Cantab
1956–1960	R Nicholson, BSc, PhD London
1956–1958	A A Wilson, BSc, PhD Dunelm
1958–1960	B A Sturt, BSc, PhD Wales [became Lecturer 1960–1970]
1960–1962	D C Turner, BSc, PhD London [Senior Lecturer 1974–1975]
1960–1962	R Beavon, BSc Wales, PhD London
1962–1965	E C Appleyard, BSc Western Ontario, MSc Kingston Ontario, PhD Cantab
1962–1964	P H Banham, BSc, PhD Nott [became Lecturer 1964–1979, Snr Lect 1979–1988]
1965–1967	D Powell, PhD Wales [became Lecturer 1967–1984, Snr Lecturer 1984–1991]
1966–1968	E P F Rose, MA, DPhil Oxon [became Lecturer 1968–1985, then RHBNC]

Lecturers in Geology

1910–1920	C A Raisin, Morton Sumner Lecturer
1919–1920	Miss G Elles, DSc (temporary lecturer)
1926–1930	Miss E W Gardner, MA Cantab, FGS (1929)
1930–1947	Miss E Dix, MSc, DSc Wales, FGS (1935)
1947–1952	N F Hughes, MA Cantab
1952–1966	C H Holland, BSc Manchester, PhD London
1958–1985	Miss G M Dunlop, PhD Glasgow [Mrs Page from 1971, RHBNC to 1991]
1960–1970	B A Sturt, PhD Wales
1964–1979	P H Banham, PhD Nott [Senior Lecturer 1979–1985, then RHBNC to 1988]

1965–1969	W W Bishop, PhD Birm [Reader 1969–1973]
1967–1984	D Powell, PhD Wales [Senior Lecturer 1984–1985, then RHBNC to 1991]
1968–1985	E P F Rose, MA, DPhil Oxon [Senior Lecturer RHBNC 1985–]
1970–1979	I L Gibson, PhD London, DIC
1973–1980	A D Gibbs, BSc Glasgow, MSc London, PhD Exeter, DIC
1979–1983	A D Saunders, MSc, PhD Birm
1980–1981	J S Myers, PhD London, DIC
1984–1985	M F Thirlwall, MA Oxon, PhD Edin [then RHBNC 1985–]
1974–1977	G A Worrall, MSc, PhD London [note: special attachment from Geography]
1977–1977	S J Lippard, PhD London [temporary replacement for Gibson]
1979–1979	N B W Harris, MA, PhD Cantab [temporary post]
1985 (July)	M A Menzies, BSc Aberdeen, PhD Cantab [then RHBNC 1985–]

Chapter 9

German

Patricia Howe

Only a year after the first public allusion to a "'Ladies College', a recent institution, much wanted and likely to succeed",[1] the German writer and traveller Fanny Lewald visited "the modest beginning of an institute which, in a few years, will be a university for women".[2] She described the activities and purposes of the College, where, with 'Miss S', she attended a lecture on Ancient History by Professor Carpenter. A year later, the Swedish writer and traveller, Frederika Bremer, whose writings were translated into English from their German versions, described both Queen's College and the Ladies' College as "praiseworthy attempts" to provide "for the intellectual culture of women".[3] Their approval of the advances in women's education were not just compliments to their hosts, but messages for their readers at home. Lewald's companion 'Miss S' was most probably Anna Swanwick, an early student, and with her mother, one of the first lady visitors. She had a lifelong interest in the college and in Germany, and her publications include many translations from eighteenth-century German dramatists. She was a member of the Weimar Goethe Society and of the English Goethe Society, founded in 1886, eventually becoming one of its Vice-Presidents. Another lady visitor, the well-known author Anna Jameson, friend of Ottilie von Goethe, and professional translator, shared this scholarly interest in German. These women, like others of their generation, enjoyed an easy familiarity with German life and culture, which helped to counteract the mid-century trivialisation of girls' education ascribed to the influence of Prince Albert's "German ideal of the Hausfrau".[4] Moreover, Mrs Reid knew from her friend Julia Smith that some Germans were challenging this ideal by establishing better schooling for girls. Given this awareness of German intellectual tradition and of the beginnings of parallel developments in "that everlasting theme 'female education'", it is not surprising that, despite Prince Albert, German was offered from the start.[5]

There was no shortage of teachers of German, for London had a considerable population of German intellectuals, refugees from the aftermath of the 1848 revolution. Many earned their living in London by private tuition, by teaching in schools and colleges, or by translation and journalism, unless or until they were able to secure academic positions.[6] They include the first two professors of German: Dr Adolph Heimann who taught at Bedford from 1849–1868 and at University College, and Charles Adolphus Buchheim, who taught at Bedford for five years while he was professor at King's.[7] The rest of the nineteenth century followed this pattern of teachers, attached primarily to other institutions in London and elsewhere, providing tuition for brief periods. As might be expected under these circumstances, the teaching and learning of German was at first modest and somewhat haphazard. In the early years the number of students taking German was small–in 1856–57, three students took German in the first term, rising by 1859–60 to fifteen.

The supplementary charter in 1867 established special examinations for women, a General Certificate, corresponding to the University's requirements for the Matriculation Examination, and a Certificate of Higher Proficiency equivalent to the Intermediate Examination in Arts for Honours. But few students took advantage of the new examinations. Although they were simplified for their benefit–for example, the *viva voce* becomes 'Conversation in German'–the actual papers make no concessions to what might be perceived as women's interests. While in 1867 French offered female candidates passages of translation in praise of Madame de Sévigné and George Sand, German had Schiller on Greek and Roman poetry and William Cowper in his greenhouse. When in 1878 a further supplementary charter made every degree, honour and prize–except membership of Convocation–available to women, they could move from matriculation in German, an examination consisting of grammar and passages of translation, to an Intermediate examination of a similar kind. To give a flavour of what was expected in the latter, the translation into German in 1889 consisted of twenty-four lines from Scott, beginning:

> The Abbess was of noble blood,
> But early took the veil and hood,
> Ere upon life she cast a look,
> Or knew the world she had forsook...

If they negotiated this,–and were undeterred by the implied warning in it–they might proceed to the Honours examination, consisting of papers for translation into and from German; Grammar, Historical Grammar and Versification; general outlines of literature, together with a special study of prescribed texts from the Old High German period onwards; dictation and the *viva voce*. This scheme, with some elaboration, provided a basis for the federal degree in German until it ended in the 1980s.

Bedford students of the 1880s and 1890s prepared for these examinations in classes that met twice a week at fixed times, except for the conversation class. The growing formality of these arrangements disguised the pedagogic and social realities: Ida Samuel, a student from 1897–1901, who was 'a loafer', ie preparing for the Higher Local examinations in English, French and German, had "German lessons with Mr Rippmann–the only pupil and I think he was relieved to find I had got past the elementary stage. Although the system of chaperons in omnibuses had at that time almost died out, my mother was very doubtful whether I should have lessons alone with Mr Rippmann".[8]

Nevertheless comparisons with German educational methods, especially for women, are favourable. The calendar for 1890–91 records an "occasional lecture" where Dr A W Schüddekopf, professor of German from 1888 to 1890 gave:

> a vivid account of German University life, and somewhat horrified his numerous and sympathetic hearers by a description of the lengthy examinations German students have to undergo. At the close of his lecture he alluded to the "Frauenverein" which is seeking to win for German women the educational battle which has been fought and won in England. It will interest the College to know that one of the Leaders of the "Frauenverein"–Helene Lange–came over to England last year for the express purpose of studying Colleges for Women. She has recently published a pamphlet, in which there is special mention made of Bedford College and its "richly blessed work", and the following quotation will show that Fräulein Lange apprehended this, which at home seems often overlooked:- "Many capable and highly-cultivated women, who have spent their lives in the service of their own sex and wrought great things for women's cause, received their training here".[9]

The writer is cheered by Lange's appreciation of the fact that:

> at Bedford College, some who have since become Heads of Women's Colleges received their training and gathered their experience which alone fitted them for the larger liberty, the wider sphere of work, the greater responsibilities that have been laid upon them.[10]

From 1898 to 1920 arrangements for the teaching of German in the University were gradually formalised. These years are marked by a struggle to keep and expand the subject at Bedford, a struggle that took place against the threat and then the reality of a war with Germany. In 1898 a Board of Studies for English and German was established, and in 1900–01:

> On the recommendation of the Lecturers in English and German (both of whom were also Lecturers at UC), supported by the approval of the Staff, Council sanctioned a scheme for the Honours teaching in these two subjects to be given jointly by the Lecturers of University and Bedford Colleges.[11]

At the same time it was announced that the University would assume the organisation of German. In 1902–03, when the University had six staff in German–two professors, three readers and one assistant–the College reported that "the University has endowed and organised a scheme for the teaching of German in Schools and other Institutions of the University of which Bedford has availed itself through courses given in the College by both Professors and Readers".[12] By 1905–06 Bedford edged towards a stronger presence in German when Robert Priebsch resigned his teaching post and his share was taken by J G Robertson, "who will act as director of German studies in the College".[13] In Robertson–of whom more later–Bedford had acquired a formidable champion.

A correspondence between the Principal of the University, Sir Arthur Rucker, and Margaret Tuke, shows her interest in the growth of German in the college during this period, and her steady defence of the institution and its students. In 1908 she reminded Sir Arthur of an earlier request for German at Bedford "to have the services of one of the University professors and to secure that a fair share of the Honours teaching should be carried out within its walls".[14] Bedford students were clearly conscientious attenders, since she based her claim on them being "first in the number attending Professors' lectures" and the College being the "second largest contributor to the fees for the provision for German". In 1910 funds from London County Council strengthened this provision, providing posts in Economics, Engineering, German, Pedagogy and Science. By 1911 Miss Tuke was satisfied with the arrangements for fees, but not with "the excessive number of lectures demanded of students on the philological side".[15] She complained about the numbers of lectures–350, compared with 250 in English and 205 in

French–and about their uneven distribution:

> "As the lectures are not evenly distributed throughout the terms, the lecture list in some cases amounts to 16 hours a week in German. Of these 3 or 4 hours are devoted to composition and literature, 2 to a subsidiary subject, the remaining hours are devoted to philology.
> I do not think it is possible for a student to do good independent work if so large a proportion of his time is taken up with lectures and the necessary immediate preparation for them."[16]

Despite a regressive move by the professors of German in 1912 to concentrate teaching in a single institution–needless to say, not Bedford–progress continued. The professors welcomed the growing numbers of students and planned to extend the period of study to three years "as the previous training of our students is, in almost every case, very inadequate and the field to be covered large".[17] Things improved so much for Bedford that by July 1914 a lecturer was to be appointed by the Principal of Bedford and the German professors, to work from September 1st 1914, mainly at Bedford. The appointment was brief and unrenewed, and repeated requests during the First World War were refused. To what extent hostility to Germany affected the Department is unclear, since references to German during the period are scant, but the finance committee believed "that in view of the diminished attendance at the German classes and the unwillingness of the College to maintain their contribution, the expenditure on the teaching of German is excessive".[18]

Robertson, however, looked to the future, describing to Miss Tuke his view of a stronger, more autonomous department:

> "it seems to me that, if changes are desired by the College, it would be advisable that they should be formulated by the Council of the College. I can only repeat what I have urged at earlier periods that the department of German would benefit greatly by having the Reader and assistant closely connected with the College. I should

like, indeed, to claim a full time occupant for the post. It will, I daresay, be urged that the classes are small–as a matter of fact, they have kept up surprisingly amidst the adverse conditions of the past years, and doubtless the numbers will increase as the war passes into history."[19]

He suggests extending the teaching programme, adding classes in phonetics and modern literature, which he would share with a capable assistant, who could "at least keep up an interest in a 'German society' for conversation and reading", give students advice, "look after the library for German reading which we are trying to get together" and show students "what to read and how to read".[20] The Principal put this to the University on December 21st 1918 and when the Senate resolved to attach Professors and Readers to specific colleges, it was agreed that a chair of German would be tenable at Bedford College from June 1920 and that Robertson would have his assistant.

When the College Secretary wrote to Robertson in 1933 to obtain a record of his appointment to Bedford, he replied:

"My appointment was expressly non-collegiate, and (together with my colleague Priebsch who was made University professor of the philological and medieval side of the subject) with jurisdiction over all the German work throughout the University (including even the Polytechnic). The University began the reorganisation of the new teaching university–the model in those days was the University of Berlin–by taking the subject of German out of the hands and control of the individual Colleges. For this purpose the LCC provided the endowment."[21]

He relates how, in the early years, the Honours work was done at University College, but he also taught at King's. He only knew that he had been attached to Bedford from the Income Tax Office, but eventually decided to transfer some of his work there:

"When the students of German at Bedford began to increase, and especially when your new building offered greater and very

> pleasant facilities, it seemed to me only fair that I should transfer some of my UC work there. I confess there were purely personal motives too. I liked the atmosphere at Bedford and particularly admired Miss Tuke's wise principalship, and disliked frictions at the other places. But I did this purely on my own initiative. UC did not like the idea, but they could not interfere as they had renounced their control of the German department, and the University had given me a free hand to organise the subject as seemed best to me."[22]

But Robertson's struggle for German at Bedford is part of a wider pattern. As John Flood records, "it was largely thanks to his influence that, despite the pathological hatred engendered by the First World War, the study of German won its place as an essential part of the curriculum of British Universities".[23]

John George Robertson (1867–1933) was a Scot, the eldest of five children of a lecturer in the Glasgow Church of Scotland Training College and later headmaster of various schools. His father encouraged him to study science, and, after school, he read Classics and then Natural Sciences at Glasgow University. But scenes from Goethe's epic poem *Hermann und Dorothea* on the walls of his family home, and his reading of Carlyle and Goethe's *Faust* in translation inspired him to learn German. He also learnt Norwegian and Spanish, and gained a thorough knowledge of music. After his MA in 1886 and BSc in 1889 he gave up science, and went to Leipzig to study German. In Leipzig he met others with artistic and musical interests, among them his future wife, Ethel Richardson, a student at the Conservatoire and 'wooed her by inviting her to the autumn cycle of Wagner's operas'. Before their marriage in 1895 Robertson returned briefly to Glasgow, applied unsuccessfully for a number of university appointments, and moved to Munich to work as a freelance teacher of English, preparing textbooks and writing about literature for several journals. In 1896 he was appointed lecturer in English in Strasbourg, then a German city, and was later promoted to Professor Extraordinarius, a rare distinction for a foreigner. His wife began her career as a writer and under the name of Henry Handel Richardson published novels such as *Maurice Guest*, about the lives of music students in Leipzig. In 1902 he published the book for which he is best known, his *History of German Literature*, "the first of its kind in English, this work long remained a standard authority, praised for its broad sweep (from the earliest mention of Germanic peoples by Roman historians to the twentieth century) and for its sober assessments and reliable presentation of essential facts". It has since been published in several revised editions, to which his successor, Edna Purdie and other members of the German department, contributed, and was published in a German translation in 1968. As Flood says, it established Robertson's reputation as the foremost German scholar in the English-speaking world, and he was immediately offered a post as professor at the University of Michigan, but he refused and in 1903 accepted an invitation to come to London as University Professor in German, teaching at University College and at Bedford. He wrote later that it seemed ridiculous in retrospect how difficult it had been for him and his wife to decide to leave Strasbourg where they were happy–"hopelessly Germanised, I suppose".[24] But his happy 'Germanisation' may have sustained him through his struggles in London, especially through the war, which as his widow writes to Edna Purdie–another war already looming large–was a personal source of grief to him.[25]

Robertson produced a large number of books and shorter writings, on eighteenth century German literature, but also on comparative subjects relating German literature to aspects of European thought and literature through Shakespeare, Carlyle, Byron, Italian thought and Classical mythology. These broad interests are also reflected in *The Modern Languages Review*, which Robertson founded and edited from 1905 to 1933. He was also deeply involved in the English Goethe Society and served as its president from 1930–1933. He was a Fellow of the British Academy and of the Royal Society of Literature, and was chosen to represent Britain at the centennial commemoration of Goethe's death in Weimar in 1932, where he received from President Hindenburg a silver medal struck for the occasion. When Robertson died on the point of retiring, the sum collected to mark his retirement went instead towards the prizes to which his name is attached, the J G Robertson Prize awarded every other year to a new graduate in German at Bedford, and the prestigious prize awarded triennially for outstanding published work in the field of Germanic Studies.

Robertson was followed by Edna Purdie (1894–1968), who thus became the first woman Professor of German. Born in St Albans, the daughter of an inspector of schools, she was educated at home and by local tutors–she recalled cycling to Hatfield for tuition in French–and through travel abroad. At first she hesitated between studying music and languages, attending Trinity College of Music and at seventeen playing the Liszt Piano Concerto in E flat at the Queen's Hall. But in 1910 she went to King's College for Women, gained a first class degree in German in 1913, and another in English as well as an MA in German. She went to Oxford as a postgraduate, but as women were not full members of the university, she could only be awarded the 'Certificate of Merit in Letters equivalent to the BLitt degree' for her thesis on *The Literary Ballad in England during the Romantic Period.* After university posts in Liverpool and Bangor, where she taught both medieval and modern literature, she succeeded Robertson at Bedford, remaining until her retirement in 1961, and serving the College and the University in many capacities: on committees in the university, at the Royal College of Music and the Warburg Institute, and in the establishment and work of the Institute of Germanic Studies. Both before and after her appointment to the Bedford Chair she published, like Robertson, in what would now be considered to be comparative literature. Her DLitt thesis in 1925 on the *Story of Judith in German and English Literature* led to many publications on Friedrich Hebbel and German drama. But she was an unselfish scholar who, as Robertson's literary executor, edited, completed and revised some of his works. This unselfishness was also evident in her interest in her students–until the end of her career she taught first-year students and to their surprise knew their names; she continued to encourage postgraduates, even after her retirement, counteracting the debilitating tendency to see a thesis as a life's work by encouraging them to treat it as an academic exercise.

Like Robertson, Edna Purdie held the chair at Bedford during a war with Germany. But their familiarity with Germany's culture and with values that transcended contemporary problems and obsessions, enabled them to survive personal distress and practical difficulties. Yet these should not be underestimated. As well as evacuation, there was the problem of obtaining materials when nothing could be imported. It is not surprising that Purdie and other members of her department, both at this time and later, created editions of classical texts with carefully researched prefaces and annotations for Anglophone students. Beyond this there was the difficulty of maintaining links with the Germany they knew. Like other Germanists and other members of the College, Edna Purdie worked to obtain entry permits and work for a number of refugees, most notably and successfully for Robert Pick and his family. His daughter, Marianne Pick, became an assistant in the German department. Robert Pick was sent to Dachau in November 1938 but soon released because of the efforts of Edna Purdie and Lillian Penson; a few weeks later he and his wife, Paula, managed to leave Austria, to be met at Croydon airport by Edna Purdie and Lillian Penson. Robert Pick eventually became librarian of the Institute of Germanic Studies, and, as his letter to Edna Purdie on the twentieth-fifth anniversary of his arrival in Britain shows, never forgot their kindness.[26]

These efforts to help refugees from Nazi Germany did not deprive her students of her attention and help. Although the Department was housed in Cambridge, she continued to supervise postgraduates trying to work in London and to help them find posts. Letters from Elizabeth M Wilkinson, later Professor of German at University College and a Fellow of the British Academy, who was then a postgraduate student, give a vivid sense of the difficulties for students and teachers, but also show how the war created opportunities for female graduates in German. She recorded in July 1940 that she had been asked to work as an assistant at University College, where Professor Willoughby's German assistant had been interned and his English colleague called up, and only later discovered that Edna Purdie had suggested her.

Wilkinson's letter refers to the bombing of Bedford, "I hear the poor students were disturbed during their finals. So much misery has happened since I saw you last–it is impossible to write about it".[27] In September 1940 her lodgings were bombed and she asked Edna Purdie for her copy of chapter III of her thesis "because the copy which I kept has unfortunately been lost through bombing so I would like to try to have another made. If it can be avoided, I don't want to have to re-write it. 2 Gordon Street was wrecked by the same H[igh].E [xplosive]. bomb which demolished the Great Hall of U.C. a week last Wednesday."[28] She described her attempts under the stern gaze of a policeman to salvage two bags of possessions from the collapsing house, and the damage to University College and the British Museum Reading Room, both vital to her research.

Edna Purdie also recommended graduates for intelligence work and code-breaking at Bletchley. They were so impressive that the invitation was repeated:

> "Whilst it is unlikely that you can provide us with two more girls so admirable as translators and as keen and conscientious workers as Miss Williams and Miss Holland, we should be most grateful if you could suggest the names of any young graduates in German who might wish to apply.
> The work is conducted in the neighbourhood of Bletchley...is definitely of national importance and requires both good natural intelligence and a sound knowledge of German.[29]

But she did provide candidates to meet the exacting requirements of the Foreign Office, among them Dorothy Reich (née Knight), who later joined the Bedford department as lecturer and senior lecturer.

The end of the war brought a gradual expansion of activities. The numbers of staff and students grew, although the staff were housed in odd parts of the College, some in Tuke Building, including its gloomy basement, some in the most modest corners of The Holme, until in the mid-sixties the department moved to the first floor of Reid building with its view over tennis courts and the lake. Direct exchange with

German-speaking countries was resumed: in 1945 it was possible to appoint a student assistant from Switzerland; in 1949 Edna Purdie lectured by invitation at the Universities of Bonn and Berlin, and at the Goethe bi-centenary celebrations in Bielefeld. Students also went to Germany: in 1946 the College Secretary promises financial help for students who were expected to spend parts of the vacation in a German-speaking country, and by the early sixties there were student exchanges with German universities, initally for a semester and later for a year. Although the size and bureaucracy of German universities usually shocked students accustomed to college life, one or two made themselves so much at home that they did not return.

Although by this time most teaching took place in the College, intercollegiate activities were important. On Tuesday mornings students from Queen Mary and Westfield Colleges visted Bedford to hear Professor Purdie's monumental two-year cycle of lectures on the history of German literature; on Tuesday afternoons second and third year students attended one of nine special subjects, travelling to hear the expert in his or her own college; and on Thursday mornings finalists attended intercollegiate lectures, first in the cramped Physics lecture theatre at Birkbeck and later in the grander surroundings of Senate House. Clearly the system depended not only on the collective good will and expertise of London's Germanists but also on the efficiency of its public transport.

In the period between Professor Purdie's retirement in 1964 and the merger twenty years later, there were two more professors, Ronald Peacock and William E Yuill. Both shared with their predecessors a broad range of interests in German, in comparative literature and in the arts, and, like their predecessors, were alert to talent in others. Ronald Peacock (1907–1993) came from Leeds, where he also studied before going as a post-graduate to Germany. He was reputedly the youngest Professor of German when appointed, at the age of thirty-two, to the chair at Leeds. In 1945 he moved to the Henry Simon chair at Manchester, which became a nursery for professors of German, and where he published three of his best known books, as well as becoming

Dean of Arts and Pro-Vice-Chancellor. In 1962 he moved to Bedford, where he remained until his retirement in 1975; he became an Honorary Fellow of the College in 1981. He was personally acquainted with distinguished scholars in Germany and the United States and brought them to London; in turn, he held visiting professorships in Cornell, Heidelberg and Freiburg im Breisgau. He was a member of many committees in the universities he served and beyond, such as the Manchester University Press, the joint Anglo-German Postgraduate Scholarship of the British Council and the German Academic Exchange Service, which he chaired from 1962 to 1975.

His scholarship reflects the breadth and depth of his interests in literature, music and the other arts. Among the honours he received were the J G Robertson Prize in 1942 for his ground-breaking study of Hölderlin, the first in English, and in 1969 the Gold Medal of the Goethe Institute for *Goethe's Major Plays* (1957, reprinted 1960, 1970), the book by which he was probably best known. During his time at Bedford he immersed himself in questions of aesthetics, and especially in what would now be called 'reader response theory', although he was the most undogmatic theorist with a profound awareness of individual sensibilities. In his final book, *Criticism and Personal Taste* (1972) and in his reflections on modern languages as a university subject, particularly on the distinctions between classes of degree, he anticipated present problems and interests.[30]

As the university system expanded in the 1960s, changes took place, including the arrival of male undergraduates, who were at first more numerous in German classes held for scientists than in the rest of the Department's activities. The number of students and of staff grew, Combined Honours degrees were introduced as were more formal procedures for providing pastoral care, and extra-curricular activities developed, mainly focussed on the German Society, but also including memorable parties for finalists at which the staff showed their skills as caterers.

Peacock's successor, William E Yuill (1921–1997), was born in Glasgow and educated principally at Robert Gordon's College in

Aberdeen. After matriculation in 1940 and two years at the University of Aberdeen, he joined the army, serving in the infantry before being sent to the School of Slavonic and East European Studies to study Serbo-Croat. After being parachuted into Bosnia he spent the period from June 1943 to March 1946 in liaison work with the Yugoslav National Liberation Army, and then on security duties in Trieste. Returning to Aberdeen, he graduated in 1947 with First Class Honours in French and German, and was awarded the Senatus Gold Medal in Modern Languages. He taught at King's College London, and gained an MA with a thesis on German Romanticism, then in Sheffield, where he also undertook translation and interpreting in German, Serbo-Croat and Czech. In 1965 he was appointed to the Chair at Nottingham, spent time as a visiting professor in Chicago, and in 1975 took up his chair at Bedford. He was a gifted linguist who loved jokes and verbal games, and could invent them in several languages. At his inaugural lecture he spoke of the mantle of J G Robertson having fallen on him, almost literally, as it was indeed Robertson's gown, green and shiny with age, that he wore on that occasion. His wit and geniality led him to authors such as Wieland and to the robust humour of Brecht, but he also wrote on a wide range of literary topics as well as compiling language text-books and editing literary and critical texts. After his retirement to Zagreb, he had a second career as a translator from German and from Serbo-Croat, which was crowned in 1995 by the award of the Tieck-Schlegel Prize for his translation of Ulrich im Hof's *The Enlightenment*. His translation of Wedekind's diaries shows his thoroughness, for he went back to the original, and insisted on including parts that had been omitted because of their supposed illegibility. His translation of Fontane's ballad about the Tay Bridge disaster featured in the programme of the Fontane centenary celebrations in Neuruppin in 1998.

Like his predecessors Yuill encouraged talent in others. He broadened the activities of the Department at all levels: a German play became an annual event, in which he often acted. These productions included such classics as *Urfaust*, which was supported by the Goethe

Insitute, which proposed to use for educational purposes the video-recordings made during rehearsals. With the support of the Austrian Cultural Institute he organised a series of literary symposia, usually in the impressive surroundings of The Holme or St John's, which brought together scholars from Britain and Austria, and fostered research in the Department. The Department also hosted visits by a Viennese theatre group, and in 1980 was invited to provide a British contingent to participate in the celebration of the twenty-fifth anniversary of the State Treaty which ended the occupation of Austria by the allied powers and the establishment of a republic. On this occasion Yuill and six students spent two week as guests of the Austrian government.

Professors of German, except at the beginning of Bedford's history, did not work alone, but increasingly shared their teaching with dedicated and gifted colleagues–too many to name individually. One of these, Maurice Walshe, used to tell students that, unlike them, he had been taught by giants, a contrast which some viewed with scepticism and others with relief. Giants or not, the teaching staff at Bedford offered scholarship and practical concern–whether, like Walshe, explaining late medieval mystical poetry or urging them to learn the London bus routes, or, like Dorothy Reich, introducing students to eighteenth-century aesthetics or giving her dinner to a hungry student.[31] The Department itself produced many graduates and postgraduates who went on to academic careers–as well as to a wide variety of other occupations–and, especially through its Tutorial Assistantships, a post rather like that of a contemporary graduate teaching assistant, gave a start to young scholars from many places.

Like the history of any department, that of German must be seen in the context of other histories–of women's education and of the development of London University, for example. But it must also be seen against Anglo-German relations during this period. Britain and Germany met fruitfully in the familiarity of scholars and students with a culture beyond contemporary obsessions, and in the exchange of information between people sympathetic to women's education. When they clashed, they brought distress and disruption, and threatened the precarious stability of the emerging department; but they also created challenges and opportunities, and, repeatedly, brought gifted refugees and exiles who came to study or to teach.

References

1 Margaret J Tuke, *A History of Bedford College for Women*, 1849–1937, Oxford University Press, p61.

2 Fanny Lewald visited England and Scotland in 1850; she records her visit in Fanny Lewald, *England und Schottland*, Braunschweig: Druck und Verlag von Friedrich Vieweg & Sohn, 1851, 2 vols. She appears to confuse Queen's College and the Ladies' College, because she says that she visited Queen's College, but her account of its origins, organisation and intentions, the reference to Professor Carpenter and to Miss S, one of its twelve lady visitors, seems to describe the Ladies' College. The quotation is translated from her remark on p284 "der bescheidene Anfang eines Insitutes, das in wenig Jahren eine Universität für Frauen sein wird". The translation is mine. Fanny Lewald was also friend of Gottfried Kinkel, who taught History of Fine Art, Roman History and Geography at Bedford, and of his wife, the author Johanna Kinkel.

3 The Swedish traveller and writer Frederika Bremer made her first visit to England in 1851, visiting as many institutions as possible concerned with the education of women, including Queen's College and the Ladies' College. The quotation is from Frederika Bremer, *England in 1851 or Sketches of a tour in England.* Translated from the German by L A H Boulogne: Merridew, 1853, p116.

4 Tuke, p19, refers to this ideal, saying that under its influence "The vigorous cramming in accomplishments, the German and Italian expected of a girl in society earlier in the century, seem to have given place to a less exacting regime".

5 Tuke, p44, says that Mrs Reid's friend, Julia Smith, also a friend of Anna Jameson, drew her attention in 1840 to a school in Berlin founded by Queen Elisabeth of Bavaria, wife of Fredrick Wilhelm IV, and comments that if all schools were like that "there would be little fault to find in that everlasting theme 'female education'". The school was in fact founded in 1747 and taken under the protection of Crown Princess Elisabeth, future wife of Friedrich Wilhelm IV in 1827. See: James Albisetti, *Schooling German Girls and Women. Secondary and Higher Education in the Nineteenth Century*, Princeton University Press, New Jersey, p25 ff.

6 Accounts of their lives in England are given in Rosemary Ashton, *Little Germany: Exile and Asylum in Victorian England*, (Oxford 1986), and in Peter Alter & Rudolf Muhs (eds), *Exilanten*

und andere Deutsche in Fontanes London, (Stuttgart and London: Stuttgarter Arbeiten zur Germanistik 331, Publications of the Institute of Germanic Studies 66, 1996).

7 An account of Buchheim's life and career can be found in: Derek Glass, 'From Moravia to the Strand. The Career of Charles Adolphus Buchheim', in: Peter Alter & Rudolf Muhs (eds), *Exilanten und andere Deutsche* pp41–76; Glass does not mention Buchheim at Bedford.

8 Liz Bennett, 'Women's College Education–the Bedford experience', *Lectures 1886–1986,* p80, quotes this reminiscence on the occasion of the centenary celebrations of 1949; Walter Rippmann, of Gonville and Caius College, was professor at Bedford from 1896–98.

9 *Bedford College Calendar,* 1889, p5.

10 *Bedford College Calendar,* 1889, p5; see also: Helene Lange, *Lebenserinnerungen,* Berlin 1930, pp140–1; for a discussion of the expedition by Lange and others to women's colleges, including Bedford, Girton and Royal Holloway, see: James Albisetti, *Schooling German Girls and Women,* p151 ff; one of Lange's supporters was the Empress Frederick, who in March 1891 was Bedford's first royal visitor.

11 *Bedford College Calendar,* 1900–1, p11.

12 *Bedford College Calendar,* 1902–3, p8.

13 *Bedford College Calendar,* 1905–6, p9.

14 Letter from Margaret Tuke to Sir Arthur Rucker, 3/6/08; College Archives.

15 Letter from Margaret Tuke to Sir Arthur Rucker, 29/1/11; College Archives.

16 Letter from Margaret Tuke to Sir Arthur Rucker, 29/1/11; College Archives.

17 Report from the University Professors of German, 5/2/12; College Archives.

18 Report of the Academic Council, 11/3/1918; College Archives.

19 Letter from J G Robertson to Margaret Tuke, 2 December 1918; College Archives.

20 Letter from J G Robertson to Margaret Tuke, 2 December 1918; College Archives.

21 J G Robertson to the College Secretary, 26/1/33; College Archives.

22 J G Robertson to the College Secretary, 26/1/33; College Archives.

23 I am very much indebted to Professor John Flood, Deputy Director of the Institute of Germanic Studies, for allowing me to read an advance version of his article on J G Robertson to be published in the *New Dictionary of National Biography* (forthcoming), on which much of my account of Robertson's life is based.

24 J G Robertson to the College Secretary, 26/1/33; College Archives.

25 Letter from Henry Handel Richardson to Edna Purdie, 2/10/38: "I have thought of you more than once during the past week, knowing something of what you must be feeling from what JGR went through in 1914". Purdie Papers, College Archives.

26 Purdie's papers in the College Archives contain a number of letters, including the correspondence with the Pick family, that testify to her efforts to help refugees from Germany. See also: John L Flood, 'Emigré Germanists and the University of London', in: Charmian Brinson *et al* (eds), *Keine Klage über England? Deutsche und österreichische Exilerfahrungen in Großbritannien 1933-1945*, Munich: iudicium, 1998, pp224–240.

27 Elizabeth Mary Wilkinson to Edna Purdie 18/7/40.

28 Elizabeth Mary Wilkinson to Edna Purdie 28/9/40.

29 January 17th, 1941, Purdie papers, College Archives.

30 See: 'Two One and Two Two', *Universities Quarterly*, 9, No 2 (March 1965) pp176–181.

31 An account of the life of Maurice O'Connell Walshe (1911–1998) is to be found in the *Institute of Germanic Studies Friends Newsletter*, 1998, pp2–4.

APPENDIX

Heads of German Department, 1906–85

1906–33	John George Robertson FBA, FRSL
1933–64	Edna Purdie
1964–75	Ronald Peacock
1975–85	William E Yuill

Biochemistry

1. *Professor Dudley Cheesman, first Head of the Biochemistry Department.*

2. *Biochemists, 1963.*

Botany

3. *Dr Ethel Nancy Miles Thomas, first Head of the Botany Department.*

4. *The Müller House for unravelling the nutritional requirements of conifer seedlings.*

5. *The Siemans übermikroscop with which the Electron Microscopy Unit was started.*

Geography

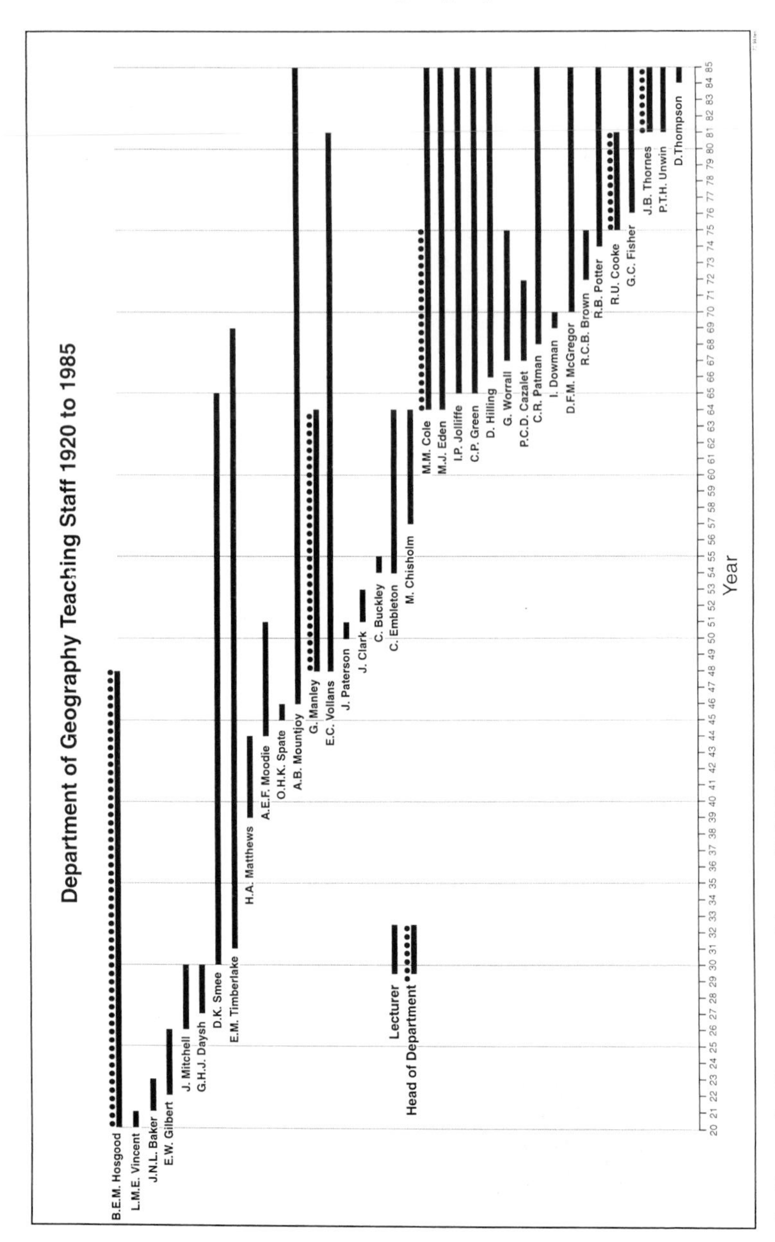

6. Geography Department teaching staff, 1920–85.

7. The Geography Department, 1951. Staff seated from left to right: Eleanor Vollans, Alan Mountjoy, Dora Smee, Gordon Manley, Eunice Timberlake and John Paterson.

8. *Field class, Hadrian's Wall, 1959, Gordon Manley and Eleanor Vollans at back right.*

9. *Off to Egham, 1985.*

Classics

10a. Dorothy Tarrant, Professor of Greek, 1936–50.

10b. Max Cary, Professor of Ancient History, 1908–46.

History

11. S R Gardiner: our greatest historian, Head of Ancient and Modern History 1862–81.

12. H W Nevinson: radical activist, Head of Ancient and Modern History 1885–91.

13. J W Allen: political theorist, Head of Medieval and Modern History 1891–1926.

14. Dame Lillian Penson: first woman Vice-Chancellor, Head of the History Department 1930–61.

15. *From the left, Ilse Crawford, Dorothy Wedderburn, Caroline Barron, Joe Mordaunt Crook, Nicola Sutherland and Karen Bull, St. John's Lodge, 16 January, 1982.*

Zoology

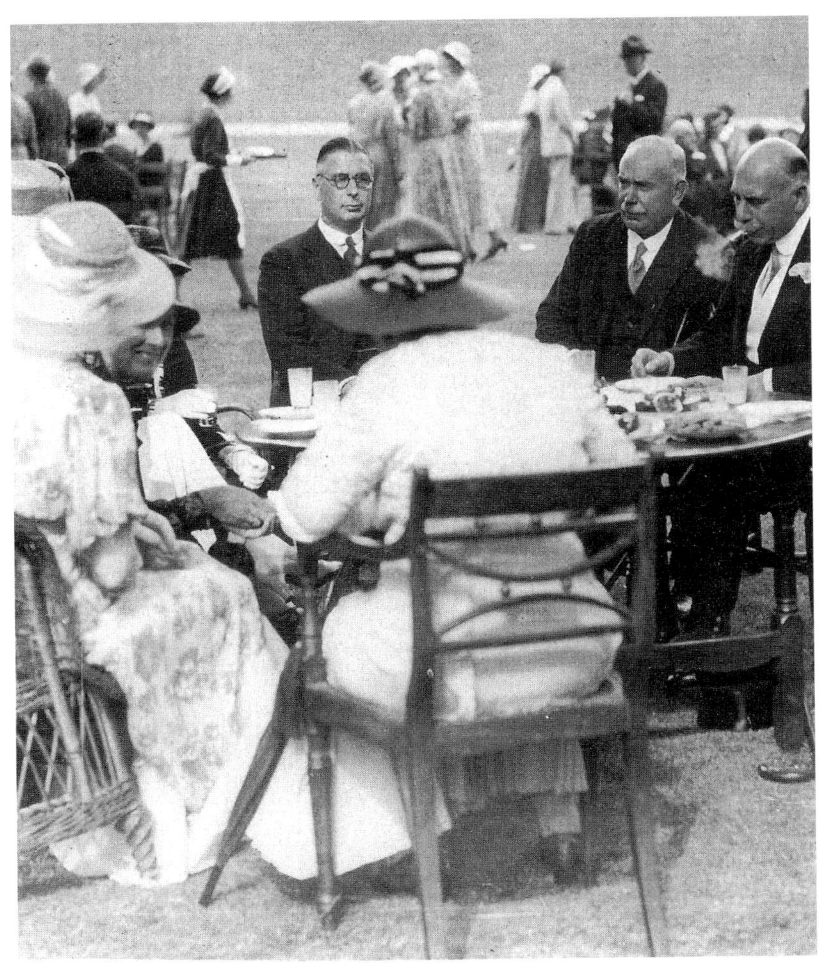

16. C L Boulanger, Head of Zoology Department 1923–40, with glasses, facing the camera, in 1933.

17. *H Munro Fox FRS, Head of Zoology Department 1941–54, in his Cambridge laboratory between 1941 and 1944.*

18. *Norman Millott, Head of the Zoology Department 1955 –69*

19. Rodney Dales, Head of the Zoology Department 1971–85 (and RHBNC 1985–1992) c. 1971.

20. H W Marrett Tims, back left, Head of the Zoology Department 1898–1922 with Dr John Edkins (back right) Head of Physiology, Professor Harding (front left), Mathematics and Miss Ethel Hurlblatt, Principal.

21. Miss Ince, 1929–68.

22. Philippa Esdale 1915–19, probably taken on the occasion of her DSc in 1917.

23. C W Blaxland Benham, 1885–98.

24. Don Field 1951–85 (and at RHBNC 1985–98) in 1971. Chief technician to three departmental professors.

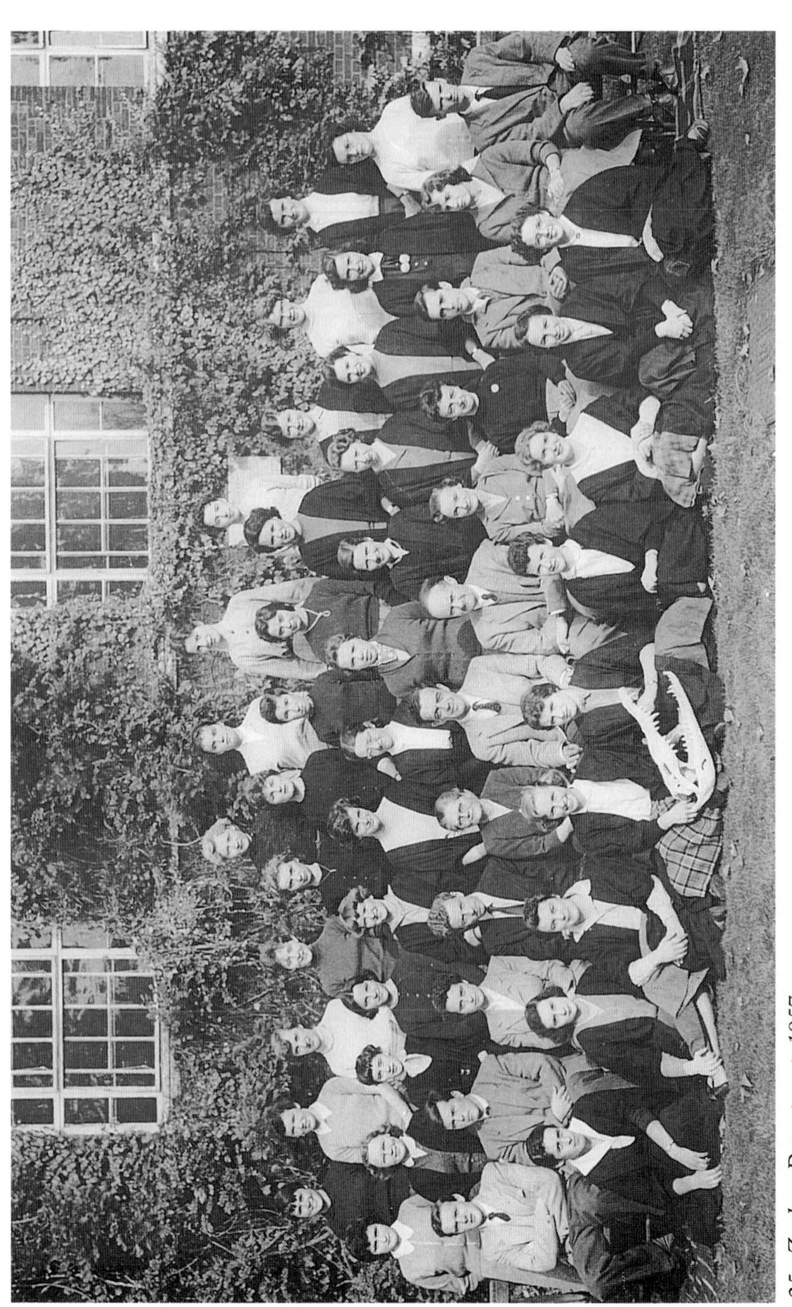

25. Zoology Department, 1957.

Chapter 10

History

J Mordaunt Crook

A volume like this is an occasion for looking back, for retrospection. A dangerous occupation, looking back: remember what happened to Lot's wife! Still, why not. If we don't blow our own trumpet, nobody else will. 1983 was the last year History was taught independently at Bedford. After 134 years. We were not exactly abolished. In the language of new management, we were not even amalgamated; we were merely redeployed.

Bedford College, of course, was founded in 1849, in Bedford Square, by the daughter of a Unitarian ironmonger, Mrs Reid. Teaching had begun in 1847. We arrived in Regent's Park in 1908–formally in 1913–via premises in Baker Street. It was the first college–well before anything at Oxford or Cambridge–to provide something approximating to university education for women. That is, specifically for women. University College and King's did in fact accept female students on an equal footing from 1878. But Bedford was a women's college. Initially, that was its strength; latterly, it was also its weakness. The attempt to maintain a women's college with multi-faculty status–that is with full coverage of science as well as arts–proved ultimately self-defeating.

From the start, the image of our college was secular, progressive, libertarian. There was never a chapel at Bedford. Westfield College and Royal Holloway College, founded later in the 19th century, were both–in different degrees–Christian foundations, catering for a rather different sort of person. The story goes that, of the three, it was Westfield College for ladies, Royal Holloway College for girls, and Bedford College for women. Westfield and Holloway were basically residential colleges; and so, initially at any rate, most of their teaching staff were women. Bedford was only partly residential; and most of its lecturers were men. That was an anomaly which would come back to haunt it in future years. Some would say that when Bedford went fully mixed in 1965, it lost its *raison d'être*, and was ultimately ripe for takeover. Others would say that segregated women's education had been so successful that, in the end, it made itself unnecessary. The debate continues.

In its earliest days, History at Bedford was certainly not a university programme as we would know it today. Many of the students were extra-mural; many were what we would now call sixth-formers; few were hoping to become professionals. The BA History, London, was not established until 1896; and as late as 1906 there were only 9 candidates in the whole university, though two of those got Firsts. Before the 1890s, History was taught in London as a supplement to serious subjects like Classics, or in conjunction with other 'modern' subjects like English and Education. As late as 1903 the total History faculty of London University consisted of only 9 members of staff: 2 professors and an assistant at University College, 1 professor and 1 lecturer at King's, and one lecturer each at Royal Holloway, Queen Mary, Westfield and Bedford.[1] In other words, the Victorian scholars who taught History at Bedford taught History in conjunction with other subjects; and they taught the whole of history: English and European, Medieval and Modern–and in some cases Ancient History as well. One member of staff taught everything. These early Bedford professors were–like Carlyle's Teufelsdröch–'Professors of things in general'. They lectured to small audiences on very large themes. They had only the courtesy title of 'Professor': they were college 'professors', not University Professors. They were paid meagerly, by a system of fees based on their number of pupils. There was no such thing as tenure. Inevitably, they had outside interests and employments. But because Bedford was a central London college, it managed to attract scholars who were working elsewhere in the metropolis, as lawyers, or journalists, or social workers. And because Bedford was a non-denominational foundation–a secular college like UC–it was able to attract men of ability who for one reason or another were excluded from the academic establishment. Remember, until 1870, commiting matrimony was enough to lose one an Oxford Fellowship. So dissenters, and married academics, went to London.

In this way, Bedford built up a strong line in rebels, eccentrics and uxorious polymaths. Johann Gottfried Kinkel (1815–82), for example, the first and last Professor of Fine Art at Bedford: from 1854 to 1866, he managed to combine Fine Art with the chair of Geography, and–for a while–the chair of Ancient History, at the same time examining in German literature. Kinkel was an Austrian who had been Professor at Bonn. He was involved in the 1848 revolution, and was imprisoned at Spandau. He escaped, and fled to England in 1850. After the failure of the various revolutions of 1848, London was filled with exotic exiles: Karl Marx from Germany, Louis Blanc from France, Mazzini from Italy, Kossuth from Hungary, and Kinkel from Austria. Having escaped from Spandau, Kinkel enjoyed a special glamour. He was eulogised by Dickens in *Household Words*; he was lionised in fashionable drawing rooms, notably that of the Baroness von Brüningh in St John's Wood; and he gave a series of public lectures, priced–amazingly–at one guinea per ticket. Marx was madly envious. In a pamphlet sarcastically entitled *The Great Men of the Exile* (1852) he poured scorn on Kinkel as a "false liberal", one of the "more noteworthy jackasses" and "democratic scallywags" who were giving revolution a bad name. Kinkel seems to have been very much a ladies' man; he was certainly popular at Bedford. One day, apparently, Karl Marx sent him an abusive letter dressed up as a Valentine card–pretending it was from one of Kinkel's young lady admirers! Anyway, Kinkel stayed at Bedford until 1866, when he became Professor of Archaeology at Zurich. By the time of his death in 1882 he had published no less than 50 books in Basle, Bonn, Berlin, Cologne, Essen, Hamburg, Hanover, Leipzig, Stuttgart, Vienna and Zurich.[2]

Our first Professor of History, in 1849, was the Reverend J S Brewer (1810-79).[3] He was also in charge of Latin. He was rather too Anglican for Bedford, and didn't last long. But he's a very good name at the head of our list.

Brewer came from a Baptist background–he was the son of a Norwich schoolmaster–but he became an Anglican at Oxford. There his brilliant Classical career was cut short by matrimony. So he moved to London. Under Newman's influence, he became an Anglican priest, and took up a post as chaplain in a workhouse on the seamier side of Bloomsbury.[4] For eight years he worked among the very poor, lecturing at the same time in Classical Literature at King's. Later on he succeeded the Christian Socialist F D Maurice (his colleague and friend at King's) as Head of the Working Men's College in Great Ormond Street. And eventually he followed Maurice as Professor of English and History at King's.

Brewer will always feature in every bibliography of Tudor history. It was he who edited the first four volumes of *Letters and Papers, Foreign and Domestic, of the reign of Henry VIII* (1862).[5] That is a work to which the adjective pioneering can truly be applied. He strode the Public Record Office like a colossus. But he was no dryasdust bookworm. He was a popular preacher[6] and a fluent journalist.[7] He was known for his knowledge of architecture, and his enthusiasm for Gregorian chant. He was first a High and then a Broad Churchman; but High or Broad, he was always a Tory. He was a strict disciplinarian; and he was a dedicated pastoral priest. He began as a workhouse chaplain, and he eventually died after visiting a sick parishioner in the snow. He seems to have had an awkward streak: he hated being in a majority–a very academic disease. As one contemporary put it, "he was consistently on the side of Cato against the divinities of the hour. No matter whether it was the Tractarians, or Mr. Maurice, or Bishop Colenso, or the Athanasian

Creed, or the Irish Church, some warm sympathy was sure to be given by him to the truth or the party which was being overridden under the predominant popular impulse. This temper of mind deserves...to be dwelt upon, because it was probably connected with his power as an historian".

Well, maybe. But that same cast of mind impelled Brewer to resist the disestablishment of the minority Anglican Church in Ireland.[8] That was surely a mistake. He was perhaps better occupied in the Public Record Office, or in revising Hume's *History of England* (1858), or in editing the works of Roger Bacon and Giraldus Cambrensis.

Brewer left Bedford in a hurry, after a religious dispute. King's was a more suitable home for him. A substitute had to be found, and Bedford found the Rev William Elliot. Now Elliot's obscurity seems to be impenetrable. If he had one T in his name, then he was the Elliot who ended up in a remote Herefordshire parish, after publishing a book on *Ecclesiastical Dilapidations* (1872). But if he had a double T in his name–and if Tuke's *History of Bedford College* mis-spells that name, which is quite possible–then he is the Elliott who was at that time Assistant Minister at St Mark's, Hamilton Terrace, and the author of *Four Sermons preached to young persons on... Confirmation* (1847). And I rather think that he is our man: Elliott of St John's Wood.

Anyway, he only lasted a year. He was followed, in 1850–56, by J Langton Sanford (1824–77). Now Sanford was a historian. A dissenting graduate of University College, probably a Unitarian,[9] he was a friend of Walter Bagehot and W C Roscoe, and a prolific journalist.[10] He did original work on Civil War MSS in the 1840s; but his *Studies and Illustrations of the Great Rebellion*[11] didn't appear until 1858–so he was pipped to the post by Carlyle and Forster. His view of the 17th and 18th century was resolutely Whig: Charles I was "a weak and bad King"; George III was simply "absolutist", "inefficient and unfortunate".[12] But one of Sanford's books survives in every bibliography of social history: with Meredith Townsend he wrote *The Great Governing Families of England*, 2 vols (1865), a foundation for much later work on the distribution of landed estates.

Sanford's successor, in 1858–9, was Thomas Spencer Baynes (1823–87). He was also in charge of English Language and Literature. Baynes was only at Bedford briefly, but he seems to have been a man very much in the Bedford image. Brought up as a Baptist in Bristol; educated at University College; he was teaching philosophy in Edinburgh and writing newspaper articles, when illness forced him to go home to Somerset for two years. Then he returned to London, married, set up house near Regent's Park, and combined teaching at Bedford with journalism–he was assistant editor of the *Daily News*.[13] Illness again–"he had a weak heart and only half a lung"[14]–so he took up what is described as "a less exacting profession" as Professor of Logic, Metaphysics and English Literature at St Andrew's. Baynes was at St Andrew's for 23 years, and is described as "the idol of the students....the universal favourite of old and young. Urbanity, *bonomie*, human kindess, unfailing cheerfulness, faithful comradeship, inalienable affection... He was one of the best men whom many of us have known".[15] His range was really extraordinary: he began as a logician[16] and ended as a philologist, while writing extensively on 16th century literature[17] and on contemporary religion[18] and politics. Whether it was editing the 9th edition of the *Encyclopaedia Britannica* (1873–87)–and himself writing the "matchless" entry on Shakespeare–or whether it was translating the Song of Solomon into the Somerset Dialect in 1860 for Prince Louis Lucien Bonaparte[19]–Thomas Spencer Baynes maintained his credentials as scholar, radical, humanist and wit.

Of Bayne's short-lived successor, Newenham Travers, little need be said. He only wrote one pamphlet, on *Marriage With a Deceased Wife's Sister* (1850).[20] He was against it, arguing passionately from evidence in Leviticus and Deuteronomy that such unions were against the laws of God and against the laws of nature.

But Travers was succeeded by a man who does deserve to be better known, Samuel Harvey Reynolds (1831–97).[21] Reynolds was the son of a London doctor, a brilliant classicist at Oxford, fellow and tutor at Brasenose College; in fact, he shared the classics teaching there with no less a luminary than Walter Pater, prince of aesthetes.

Reynolds' range was certainly impressive. He edited 12 books of the *Iliad* (1870); he was an essayist and minor poet, and a speculative historian; speculative in the sense that he produced slim volumes with titles like *The Reciprocal Influence of the Condition of Countries upon each other* (1856), and the *System of Modern History* (1865). He was a progressive Liberal in university politics. And he could write: George Saintsbury noted "the freshness, the vigour, and above all the geniality (in the foreign as well as the English sense) of his mind".[22] In fact Reynolds was enough of a critic to be considered for the Professorship of Poetry at Oxford in succession to Matthew Arnold.[23]

How did he come to be teaching at Bedford? Well, at one point he decided to become a barrister, and while reading for the bar at Lincoln's Inn, he did some teaching here. He might have stayed at Bedford longer but he had an accident to his eye, and decided–curiously–that he could be a scholar with defective eyesight but not a barrister. So he went back to Oxford and took Holy Orders. When he married in 1871, Brasenose presented him with what was then a valuable living, in an obscure, quiet place: East Ham. When he arrived the population there was under 2000; when he left it was 45,000. He needed a sense of humour, and a generous spirit–in fact, a Christian spirit–and he had both. It must have required more than ordinary dedication to keep going, at the same time producing scholarly editions of Selden's *Table Talk*, and Bacon's *Essays*, and about 2000 articles in *The Times* over a period of 20 years.[24] When he retired, he settled at Abingdon–"to be near enough to the Bodleian for study, and not near enough to Oxford for society". His *Times* obituary noted his Swiftian tolerance, "sturdy common-sense,...hatred of cant...and...abiding sanity of judgement, not unworthy of [Dr] Johnson himself".[25] Among Oxford men, he was a noted wit, a famous raconteur, a stylist and a scholar–he even rowed in the Brasenose first eight about the time he was examining young Lord Rosebery in Greats.

Reynolds was followed by L B Seeley, who stayed at Bedford seven years, from 1862 to 1869. Seeley was the younger brother of the great S R Seeley, Regius Professor at Cambridge and founding father–after Lord Acton–of the Cambridge History School. At Cambridge young

Seeley had a dazzling career, with a triple First at Trinity, followed by a Fellowship. He came down to London to practise at the bar, or near it, as a conveyancer and equity draughtsman. In his spare time he produced an edition of Euclid (1875), and he dallied with history. What did he write? *Horace Walpole and His World* (1884); *Fanny Burney and Her Friends* (1890); *Mrs. Thrale's...Diaries* (1891)–these are some of the books which appeared from the pen of L B Seeley.[26] Volumes, we might think, unworthy of his talents.

Seeley was succeeded in 1869 by our greatest Bedford historian, S R Gardiner.[27] Now people from King's will tell you that Gardiner is their greatest historian. Well, so he was. But he was teaching at Bedford before he was teaching at King's, and he taught in both colleges simultaneously for many years. Gardiner was descended from Puritan stock: in fact he descended from Oliver Cromwell–via Bridget, Cromwell's eldest daughter, through her marriage to Henry Ireton. Both Gardiner's parents were Irvingites, that is they were members of a sect founded by Edward Irving and known as the Catholic Apostolic Church. They managed to combine Presbyterian theology with Anglo-Catholic ritual; their cathedral was the present London University Church in Gordon Square, Bloomsbury. And Gardiner was more apostolic than most: while still at Oxford he married a daughter of Edward Irving himself. That put paid to Gardiner's Oxford career. So he fled to London, and Bedford took him in, from 1862: first as Professor of Ancient History, then as Professor of Ancient, Medieval and Modern History. He stayed there just under 20 years, lecturing in Bedford Square and Baker Street, working in the British Museum and Public Record Office, and cycling round Civil War battlefields in the vacations.

It is clear that Gardiner depended on his salary from Bedford; calculated, remember, in terms of fees per student in those days: market economics with a vengeance. He was only able to give up lecturing at Bedford in 1881, when Lord Acton persuaded Gladstone to award him a Civil List pension of £150 p.a. Since 1877 he had also been lecturing at King's, besides doing extra-mural teaching in the evenings in the East End. And he retained his post as Professor at King's till 1884, when he became the first research fellow at All Souls, on £200 p.a.[28] From 1882 to his death he was research fellow at Merton College, Oxford, though he actually lived in London.

These details are important: it was only by a series of lectureships and fellowships that Gardiner was in a position to do research in London, and to write his 16 monumental volumes on the *History of the English Revolution*. The first two volumes of that great work sold only 140 copies; the next two 580. They all made a loss. The next two broke even: Gardiner never made much money. He was not a man of the world. Nor was he a popular prophet like Carlyle.[29] He was what we call a working historian. In Christopher Hill's words, Gardiner was a master of primary material; "almost perfect", "he missed nothing".[30] And that meant working in London. He even declined the Regius Chair at Oxford, when Rosebery offered it to him in 1894, because it would interfere with his research.[31]

So what makes a great historian? Gardiner had precision, lucidity, industry, integrity, a talent for generalisation, and a genius for detail. And he had a singlemindedness which amounted to monomania. He worked alone: no secretary, no research assistant; and he wrote everything out in longhand. No xeroxes or computers, of course. He didn't work long hours–about 5 hours per day–but every day. He was as punctual as a metronome. Listen to F York Powell's obituary of Gardiner in the *English Historical Review* for 1902.[32]

> "[Gardiner] was well prepared for his task: he had a careful classical training; he was of sound health, of enormous perseverance and determination; he had the faculty... of getting rapidly and surely at the contents of a book or paper; his eyesight was good; his temper even and contented; he desired neither wealth nor fame, but was satisfied if he could make time enough to permit daily and constant application to his studies; he had the gift of concentration, so that he was able not only to read and make notes, but even to write his book in the busy reading room of the British Museum... He learnt Dutch, Danish and Spanish (being

> already acquainted with French, German and Italian)...He went regularly to his business at the Museum every morning like a good city man...He did a good deal of teaching [at Bedford; that is lecturing of course: there were no tutorials then, and little or no administration]; and he wrote a number of school books...He lectured out of the fullness of his knowledge, without an effort at rhetoric, but with the vivid conviction that is sure to interest and stimulate...he made himself master of a plain nervous style...His editions of original documents are exact, straightforward, and businesslike...He...found the story of the first Stewarts and [of] Cromwell legend, and [he] left it...history".

Gardiner was briefly followed by somebody very different: a pathological eccentric called J Bass Mullinger. "As a young man, in 1871", so it is recorded, Mullinger "served a term of imprisonment for an attack upon his sister-in-law with a carving knife. Always eccentric in his conduct, many stories were current about his intolerance of the slightest noise when lecturing, and of his threats to those with whom he came unexpectedly into contact".[33] Well Gardiner at any rate had faith in him: they were working together on *An Introduction to English History*[34] when Gardiner retired from Bedford, and Mullinger–as his co-author–became his successor. Before he came to Bedford he had already made a name for himself with books on *The Ancient African Church* (1869) and *The Schools of Charles the Great* (1876). And from Bedford he went back to Cambridge as Librarian and Lecturer, and there completed his magnum opus in 4 volumes, *The University of Cambridge from the Earliest Times to the Decline of the Platonist Movement* (1873–1906)[35]. So Mullinger is remembered as an historian of the medieval university. And he had pretty definite views on modern universities too. In 1878, for example, he came out against the creation of new universities in Manchester, Birmingham etc–because he thought it better to expand the older universities rather than create new ones: quite a perceptive viewpoint. His ideal–the medieval university–was not local, not provincial, not even national, but essentially international. "A university", he believed, "if it is to rank as a national institution, postulates not merely adequate material resources, but a certain numerical strength". That was why he supported London University; and no doubt he would have approved of our recent reorganisation in five large units. "A university", he stated, "should stand for the elimination of all that is provincial, petty and sectarian".[36]

There was nothing provincial or petty about Mullinger's successor, Alice Gardner (1854–1927), the first woman to teach History at Bedford. But there was perhaps a little of the sectarian. She was a Byzantinist by profession, with a first at Cambridge to her credit, and she only stayed with us a year, in 1883–84, before going back to Newnham.[37] She eventually ended up as Reader at Bristol. She wrote seriously about religious training,[38] about women's suffrage[39] and about women's education.[40] She was much given to country walks and to Anglicanism of a Broad church kind.[41] And–something of a first for Bedford–she was a historian of medieval London.

Listen to Miss Gardner on the education of women. She was progressive but pragmatic. "The question of the equality or inequality of the sexes", she maintains, is as relevant to "a discussion of the educational claims of women..." as "an investigation of the comparative merits of wheat and oats" would be "in a discussion on systems of irrigation". In other words equality was a red herring; the real issue was simply this: what is the best education for girls? "The female mind is not essentially different from the male", she wrote; but there is a difference of physique: hence, she believes, the danger of nervous breakdowns. And hence the need for a selective junior education (no need for classics or maths except for the ablest girls); and all this punctuated by lots of healthy exercise. "The invention of lawn tennis", she concludes, "has come at a most opportune moment" for women.[42] No doubt very true. But there was something a little too solemn about Miss Gardner. Not so her successor, Lloyd Sanders.

Lloyd Sanders was a littérateur, and an historian of Society. While at Christ Church, Oxford, he won the Stanhope Prize with an essay on the Stuart Cause.[43] Biographical studies of Melbourne, Palmerston,

Sheridan, Bubb Doddington and *The Holland House Circle* made him a popular writer. But he was best known for the Victorian volume which he wrote with Sydney Low of King's in Longman's Political History of England series: those pale red volumes which many students will remember as standard textbooks until they were superseded by the black-bound Oxford Histories.[44] At Bedford Sanders was also in charge of Ancient History.

If Sanders was a well known writer, he was quite eclipsed by his successor, H W Nevinson (1856–1941)[45], the father of the First World War artist, C R W Nevinson (1889–1946). Now Nevinson stayed at Bedford six years, and given his globe-trotting, trouble-shooting reputation, that says something about his commitment to progressive education. Nevinson was not an academic historian: he was a Romantic Radical with a libertarian world-view; and he wrote like an angel. John Masefield, then poet laureate, noted: "it would be difficult to discover in [Nevinson's] writings…an error of fact, a clumsy sentence, or a limping rhythm". And he produced a couple of dozen books and literally hundreds of articles over half a century of journalism.[46] In fact his life as a war correspondent and freedom-fighter now seems almost incredible. He once summed up his code of honour in these words: "the impulse of every decent Englishman is, of course, to favour the underdog".[47] "When the bullets flew", it was said, "there was Nevinson, pen in hand…eight wars…six rebellions…he was a passionate champion of all victims of oppression and injustice".[48]

Nevinson's roots were in Westmorland. For centuries his family farmed the bleak uplands beyond Shap Fell.[49] They moved south in the 18th century, and became doctors and lawyers. So Nevinson happened to be born in Leicester where his father practised law. And there he was brought up in a strictly Evangelical household. Most of his life he lived in London, but he punctuated this with travels as a newspaper correspondent to the four quarters of the globe. He had a gift for language, and a romantic's love of solitude, hardship, danger. But then his ancestors had chased sheep over the fells for centuries. He was educated as a Classicist. He trained himself as a journalist. But he was born to be a war correspondent. I think the greatest influence on his life was Ruskin. At Oxford he revelled in Ruskin's writing, and listened spellbound to the great man's lectures. And he absorbed Ruskin's social gospel: his horror of industrialism and his hatred of the liberal ethic. At Oxford Nevinson took up Christian Socialism under the influence of Canon Scott Holland. Later on he became an agnostic. In London as a young man he worked at Toynbee Hall and lived in the slums of Whitechapel at the time of Jack the Ripper's murders–quite a dangerous place to be. And while he was living there, he taught at Bedford College, from 1885 to 1891. Now Nevinson later claimed that he hated teaching at Bedford, that he knew nothing about history, in fact that he was only "pretending".[50] But that seems to me like mock-modesty. He knew a great deal of Ancient History–and he was responsible for Ancient, Medieval and Modern. He was a passionate believer in women's rights; with a classicist's feeling for words, and a romantic's commitment to truth, justice and freedom. With his striking presence and glorious prose style he must have been an inspiring lecturer. In 1889 he joined H M Hyndman's Social Democratic Federation. But he was never a real Communist. He seems to have been more permanently influenced by Kropotkin's anarchist views than by Hyndman's collectivist Marxism. He was really a political agnostic, hating all forms of dogma. Edward Carpenter's socialist ethics had a strong appeal for him, and for many years he was a Labour party activist. But he was really a Radical, free of all parties. What stirred his imagination was a great cause: he found his métier as a campaigning journalist all over the world. For the *Daily Chronicle* he covered the Greco-Turkish War, the South African War–he got himself besieged in Ladysmith–and the abortive Russian Revolution of 1905-6. In 1904-5 he was investigating slavery in Angola. For the *Manchester Guardian* he was in India in 1907–8, and in Bulgaria soon after. In the First World War he was a correspondent on the Western Front; he was a founder of the Friends Ambulance Unit in Flanders; and he was wounded at the Dardanelles. And that was only the beginning. He was a fierce supporter of Irish Home Rule, and a friend of Roger Casement. In 1909 Lloyd George had him thrown out of the Albert Hall for supporting the suffragettes. In the Second World War he was still making speeches, at the age of 84, with Aneurin Bevan and Michael Foot and E M Forster. This fierce romantic Radical, with staring blue eyes, and hooked nose, goatee-beard and knee-breeches–at times of crisis he would walk alone all night, tramping through the fields by moonlight–what did all those future schoolmistresses at Bedford make of him in the 1880s? Alas, his diary for those years does not seem to survive.

After Nevinson came J W Allen. Allen taught at Bedford for 35 years–1891–1926–a record parallelled three times in the history of Bedford History–by Professor F R H Du Boulay, by Professor C H Lawrence, and by myself. Professor Pilbeam and Professor Barron look set to beat all four of us. Allen will probably always be remembered for two, well-thumbed textbooks: *A History of Political Thought in the 16th Century* (1928; 1951) and *English Political Thought, 1603–60* (1938; 1967). He seems to have been a devoted, if eccentric, teacher. He began brilliantly at Balliol.[51] He had a clear mind and a stylish pen. In the Bedford tradition he was a link between the gifted amateurs who preceeded him–though S R Gardiner can only be called an amateur in the sense that W G Grace was an amateur–and the new academic professionals who followed him. But he paid the penalty of that ambivalent position: for all his 35 years' teaching, he never became a University Professor.[52]

One pupil, Vivian Hughes, remembered what she called his "revolutionary" approach. In lectures he "poured forth his indignation [against romantic historians] in a stream of extempore fervour". Obviously a reaction against too much Nevinson. His experience of all those years at Bedford led him to the conclusion that there was no real difference between the male and female intellect: far from being weaker, he believed, girls had "a special aptitude" for economic and constitutional history.[53] In tutorials, apparently, he was a rather comic figure. Vivian Hughes again: Allen "was so earnest that he twisted himself into a kind of a knot round his chair and barked out his opinions like a Hyde Park orator. He was dead against all the usual methods of teaching history, training his biggest guns against any attempt to draw morals or any effort to make it picturesque. Science, that was the thing. History was merely a branch of biology. The doings of human beings in the past were to be studied and recorded as cold-bloodedly as the wrigglings of insects under the microscope. The students were too much overawed to ask him how this method was [actually] to be carried on in [their future lives as] school [teachers], but they were wholesomely headed off anything like an emotional touch in their history lessons".[54] After reading some of Allen's essays, I think this hard line on romanticism–so very different to Nevinson–may well have been an attempt to control an impulsive and romantic streak in his own nature. In 1914–15 he was belligerently anti-German–giving lectures as part of the war effort: he put Teutonic militarism down to a misuse of political theory.[55] Every long vacation he would set out on a bicycle, revelling in solitude, fresh air, bread and cheese, and beer, and old England. "The perfected cyclist", wrote Allen, "is a wandering spirit, full of eyes, like the beast in the Revelation. All the burden of humanity falls from him as he mounts. He has no past, neither does his future extend beyond the flying day".[56] In 1909 he published a book of essays called *Wheel Magic, or revelations of an impressionist.* Today it seems a marvellous period piece–Edwardian *belles lettres*–with Allen as the "Izaak Walton of cycling". There is a wonderful description of an 'Abbey Church'–Malvern perhaps–in the romantic tradition of Morris or Carlyle.[57] But all those years at Bedford seem to have turned him into a philosophical bachelor: "Love is a fever or a habit", he wrote; "–a bad habit. You gain a woman and you lose your own soul".[58]

As to Allen's philosophy of history, far from being 'scientific' in his approach he worried about the dangers of determinism, the dangers of impersonal, mechanistic history. He had more than a little sympathy with history as pageant–"our Baedeker to the past" he called it:[59] the food of imagination in young minds–and for Shakespeare and Scott as in some ways our greatest historians. Somehow, he believed, the historian had to reconcile the clinical and the practical approaches, the scientific and the picturesque. The scholar, he felt, had to balance a double responsibility: to hand on the heritage of the past–the achievements of mankind, the cumulative wisdom of generations–and at the same time to question and re-phrase those traditional assumptions and values. He saw this as a double responsibility. He liked to echo Macaulay: "No past event has any intrinsic importance" (or as Alfred Cobban used to say: "all facts are not born free and equal")–as well as quoting Francis Bacon: "histories make men wise". Our task, as teachers of history, Allen believed, is "to set the feet of our children on the way to intellectual freedom". "This emancipation of the intelligence", he wrote, "should...be the primary aim of intellectual training...We want to develop a power of suspending judgement...We want a logical habit and we want an analytic habit...and...we want...a training in the medium and means of thought - that is, in language".[60] In other words, and this is rather my own opinion, an historian must have a mission to explain the past, a talent for exposition, a sturdy independence of mind, and a feeling for the magic of words–because writing History is above all a form of communication. A book which is unreadable communicates with nobody except its author. And having said all that, Allen was big enough to spot the one major weakness in his own approach: the lack of any historico-visual sense. To discuss "the intellectual and moral aspects of education", he notes, "with hardly any reference to aesthetics is, perhaps, characteristically English".[61] That at least, I hope, is a weakness I have avoided.

Allen's successor, J D Mackie, was the first University Professor of History at Bedford College. He stayed four years, 1926–30, in between long stints at St Andrews and Glasgow.[62] In fact, although he will always be remembered for his Oxford History volume on the *Earlier Tudors*, Mackie was by birth, by instinct, and by profession a Scottish historian, ending his long life–he lived to the age of 91–as Her Majesty's Historiographer in Scotland.[63] His appointment in 1926 must have been A F Pollard's doing. Pollard was due to retire in 1927, and he needed another big name to carry on the London tradition of Tudor historiography. When Mackie's Oxford History volume eventually appeared in 1953 he was already 66, and inevitably it was savaged by young Turks half his age. When I attended lectures on the gentry at Oxford in 1955, by Trevor-Roper, Stone, Hill and Cooper–and you could hear them all in one week, attacking each other–the only thing they seemed to agree on was that Mackie had got it all wrong. Well, they in their turn have gone the way of all historians–savaged by lesser men in search of a reputation.

Of Mackie's successor, Dame Lillian Penson, there must be many who can speak with rather more authority. I can simply set out the facts of her remarkable career.[64] She was born in Islington in 1876, from a dissenting background–Plymouth Brethren, apparently–the daughter of a wholesale dairy manager. She enrolled as a student at Birkbeck College but spent much of her time at lectures at UCL, KCL and LSE; and took a First in Modern History in 1917. She was the first London history student to be awarded a PhD, in 1921. She was the first woman to become a Professor of History in any British university, in 1930, and that at the age of 34.[65] And in 1948 she became–famously–the first woman to be Vice-Chancellor of any university in Britain or the Commonwealth, at the age of 52. She was a formidable diplomatic historian, trained in the school of Gooch, and Grant, and Temperley, at a time–between the two world wars–when diplomatic history was in the ascendant. In some ways, she took over from Temperley as the Stubbs of diplomatic history. But she was a still more formidable *politique*, a legendary power in the Senate House and in Whitehall. And in the emerging countries of Africa she was the godmother of a whole string of nascent universities. Most unusually at that date, she was a woman who combined influence in academia, in government, and in foreign affairs–notably Anglo-American relations. For years she dominated the Fulbright programme. She spent the First World War in the Department of Labour Supply and the War Trade Intelligence Department. She spent the early part of the Second World War in the Ministry of Information and Intelligence Division. In both she built up a network of government contacts which stood her in good stead in post-war educational politics. Her research seminar at the Institute of Historical Research, from 1928 to 1962, was legendary. One of its last products was

Valerie Cromwell (Lady Kingman), later Director of the *History of Parliament*. In 1948, when Cambridge at last agreed to confer degrees on women, three symbolic recipients were chosen for LLD: Dame Myra Hess, HM the Queen (now Queen Elizabeth the Queen Mother), and Lillian Penson. When Oxford gave her a DCL in 1956, the other recipient was ex-President Truman of the United States. For over 30 years Dame Lillian, as she became in 1951, was Head of our Department at Bedford, and of much else besides. Dressed always in a dark tweed suit and white blouse; speaking in calm, measured tones; her lectures were polished performances, her comments in conversation trenchant.[66] During her time as Professor she appointed or promoted scholars of distinction: Darlington, Deansley, Du Boulay and Lawrence in medieval studies; Hussey in Byzantine history; Tooley in political thought; Russell in 17th century history. These appointments surely vindicate her judgement. It is hard to believe, today, that Bedford College once produced a Vice-Chancellor. Somewhere, wherever Vice-Chancellors go in the end, she must surely be fulminating at the unhappy chain of events which destroyed the independence of her old college.

With the passing of Penson, I come to my own time at Bedford. And not everyone can be mentioned. When I arrived in Regent's Park as a Tutorial Research Fellow, in October 1962, it was the time of the Interregnum. Dame Lillian lay prostrate as the result of a stroke. My first Head of Department–Dame Lillian's successor–was R W Greaves.[67] I owe him a great deal. Like Nevinson, he was a Leicester man. Like Brewer, he was a High Anglican and a Tory. Like Sanders and Seeley, he had a weakness for 18th century gossip. Like Reynolds, he had the gift of anecdote and epigram. How can I catch the flavour of Bob Greaves? When I reappeared at Bedford–as a Lecturer–in 1965, he fixed my salary at an appropriate point on the Lecturer's scale. I can almost hear him telling the College Secretary: 'I suggest he starts at £1485'. I was once talking with him at the Reform Club in Pall Mall; and I suggested it was time he moved to a proper Professors' club, like the Athenaeum. "Certainly not", he replied. "Why should I exchange a club where I know nobody, for a club where I should know everybody?" Bob was a bespectacled, Pickwickian bachelor; he married late in life, at the age of 53, but even then he was really a married bachelor. I can see him emerging from Sung Mass at St Cyprian's, Clarence Gate; then lingering in the Common Room after lunch, remembering his days as a wartime civil servant in Whitehall. In 1939 Dame Lillian took him with her to the Ministry of Information; then he moved to the Treasury and the Ministry of Production: at one time he was Assistant Private Secretary to the Chancellor of the Exchequer. Then he returned to the bombed-out buildings of Bedford in 1945. Bedford College had, of course, moved to Cambridge between 1939 and 1944, and the students of those years enjoyed, uniquely, the London experience in a Cambridge context.

Lecturers in those days had to cover–by modern standards–an extraordinary range. In 1939, for example, Greaves was offering the following courses: European History, 1494–1914; English Economic History, 16th-20th centuries; English Constitutional History, 1450–1782; and, just for good measure, 'Outlines of French History, 1494–1914', "as required". At least in that year he didn't have to lecture on medieval history, as he had previously done at Queen's University, Belfast. On the other hand, there were very few tutorials or seminars in those days, and–again by modern standards–precious little administration. So there was time to do some solid, primary research; and Greaves made himself a master of the minutiae of 18th century church politics. But I suspect he lived too long under the shadow of the Dame; and - looking back–his tenure of the chair now seems rather an anticlimax. Though he survived to the age of 70, he never lived to see the publication of the *Autobiography and Court Papers of Archbishop Secker*, on which he had set his heart; still less the general survey of *The Erastian Age, 1650–1850*, a moderate phase in the evolution of Christianity which he was ideally suited to explain. He left for America–and the distant fields of Kansas–in 1968, and died there in 1979.

Of his immediate successor, Professor F M L Thompson–steady as a rock throughout the troubles of the late 1960s and early 70s–it can truly be said that he presided over a History Department of All the

Talents. Our success in those years owed much to his genial leadership. After nearly a decade at Bedford (1968–77), with Sheelagh Taylor as secretary, he moved to the Institute of Historical Research, thus taking his rightful place at the centre of historical studies in London. Not the least of the Talents in those happy days at St John's was, of course, Conrad Russell, now Professor at KCL, having previously been Astor Professor at UC. How can I characterise Conrad's unique *persona*: the last of the Whigs, doyen of 17th century revisionists, hero of innumerable anecdotes from Cumberland Lodge to Regent's Park, and now mouthpiece of Liberalism in the House of Lords. In his attic room at St John's, I can still imagine him putting down his cigarette, picking up the telephone and intoning: "History speaking"! Conrad has an hereditary sense of history, and of his own oracular function in its explanation. I think he would like me to tell you one story. He once recommended a particular student for a prize with these words: "Miss X is an excellent student, unusually perceptive–in my lectures, she is invariably the first to see the jokes…" I remember asking one student in 1962 whether she found it a good department. "Oh, yes", she replied; "it's a wonderful department–Mr Russell is so clever, and Dr Lawrence is so handsome." It wasn't long before I discovered that clever Mr Russell and handsome Dr Lawrence had at least one thing in common: they had both committed matrimony with a student–not, I hasten to add, the same student!

I like to think of the Civil-War mantle of S R Gardiner descending on to the shoulders of Conrad Russell. Or the political-theory mantle of J W Allen descending, via Marion Tooley, to Penny Corfield. Or Langton Sanford's concern with estate history descending to Michael Thompson. Or the Tudor, state-paper mantle of Brewer and Mackie descending on Nicola Sutherland. Of professional medievalists, the department had, until the 1950s, strangely few; but their number has been less significant than their distinction. Darlington's eminence–if not his acerbic manner–was amply replaced by the two young Oxonians who arrived in 1947 and 1951, Robin Du Boulay and Hugh Lawrence. Like S R Gardiner, Robin Du Boulay eventually retired to Sevenoaks, though he is now in retreat at Beverley, Yorkshire. Like S H Reynolds, Hugh Lawrence planned for a long time to retire to the hinterland of Oxford, though in the end he stayed put in Wimbledon. In Byzantine studies continuity is also striking: from Alice Gardner to Joan Hussey; and with Joan Hussey–as with Peggy Deansley–comes our first teaching link with Royal Holloway. The terrifying J Bass Mullinger–historian of medieval Cambridge–had, of course, his successor in Hugh Lawrence, though Hugh's cool temperament was a long way from the histrionics of that ferocious disciplinarian. Dame Lillian–I suspect–will have no successor, though perceptive colleagues have noticed that Professor Barron has taken to wearing Dame Lillian's gown.

As for me, which of my predecessors might I identify with? Gottfried Kinkel perhaps?–art historian, polymath and lady-killer? No; far too risky. Safer to choose the Rev. Samuel Harvey Reynolds–colleague of Walter Pater at my old college, Brasenose; critic, *Times* leader-writer, raconteur and wit. But, alas, I could never have survived for 20 years in the parish of East Ham.

So now we have moved from Regent's Park to Egham. This is not the place to rehearse the debates which led to that decision. But I will remind you of one nice story. A 19th century poet is said to have ended his days in a lunatic asylum. One day a visitor asked him how he came to be there. He replied: "Well, I said the world was mad; and the world said I was mad; and the world outvoted me". When the great medievalist Stubbs took up his second Bishopric, he was translated from Chester to Oxford: "like Homer", he remarked, "I lose everything in translation". Clearly we have lost something. But we have gained something too: not least some of the most dramatic campus architecture in the world. And we left Regent's Park–thanks to the generalship of Hugh Lawrence–with our academic banners flying. Our new colleagues at Royal Holloway include scholars and eccentrics–so we feel quite at home.

I have given you something of our early history. What of more recent times? Well, this is the moment to blow our own trumpet. The years at St John's were the vintage years, 1966 to 1982. A department which from among its students produced a series of Presidents of the

Union, and a respectable sequence of Firsts, when Firsts really were Firsts–17 Firsts in one decade, including 4 in 1974 and no less than 5 in one record year, 1973; a department whose graduates–only 30 per year remember–eventually included the Keeper of the Public Record Office (Sarah Tyacke), the Director of the London Museum (Simon Thurley), top civil servants like Dinah Nichols and Dave Wilkinson and several notable writers (Ann Wroe, Richard Dowden, Amanda Vickery); a department which in the space of 30 years produced–from a regular teaching staff never in double figures–four Fellows of the British Academy (Robin Du Boulay, Michael Thompson, myself and Conrad Russell), two senior Professors at Yale and Princeton (Conrad Russell and Peter Lake), a Slade Profesor and Wayneflete Lecturer at Oxford (myself); a Director of the Institute of Historical Research (Michael Thompson), and the first woman Vice-Chancellor in any British university (Dame Lillian)–such a department can hardly be said to be without distinction.

That department is no longer an independent unit. We have had to learn new tricks. We have become entrepreneurial. In my own case, for example, in the first five years after amalgamation, I took up visiting duties in Oxford, Cambridge, America, Australia and New Zealand. And in the ten years after that I ran a largely self-funding Victorian Studies Centre, catering for MA, MPhil and PhD research. Such diversification, I think, is in the best London tradition: London University must be the least ivory-tower of all major universities. Even the great S R Gardiner was something of an entrepreneur, lecturing on different days of the week at Bedford and at King's, and teaching in the evening as well.

When A F Pollard of University College reorganised the London History School early in the 20th century, he used as his model an expanded version of the Oxford system of intercollegiate teaching. And that has served us in good stead: although we have emigrated to Egham, we have managed to keep our roots in Bloomsbury. Wisely, we took one key thing with us: the heritage of the intercollegiate syllabus, the intercollegiate process of teaching and examining. Despite so much reorganisation–and it still goes on–that is what we must hold on to. If we throw that away–the intercollegiate inheritance–we throw away membership of what A G Dickens once memorably described as "the finest History Faculty in Europe". In that extended family of history, Bedford historians have played–and I hope will continue to play–a considerable part.

References

1 See A F Pollard, *Factors in Modern History* (1907). The first chair of History established independent of fees, was at King's College London. The growth of History posts was quite uncoordinated: "the titles themselves are a study in anarchy" (*ibid*).

2 Boase, *Modern English Biography* iii; F Wheen, *Karl Marx* (1999), 194.

3 *DNB* (J Gairdner); *English Studies*, ed H Wace (1881), including a list of works, p xi.

4 J S Brewer, 'Workhouse Visiting', in *Lectures to Ladies on Practical Subjects* (1855).

5 Brewer's prefaces were later edited by J Gairdner as *The Reign of Henry VIII* (1884).

6 At the Rolls Chapel, Chancery Lane, 1857–79.

7 For example, 1854–1860 for the *Morning Post* and *Morning Herald*; he resigned from the *Standard* when the editor refused to employ a Roman Catholic contributor. See also *Wellesley Index of Victorian Periodicals* I, 821; III, 735.

8 *What is Establishment? Or Letters on the Church in Ireland* (1868). Disraeli rewarded him with the Crown living of Toppesfield, Essex, 1876–79.

9 He was joint editor of the Unitarian *Inquirer*, 1852–55; he was buried in the Oat Street Chapel, Evesham (*DNB*; Boase, III, col 410).

10 For example, contributions to *The Spectator*, 1861–77, and *National Review* (*Wellesley Index*, III, 883). See also obituaries in the *Law Times* 11 Aug 1877, 273; and *Inquirer* 4 Aug 1877.

11 Originally articles signed 'Sigma' in the *Christian Reformer*.

12 J Langton Sanford, *Estimates of the English Kings from William the Conqueror to George III* (1872).

13 1857–64, writing for example in support of the federal cause in the American Civil War. In 1850–54 he had contributed humorous articles to the *Edinburgh Guardian* under the pseudonym of 'Jupiter Agate' (*DNB*; Boase, supp I, col 317-8). A portrait by Lowes Dickenson was presented to his widow.

14 J Skelton, *The Table Talk of Shirley* (3rd ed, 1895), 38–59.

15 L Campbell, *Speculum universitatis: alma mater's mirror* (Edinburgh, 1887), p vii.

16 For example, he edited *Translation of the Port Royal Logic* (1851; 7th ed 1874).

17 For example, articles in the *Edinburgh Review* etc (*Wellesley Index* I, 807; II, 831); *Shakespeare Studies* (1894), with memoir by L Campbell.

18 For example, 'Churches and Creeds', *North British Review* xlviii (1863), 397–428.

19 See also his *Somersetshire Dialect* (1861).

20 Signed Newenham Travers, BA, FSA.

21 *DNB* ('ISL'); Boase, III, cols 126–7.

22 S H Reynolds, *Studies in Many Subjects* (1898).

23 T D Raikes, ed, *Sicut Columbae: 50 Years of St. Peter's College, Radley* (1897), 19 . He considered Arnold "the very best critic we possess"; Ruskin he thought "deficient in the true critical temper", but "a man of true genius" who "can write even nonsense well" (*Studies on Many Subjects* 1898).

24 Memoir, *Essex Review* vi (1897), 69–71.

25 *The Times* 10 Feb 1897, p10.

26 *DNB*; Boase III, col 478; *The Times* 2–3 Nov 1893, p8; *Publisher's Circular* 15 June 1886, pp601–2, portrait; *The World* Nov 1893.

27 *DNB* (C H Firth); *EHR* April 1902 (F York Powell);

28 Anson supplied the bulk of the funds anonymously (*ex inf* J S G Simmons, All Souls College).

29 J F Rhodes, *Historical Essays* (1909), 143–50.

30 Intro to Gardiner's *History* (1987 ed).

31 That is, on Froude's death. The post went to F York Powell, who is reported to have delivered his inaugural briefly, impromptu, and in haste.

32 *EHR* April 1902.

33 Venn, *Alumni Cantabrienses* II, iv, 495; *Who Was Who* ii.

34 "History is the record of change... Savage tribes have no history because they have no change" (p1)–their study is, presumably, anthropology.

35 See also his *Cambridge Characteristics in the 17th century* (1867); *History of St. John's College, Cambridge* (1901).

36 J Bass Mullinger, 'The Multiplication of Universities', *Fraser's Magazine* NS xviii (1878), 279–95. He attacked Goldwin Smith's view (*Fortnightly Review* Jan 1878; *British Quarterly Review* April 1878) that the new universities should break away from traditional university forms.

37 *Who Was Who* ii. She was the sister of Professor Percy Gardner, and a Cambridge friend of the Rev J B Mayor, University Librarian, and Flora Macdonald Mayor, the novelist.

38 Alice Gardner, *The Conflict of Duties* (1903); *Sound Learning and Religious Education* (1904); *Within Our Limits* (1913).

39 She argued that the campaign for women's suffrage should be held in abeyance during the Great War (*Our Outlook as Changed by the War*, Cambridge, 1914).

40 'A Transition Period in Female Education', *Modern Review* v (1884), 70–90; *Short History of Newnham College* (1921).

41 For example, *History of Sacrament in Relation to Thought and Progress* (1921). She contributed a chapter to *The Faith and the War* (1915).

42 'A Transition Period in Female Education', *Modern Review* v (1884), 70–90.

43 BA 1880. His father was Rector of Whimple, Devon.

44 With J Bass Mullinger, Sanders also contributed to Low's *Dictionary of English History* (1884 etc).

45 *DNB* (H N Brailsford); *The Times* 10 Nov, 1941, p6. There is a portrait at Christ Church, Oxford, by J Southall.

46 For example, *Wellesley Index* I, 1027; II, 1026.

47 *More Changes and Chances*, intro.

48 *The Times* 12 Nov 1941, p7 (Janet Leaper).

49 Newby Manor, near Moorland, Westmorland (H W Nevinson, *Visions and Memories*, ed Evelyn Sharp; *Last Essays*, intro Gilbert Murray, 1944, 184–6).

50 *Fire of Life* (1935), 39.

51 Brackenbury Exhibitioner.

52 In 1909 he describes himself as Hulsean Professor of Modern History [? Sir Edward Hulse, Bt 1809–99, Fellow of All Souls]; in 1914 'Barclay Lecturer in Modern History'; in 1915 'Lecturer in History'. His death was reported in *Bedford College Annual Report* 1945–46.

53 J W Allen, *The Place of History in Education* (1909), 182.

54 M Vivian Hughes, *A London Family, 1870–1900* (1946), 415, 416.

55 J W Allen, *Germany and Europe* (1914); *The Danger of Peace* (1915).

56 J W Allen, *Wheel Magic, or revelations of an impressionist* (1909), 119.

57 *Ibid* 142–50.

58 *Ibid* 77–8. His travelling companion was often Thomas Seccombe, with whom he wrote *The Age of Shakespeare*, 2 v. (1903).

59 J W Allen, *The Place of History in Education* (1909), 88.

60 *Ibid*, 123.

61 *Ibid*, 135.

62 *Who Was Who* vii; [University of Glasgow] *Newsletter*, 7 Dec 1978, no 17; *The Times* 1978, p16g. He took a First in History at Jesus College, Oxford, in 1908 and earned an MC in the First World War.

63 For example, his edition of the *Calendar of State Papers relating to Scotland and Mary Queen of Scots xiii, 1597–1603* (1969).

64 *Who Was Who* vi; *The Times* 20 April 1963 p12a; 2 May 1963 p23b; 13 May 1963 p16a; 8 June 1963 p12d. She was author of *The Colonial Agents of the British West Indies* (1924); co-author (with H Temperley) of *A Century of Diplomatic Blue Books* (1938) and *Foundations of British Foreign Policy* (1938); contributor to (Gooch and Temperley), *British Documents on the Origins of the War, 1898–1914*, vols I-IX (1925–38); and editor of (Grant and Temperley), *Europe in the 19th and 20th centuries* (1952). For her private papers, see Bedford College Archives, RHBNC.

65 Lillian Knowles (d1926) was previously Professor of Economic History at LSE. (*Who Was Who* ii; *The Times* 27 April 1926, p18a).

66 For a sympathetic account, by R W Greaves, see *DNB*. Penson's policy as regards higher education in the colonies is summed up in her Montagu Burton lecture at Glasgow, *Educational Partnerships in Africa and the West Indies* (1954).

67 *Who Was Who* vii. He was the first pupil from Alderman Newton's School, Leicester, to win an Oxbridge scholarship; he took a First in Modern History at Merton College, Oxford, in 1930; his DPhil, supervised by Dr Lucy Sutherland, was published as *The Corporation of Leicester, 1689–1836* (1939). In 1963–64 he was Birkbeck Lecturer in Ecclesiastical History at Trinity College, Cambridge. For details of his career, see Bedford College Archives, biographical files.

Chapter 11

Italian

Peter Armour

The Ladies' College, Bedford Square, which was to become Bedford College, was founded at a time when there was widespread enthusiasm in Britain for the movement towards Italian liberation and unification. Elizabeth Jesser Reid herself had visited Italy in 1839 and made a prolonged sojourn there, mainly in Rome and Sicily, in 1845–47. For her, Garibaldi was a hero.[1]

Nineteenth-century Britain, inheriting the traditions of the European Grand Tour, was marked also by a growing interest in Italian culture of the Middle Ages and the Renaissance. Following the translation of the *Divine Comedy* by Henry Cary, the father of Francis (the College's Professor of Drawing 1849–70), Dante had become a focus of attention not only for poets, such as Shelley and Byron, but also for many scholars and dedicated readers in London, Oxford, and elsewhere, and including even Gladstone. The Victorian age saw also a surge of enthusiasm for Italian Renaissance art, with the Pre-Raphaelite movement and the scholarship of Ruskin, Pater, and Symonds. One of Mrs Reid's closest friends, Mrs Jameson, made her own, now forgotten contribution here with her *Legends of the Saints*, which became an indispensable guide for mid-Victorians to the subjects of sacred art in

Italy;[2] and, of course, one of the College's first students was to go on to write a novel set in Renaissance Florence–George Eliot's *Romola* of 1863. More generally, in the period, especially in the new universities, the study of Modern Languages and Literatures was developing as a respectable academic discipline alongside the traditional subjects of Latin and Greek. Indeed, knowledge of French, German and Italian was considered a more appropriate accomplishment for young ladies of the time than was Latin, the study of which was held 'unwomanly'.[3] As regards the new Ladies' College, moreover, Italian would have been a most useful accompaniment for Mrs Reid's students of music and art.

Whereas both University College and King's College had already established Chairs of Italian, the origins of Italian at Bedford College were rather more modest. The Prospectus for 1849 announced that there would be classes in Italian given by a Signor Incoronati, who had three students in the first term, after which he was succeeded by Ignazio Valetta, who had nine students in the second term, and eight in the third[4] Unlike French and German, which received greater prominence, Italian appears to have been taught in these early decades of the new College on an occasional, though renewable, basis, that is, when it was requested by students, and a series of Italians was employed, presumably paid at the normal hourly rate and according to the number in the class. In 1879, Margaret Tuke, the future Principal and historian of Bedford College, enrolled for Italian, and a teacher was provided, but unfortunately, after only two or three lectures, 'the difficulty of providing the then essential chaperon was found to be too great and the attempt was given up.'[5] Very little seems to have survived concerning the contributions to the College by its earliest teachers of Italian apart from their names,[6] although at least their occasional status allowed them to escape the fate of the Professors of French and German, dismissed for poor teaching in 1868-69.[7] In passing, it may be noted here that during these decades Thomas Holloway was amassing the fortune that was to provide the eventual destination for Bedford College and that this too had its origins with an Italian *émigré* of a very different sort, the Turinese leech-seller, Felix Albinolo, whose formula for a cure-all ointment had been taken over by Holloway in the late 1830s.[8]

The founder of the Department of Italian as such at Bedford College was Signorina E (for Emma) Bice Dobelli.[9] Educated in Rome, she came to London in 1903 and, in 1905, was appointed to teach Italian at the College at the rate of 7s. per hour for one student, 10s. for two at Advanced, and 5s. and 7s. 6d. respectively at Elementary level. Her appointment was renewed annually until 1913 when, dissatisfied with her position, she resigned; however, she was persuaded to stay on, becoming a Recognized Teacher of the University and Head of the Department of Italian in 1915 and then Senior Lecturer from 1921 until her retirement, at the age of 65, in 1936. In her 31 years, she guided Italian through major events in the history of the College, from its move to its new home in Regent's Park to the construction of the new building (the Tuke Building) where the department was situated from 1929.[10]

Signorina Dobelli was not herself a researcher; the College Calendars record only one publication by her, the translation of work by G M Trevelyan on Garibaldi.[11] Nevertheless, she developed Italian at the College in several important ways, providing courses not only in the language but also in Italian literature from Dante to the early nineteenth century, thus enabling the department to contribute to the University of London's Honours degree in Italian, which was established in 1917. Besides Intermediate, General, and Honours Italian, the department taught a course in Italian for History students, which came to include 'Readings from Renaissance Texts' and whose numbers reached a peak of over 40 in 1926–28 before dwindling to only two in 1932. There was also the occasional postgraduate student.[12] Crucial too was the expansion of the department with the appointment of Violet M Jeffery as a full-time assistant in 1922.

The College Calendar for 1922–23 gives an idea of the pattern and range of teaching provided by the department. Intermediate students took classes in 'Grammatical Morphology and Syntax' with Signorina Dobelli, and, with Miss Jeffery, 'Translation and Composition', the quaintly named 'Training of Ear and Accent, with Readings from Modern Literature', and six lectures on the Italian Risorgimento. Pass degree students followed courses in General Literature: the 13th–14th centuries (first year) and Dante's *Purgatorio* (second year) with Signorina Dobelli, and the 15th–19th centuries with Miss Jeffery. The schedule for Honours students was as follows:

Class A.–Honours

Signorina Dobelli.	2. Early Literature XIIIth-XIVth Centuries (First year).
" "	4. Dante Alighieri: Life, Times and Minor Works. Special Study of *La Vita Nuova.* Boccaccio: *Trattatello in laude di Dante* (First year).
" "	6. Special Period: Early Renaissance 1441–1503 (Second year)
" "	9. Renaissance Prescribed Texts: Sannazaro: Arcadia;.Ariosto: *Satire; Orazioni Scelte*; Castiglione: *Il Cortegiano*; Guarini: *Pastor Fido* (Second year).
" "	12. Modern Prescribed Texts: Gozzi: *La Gazzetta Veneta*; Alfieri: *Prose e Rime scelte*; Parini: *Poesie scelte* (First year).
Signorina Dobelli.	19. Composition and Translation (First year).
Miss Jeffery.	20. General Literature, with readings and Practical Exercises. (First year) (Second year).
" "	21. Comparative Syntax and Translation into English (First year).[13]

Over the years, of course, different authors and 'Prescribed Texts' were introduced, and between 1924–34 Professor Edmund Gardner of University College gave courses on the 'History of the Italian Language and Historical Grammar' and 'Old Italian Texts'. By 1937, the Departments at Bedford College and University College had developed an intercollegiate syllabus for Honours students that included History of the Italian Language, a Special Subject, and Italian literature from Dante to 'Contemporary Italian Literature' (which by 1939–40 went as far as Pascoli, 1855–1912). The General degree courses had acquired titles such as 'Literature from Dante to the death of Tasso' and 'Modern

Literature to the present day' (which by 1939–40 had arrived at D'Azeglio, 1798–1866). Such courses would, with variations, be familiar to later students of the University of London degree up to its replacement by the individual Colleges' course unit syllabuses in the early 1990s. Whilst today it seems more of an Italian than a British convention to term late eighteenth and nineteenth-century authors 'modern', it was not uncommon then, or even later, to ignore the writers of early twentieth-century Italy who have since become classics, although in 1935 Miss Jeffery travelled to Manchester to lecture to the Dante Society there on the theatre of Pirandello.[14]

Violet May Jeffery (later Mrs Saunders) was Signora Dobelli's colleague throughout these years. A student at Bedford College (1916–20), MA (1922), and DLit (1927), she first joined the department as part-time Assistant in 1921, becoming full-time in the following year, Junior Lecturer (1926–28), and Lecturer from 1928. Her particular field of research was pastoral drama in Renaissance Italy and England on which–with the help of a grant of £28. 3s. 4d. from the College's Research and Publications Fund–she published her book, *John Lyly and the Italian Renaissance* (Paris: Champion, 1928). Her articles included research on Italian sources for Peele's *Arraignment of Paris*, Daniel's *Queen's Arcadia* and Randolph's *Amyntas*, and Fletcher's *Faithful Shepherdess*, and studies of Shakespeare's Venice and Boccaccio's *Corbaccio*.[15] Moving into the nineteenth century, in 1937 she published an annotated selection of Leopardi's *Canti*.[16]

As Signorina Dobelli's retirement in 1936 approached–and perhaps inspired by the existence, by then, of several Chairs of Italian outside London, in Manchester, Oxford, Cambridge and Birmingham–the College requested the University to establish a Readership and, somewhat to Signorina Dobelli's displeasure, appointed a German, Curt Sigmar Gutkind, to the post.[17] Born in Mannheim in 1896, and after war service in 1914–18, he had obtained a DPhil (Heidelberg) in 1921. Having lectured in German in Florence (1922–28), he returned to Heidelberg as Reader in Romance Philology (1928–30). A founder member and Director of the Dolmetscher-Institut in Mannheim

(1930–33), he was elected Professor at Heidelberg but forced to resign because of his non-Aryan origins. Coming to England, he was Deputy Taylorian Lecturer at Oxford in 1935 before being appointed Reader and Head of Department at Bedford College in 1936 for what was to prove, however, a tragically brief tenure of his post.

Apart from a selection of Italian poetry, published in Heidelberg in 1923, Dr Gutkind's field of research in Italian studies was the Renaissance. He had published two articles on the fifteenth-century burlesque poet Burchiello,[18] and his inaugural lecture, delivered at the College on 1 December 1936, was entitled 'Cosimo de' Medici and Humanism'.[19] The founder of the Medici dynasty in Florence was the subject of his book, *Cosimo de' Medici, Pater Patriae, 1389–1464*, whose publication by the Clarendon Press in 1938 was received as "an event of prime moment in the history of Italian studies in this country", and its author praised for his "great learning and occasionally brilliant style" and his "superb" bibliography.[20] His work earned him a London DLit (1938); in the following year he gave a lecture in Oxford on Manzoni and Goethe[21] and published a short article describing a medallion, illustrated in a German book of 1627, as evidence of a tradition, revived during the Renaissance, that Dante had been an alchemist.[22]

Most of the surviving correspondence concerning Dr Gutkind is, however, of more sombre import. Having acquired Italian nationality in 1936, he was deprived of it in 1938, again because of his Jewish ancestry, and the College had to apply annually to the Ministry of Labour, Aliens Branch, to renew his appointment. His own attitude to the current cultural situation in his native land was expressed in a letter of 16 December 1938 to *The Tablet* in which, attacking a Nazi-orientated review of German writers, he wrote, among other things, that: "Nazidom has killed the spirit of free creation in Germany, and those who still write do so as 'die Stillen im Lande' (the Silent Ones in the Land)".

In January 1940 he applied for British citizenship, but world events soon intervened fatefully for him, as for countless others. In May, when Bedford College had been evacuated to Cambridge, he arranged with the Principal, Miss Jebb, to approach the Chief Constable with a view to lifting the restrictions of movement imposed on aliens in the Cambridge area, but on 11 June, the day after Italy entered the war, he was interned as an enemy alien. Also interned was Piero Treves, then an assistant in the Department, but only until 22 June when he was released and saw Dr Gutkind for the last time.[23]

Miss Jebb took up Dr Gutkind's case, writing on 5 July to Sir Alexander Maxwell that he had been expelled from Germany and Italy "on account of his Jewish extraction" and that he strongly disapproved of the German-Italian alliance; a reply sent on the following day assured her that the case would be investigated "to see if there were any grounds for release". On 8 July the Society for the Protection of Science and Learning in Cambridge also offered Miss Jebb help in freeing him as an interned refugee scholar. By this time, however, it was already too late. Dr Gutkind was one of the civilians and genuine refugees who had been mistakenly selected for deportation and, with over a thousand German and Italian prisoners of war, put on board the *Arandora Star* which set sail from Liverpool for Canada. On 2 July it had been torpedoed and sunk by a U-boat in the Atlantic with the loss of over 700 lives.[24] The news reached the College in a telegram of 10 July: 'Jebb Bedford College S[i]dgwick Avenue Cambridge. Gutkind is missing believe[d] drowned. Beaumont.'

The remaining correspondence concerning Dr Gutkind has an added poignancy because of its relative triviality. A telegram sent to London on 11 July advised the Examiners' meeting not to look for 'Jutkind' (sic) as he was on the casualty list. Unaware of his death, the Cambridge University librarian had already sent him a fine notice for the non-return of two books, and later letters deal with the possibility that these, and some books from the Bedford College library, might be in his London flat. Dr Gutkind's widow, Laura Maria, sent Miss Jebb two sealed letters which were forwarded, unopened, to Queen Mary and Anthony Eden. The College subsequently had to arrange for the payment into his estate of his remaining salary, the surrender value of his pension policy, his examination fees, and even the deposit of one guinea on his library keys.

During the war years, Violet Saunders (Jeffery) looked after Italian as Acting Head and, from 1944, Reader and Head of Department. Mrs E H Thorne (née Bigg-Wither) was employed as temporary Lecturer and then Lecturer (1944), and Italian received much teaching help from colleagues in Cambridge: Angelo Crespi, Dr Decio and Mrs A Pettoello, and, above all, two illustrious Italianists, Kathleen Butler and Barbara Reynolds.[25]

Upon the return to London, Dr Saunders, one of the earliest members of the Society for Italian Studies, helped to bring it "back to active life after six years of hibernation" by hosting a conference at Bedford College in July 1945.[26] She continued to run the department until her resignation, for reasons of ill health, in 1947; an indication of her personal interests is perhaps given by her leaving presents: binoculars and a handbook of British birds. Her obituary, following her death in 1950, paid tribute to her work, noting that "generations of students of Bedford College for Women, University of London, will remember her as a devoted teacher".[27]

On Dr Saunders' resignation, the College took what was to prove its most important step in the development of the Italian Department by deciding to establish a Chair.[28] In the meantime, Mrs Thorne, who had obtained her PhD in 1946, took over as Acting Head of Department. With research interests in the field of Anglo-Italian links and Italians in England in the eighteenth century, she was to become a Senior Lecturer in 1954 and remain an important member of the teaching staff until her retirement, because of serious ill health, in 1967.[29]

While the College searched for its new Professor, teaching help in Italian was provided by Decio Pettoello from the Cambridge days and by F M Guercio, who also taught Italian for the Renaissance Special Subject at the London School of Economics for many years. For the first term of 1947–48, Professor J H Whitfield travelled from Birmingham to give lectures on Tasso, Manzoni, Leopardi, and Pascoli. In August 1948, although it had received 27 applications for the Chair, the College's Board of Advisers decided to postpone a decision and offered a temporary Lectureship for the session 1948–49 to Fredi

Chiappelli (1921–90). He, however, had already committed himself to the University of Zürich, though he declared himself willing to take up the post at Bedford College in 1949–50.[30] By then, of course, the position was no longer available, and Professor Chiappelli, after remaining for a further twenty years in Switzerland, went on to become one of the most illustrious Italian scholars in the United States, as Professor at the University of California, Los Angeles, and then Director of the UCLA Center for Medieval and Renaissance Studies (1972–88). Thus, but for a matter of timing and finance, the Department might for a time at least have contained both Fredi Chiappelli and the scholar who was appointed to the Chair of Italian in 1949–Carlo Dionisotti.

Professor Dionisotti (1908–98), from Turin, had already established himself as a scholar while still a schoolteacher in Italy and had worked as a researcher in Turin and Rome before coming to England to take up a Lectureship in Oxford in 1947. He occupied the Chair at Bedford College from 1949 until he reached what was then the first retiring age of 62, in 1970. His Inaugural Lecture, delivered at the College on 22 November 1949, has proved to be especially famous, "the best known work of not only the greatest Italianist to have worked in Britain but the greatest Italian literary historian of the twentieth century".[31] Entitled 'Geografia e storia della letteratura italiana', the lecture set out to challenge the "unitary line" of earlier literary historians in which Tuscan literature evolved into a literature that is "linguistically and geographically Italian". Instead, he proposed a revision that would take account, particularly, of regional developments in the peninsula before unification, and would arrive at necessary distinctions and definitions by "paying attention to geography and to history, to the circumstances that constrain and uplift the lives of human beings in space and in time". Published as an article in 1951,[32] it was republished and gave its title to Professor Dionisotti's most celebrated and influential book, a collected volume of his major articles (Turin: Einaudi, 1967), in which "for the first time Italian literature as a whole was being reconsidered from a rigorous diachronic and synchronic angle, that is historical as well as geographical, the emphasis being on the latter as revealed by the title itself".[33]

Professor Dionisotti's scholarly work will always be associated principally with the Renaissance in the sixteenth century. It includes his editions of works by Pietro Bembo (1931, 1932, 1950, 1960, and 1966), his *Machiavellerie* (1980), and many articles on humanism, language, and regional cultures and literature (in the context, for instance, of the Council of Trent and the war against the Turks). To these researches he brought a European dimension in his Taylorian Lecture of 1971.[34] His work was not, however, limited to this one century but spanned the whole range of Italian literary and cultural history. With Professor Cecil Grayson of Oxford, he produced an expertly annotated selection of *Early Italian Texts* (Oxford: Blackwell, 1949 and 1965) that became a standard source for students of the history of the Italian language. He revised and updated *The Oxford Book of Italian Verse* (Oxford: Clarendon Press, 1952), containing poems from the thirteenth to the early twentieth centuries. One of his most important articles (1966) surveyed attitudes towards and critical opinions of Dante from the eighteenth to the twentieth centuries; his British Academy lecture of 1973, following his election as a Fellow, took as its subject 'Manzoni and the Catholic Revival';[35] and in 1988 he published his collection of *Appunti sui moderni*, his 'notes' on Foscolo, Leopardi, Manzoni, and others. Unlike many of his contemporaries, moreover, he wrote in a clear Italian style, and one reviewer summed up this combination of depth and accessibility as follows: "Every utterance of his is the tip of an iceberg: the vertical fund of learning which supports it lies modestly beneath the surface".[36] Undergraduates whom he taught at Bedford College may have "both feared and respected" him, but they also came to appreciate the breadth of his knowledge and teaching, the perfect timing and "masterly" delivery of his lectures, his wit, and his sensitivity to gaps in students' knowledge in his tutorials, which could last up to three hours at a time.[37] In his nearly thirty years of retirement, he remained in London for much of the year, continuing to work in the British Library, whose rich resources he had mastered and made available to other scholars in his publications.[38]

Professor Dionisotti was succeeded in 1970 by Giovanni (Gianni) Aquilecchia, previously Reader at University College London and then Professor of Italian at Manchester University, who occupied the Chair at Bedford College until the merger with Royal Holloway and subsequently in the new College until his retirement in 1989. Like Dionisotti, he too is best known for his scholarly work on sixteenth-century Italy, based largely on his extensive knowledge of the holdings of the British Library in this area, though he has published work on other periods too, notably a selection from the fourteenth-century Florentine Chronicle by Giovanni Villani (1979). His principal research subjects–before and during his tenure of the Chair at Bedford College, and since his 'retirement'–have been the poet, playwright, and letter-writer, Pietro Aretino (1492–1556), and the philosopher, Giordano Bruno, whose unorthodox views included the suggestion that the universe contained innumerable suns with orbiting earths, and who was burnt at the stake in Rome in 1600. Professor Aquilecchia's critical edition of Aretino's *Sei Giornate*, with prostitutes as its interlocutors, was inevitably one of the scholarly publishing successes of 1969; he rediscovered and edited the same writer's 'Sonnets on the Sixteen Positions' (originally printed with graphic sixteenth-century illustrations), and co-edited Aretino's poetry for the National Edition of the complete works (1992). Having provided a critical edition of Bruno's *Cena de le ceneri* (*Ash Wednesday Supper*) in 1955, he has continued to edit the philosophical and literary texts and to publish articles on Bruno's life, thought, and writings in Italian, dealing, among many other things, with his sojourn in England in 1583–85 and his possible influence on Galileo. He has also revived interest in the arcane Renaissance science of 'metoposcopy', the reading of a person's character, moral nature, and destiny from the positions of the lines and moles on his or her face; he discovered in the British Library and then edited an illustrated manuscript on this topic by Giovan Battista Della Porta (1990).[39]

From 1949, therefore, the Department had two leading Renaissance scholars at its head. Other Lecturers during this period have included: G H McWilliam and P M J McNair (future Professors of Italian at, respectively, Leicester and Birmingham); Dr Thorne, Dr Glynn Faithfull, and Dottor Giuliano Dego until their retirements in 1967, 1979, and 1984, respectively; in 1972, Francis E Rutland was replaced by Mrs Prue James, and in 1979 Dr Faithfull by Dr Peter Armour.[40] Students of Italian will probably remember two aspects in particular of their life at Bedford College. One will be the integrated system of intercollegiate teaching, by which they attended lectures at University College on Mondays and Tuesdays, whilst UCL students came to Bedford College on Thursdays and Fridays, Wednesdays being left for language classes and tutorials in the separate Colleges. Above all, they will remember The Holme, the Regency villa which Italian shared with the Department of English. Situated on the Inner Circle in Regent's Park, it provided what was certainly the most beautiful setting of any of the London Colleges. Indeed, it would occasionally dawn on a lecturer that performances by swans or squirrels on the lawn leading down to the lake were attracting more attention from the audience than the lecture itself.

The financial pressures imposed on Universities in the early 1980s by the government of Britain's first woman Prime Minister had a severe impact on Bedford College for Women. The Holme was returned to the Crown, and the Italian Department was moved back into the Tuke Building on the main College site. After the merger of Bedford College and Royal Holloway in 1984–85, the intercollegiate teaching arrangements established before the war were continued on a reduced scale until 1989, with students travelling from Egham to University College for lectures in medieval and Renaissance courses. Though the site was changed, however, Bedford College Italian had endowed the new College with several important and more permanent gifts: the full range of Honours courses, Single and Combined (now called 'Joint'); an excellent collection of Italian books in the library; and a tradition of scholarly research that, despite the new pressures in contemporary academic life, should stand as an example, and not merely a memory, for teachers and students of Italian in Britain in the century to come.

References

1 Margaret J Tuke, *A History of Bedford College for Women 1849–1937* (London, New York, & Toronto: Oxford University Press, 1939), pp10–11, 13; see also pp214–15 on the similar enthusiasm of Mrs Carlile, mother of the College's future benefactor, Sir Hildred.

2 *Ibid*, pp58, 306.

3 *Ibid*, p19.

4 *Ibid*, pp323-24.

5 *Ibid*, p250, n1.

6 The list given in the *Calendar of Bedford College London*, 1888, p53, reproduced in that of 1899, p72, and in Tuke, *A History*, p343, is as follows: Ignazio Valetta (1849–58), Vital de Tivoli (1858–61), Cesare de Tivoli (1861–65 and 1868–71),–Biaggi (1865–68), Giovanni Toscani (1871–76), C. F. Coscia (1876-78),–Savazzi (1878-84),–Balestrieri (Signorina) (1901–03), and E Degani (Miss) (1904-05).

7 Tuke, *A History*, pp115-16.

8 Anthony Harrison-Barbet, *Thomas Holloway, Victorian Philanthropist* (revised edition, Egham, Surrey: Royal Holloway, University of London, 1994), pp21-22, 28-29, 68, 70; John Elliott, *Palaces, Patronage & Pills. Thomas Holloway, His Sanatorium, College & Picture Gallery* (Egham, Surrey: Royal Holloway, University of London, 1996), p6.

9 For what follows, see the Bedford College Archives (Founder's Library, Royal Holloway) (herafter BCA), AR 150/24 (Staff files), D 304 (Dobelli); for additional information, see also AR/333/3/1 (Correspondence with the Italian Department 1915-49). I am most grateful to Jill Sherlock and Gavin Fearnley for their invaluable help in my work in the archives.

10 Tuke, *A History*, p241. Signorina Dobelli eventually retired, after the war, to Italy where she died in 1955.

11 *Calendar*, 1912-13, p131.

12 BCA, AR/333/3/1 contains a typed list of student numbers in the Department 1912–35, including one postgraduate for each of the years 1918, 1921, 1932–35; see also Tuke, *A History*, p347, on Higher Degrees 1920–37, in which there were three MAs, one PhD, and one DLit (presumably Miss Jeffery) in Italian. BCA 325/3/1 contains material about three prints given by the Italian government in 1921 to be awarded as prizes for an essay. The first was won in 1924 by a Mrs Knox for an essay on Lorenzino de' Medici's *Apologia*, Alfred de Musset's *Lorenzaccio*, and Sem Benelli's *Maschera di Bruto*. The remaining two prints had not been

awarded by 1926.

13 *Calendar*, 1922-23, pp74-75.

14 For what follows, see BCA, D 451 (V M Jeffery); also AR/158/8 (Applications for Chairs and Readerships 1921-60) and AR/333/3/1 (the correspondence file; see note 9, above).

15 Published in the *Modern Language Review* in 1924, 1926, 1932, and 1933; see the *Calendars* for 1924–25, 1925–26, 1926–27, 1932–33, 1933–34.

16 Cambridge University Press, 1937; reviewed by Walter Ll Bullock, Italian Studies, 1 (1937–38), 187–89.

17 For what follows, see BCA, D 349 (C S Gutkind).

18 *Burchielliana: Studien zür volkstümlichen Kehrseite der italienischen Renaissance* (Geneva: Olschki, 1931, from *Archivum Romanicum*, 15/1, 1931); 'Bemerkungen zu Melin de Saint-Gelais. Paraphrase einer Priamel des Burchiello', *Zeitschrift für Romanische Philologie*, 55 (1935), 199–203. The former has recently been described as 'fundamental' by Mauro Cursietti, *La falsa tenzone di Dante con Forese Donati* (Anzio: De Rubeis, 1995), p9.

19 Published as 'Cosimo de' Medici il Vecchio and Humanism', *Italian Studies*, 1 (1937–38), 116–31.

20 Review by C Roth, *Italian Studies*, 2 (1938–39), 186–87.

21 *Ibid*, 152.

22 'Dante Alighieri Alchymicus Amoris', *Journal of the Warburg and Courtauld Institutes*, 3 (1939–40), 153–55.

23 BCA, AR/333/3/2. Paolo Treves had been a student assistant and, when he was appointed to the BBC, his younger brother Piero took over for the Summer Term 1940. In a letter to the College of 14 July 1940, he enquired about Dr Gutkind 'whom I lost sight of when I left Bury Internment Camp on June 22nd.'

24 See http://www.iinet.au/-gduncan/maritime.html (with my thanks to Dr Anne Mullen for supplying this information). One of the Italian Jewish refugees rescued from the sea after the disaster was Uberto Limentani, later Professor of Italian at Cambridge.

25 BCA, AR/333/3/1 (see note 9, above); D1125 (E H Thorne).

26 Uberto Limentani, in his obituary of E R Vincent, *Italian Studies*, 35 (1980), 1.

27 *Italian Studies*, 5 (1950), 90.

28 For what follows, see BCA, AR/333/3/1 (see note 9, above); also AR/158/6. The Advisory

Board consisted of Miss Jebb and Professors Lillian Penson, Edna Purdie, and Gladys Turquet.

29 For her articles on Baretti, Badini, Martinelli, and Pindemonte, see, respectively, *Italian Studies*, 1 (1937–38), 132–36; 2 (1938–39), 153–70; 11 (1956), 92–107; 22 (1967), 62–77. Although she resigned in 1966, the College advised her to take unpaid leave until she reached the age of 60; however, she died before then, in January 1968.

30 See BCA, AR/333/3/1 (see note 9, above).

31 Brian Richardson, 'Carlo Dionisotti', *Italian Studies*, 54 (1999), 13–16 (p13).

32 *Italian Studies*, 6 (1951), 70-93.

33 G Aquilecchia, 'Carlo Dionisotti's Taylorian Lecture', *Italian Studies*, 27 (1972), 104–09 (p104).

34 *Europe in Sixteenth-Century Italian Literature* (Oxford: Clarendon Press, 1971).

35 Published by Oxford University Press, 1974, from the *Proceedings of the British Academy*, 59 (1973).

36 Philip McNair, review of *Manzoni and the Catholic Revival, Italian Studies*, 31 (1976), 119–20 (p119).

37 Nelia Saxby, in *Italian Studies*, 54 (1999), 16–17 (p16). Further information on the Italian Department 1958–69 is in BCA, AR/333/3/4, and on student assistants 1951–62 in AR 333/3/3.

38 See J H Whitfield, review of *Machiavellerie, Italian Studies*, 36 (1981), 97–100 (p97).

39 Collections of his numerous articles are in his *Schede di italianistica* (1976), *Schede bruniane* (1993), and *Nuove schede di italianistica* (1994).

40 Dr Faithfull died in 1998. For some further information on the Department 1970–76, including staff and language assistants, see BCA, AR 333/3/5; and on staff and their publications, see the College's *Calendars* 1949–69 and *Reports of the Council* 1969–84.

APPENDIX

Heads of Italian Department, 1905–85

1905–36	Emma Bice Dobelli
1936–40	Curt Sigmar Gutkind
1940–47	Violet Saunders, née Jeffery
1947–49	E H Thorne, née Bigg-Wither
1949–70	Carlo Dionisotti-Casalone FBA
1970–85	Giovanni Aquilecchia

Chapter 12

Mathematics

Paul M Cohn

In the thirteenth century, when the first universities were founded in this country by scholars migrating from Paris, the site of Regent's Park was a tiny part of Middlesex Forest, "a great forest with wooded glades and lairs of wild beasts, deer both red and fallow, wild bulls and boars".[1] Six hundred years later this had become Regent's Park, created by John Nash and his Royal Patron, the Prince Regent, at the beginning of the nineteenth century. It is to one of its residents that Bedford College owes its existence. She was Elisabeth Jesser Sturch, born in 1789, the daughter of a wealthy ironmonger, who lived with her parents at York Terrace, Regent's Park. In 1821 she married Dr John Reid, but after only 13 months of marriage she became a widow. This left her financially well off and her situation improved still further after the death of her parents. Throughout her life she had cherished the dream of "a College for women or something like it", and this she was able to realize in 1849, when she founded a Ladies' College in central London. The College was at first called 'Ladies' College, 47 Bedford Square', but later, in 1859 became 'The Bedford College for Ladies' and after several minor changes eventually became 'Bedford College'. It was the first establishment for the higher education of women in this country, although this was an ideal to be fully realized only later. According to its first prospectus "Ladies are admitted over the age of 12 years", and the Council report for 1849 states that "the total number of attendants at College lectures we find to be 68. Of these, as many as 42 attend only one set of lectures each, a considerable fraction of the 42 being ladies of mature age…"[2]

Through personal acquaintance Mrs Reid had persuaded an impressive array of professors to help in the teaching, in some cases without taking fees. They included Augustus De Morgan, who had in 1828 at the age of 21 been appointed the first Professor of Mathematics at University College. De Morgan taught for two terms at the new College but left at Easter 1850 on the ostensible ground of pressure of important work. Mrs Reld herself sets it down to "no remuneration", but Dame Margaret Tuke (the College Principal 1907–29) is probably nearer the mark when she writes in her history of the College that "a man who has been spoken of as 'an unfathomable fund of mathematics' may well have felt his time wasted in lecturing to girls who had only a very elementary knowledge of arithmetic".[3] The Rev James Booth FRS (1806–78), Professor of Astronomy and Scientific Geography, looked after mathematics instruction until a more permanent replacement could be found, but for the next decade or so mathematics was in the charge of men whose distinction usually lay in other fields. Booth's successor was Francis William Newman (1805–97), the free-thinking younger brother of the future cardinal. He had been Professor of Latin at University College and as a promoter of Mrs Reid's scheme was one of the main influences on the new foundation. He was brilliant but eccentric. He condemned urban life because he disapproved (in principle) of drains. He said of himself that to be in conflict with current opinion was to be in his element. When the lectures of the Professor of English, Geography and Astronomy, Rev Thomas Wilson, were censured as being too heterodox (for example, Wilson did not subscribe to the 39 Articles of the Faith), Newman supported him. Religious antagonism was rife and caused a number of resignations in 1851, including Newman's. This was a bleak time for the College; its finances were low, partly because the fees charged were inadequate, and

Mrs Reid became so depressed that she resigned from the Council, though after a while she returned. In later years she took a less active part in the direct management of the College. As her health declined, she created in 1860 a trust of the greater part of her property, to be administered for the benefit of female education. She died on Good Friday, 1866. Earlier a friend had summed up her character in the words "as to dear Mrs Reid, her failures are better than other people's successes; they are worthier, and they sometimes also produce more visible good effects, though not exactly the effects she looked for and worked for".[4]

The next few years were uneventful for Mathematics at the College and little survives on record save the names of the Heads of Department: Rev William Cooke 1851–53, Rev Henry J Hose 1853–56, Rev Walter Mitchell 1856–57. In the early days of the College the emphasis was on liberal Arts, though courses in both Mathematics and Natural Science were also taught from the beginning. However, many of the students were insufficiently trained to benefit by the lectures and from 1853 to 1868 a school was conducted in the same building, in association with it but under separate management. From 1858 to 1865 Mathematics was in the charge of Richard Holt Hutton (1826–97), who had been educated at University College School, University College London, and at Heidelberg and Berlin. He was a theologian and man of letters, who had been Principal of University Hall, London, before coming to Bedford College. Before coming to the College he had been Editor of *The Enquirer* and later became joint Editor with Walter Bagehot of the *National Review*; from 1861 to 1897 he was joint Editor and Proprietor of *The Spectator*, a feat unequalled by any of his successors. He also instituted a prize to be offered to mathematics students. He was followed by Jonas Ashton 1865–69 and Olaus M F E Henrici FRS, 1869–70, who was at the same time Professor at University College. He had written a book on bridge building and in 1882 became President of the London Mathematical Society (LMS).

In 1874 the College moved to new premises in York Place, Baker Street. Its work received great impetus in 1878, when the University of

London opened its degree examinations to women. This led to considerable changes in the teaching of science in the College, including the institution of a 'higher mathematics' class for the first time in 1879–80. Until then the University had merely been a degree-giving body, having been constituted in 1836 as a Board 'holding examinations and granting degrees' under the title of 'University of London'. Now the lack of a university in the full sense, teaching as well as examining, began to be felt, and this resulted in the formation in 1884 of the 'Association for promoting a Teaching University in London'. A number of schemes were put forward, both by the University and by outside bodies, including an attempt by University College and King's College to obtain a charter enabling them to give degrees and thereby create a second University in London, the 'Albert University', but this came to nothing. After repeated attempts, a charter for 'Gresham University' received the assent of the Privy Council and in 1892 was laid before the House of Commons, but then foundered amid the storms of hostile criticism from many quarters (including Bedford College). A Royal Commission was appointed, with Lord Cowper as Chairman, and its report in 1894 formed the basis of the constitution of the University of London Act (1898).

In 1900 Bedford College was recognized in the Faculties of Arts and Science as one of the first Schools of the reconstituted University. This was followed by the granting of a Royal Charter in 1909. The lack of proper premises was now more keenly felt. An Appeal was mounted and its success enabled the College to purchase the lease of South Villa in Regent's Park. This was a property dating from 1827, standing in eight acres of ground on the edge of the lake, and the College had permission to replace it with a fully equipped academic building. A design by Basil Champneys was completed in 1913 (not without protests staged in the park by outraged residents), and it was opened in July by Queen Mary, who had earlier that year become joint Patroness with Queen Alexandra.

Henrici was succeeded by Percy John Harding, who was connected with the College for more than 50 years, as Head of the Mathematics Department from 1870 to 1907 and then as Honorary Lecturer until his death in 1925. His services to the College are commemorated by the Harding Prize in Mathematics. In 1907 Harold Hilton was appointed Head of Department, and when in 1912 the first University Chair for the College was instituted in the Mathematics Department, he became the first holder of this Chair. His annual salary was then £600 and being required to "live in London", he writes (from his address in Platt's Lane, Hampstead) wondering whether he qualifies, and whether it might not be better to require the Professor to live "in London or its suburbs". Hilton (who in 1939 changed his name to Simpson) wrote on geometry, group theory and crystallography and is well known for his books on these subjects; his books on algebraic curves and on groups are almost forgotten now, but his book on crystallography was reprinted in 1963, 60 years after its first appearance. From 1914 to 1944 he was Librarian of the LMS. In the department he was known for the dedication he brought to teaching and to the general welfare of his students. In October each year his former students (the 'old girls') organized a gathering, which he attended throughout his retirement (until just before his death, in 1974, at the age of 97). I attended some of these meetings and met Professor Simpson there; he was very sprightly and perfectly lucid, but he made it clear that he did not want to talk about mathematics. After his death there was a further meeting at which over £2000 was subscribed, to be presented to the Principal for his hardship fund. Later a Simpson Prize was established in the Department.

Bedford College had no substantial endowments; it was launched with a loan of £1500 from Mrs Reid, later converted into a gift, and it was always run very much on a shoe-string. For example, in the spring of 1925 Professor Hilton was informed that the departmental grant for 1925–26 would be £5, with the rider "should unforeseen financial pressure make it necessary to reduce this grant, due notice will be given to you before the end of the Easter Term".[5]

Professor Hilton's successor was Wilfrid Norman Bailey (1893–1961), who had previously been at Birmingham and Manchester and whose work was on hypergeometric series. Soon after his appointment in 1944 the College began to take men postgraduates, although undergraduate classes did not go mixed until 1965. Between 1944 and 1955 Professor Bailey was successively Librarian, Proceedings Editor and Secretary of the LMS. As Librarian he had been instrumental in salvaging some of the Society's books that had suffered war damage at the University College Library. Bedford College had also suffered badly from the bombing; during 1945–48 repairs were carried out and three new buildings put up. An upper floor in the new Oliver Building (named after Richard Oliver whose wife Louise, née d'Este Courtenay (1850–1919) had provided a substantial gift; she had been a student of the College in 1864–65 and from 1912 until her death was a Council member) was allocated to Mathematics, and the department moved there in 1949, the centenary year. In 1946 Dr Geoffrey T Kneebone joined the department; originally a geometer, he turned to logic at this time and started one of the first logic groups in London. More recently a strong research school in model theory was established by Dr Wilfrid A Hodges, whose appointment in 1968 had been shared with Philosophy, and by the time Dr Kneebone retired in 1983, the department had acquired an international reputation in logic.

Professor Bailey retired in 1958 and was succeeded by H Gordon Eggleston, an analyst whose interests were in convexity and Hausdorff measure. During his eight years at the College (he left in 1966 for the Chair at Royal Holloway College, which he held until his retirement in 1981) he oversaw the substantial changes that took place in the department, at a time of general expansion in the universities. Staff numbers increased, a full-time secretary was provided, and in 1964 a second Chair for the department (in Applied Mathematics) was created, to which John S Griffith was appointed. He was a theoretical chemist with a mathematical background and an interest in artificial intelligence. As the College opened its doors to male undergraduates, the University abolished the common syllabus and instituted the Course Unit system (at least in the Science Faculty). This meant that each College would henceforth conduct examinations to its own syllabus, of course with appropriate cheeks and visiting examiners, to keep some degree of comparability. This had a great liberating effect on the syllabus, which for the first time could be truly up to date, as well as being responsive to the needs of the staff.

In 1967 I was appointed to the Chair of Mathematics, which had been vacant for a year; at this time the Head of Department was Dr Gordon L Clark (1914–82), who was reader in Applied Mathematics. I found a Department of 11, or rather 10 and 2 halves, one post being shared with the Institute of Computer Science and one with the Philosophy Department. In the course of the next few years both were converted to full posts, giving us a strength of 12. Professor Griffith left in 1968 to take up a split appointment between Indiana University at Bloomington and the CSIRO in Sydney (sadly he died only 5 years later, at the early age of 46). He was succeeded in 1969 by Raymond F Streater, an applied mathematician with very broad interests in pure mathematics. During the next dozen years British universities suffered from the brain drain, when lecturers were relatively scarce. We had a turnover of about one staff member per year, and we were usually able to get as replacement a lecturer whose interest was represented in the department, with the result that distinct research groups could be formed, in algebra, logic and quantum field theory. This was also reflected in the growing number of research students, research fellows and the steady stream of overseas visitors to the department. At the same time the interests of the undergraduates were not forgotten; the syllabus had become more 'algebraic', but efforts were made to provide a balanced fare. In the third year it was possible to attend courses at other colleges, and there was a two-way interchange with University College and Westfield College, and to a lesser extent with King's College. At the postgraduate level there was the MSc which was truly intercollegiate, and it could easily happen that the class for an MSc course was larger than one for an optional second year course. In 1958 an Easter conference was organised by Dr N Jessie Hardiman in the department. About 120 sixth-formers and their teachers were offered a glimpse of university mathematics in half a dozen lectures by the staff. This was so successful that it was repeated and soon became an annual event, with the lecturers often drawn from further afield.

In 1972 the Murray Commission was appointed, the latest in a series of Royal Commissions to examine the problems of London University. One suggestion, at the end of one of the 600-odd paragraphs, was that the smaller Colleges like Bedford, Westfield and Queen Elizabeth Colleges should look at ways of combining their efforts to make overall savings. In consequence the College spent a busy six months discussing various possibilities, such as moving out to Hatfield, but the only conclusion to emerge was that it was impossible to devise changes to produce significant savings without spending a great deal of money. However, the debate made many of us conscious of the great advantages of our superb site. The next crisis came in 1981, when the University Grants Committee, anticipating the impending fall in the number of 18-year-olds, wrote to all universities, setting lower student targets. At that time Bedford had about 1600 students, and as a College was just managing to survive. No doubt with a student population of 2000 its future would have been more secure; instead the University Court, parcelling out the targets, reduced Bedford's allocation to 1350. This left only two possibilities: either to cut drastically the number of departments and perhaps to function as an Arts College together with mathematics, an option briefly considered (but strongly opposed by us) or to merge with another College. From October to December 1981 talks were pursued with King's College which had proposed a merger, but this came to nothing. Early in 1982 the possibility of a merger with Royal Holloway College was first mooted. This would mean the end of the Regent's Park site, but in any case the lease on most of it would run out in 30 years' time, and the RHC site at Egham was spacious enough to accommodate both Colleges, while the sale of the lease would provide some funds towards the cost of the new buildings that would be needed at Egham. The prospect of new purpose-built laboratories for the larger departments formed by the merger held an attraction for several Science Departments; enthusiasm on the Arts side was less marked, but everyone recognized that this was a critical situation that required a drastic remedy. In Mathematics the contacts between departments in the different Colleges suggested that something could be done to take advantage of the various mergers that were under consideration, to form five strong departments of comparable size, but not necessarily along present College lines. It took a number of meetings in smoke-filled rooms to work out the details, and the University recognized this activity by setting up a committee under the chairmanship of Professor (later Sir Michael) Atiyah, which met early in 1983 to complete the arrangements.

Meanwhile wild rumours circulated about possible purchasers of the Regent's Park site, ranging from an Arab State (to build a Moslem Museum) to a sect of transcendentalists. Several thousand glossy prospectuses were sent all over the world and there were hundreds of enquiries. The eventual purchaser was Rockford College, Illinois (founded in 1847, two years before Bedford College), which had formed a consortium of American universities to use the site for a new institution, Regent's College, that would enable their students to spend their junior year in London.

By now the Mathematics Department staff had shrunk to nine by the retirements of J C Fernau (1927–96), N J Hardiman and G T Kneebone, the latter two after more than 30 years with the Department. The remaining staff were soon dispersed: the algebra group (P M Cohn, W Dicks, W Stephenson) to University College, though Dr Dicks left in 1986 to take up a chair at the Autonomous University in Barcelona; the applied group (R F Streater, L J Landau, H C Rae, I F Wilde) to King's College; and the remaining logician (W A Hodges) and the relativist (P J McCarthy) to Queen Mary College, later Queen Mary and Westfield College.

There was general sadness among all who had worked at the College, that this phase in its life had come to an end. Reflecting on my seventeen years with the College, I found the atmosphere, both physical, in one of London's finest parks, and mental, surrounded by colleagues who were both stimulating and sympathetic, very conducive for productive research and rewarding teaching. Writing fourteen years ago, I expressed the hope that "the resulting reorganisation will give the

University the strength and stability to cope with the needs of the 21st century". That hope remains, though it is clear that much will depend on the recognition by the government of the essential role the universities are playing and will continue to play.

Acknowledgements

This article is a revision of a piece I contributed to C W Kilmister's essay on 'The teaching of Mathematics in the University of London', which appeared in the *Bulletin of the London Mathematical Society*, 18 (1986), 321–337, and I am grateful to the Society for their permission to use the earlier article. I should also like to thank my former colleagues Dr N J Hardiman and Dr G T Kneebone for providing me with details and some reminiscences of the early post-war period.

References

1 Fitzsteven's 'Description of London', in Ann Saunders: *Regent's Park, a study of the development of the area from 1086 to the present day* (1969), p9.

2 Margaret J Tuke, *A history of Bedford College for Women 1849–1937*, (1939), p18, 61.

3 *Ibid*, p65.

4 *Ibid*, p17.

5 Bedford College Archives.

Chapter 13

Philosophy

Mark Sainsbury

The teaching of Philosophy at Bedford College seems to have begun (if the earliest prospectus is to be believed) on Wednesday 10 October 1849 at 2 pm with a lecture entitled 'Moral Philosophy' given by A J Scott, a professor of English Literature at UCL, to around 50 students. It ended on 12 July 1985 with a 'Concluding Philosophical Exercise' at which various past and present members and friends of the department gave papers before a rather smaller audience than Scott's. The event included refreshments in the Botany garden, and my recollection is dominated by the swarming of a former student's bees, making the air black. This caused no panic in the assembled dignitaries, though I'm not sure whether this was because they didn't notice or because the refreshments were so distracting or because the guests were well informed about the habits of bees. Before they swarm, bees eat as much honey from the hive as they can, to take with them to their new abode. This puts them in a very sweet temper, so although there is a lot of buzzing there is nothing to be afraid of.

One strand of interest in the history of philosophy at Bedford is the relation between this subject and psychology (many details of which can be found in Dr Valentine's contribution, chapter 17). 'Logic, psychology and ethics' is a triad which appears on many records in the last century and the early years of this. One should not assume that what was offered under the heading 'Psychology' was devoid of philosophical interest. When Sophic Bryant lectured on Elements of Psychology in the Training Department in 1892, her syllabus included questions like "Answer carefully the question, What is Truth?" and "What are your grounds for supposing that any other persons except yourself exist". The Training Department must have been notable for the breadth of its education. In 1892, the Reverend W C Stewart (gold medallist in ethics and logic in Dublin) gave a lecture on John Locke in a series whose next lecture was 'Why Teachers should know Something of Hygiene' by Mrs Clare Gosiett, an Associate of the Sanitary Institute.

Many glamorous names were associated with the department over the years, starting with one familiar to every student of Elementary Logic, Augustus de Morgan. He was listed as a lecturer in Mathematics in the very early years (1849–50), though his main post was at King's. I have not been able to discover whether Bedford students were introduced to de Morgan's laws by their inventor, though it seems that Logic was not always listed as a separate curriculum subject, and first appears as such only in 1851. Some of the course titles sound ahead of their time, for example, the course listed in 1855 entitled 'Elementary Principles of Morals: Applied more particularly to the Duties and Pursuits of Women'. Strangely, and one hopes unconnectedly, no Philosophy courses are listed for 1856 (though in the accounts for that year one unfortunate student out of 118, Mary Ireland, is recorded as having paid for Philosophy courses). There are other little signs of momentary decline in 1855: elocution has sunk to "reading aloud".

Other distinguished names associated with the Philosophy Department as Visiting or Occasional lecturers include those involved in a lecture series on time given in 1934–35 (C D Broad, Arthur Eddington, F C Bartlett); and, in that rich year, Rudolph Carnap and Ernest Cassirer. More recent Bedford-related luminaries include: John Hospers (1954–55), Noam Chomsky (1964–65), Alfred Tarski (1965–66;

these lectures included a version of his famous "Truth and proof", and of a paper, published only in 1986, on logical constants), Fred Dretske and Anil Gupta. The lectures on time were organized by Susan Stebbing, then Professor and Head of the Department of Mental and Moral Science (1933-43). She was in touch with Bertrand Russell and other eminent philosophers in this country and in the USA, and is remembered above all for her work in logic. She passionately believed that this was no mere academic subject, but one whose lessons needed to be suffused through any society in which democracy could flourish.The Susan Stebbing Professorship at King's marks Bedford's contribution to the present King's department.

The Departments of Philosophy and of Psychology went their separate ways in 1944, nearly twenty years after the idea of division was first mooted, and subsequently there were only three professors of Philosophy and Heads of the Philosophy Department: H B Acton (1944–64), Bernard Williams (1964–67) and David Wiggins (1967–1980).

Acton initially headed a Department of just two people (himself and Dr R L Saw), and for some time operated from the Ministry of Supply. He was a political philosopher whose book on Marxism still earns praise. Margaret Macdonald came to the Department in 1946 first as lecturer and later as Reader, replacing Dr Saw who had been appointed to a Readership at Birkbeck in 1945. Net expansion began in 1954 with the appointment of Dr Alan Lacey; in 1956 Ruby Meager replaced Margaret Macdonald, who had died earlier in the year; and in 1958 Doreen Tulloch was added to the strength. Aurel Kolnai joined the Department in 1959, remaining until his death in 1973. He had escaped Nazi persecution, and is said to have written his well-known *The War Against the West* (1938) in a café in Vienna.

Bernard Williams is one of this century's most distinguished moral philosophers. He has also written a book on Descartes, and has made important contributions to our understanding of personal identity and related topics. He left Bedford to become the Knightbridge Professor of Philosophy at Cambridge and then Provost of King's College Cambridge, before going for some years to Berkeley, and then, in 1990, returning to England to be White's Professor of Moral Philosophy in Oxford. During his tenure of the Chair, David Lloyd Thomas (1965) and Anthony Savile (1966) came to the Department, and in 1967 Brian O'Shaughnessy replaced Ruby Meager, who followed Dr Saw's course of moving to a Readership at Birkbeck. The logician Wilfrid Hodges was in the Department between 1968 and 1974, when he moved to the Mathematics Department. I arrived in 1978, replacing Doreen Tulloch.

David Wiggins was my Head of Department, a man of great charm and well as distinction, whose well known *Sameness and Substance* was written while he held the Chair. His contributions to philosophy range widely: metaphysics, moral philosophy and philosophy of language are some of the main areas to which he has contributed, and in all cases he has brought to bear his deep knowledge of ancient philosophy, and in particular of Aristotle. As Head of Department, he allowed us to live charmed lives, never letting the rest of us sense the existence of administrative burdens, while welcoming our contribution to organizational issues. He was a helpful reader of work in progress, encouraging by his criticism and inspiring by his example. He left Bedford to return to Oxford, coming back to London for a spell as Professor at Birkbeck before going back again to Oxford as Wyckham Professor of Logic. Rumour has it that he would ask candidates for admission whether, if the word 'pigs' came to mean what 'birds' currently means, pigs would fly. (I have placed the official version of the correct answer at the foot of this article.)

Despite its small size, the Department has been associated with many well-known philosophy journals. *Mind*, at various points in its history arguably one of the most important philosophy journals in the world, was founded by Alexander Bain (Professor of Moral Philosophy, 1851–54) as 'A Quarterly Journal of Philosophy and Psychology' (and only quite recently has it dropped pretensions to psychology). Margaret Macdonald edited *Analysis* from 1948-56, and Acton edited *Philosophy* for a long stretch, 1957–72. Anthony Savile (1972–1980) and I (1980–85) were successively Honorary Secretary of the Aristotelian Society and Editor of its *Proceedings*.

While I was in the department, the most significant event was the decision that it would transfer to King's rather than join the newly merged Royal Holloway and Bedford New College. There was a straightforward academic reason for not trying to run a London Philosophy Department at Egham: co-operation with UCL, Birkbeck and the LSE results in a system of intercollegiate Philosophy lectures to which most of the 60 odd philosophers in London contribute. These lectures cover all the compulsory and optional papers on the syllabus, and these span almost the whole history of philosophy from its pre-Socratic beginnings to the present day, and most of the main subjects. No one department could mount such a programme. Sending students from Egham to attend these would not have been practicable, and it would have been damaging to staff to lose their more or less day-to-day contact with other London philosophers. Clear as the academic case was–and it applied to other departments as well–we were no doubt helped to see its merits by the fact that in 1981 the Bedford administration compiled what it called a 'stand-alone' plan: a plan for the College's future on the supposition that it did not merge. The main point of the plan was to open the College's eyes to the merits of a merger, by showing how nasty it would be to stand alone. Doing so would apparently have involved closing several departments, including Philosophy. Looking back, this feature of the plan may not have been a good one, since Philosophy is cheap to run and student demand at all levels has been rising steadily for twenty or more years. However, the plan made us feel insecure within the Bedford framework, so we began at that early stage to consider for ourselves where our salvation lay. Happily for us, though less happily for the new College, a University-appointed SARC (Subject Area Review Committee) in Philosophy, chaired by Ronald Dworkin, took our fate as the only item on its agenda and recommended that we should, as we by then desired, move to King's.

For all the merits of the King's department, including an institutional framework that has allowed us to thrive and to grow, it is hard not to be nostalgic for the Bedford days. The physical surroundings were uplifting, perhaps the most beautiful of any academic institution of any city in Europe, with lawns, a lake, trees, a herb garden, and tutorials out of doors in fine weather. Then I knew every student by name, and had personal contacts with many colleagues in other departments. Above all, there seemed quite time enough to give the students a good education and still do some work of one's own.*

* The answer is No. The sentence "Pigs fly" would be true, but it would not mean that pigs fly.

Chapter 14

Physics

Peter Rice-Evans

Memories: 1956, my arrival in Regent's Park in the cab a of low-loading trailer. I was accompanying a large two-ton magnetic beta ray spectrometer, to the construction of which I had already devoted two years of my life as a postgraduate at Exeter University. This event signified a new direction and a new scale for physics at Bedford; Harold Richardson had just been appointed Hildred Carlile Professor and I naturally wished to continue to pursue nuclear physics with him. Not surprisingly, I was enthusiastic; I held a generous Bedford scholarship of £350 pa, I owned an open red two-seater Swallow Austin-7 and I would be surrounded by young women–all of them with beautiful minds. Indeed as a rare male postgraduate I was expected, each evening, to select an undergraduate and, gowned, accompany her to High Table for dinner. Blissful days. Two years later, the proud possessor of a doctorate and the co-author of three publications, I departed for Chicago and later Columbia University in New York. Life in the USA was intoxicating, but when in 1962 Richardson invited me to return to Bedford as a lecturer I could not resist.

I mention these facts by way of excuse; my recollections go back only forty years, not 150. Physicists by their nature are consumed by present results and future possibilities–it is not natural to examine the past. So, in this article, I cannot aspire to History with evidence fully examined and weighed, prior to preconceptions being expressed. Rather I shall have to content myself with a dip into the College archives; perhaps a few plums will emerge. After all, this is not scholarship–this is a celebration. And I shall consult colleagues.

Dame Margaret Tuke's book[1] on the History of Bedford explains that life was austere in the early days of the College: "hunks of bread" for lunch; cold baths; lights out at 9:30 pm. From today's perspective one must admire the young women's fortitude. Was it a love for learning that attracted girls into education or the necessity to establish a career? Young women aspiring to an education in the nineteenth century were one thing; an aspiration to read physics was perhaps something more remarkable. Was a yearning for Italian, pianoforte, and fine art the same inspiration that some women felt for science?

Middle class London families must have been much impressed by the public discourses held at the Royal Institution. Every Friday night in Albemarle Street, science was vividly portrayed by eminent practitioners following in the footsteps of Humphrey Davy and Michael Faraday. The power of the ideas must have turned many a daughter's head; what excitement: the challenge of the physical world. Were there job opportunities in the barely developed sciences as well as the arts? There was an obvious connection between physical knowledge and the optical and electrical industries but was it a practical prospect for women to become engineers? Perhaps the spirit of the age was just overwhelming; the possibilities of electricity and the submarine telegraph could not be resisted; the 1900 *Exposition Universelle* in Paris, representing the high point of *Art Nouveau*, had the *Palais de l'Electricité* as one of its showpieces, spectacularly lit and surmounted by the *Spirit of Electricity driving her chariot into the future*.

In the 1911 College Calendar, the entrance exam questions are presented. They consisted of demanding but rather dull exercises in estimating results for heat conduction in bars, light focusing in combinations of lenses, etc. But, at the turn of the century people had witnessed the astonishing synthesis by James Clerk Maxwell at King's College on electromagnetic theory; the electron, X-rays and radioactivity had just been discovered and quantum theory and relativity were in the offing. Some women must have been inspired by the prospects of going further in research even though the subject was dominated by men. The famous 1922 photo of the Solvay conference on quantum mechanics displays twenty men but also one woman, Madame Curie, who had discovered radioactive radium in 1905, which proved that women could make it.

From the beginning, science was offered at Bedford. Pupils signed up for courses at random; 'natural science' was offered in 1849 for one guinea a term, but 'astronomy and geography' was more popular. Natural science evolved into natural history and eventually botany. It is recorded that a course of natural philosophy in 1851 attracted seven pupils, but then there was a lapse until 1860. Tuke records that the heads of natural philosophy in these days were Rev William Cooke (1851–53), John Drew (1854–56) and Rev Walter Mitchell (1856–57); is it possible no women enrolled? In 1860 an extraordinary 47 registrations were made, and thereafter regularly about 20 per annum spread over three terms. This activity corresponded with the appointment of William Russell in 1860 as Professor of Natural Philosophy. He was essentially a chemist who researched at the Royal Institution, became an FRS in 1872 and in 1870 had left to become Professor of Chemistry at St Bartholomew's Medical School.

Serious physics commenced at Bedford at York Place with the brilliant appointment in 1875 of a talented young man, Oliver Lodge, as Professor in Natural Philosophy. Over the years 1876–81 he was to hold this concurrently with a demonstratorship and then an assistant professorship at University College.[2] His Royal Society biographical memoir[3] comments "By undertaking much additional work in examining and teaching, he was able to earn a sufficient income to obtain the consent of the parents of a student at the Slade School of Fine Art to marry her". They had 12 children. He had only graduated in 1875, having received a 'course of quantitative laboratory instruction' under Professor Carey Foster at UCL. We may assume that he introduced many of the UCL experiments to the women of Bedford. Indeed the Department still retains many beautiful mahogany and brass instruments of this time. In his autobiography,[3] Lodge recalls how "when the bell rang, the girls trooped in, and with them an elderly lady, who sat on a chair by the side, bringing some knitting with her. I understood this to be a precautionary chaperon. I was not disconcerted by it; it seemed quite natural". In the next five years he published 15 papers and numerous letters in *Nature* on a wide range of topics. Among the papers were two, with Carey Foster, 'On the flow of electricity in a plane conducting Surface'.[4] In 1881 Lodge became Professor at Liverpool University College, where he pursued his researches on wireless telegraphy which were recognised with the award of the Albert Medal. He became Principal of the University of Birmingham in 1900, gathered ten honorary doctorates and acquired national fame as an educator.

Frederick Womack was a curious recruit. Originally he had trained as a doctor at St Bartholomew's Hospital, but apparently his MB was an appropriate foundation for teaching Physics at Bedford which he did from 1882 for forty years. The period seems to have been uneventful except for the war years when he visited France to lecture to the troops in rest camps. His contributions to the advance of his subject are not easily visible, but Tuke records that he helped Carey-Foster with his 'bridge' at University College. Elderly physicists will today recall that this device may be employed to obtain electrostatic capacitance with the application of alternating potentials. And indeed the Bedford College Calendar for 1910 proudly announces that research will be possible for continuing graduates with both direct and alternating current apparatus. Tuke also records that Womack was one of the first scientists in England to apply the microscope to the study of metallic structure, and elsewhere[5] it was reported that his special subject was geometrical optics.

Presumably, the whole of then-known physics was covered by Womack but, of course, the numbers of undergraduates were small.

The 1910 College Calendar lists the Bedford graduates obtaining a BSc between 1878 (when University of London degrees were opened to women[6]) and 1905; altogether they number 66, of whom a mere 7 apparently received Physics degrees. These pioneering females were M Vickers (1888, 2nd Class Hons), E J Lewis (1891, 3rd Class Hons), G Black (1893, 3rd Class Hons), E E Humphrey (1897, 2nd Class Hons), J S Young (1901, 2nd Class Hons), A M Cooke (1904, 3rd Class Hons), and L M J Bellis (1905, 3rd Class Hons): I wonder what happened to these brave ladies.

The appointment of William Wilson as Professor of Physics in 1921 was an astonishing coup for the College. He was one of the lone intellectual giants probing the theoretical abstractions of quantum theory. The world boasted of Planck in Berlin, Sommerfeld in Munich, Bohr in Copenhagen, de Broglie in Paris and Wilson in London. While a lecturer at King's College, in 1915, he published his paper 'The quantum theory and line spectra'[7] where the equation $\int pdq = nh$ was written for the first time. At this point, he led the world. Bohr had proposed that atomic hydrogen might exist in quantised states, with definite energies and with angular momentum an integral multiple of $h/2\pi$. Wilson extended the rule to a wider variety of atomic systems. "The rule is applicable to Hamiltonian systems in which the coordinates are cyclic variables and states that the integral of each canonical momentum with respect to its coordinate over a cycle of its motion must be an integral multiple of h."[8] The Great War was on and, independently in 1916, Arnold Sommerfeld produced the same ideas which he amplified and exploited in his book *Atomic Structure and Spectral Lines*. In later years, undergraduates, in England at least, were to learn of the Wilson-Sommerfeld quantisation rules although today, only Sommerfeld is remembered in popular books on quantum theory[9]. This was an interesting example of the importance of priority in Science. Wilson must have complained to Sommerfeld that he had endowed his (Wilson's) earlier work with insufficient recognition as the Archives contain a letter from Sommerfeld acknowledging Wilson's claim and saying he will make amends in his next work.[10]

Wilson's arrival was trumpeted by his election as Fellow of the Royal Society in 1923, and he became the first holder of the Hildred Carlile Chair in Physics in 1927. (Incidentally, it appears he was a little embarrassed to belong to a Women's College as he declined to mention Bedford College in his *Who's Who* entry[11] emphasising only the Hildred Carlile Chair in the University of London–although Bedford must have paid his salary). With the aid of Maud Saltmarsh, who rose from lecturer to reader in the 1930s, and a number of demonstrators, Wilson ran the Department until 1944. During this time he produced his comprehensive work on *Theoretical Physics* in three volumes for Oxford University Press; I (1931) Mechanics and Heat; II (1933) Electromagnetism and Optics and III (1940) Relativity and Quantum Dynamics. In his preface he says the material was based on his lectures leaving little doubt that the ladies of the 20s and 30s were taught to the highest standards.

After glancing at a few pages of vol III of *Theoretical Physics*, my colleague, Alex Love, comments that he "found a little odd Wilson's use of fifth-dimensional Kaluza-Klein theory to suggest that the electron, positron and photon are components of a single particle distinguished by their momentum in the 5th dimension. Nonetheless, it is in the spirit of today's superstring theory (which also starts in higher dimensions) to have various particles in 4 dimensions appearing as components of a single state in the higher dimensional theory".

After retirement Wilson remained active in physics, but not always successfully, at his home in Essex. Letters to Wilson received from Planck, Einstein, Schrödinger, Louis de Broglie etc lie in the Archives but unfortunately not Wilson's. Not uniquely, he had difficulty with Heisenberg's uncertainty principle. A diplomatic letter from Max Born[12] starts "I enjoyed in particular the frankness with which you stigmatised some exaggerated pronouncements of extremists in 'modernity' as 'pure nonsense'. Yet I think you have fallen, to some degree, into the opposite extreme, to underrate the thoroughness of the conceptual upheaval produced by quantum theory. This is strikingly evident from your attempt to save the possibility of simultaneous determination of position and momentum by considering measurements in two consecutive time instances. Your example of a small flash does not work. You suggest a flash of light at some precisely defined place and instance. That means........"

And he got into difficulties in 1956 with Bertrand Russell. "You have entirely misunderstood my remark that there is no reason to suppose the Sun to be bright and warm. I thought the context had made it clear that I was using the words 'bright' and 'warm' as describing qualities of our sensations. What I was saying has been a commonplace ever since the time of Locke. When a statement by an author seems obviously absurd, it is well to read the passage over again to make sure that there has been no misunderstanding".[13]

His Royal Society memoir[14] records that "Wilson was a tall, broad-shouldered man with large brown moustaches.[15] He walked and moved with a striking and unusual manner, almost as if he were one of the three original mousquetaires of Dumas and about to draw and flourish a rapier. He conveyed an immense vitality and friendliness."

I met Wilson in the College gardens in 1963 as he approached his ninetieth year. He complained that he was having difficulties with the Royal Society over a paper he had just submitted for publication, and also of the iniquities of a pension with no inflation-proofing. But the fact remains that in his prime, William Wilson was a great man who brought renown to the College. It is the lot of a scientist to run for a while with the baton but then to pass it on to fresher runners.

The greatest star produced by the Department was Kathleen Lonsdale (née Yardley). She had been an extraordinary child with total memory recall–word for word of sermons etc. She was interviewed for Mathematics by Professor Hilton and entered Bedford at the age of sixteen. At some point, she changed to Physics; she later wrote: "I rather suspect that my affection for some of the Physics staff may have had a stronger influence on my decision than I would have admitted" and "Professor Wilson covered a tremendous amount of ground during the one year in which he taught me".[5] Lonsdale was one of only two students of Physics in her final year at Bedford College, but she headed the

University list in the honours BSc examination in 1922. This brought her to the attention of W H Bragg, and she jumped at the chance of a place in his research team at UCL and the Royal Institution, to work on crystal structures. Thus began an outstanding scientific career, which triumphed in her being one of the first two women to be elected to the Fellowship of the Royal Society. In 1927 she married Thomas Lonsdale and removed to Leeds. It appears she had been awarded the Amy Lady Tate scholarship by Bedford College for 1927–29, and she was granted £150 by the Royal Society to buy a new ionisation spectrometer and electroscope to set up in Leeds[5]. At the end of the War (1944) she applied for the newly vacant Hildred Carlile chair at Bedford, but withdrew from the election when she realised how much teaching would be required of her. But she had the Bedford spirit: in 1939, as the mother of three children she failed to register for civil defence duties and was fined £2. She refused to pay, and was sent to Holloway gaol for a month, where she complained of only being able to work for 7 hours a day on her physics.

The post-war period saw a healthy expansion of Physics. Again the existence of a chair at Bedford meant another outstanding theorist might be tempted away from King's. H T Flint was appointed to the Hildred Carlile chair in 1944. Richard Mansfield alerted me to his having been possibly on a par with Paul Dirac at Cambridge. And so I was intrigued when I read in Wilson's volume III[16] that "H T Flint arrives at Dirac's results by starting out with a new kind of geometry in which lengths and vectors are represented from the outset by matrices. His work is based on Kaluza's 5-dimensional relativity and he assumes the path of an electron, like that of a photon, to be a null geodesic in this continuum. An interesting feature of his work is the use he makes of Weyl's 'gauge' hypothesis. In fact Dirac's equation may be described as a 'gauging' equation." Everyone knows of Dirac's pre-eminence in quantum theory; Nobel prizewinner, etc. But had Flint really achieved as much? Had his lack of acclaim meant an injustice had been done? In fact, Flint's first paper was in exactly the same 1928 volume of the *Proceedings of the Royal Society*[17] as Dirac's and even has an earlier submission date! It is difficult material so I asked our resident polymath, Brian Cowan, for his opinion. He writes "Flint attacked the problem from the perspective of general relativity, incorporating the ideas of torsion and gauging, which had been introduced by and exploited by Eddington. The key points of the Dirac equation, viz the use of special relativity, and the appearance of internal degrees of freedom are not immediately apparent from the dense mathematics of Flint's paper. Wilson may have reinterpreted Flint's paper with the benefits of hindsight. I believe that historical justice has been done."

After Flint's arrival in Regent's Park, the leading journals *Nature, Phil Mag* and *Phys Rev* received a steady flow of papers with titles such as 'Energy in the Nuclear field'; 'Co-ordinate Operators in Quantum Mechanics', 'The Quantisation of Space and Time'. Unusually, he was not content to restrict himself to his mathematics; he simultaneously produced a classic textbook–Worsnop and Flint–on *Advanced Practical Physics*. In 1945, Flint recruited a young lady E M Williamson as demonstrator, and soon they were producing joint papers: 'Quantum Mechanics of the Electron' appeared in *Proc Roy Soc 1951*[18] adding to Williamson's earlier solo piece 'On de Broglie's Theory of the Photon'.[19] Margerie Williamson was later to distinguish herself as Principal of Royal Holloway College.

In the late forties, once Flint had settled, he set about building a modern department. In 1947 he appointed Victor Little, an expert in dielectrics, and Richard Mansfield from Queen Mary, an enthusiast for the commencing field of semiconductors. A couple of years later Leo Pincherle was recruited as a reader from the Radio and Signals Research Establishment (RSRE) at Malvern and in 1953 Nora Hill from Royal Holloway for research in liquids. Pincherle, a member of a well-known Italian academic family and a cousin of the novelist Alberto Moravia, who had had to flee from Mussolini before the war, was a prominent authority on electronic band structure theory of crystals. For a decade under Flint this team imparted a sound understanding of Physics to a generation of women while simultaneously advancing their researches. The results of Nora Hill's punctilious experiments in liquids are still being referred to today (1999) in the Science Citation Index. Mansfield's work centred on the electrical properties of semiconductors. Unlike metals, the resistance goes down with increasing temperatures, and he studied $Mg0$, Bi_20_3 and MoS_2 using temperatures up to 1700°C in a furnace purchased by the College. In 1954 he embarked on a study of III–V semi-conductors, starting with polycrystalline InSb prepared from scratch. He says he was "amazed" to discover that the product ($R\sigma$), of the Hall coefficient (R) and the conductivity (σ), was two orders of magnitude higher than that reported hitherto for any other semiconductor: a moment of elation that all scientists yearn for.

In the mid 1930s Harold Richardson, son of the Nobel prize winning O W Richardson at King's, tasted excellence as a demonstrator at Bedford College. He had been a research student with Rutherford at the Cavendish Laboratory in Cambridge, and at Bedford he continued his nuclear physics with studies on the beta decay of Radium C and Radium D. After spells as lecturer in Leeds and Liverpool, reader in Edinburgh and professor in Exeter, he was appointed to the Hildred Carlile chair. When he returned to Regent's Park in 1956 he brought with him his unique conception of a double-focusing prolate-spheroidal magnetic field beta ray spectrometer.

The 1960s were a great time for Physics. Radar had been crucial in the war against Germany; nuclear physics had won the war against Japan; nuclear fission and fusion power would solve man's energy needs; electronics held huge promise of new technologies; the Russian Sputnik presented a challenge in space; CERN was created to study the foundations of matter and indeed the universe; mastery of the world was feasible . . . . . On this surging whirlwind, universities boosted their science departments and physicists soared like golden eagles.

Naturally, Richardson played his part at Bedford. Robin Thomas from King's, Peter Rice-Evans and Noel Stewart (King's) were engaged as nuclear physicists, Stuart Owen-Jones (Aberystwyth) to work in ionospheric physics, Michael Hoare (Cambridge, Seattle and Göttingen) to theorize in molecular physics and Tom Taylor (Imperial) to embark on an experimental programme to develop a gas laser to operate in the infra red region of the spectrum. Good progress followed, SRC grants were won and a steady flow of publications resulted.

Vic Little had exploited his electronics in developing a spark chamber for detecting charged cosmic ray particles. But he became impressed with the remarkable precision offered by the Mössbauer effect and when he was appointed reader at Royal Holloway, I inherited his spark chamber. This led to a most enjoyable period for me; exploiting Russian ideas, I designed and built the first English neon/helium streamer chamber. When cosmic rays passed, a 240,000 volt Marx generator flashed and beautiful 25cm pink lines of streamers depicted the particle's tracks. Occasionally, extensive air showers (mainly muons) would occur with dozens of tracks appearing simultaneously: *son et lumière* indeed! This led to publications on streamer discharges, Lichtenberg figures, cosmic rays and even the search for fractionally-charged free quarks.

Michael Hoare was a tower of strength. Turning his back on conventional theory, he exploited interdisciplinary topics, particularly in the fields of amorphous solids, cluster physics and the statistics of energy-transfer. A dominant interest in statistical models and transport processes led him to unsuspected insights in the theory of special functions, difference calculus and distribution theory, and to solutions which could be implemented in 'everyday life' models, as equally in Physics. Disillusioned with the advent of the "cash-register university", (his words) he retired early in 1983 to devote himself to history and oriental studies.

Robin Thomas and I spent a decade on the study of nuclear energy levels but the heyday of university laboratory-based nuclear spectroscopy was past; we had to seek other avenues. Thomas pioneered the development of electronics for coincidence gamma ray measurements and successfully collaborated at the University Reactor at Silwood Park which allowed the study of neutron activated isotopes with short lifetimes.

Noel Stewart was the first member of the Department to engage in international research groups employing particle accelerators. His early work concerned neutron-proton collision cross-sections at AERE, Harwell. Subsequently, at the TRIUMF cyclotron in Vancouver he worked on polarised neutron experiments, clarifying the two-nucleon interaction from near the pi-meson threshold up to 525 MeV. Research at TRIUMF with longitudinally polarised proton beams and polarised hydrogen targets was continued in Los Alamos (USA) where he investigated the properties of dibaryon resonances below 1 GeV.

Under Richardson the Department expanded physically. With the Tuke Extension, a new third year laboratory was built together with a nuclear research laboratory, workshops and offices. Undergraduates in the teaching laboratories enjoyed the deceptively casual Vic Little, the graceful, lucid Nora Hill, the energetic Dick Mansfield and the thoughtful Robin Thomas. Mr Greenfield (I never learnt his Christian name), Frank Grimes and Wally Baldock worked valiantly as chief technicians. The admission of male undergraduates in 1965 initiated the remarkable switch from 100% women to about 20% in Physics. In the late sixties, two MSc courses were created: one, with Westfield College, on nuclear and elementary particle physics and another, with Chelsea College, on solid state physics. Both were successful, providing the students with the academic foundations for further PhD research, often in the department.

A significant change in Richardson's time was the changeover to the course unit system. Instead of undergraduates sitting 5 papers (Properties of Matter, Heat, Light, Electricity and Magnetism and Atomic Physics) common to all Colleges, each department became responsible for setting its own papers. I recall the sheer agony of sitting through the meetings where we discussed all the Bedford papers; fortunately Leo Pincherle appeared able to spot all flaws and answer all the questions!

Academic departments are notorious for their power struggles and personality clashes; an industry of campus novels has flourished as a result. A rumpus that arose in Geography and required resolution at the highest College levels led to the recommendation that all departments set up a Board with its own constitution. An important feature was that in the event of serious disputes, Board minutes would be available to the College Council for scrutiny. At the time, in Physics, there was a little dissension arising out of arcane allocations of very limited resources for research in the later days of Richardson's tenure, and the department jumped at the opportunity to write a constitution. All matters were to be discussed at regular meetings by the whole lecturing staff, minutes taken and votes recorded by a Board Secretary elected from the staff. Any member could raise any issue but the Head of Department had the ultimate responsibility, for decisions. This constitution proved a boon.

In 1973 Richardson retired. He had been an erudite scholar and a gentleman of the old school: undergraduates could regularly set their timepieces at 9.20am on his arrival for the 9.00am lecture. His obituary in *The Times* 1982 recalled the vision of his tall, spare figure bicycling in Regent's Park. Roland Dobbs was then appointed Hildred Carlile Professor. A student at University College, lecturer at Queen Mary and research fellow at Cambridge, in 1964 he had created the Physics Department at the inception of the new University of Lancaster. Earlier in 1973 Dobbs had been a member of the Science Research Council's visitation at Bedford to assess its research effort and one may conclude he liked what he saw. He planned to transfer a sizeable fraction of his low temperature research from Lancaster and brought with him Michael Lea as research associate. It transpired that there was appropriate space in the Tuke building for his main dilution refrigerator, but there was discussion at the time on whether vibrations from the Bakerloo underground trains beneath Regent's Park would limit the ultimate low temperatures attainable. In April 1976 in Regent's Park, Lea achieved the lowest temperature ever in London of 13 millikelvin and went on to study acoustic impedance in ^{3}He and ^{4}He. He was appointed lecturer in 1977.

In his inaugural lecture on quantum crystals and fluids Dobbs explained the excitements of superfluid helium 3. In practice, a move into this research would entail new millikelvin facilities (Kelvin temperatures are above the absolute zero at -273°C); which would require considerable space and financial support. Dobbs' first proposal, to set up a national low temperature centre at the Rutherford Laboratory, was killed by committee politics; instead a collaboration with Professor Douglas Brewer at Sussex University was advocated. This came to pass and a nuclear refrigerator was built at Sussex with generous SRC support (£182,000 between 1977 and 1986). John Saunders joined as a Royal Society fellow and soon ultrasonic measurements on the B phase of helium 3 were revealing a fascinating new phenomenon. This was difficult to interpret and was a controversial topic for theorists for many years until K Nagai et al showed it was due to a combination of the $J_z = O,\pm 2$ components of the $J = 1^-$ collective mode in 1996!

The arrival of Dobbs brought a brisker managerial style to the department–a new vitality. Suddenly, significant College monies became available for experiments and the staff were not merely encouraged but expected to raise grants from the Science Research Council. Mansfield began a collaboration with Lea on magnetic freeze-out in n-type indium antimonide at millikelvin temperatures; Nora Hill published both theoretical and experimental studies on the microwave properties of dielectric liquids; and Owen-Jones travelled the World on field trips with Professor Monica Cole (Geography) in connection with his development of remote sensing (satellite imaging) techniques to study the utilisation of land and analysis of terrain.

Between 1969 and 1974 I had spent the summers at CERN, Geneva, but my flirtation with particles was killed by B Gregory, the Director General. I had proposed to conduct a one-man (with spectrometer) experiment to search for low energy photons at the intersecting proton storage rings, only to be told that CERN could only countenance work by the large teams of physicists, because of the huge investment involved. (Already the European enthusiasm for bureaucracy prevailed!) Since my Chicago days at the Argonne National Laboratory, I had been enchanted by positrons–especially the question (still unresolved in 1999) of whether they fell upwards or downwards in the earth's gravitational field. There were many more realistic investigations to be made in the field of positron annihilation and I resolved to devote myself to this subject. With keen postgraduates I proceeded to design and construct a low-energy positron beam for probing sub-surface crystalline properties in thin films.

It was sad that in this period our intellectual rock and gentle extraordinary friend, Leo Pincherle, died. In 1977 Owen-Jones resigned to join the Welsh Industrial and Maritime Museum in Cardiff, Thomas took up a post in the University of East Anglia and Nora Hill unfortunately had to resign through ill-health in 1980. However, the Department was much strengthened by the recruitment of Brian Cowan as a young lecturer from Sussex to join the Low Temperature group in 1978 and by a theorist, Alex Love, also from Sussex.

Cowan's original interest was in nuclear magnetic resonance studies of helium-3 films on carbon. In Regent's Park he created a helium cryostat with which he extended his measurements to mylar and boron nitride substrates. His intellectual curiosity then drove him to contemplate and develop the theory of nmr in two dimensions, which led to new insights into three dimensions. These required further tests with new sensitive electronics devised in conjunction with Alan Betts in the electronics workshop. Incidentally, Cowan introduced me to exfoliated graphite, a material with a huge specific area and, due to a happy chance in the band structure of carbon, this led me to a unique series of experiments on positronium formation.

Alex Love had started in the early 1970s in particle theory, exploiting the renormalisation group to derive observable consequences from electroweak and QCD theory. He extended this technique to study phase transitions at finite temperature and density in the early universe in Grand Unified Theories, thence to Kaluza-Klein cosmology, especially the question of time-independence of the fine structure constant and, once in higher dimensions, it was natural to progress into super string theory.

By 1980 the clouds were gathering over the lake in Queen Mary's Garden; the roses would soon become a memory. In that year Sir Peter Swinnerton-Dyer reported on the future of the University of London and as a result the Senate established Subject Area Review Committees. The SARC for Physical Sciences, chaired by Sir Sam Edwards, propounded the view that a viable physics department should contain at least 20 staff and 200 undergraduates. At Bedford we did not approach this. At the same time the College was in financial difficulties; something had to be done.

The first subject-based proposal was that Bedford physics should join University College. The condensed matter group would complement their particle and astrophysics strengths. This was discussed at an inter-departmental meeting but foundered, partly because the necessary cryogenic facilities would have presented severe space problems in Gower Street, and partly because it was uncertain whether the whole department would transfer. The Departmental Board wished to remain undivided. The first realistic proposal resulted in our Principal Dorothy Wedderburn, and the Principal of King's signing a letter of intent that our two Colleges should merge. This had many merits and as a department we visited King's for round table discussions. However, it transpired that King's Physics favoured instead the idea of a merger with Queen Elizabeth's Physics with its expertise in image analysis; a decision that has been wondered at! Other King's departments strongly opposed the Colleges' merger and it came to nothing.

The problem was solved by a visit to the College of the Vice Chancellor, Randolph Quirk, in the Lent term 1982. He recommended the University developing two strong units outside the main bloc of IC, UCL, KCL and LSE at the centre. To the east would be QMW and to the west, Bedford would join Royal Holloway College at Egham to become RHBNC. Many staff were dismayed at the prospect of leaving central London. However the University Senate had declared it could only support science on a maximum of five sites, and the logic of the fifth site being RHBNC was overwhelming. And so we packed our books and our apparatus and embarked for Surrey, to be pleased with our welcome and our new circumstances.

How does one measure a Department? Today we are familiar with Research Assessment Exercises, league tables and Teaching Quality Audits. The idea of a group of scientists working naturally and harmoniously together, idiosyncratically teaching and encouraging undergraduates to relish their subject, trying out wild research ideas, delighting in discoveries made elsewhere, mastering difficult theoretical concepts for their own sake, fostering individual practice in their supervision of postgraduates; these notions seem so old fashioned, quaint relics of the past that we left behind in Regent's Park. Today we conform.

And to finish, on a personal level, what I appreciated at Bedford was the Collegiate spirit; we were making contributions to a whole academic community. This was evident in the conversation in the elegant Senior Common Room used by virtually all staff in all subjects and in the Joint Faculty meetings. Surrounded by the great trees and glorious gardens, the Physics Department seemed a niche in Paradise. I have only gratitude to express to the College, my brilliant and dedicated colleagues and especially my enthusiastic band of postgraduates for the opportunity to spend a life as a man of Science within the embrace of the Physics Department. I was fortunate to have made that chance arrival in 1956.

References

1 Margaret Tuke, *A History of Bedford College for Women 1849–1937*, Oxford University Press, 1939.

2 J W Fox (UCL), priv commun, 19.2.99.

3 Oliver Lodge, *Biographical Memoirs of the Royal Society, and Past years–an autobiography*, Hodder & Stoughton, London, 1981.

4 *Proc Phys Soc*, 1876, 1,113; 119.

5 K Lonsdale, *Biographical Memoirs of the Royal Society*, p449, 1975.

6 Liz Bennett, *Centenary Lectures* (1886-1986), Ed: Moreton Moore, RHBNC, 1988.

7 W Wilson, *Phil Mag* 29 795, 1915; 31 156, 1916.

8 L Schiff, *Quantum Mechanics*, p4 McGraw Hill, New York, 1955.

9 J P McEvoy and O Zarate, *Introducing Quantum Theory*, Icon Books Cambridge, 1996.

10 A Sommerfeld, Archive letters PP36/32/1 and PP36/32/9.

11 W Wilson, *Who Was Who*, 1961–70.

12 M Born, Archive letter PP 36/8/3, 1952.

13 B Russell, Archive letter PP 36/28/1, 1956.

14 W Wilson, *Biographical Memoirs of the Royal Society*, 1966.

15 In the tradition of Frederick Womack.

16 W Wilson, *Theoretical Physics*, III, Oxford University Press, 1940.

17 H T Flint, *Proc Roy Soc A*, 117 625 (1928) and 117 630, 1928.

18 H T Flint and E M Williamson, *Proc Roy Soc*, 1951.

19 E M Williamson, *Phil Mag* 39 314, 1949.

Acknowledgements

I would like to express my gratitude to Dr J W Fox (formerly UCL), Professor Dick Mansfield, Professor Roland Dobbs, Dr Michael Hoare, Professor Brian Cowan, Professor Alex Love, Dr Noel Stewart, Professor Michael Lea, Dr Paul Finch, Mrs Val Leach and Mrs Jennifer Ayres for their great help.

Chapter 15

Physiology

Maureen Young

The Foundation

Physiology was taught as a suitable discipline for women at Bedford College as early as 1882; this was eight years after instruction in the subject had begun at the London School of Medicine for Women, at the Royal Free Hospital. Physiological laboratories were opened for the Royal Free Medical School in 1898 at the new site in Hunter Street. Physiology at Bedford College had to wait for laboratories until 1913, when their new buildings were completed in Regent's Park.[1]

Dr J S Edkins, who had the distinction of discovering gastrin (which stimulates the production of acid by the stomach), was the first Head of Department and held the title of Professor. He was very active and the attainments of the department were considerable at this time. Eighty per cent of women students of London University studying Physiology separately from the full medical curriculum did so in his department at Bedford. His courses were also recognised for the 2nd MB, which allowed successful students to proceed to a medical school after graduation if they wished; the failure rate was only 4%. After graduation these women also provided all the teaching staff (excepting for the professors) in the Physiology Department at Bedford itself, as well as nearly all at the London School of Medicine for Women, and at King's College of Household and Social Sciences. About a dozen women graduates also taught in other Medical Schools where women had not yet been admitted as students! One, working overseas, became a Professor of Physiology at a medical school in India.

The experimental science of Physiology had developed in the middle of the 19th century, and it is recorded that only a few women undertook research and published their findings in the subject at the end of the nineteenth century and the beginning of the 20th century.[2] The Physiological Society, founded in 1876, started as a dining club consisting entirely of men; women were not admitted until 1915, although the admission met with relatively little resistance. The 1920s were halcyon days when the rights of women in education–and to contribute intellectually–were on a firm basis in England, at last. However, it was still not always easy for women to obtain a suitable laboratory teaching and research position, as some antagonism towards them remained.

Professor I Mary Pickford, MSc, DSc, MRCS, LRCP, FRS, one of the most distinguished women who studied Physiology at Bedford, had to challenge this hurdle when she graduated in 1925. She was not to be deterred and her enthusiasm, persistence, hard work and courage took her through qualifying in medicine, to a very fruitful research fellowship at Cambridge and finally to a lectureship in the medical school at Edinburgh in 1939.[3] From this start, Dr Pickford subsequently became Reader in 1952 and a Professor in 1966. She was the first woman to hold such a title in a department of a medical school in Scotland, and combined active research with a heavy teaching load. Her research centred on the neuroendocrine role of the hypothalamus and posterior pituitary gland requiring her gift of excellent surgical technique for this work. She was elected a Fellow of the Royal Society in 1966. During her long career Professor Pickford had experience of teaching both small and large classes of students. She considered the latter poor value for the students because they did not receive adequate attention, besides making additional work for the staff because the classes have to be duplicated. She has written to the present author quite recently in praise of the small department at Bedford: "In my opinion BC was first rate and its staff excellent; there was real contact and understanding". Professor Pickford is now in her 97th year and has lost none of her enthusiasms–or her sense of humour. She recalls with a smile the times when she was mistaken for her filmstar namesake, the US heroine of the silent picture era, and received large bouquets of flowers and dishes of fruit in her hotel rooms, when visiting the USA!

Dr Nora Edkins (née Tweedy) DSc had graduated in Physiology at Bedford College and had helped Professor Edkins in his teaching and research. After his first wife died, they married. After Professor Edkins' death, Dr Nora Edkins as Reader carried on her husband's teaching tradition and was Head of the Department from 1931–47. (It is recorded that, as a demonstrator in 1914, her salary was £120 pa.) Dr Edkins had a very active life both as a teacher and investigator; she was skilled in experimental physiology, her research being primarily concerned with absorptive mechanisms in the stomach. Three FRS's supported her application for the Readership. The following quotation from their opinions fully describes the atmosphere which was experienced by myself and fellow students when we studied in the 1930s: "The department of physiology has been markedly successful in the enthusiasm of the students for their work, the good degrees obtained by them and the keenness they have displayed to carry on their studies and to proceed to research when their undergraduate days are over".

Dr Edkins was most generous with her time for everyone, both in and out of the laboratory; there were invitations to watch the Boat Race from her flat overlooking the Thames at Hammersmith Bridge, and strawberry teas in the summer. She always made us feel that she believed in us absolutely and this, together with her realism and her dry sense of humour, prepared us well for the welcome many of us received in medical schools, other university departments, and in research institutes after the coming World War.

Her elder sister May Tweedy had also trained in physiology and medicine and taught at Bedford College at the beginning of the century.

Her joint work on Vitamin D with her future husband Dr Edward Mellanby (afterwards Sir Edward) has contributed to the eradication of the deformities produced by rickets, once seen regularly on the streets of northern towns and in other urban areas at the end of the nineteenth and in the early decades of the twentieth century. Lady Mellanby and Dr Nora Edkins were regular attendees at Meetings of the Physiological Society at which new research was reported. At the Meeting of the Society held at Bedford College in November 1971, Dr Nora Edkins chaired the meeting for those items being presented by the current members of staff.

World War II

Bedford College was a guest of Cambridge University for six years during this war, and Physiology teaching continued in the Cambridge University Physiological Laboratory on the Downing Street site. Professor E D Adrian, (later Lord Adrian), gave the staff a sizeable room on the second floor as an office, and the practical classes took place in the main labs when they were not needed by Cambridge students. Student numbers did not fall and the standard of teaching remained high. It was an exciting and hospitable time with many staff and students taking advantage of being able to attend Cambridge University lectures. Sir Joseph Barcroft, whose work on foetal physiology led to the world wide flowering of neonatal intensive care was still working though retired, and both he and Dr W Feldberg were always ready for a good discussion–the latter especially enjoyed his afternoon tea in the Bedford College room. Professor R A McCance and Dr Elsie Widdowson of the department of Experimental Medicine were also a great stimulus, and had just completed their studies of experimental nutrition, which were so important in helping the government to determine our food rationing during and immediately after the war. Optimism concerning the outcome of the war enabled the College to move back to its Regent's Park home site in London, in the summer of 1944. This was before hostilities had ceased–and there was much cleaning of benches and apparatus to be done in the empty laboratories.

Early Post-War changes and personalities

With the expansion of science as a whole within the University of London, Dr Edkins and the College successfully negotiated for the headship of the Physiological Department at Bedford College to be recognised as a University Established Chair. As she herself was nearing retirement age Margaret Murray DSc was appointed to fill the chair. Professor Murray was already well known for her research work and as a teacher, and held the post as Professor and Head of Department from 1947–1959. She herself had been a student in the Department and was a lecturer whilst Dr Edkins was acting as Head. The partnership of these two very different personalities was most successful. Dr Edkins' appreciation of her younger colleague and her own devotion to Physiology was expressed by the help which she gave by continuing with her physiological teaching in the Department during the years up to 1959, more than six years after her own retirement.

Professor Murray was a born teacher and most interested in the biochemical aspect of physiology and of nutrition; her lectures were meticulously prepared and always contained the latest information. Her standards were very high and she had a great capacity to make us think–she was a little intimidating until one discovered her delightfully dry sense of humour and her heart of gold. Professor Murray's main research centred around calcium metabolism and the influence of diet on dental enamel, especially the fluoride content of water: we all remember being 'roped in' to produce large volumes of saliva by chewing candle wax. Her research was highly respected and as students the number of scientific visitors to the laboratory who sought her advice impressed us.

Amongst these visitors was the striking figure of Lady Mellanby who had been a student and on the staff of the Bedford Physiology Department. She was mentioned earlier as Dr Nora Edkins' elder sister. She was renowned for the joint work with her husband Sir Edward Mellanby on the fat-soluble vitamins A & D.[4] Another was a student from the Chemistry Department, Rosalind Pitt-Rivers, who later was to discover the thyroid hormone T4, in Sir Charles Harington's department, for which she was elected FRS in 1954.[5] Professor Murray's capacity for work was enormous (in spite of her very poor sight which must have been a great strain, but about which she never complained), and she published as many as four papers in some years.[6] Her wide interest and quick wit made her a lively contributor at scientific meetings and an invaluable member on University committees; she was an original member of the Board of Studies in Biochemistry when the University of London set this up.

During this time there was close co-operation with the physiology departments of the medical schools at Board of Studies meetings. This included the provision of special research training for brighter medical students who had passed the 2nd MB BS examination and could study for a further year to take an Intercalated BSc in Physiology. Professor Murray ran an intercollegiate course on the chemical analytical techniques available for examining human blood. Her course entitled 'Methods in Blood Biochemistry' was much sought after by such students from other London Medical Schools. One of these students remarked that the course at Bedford College gave one the feeling of a long personal tutorial, such was the extreme generosity of thought and time given by everyone in the Department.

To help in the application of chemistry to physiological problems, in which she had specialised, Professor Murray appointed D Dudley Cheesman as a lecturer in 1948. Dr Cheesman had graduated in Chemistry from Imperial College in 1937 and had had considerable training in Physical Chemistry, which she thought an important aspect. He had been 'stuck' in Sweden for most of the war. With Professor Murray's support and Dr Cheesman's quick grasp of Biochemistry he was soon able to teach students up to the level of the required curriculum for a Special Degree in Biochemistry. The basic curriculum required for University of London Special Degrees are determined by the appropriate Board of Studies in the subject made up chiefly by Heads of Departments. After Professor Murray's retirement, Professor W F Widdas, MB BS, BSc, PhD, DSc, succeeded her in the Established Chair of Physiology and was the appointed Board of Studies member.

As the Special Degree in Biochemistry had become a viable University Degree Course for the direct entry of new applicants from Schools, a separate Department of Biochemistry seemed to be justified.

At this time, students taking Special Degrees in Physiology were encouraged to study Physics and Chemistry during the first year. More Chemistry and Biochemistry were studied during the second year, whilst the third year was devoted to special aspects of Physiology to supplement those of the first two years, which covered physiology of all the bodily systems. There was no difficulty in finding suitable instruction in the Department of Physics for the first year course, or in the Department of Chemistry for a longer two-year course, and therefore a separated Biochemistry Department could easily provide for the biochemical teaching required by physiological students.

On the initiative of Professor Widdas, the College and University agreed that Biochemistry should become a separate department with Dr Cheesman as Head and representing the Department on the University Board of Studies in Biochemistry. Although the University did not agree to an Established Chair in Biochemistry, Dr Cheesman's standing was high and he quickly became eligible for a personal chair with the title of Professor. This he held from 1964 until he retired in 1982. The Department of Biochemistry at Bedford was small but effective; its success was largely due to Professor Cheesman's encyclopaedic knowledge of his subject, his stimulating lectures and the support of the staff and technicians. His research covered many aspects of protein properties including their ability to form monolayers when spread on water (applying his early training in physical chemistry, which had influenced Professor Murray in first appointing him). His wider interests included classics, literature, music and a working knowledge of several European languages. He endeared himself to his colleagues on the teaching staff by his humanity and good company. They may be quoted as calling him an "academic in the best sense of the word–a scholar as well as a scientist".[7]

Memories of Physiological Teaching, 1931–1959

Between 1931 and 1959 teaching in the Department was little different from that in the London medical schools: Dr Edkins gave nearly all the physiological systems lectures, while Professor Murray gave those on endocrinology, nutrition and other biochemical aspects of the subject. The practical classes, histology, biochemistry and animal work were always extremely well prepared by the inestimable Mr Guildersleeves, and always 'worked'. The classes never exceeded 30 in number and there was always one demonstrator to 15 students. Dr Gertrude Glock, who later had a distinguished career in Biochemistry at the Middlesex Hospital Medical School, and Dr Grace Eggleton from University College, were two whom we remember well and, later, the tall Dalene Lewis who had graduated from the Department.

Development of Opportunities after Graduating

Both teaching and research posts in biological subjects were still relatively scarce for women during the 1930s in spite of the declining male antagonism to them as scientists. But this was to change rapidly at the end of the decade. As World War II approached many opportunities arose, especially in laboratories related to medicine. For instance, Blood Banks were set up in preparation for war casualties and two of us from the Bedford Department graduating at this time were lucky enough to find ourselves helping in these. We trained in the Epidemiology laboratory at University College in London where blood from soldiers in the London barracks was collected and grouped, for storage. It was interesting to observe the response of these men to the sight of their own blood. During the war we served at the MRC emergency blood bank in south-west London. There were many exciting nights when the bombs seemed to be destined for us and we dived for a place under a very solid table in the common room. The sound of shrapnel whizzing down as we fire-watched in the streets is unforgettable. Barbara Dodd remained in the service until 1955 as part of a group pioneering the diagnosis and treatment of haemolytic disease of the newborn. She was invited to join the Department of Forensic Medicine at the London

Hospital Medical School where she applied her knowledge of blood grouping and other genetic markers to medico-legal problems and co-authoring a book *Blood Group Serology* which ran to six editions. She obtained a DSc and was given a personal chair eight years before retiring. Barbara Cheek enlisted in the army during the war and remained in Malaya to help with the intricate problems of food and feeding carried out by the new Division of Nutrition, at the restored Institute of Medical Research in Kuala Lumpur.

With the end of the war, more opportunities were opened up for women physiologists; all medical schools which had not previously admitted them were now obliged to take 15% of women students and this led to the concept that there should also be more women on the teaching staffs. Three of us from Bedford who had graduated before the war were given this opportunity and served for upwards of 35 years. Dr Majorie Nutt, employed her teaching and administrative expertise at Birmingham University Medical School; Dr Anne Cole became a demonstrator in Physiology at King's College in London and subsequently taught for 18 years as a lecturer at the University of Bristol, changing to Biochemistry as a senior lecturer for another 18 years. She was the initiator and major editor of the first textbook on Biochemistry for dental students, *Biochemistry and Oral Biology*. The author (of the present article) had worked at the South West London blood bank during the war with doctors from St Thomas's Hospital, contributing to the development of the acid-citrate solution which improved blood storage and was used exclusively for some years after the war. After demonstrating at Bedford College for 5 years she was appointed lecturer in the Physiology Department at St Thomas's Medical School in 1946.

The post-war atmosphere was very exciting with enthusiastic doctors and students returning from the war keen to get their lives going again. The present author helped to initiate research in the Department of Paediatrics and from 1964–82 had a small unit of Perinatal Physiology in the new academic department of Obstetrics and Gynaecology. She was given a personal chair of the University in 1976. This unit was the first of its kind in Britain and undertook an experimental study of foetal nutrition because of the increasing awareness that there could be malnutrition of the foetus *in utero*. Pearl Scott (another Physiology graduate) continued in the tradition of Bedford providing teaching staff for the Royal Free School of Medicine and was given a personal University chair.

Opportunities for research assistants in academic departments and research institutes also increased rapidly after the war. I remember two of the bright students who graduated during the war, Betty Wilkinson and Christine Walsham, who went to work with Professor McCance and Dr Widdowson at the Department of Experimental Medicine in Cambridge. I remember, too, Jean Hanson as a very diligent student who obtained a First Class degree and later made a major contribution to our understanding of muscle contraction, with H E Huxley, for which she was elected FRS in 1967. After graduating she first worked at the Strangeways laboratory in Cambridge on wound healing. In 1948 she was a founder member of the NARC Biophysics Research laboratory at King's College in London and, with the newly available technology designed to study the structure of biological tissues, she began her studies on muscle which continued until her early death at the age of 54 years. She was one of that breed of women scientists who display boundless energy and enthusiasm coupled with a great capacity for clear thinking. She also had a considerable administrative aptitude besides her research imagination.[8]

The End of Bedford College for Women and the Entry of Men Students

Following the Robbins' Report and the general acceptance that all University courses should be open to adequately qualified girls and boys on an equal footing, it was represented that the women-only Colleges should reciprocate by admitting a proportion of men students. Thus, the Council approved a supplemental charter in 1963 and men students were admitted to Bedford College from 1965.

The Physiology Department received applications from very able candidates who for one reason or another just failed to obtain a place in a medical school. Several of these matured rapidly as University students and were readily accepted for medicine after graduation in Physiology. One became an ENT specialist in a London teaching hospital. Besides those going on to medicine, many have found employment of their University training in hospital posts involving clinical investigation of the cardiovascular, nervous, genito-urinary and other bodily systems of patients. Yet others have been taken up by pharmaceutical firms or by teaching departments in Universities.

As an example John Laycock, the son of Mrs Laycock, for many years a stalwart teacher in the Bedford College French Department, is now working in the Physiology Department at Charing Cross Hospital Medical School after graduating from the Department. He has become a recognised expert on the clinical problems related to neuro-endocrinology. Mary Forsling, who did a period of postgraduate study to obtain the PhD degree in Physiology (1967), is now Professor of Neuro-Endocrinology in the Division of Women's and Children's Health at St Thomas's Hospital Medical School (now associated with King's College). Besides teaching and research Mary Forsling has combined her career with marriage and the raising of her family–an active life not unknown amongst professional academic women. Another postgraduate student Jennifer Remfry went on to study Veterinary Medicine. With this dual background she was able to make significant and helpful contributions in drafting the Guidance Notes for new licensees during the debates leading up to the Animals (Scientific Procedures) Act of 1986. David West, another graduate, stayed on to study for a PhD degree with Mrs Beth Hilton. He is currently doing neurological research work at the Institute of Ophthalmology in London. There are many others such as Alex Thomson who after graduating at Bedford took a higher degree at Oxford, and is now Professor of Physiology at the Royal Free School of Medicine. Peter Sutton, another graduate, is now working on the mechanisms of cardiac arrhythmia in the human heart at University College Hospital, London. Besides carrying out research important to medicine these Physiology graduates are also teaching future doctors.

Amongst the men who qualified with the Special Degree in Physiology, special mention may be made of Dr G F Baker who made significant contributions to the study of the membrane transport of glucose and obtained his PhD in 1973. He continued to help in this research with David Basketter (now in a Pharmaceutical firm) and with others. A research project was part of the final year students' practical work, the significance of which was only analysed and published jointly after Professor Widdas had retired and had time to collate the results on his home computer. This was while caring for his terminally ill wife who died of Parkinson's Disease and cancer in 1983, two years after his retirement.

During the two decades 1960–1981 Professor Widdas had continued the tradition of giving thoroughly up-to-date and friendly teaching of Physiology at Bedford College. The College provided well-trained physiologists (both men and women) who were most welcome in the rapidly expanding medical scientific scene. They met an expanded demand in university medical schools, in hospital clinical measurement laboratories and in the pharmaceutical industry. The Professor of Medicine at King's College Medical School in Denmark Hill, (Professor John Anderson MA, MD, FRCP), had appointed a full-time Physiologist to the medical unit at the hospital. Although not a Bedford graduate he appreciated how teaching kept one up-to-date and sent him to Bedford College to help in teaching duties one day each week. The teaching was also well supported by Dr George Darlow, Dr G H Wright and by Mrs Beth Hilton, several of whom had been appointed by Professor Murray. An assistant lecturer Alan Hall BSc (a graduate from UCL) was appointed on the advice of Sir Andrew Huxley and Dr D Noble FRS. Mr Hall proved to be an enthusiastic teacher particularly of the nervous system. He and Dr Darlow gave a popular one year course on the anatomical structure and physiological functional mechanism of the brain to the first year Psychology students, many of whom had very little background knowledge in the basic sciences of Physics, Chemistry and Biology.

Professor Widdas combined an active life teaching, helping his postgraduate helpers with research, while heavily engaged in College and University administrative affairs. He served as University Dean of the Faculty of Science both on the Academic Council and University Senate up to his retirement in 1981. These duties included work on the Management Committee of the newly established Marine Biological Laboratory at Millport on the Isle of Cumbrae in the Firth of Clyde. This had been adumbrated by the Bedford College Professor of Zoology (Professor Millott) and was a joint venture with the University of Glasgow.

In College administration Professor Widdas was Chairman of the Board of Examiners responsible for combining all the Course Unit examination results from both science and arts Departmental Courses, which became available to students for the new University Course Unit Degrees. In non-academic matters, the men students–far fewer than those in larger colleges–had acquired an aptitude for football, having been coached and trained by Mr Grimes (a Chief Technician) to a high standard. Mr Grimes' coaching was so effective that the Bedford College football team won the University cup in one of the years in which Professor Widdas was the Club's Academic President. After the death of his wife, Professor Widdas as Emeritus Professor of Physiology has continued in part-time physiological research with his former PhD student Dr G F Baker, whose expertise lies in the same field of Physiology. More than forty publications have been made and reprints of the more important of these have been deposited in the Bedford Library for reference by any future research personnel who may be interested.

Progressive Tightening of University Funding and Joining with Royal Holloway College

During these two decades (1960–1980) the University as a whole had witnessed a progressive tightening of University funding, which reflected severely on the College and its departments. When Professor Widdas retired in 1981, the refilling of the University Established Chair in Physiology was deferred due to the current financial difficulties and a shift in University policy. The new University policy was to encourage Physiology teaching at Queen Mary College (which previously had none) as the University was trying to combine the independent medical schools with one or other of its multi-faculty Colleges. It was envisaged that Physiology at Queen Mary College would facilitate its amalgamation with the Medical School of St Bartholomew's Hospital and that of the London Hospital.

The co-operation of the administration of Bedford College with these wider University aspirations coincided with still further reductions in Government funding so that many of the University's smaller colleges were obliged to seek mergers with the larger colleges, to pool and reduce overhead expenditure. For Bedford College the Crown lease of the Regent's Park site would involve a costly renewal, so a merger with Royal Holloway was negotiated. The established Chair in Physiology was never filled and teaching in Physiology was left to the remaining, hard-pressed staff, initially headed by Mrs Hilton, then by Dr G Darlow, who had Dr Wright and Mr A Hall BSc to help. Dr Baker also helped at this time. For some four years teaching was divided between the Regent's Park site and Royal Holloway more than twenty miles away at Egham. Administrative support at this time was to be given to Physiology as a 'sub-department' of Psychology, but in effect the staff received little or no support from that Department or from College Administration, and there was little time for research. Events during the early 1980s, up to the official merger in July 1985 and immediately afterwards, now seem somewhat confused. However, during this phase there was further rationalisation of University Physiological resources. Dr Olof Lippold, vacating his Readership post at UCL, was invited to head the physiological teaching from a Human Physiology standpoint. Again there was little support for Dr Lippold and little opportunity for research. Initially some of his lectures were given on buses transferring students from the Regent's Park site to Egham. A few years later the Moore Laboratory was vacated for Business Studies and Drama. The teaching for the Special Degree in Physiology was discontinued, as was that for the Special Degree in Chemistry.

These two courses required extensive laboratory space, apparatus, and technical staff. They were thus more expensive per student. In the climate of cost effectiveness, degrees of less value to the health and future prosperity of the country were substituted, some of which have attained high repute in their own field.

However, during all this time leading up to the merger, the Physiology degree results compared most favourably, in numbers and degree category, with those in the other biological science subjects, and Physiology graduates continued to fill numerous posts in hospitals and universities throughout the country. Naturally those who had enrolled to study for a Special Degree in Physiology in 1984 thought they had been badly treated when this was not provided. The Zoology Department then came partly to the rescue, since half of their students took Physiology, and so the Department became a sub-department of Zoology. This continued until all biological departments became combined in a new Department of Biological Sciences.

This unhappy situation is abundantly clear from a careful reading of the final 'Report of the Council 1984–1985'.[9] Thus, although the Council of Bedford College has been required to make an annual report of the work of the College ever since the granting of a Royal Charter in 1909, in making the 1984–1985 report, all Departments receive mention in the 'Section 2: Academic' except for Physiology. The preamble to this last report (see page 2) describes the setting up of a committee to advise on the Department of Psychology with its sub-department of Human Physiology. The Department of Latin headed by a Reader has a short separate report as required by the Royal Charter but the full report on the Department of Psychology makes no mention of a sub-department of Human Physiology. The Established Chair of 1947 was in Physiology and the invitation to Dr O C J Lippold MD to organise teaching in Human Physiology was envisaged to take effect after the merger. Professor Widdas had retired when all the above decisions were made by academics without the benefit of advice from any medically qualified scientist.

Physiology in the Future

Professor Widdas has told the present author that he considered the combined site at Egham might have had potentialities as one of the multi-faculty medical Colleges of the University of London, if Physiology and other medically-related sciences had been developed. Large teaching hospitals thrive within a locality that has a large resident population. In this respect Egham was well placed for the outer migration of medical teaching into the growing population of the Surrey commuter belt. Many Universities outside London find it rewarding to have a medical faculty associated with a teaching hospital. Nottingham has degree courses for nurses, and there the postgraduate courses in Sports Medicine are linked to the Orthopaedic Department of the hospital. Such opportunities for scientific work of direct application to national health will surely appeal to both men and women students of the twenty-first century. Meanwhile former staff and students of Bedford College may exult in the knowledge that opportunities for training in Physiology were presented to women for more than one hundred years, and that enduring benefits to the nation's health have resulted from their contributions to teaching and research.

The Tennyson family whose long association with the Council of Bedford College, (cf Tennyson Hall), has been greatly appreciated may feel deep satisfaction from the achievements of the women physiological graduates from Bedford. Their many research contributions have helped in the introduction of new medical and nutritional practices, which have largely succeeded in eradicating nutritional diseases, and thus, carrying out the first of the far-reaching philosophical needs enunciated by their forefather Alfred Lord Tennyson (1809–1892).

Ring out old shapes of foul disease;
Ring out the narrowing lust for gold;
Ring out the thousand wars of old,
Ring in the thousand years of peace.

'Phoenix will arise again from the ashes'

The main block of Bedford College in Regent's Park was badly hit by bombs in World War II but was rebuilt and operating again within four years. This was largely due to the persistence of the then Secretary, Miss Olive Monkhouse. Similarly, perhaps, the Department of Physiology at Royal Holloway and Bedford New College may one day be refurbished in suitable laboratories, with its Established University Chair of Physiology, first awarded to Bedford College in 1947.

Acknowledgements

With grateful thanks to Professor W F Widdas, Miss M Pakenham-Walsh and Dr M M Harris for helpful suggestions during the preparation of this manuscript.

References

1 M J Tuke (1939) *A History of Bedford College for Women*, 1849–1937, Oxford University Press.

2 E M Tansey (1993) 'To dine with ladies smelling of dog. A brief history of women and the Physiological Society'. In *Women Physiologists*, p3. Portland Press, London.

3 M Phillips (1993) 'Mary Pickford FRS (1902–)'. In *Women Physiologists*, p41. Portland Press.

4 E M Tansey (1993) 'The Tweedy sisters–May Mellanby (1882–1978) and Nora Edkins (1890–1977)'. In *Women Physiologists*, p10.

5 J R Tata (1994) 'Rosalind Pitt-Rivers (1907–1999)'. *Biographical Memoirs of the Royal Society*, vol 39: 325–348.

6 M Young (1993) 'M M M Murray (1899–1974)'. In *Women Physiologists*, p111.

7 J N Prebble (2000) 'Professor D F Cheesman', chapter 2 in this volume.

8 S Page (1993) 'Jean Hanson (1919–1973)'. In Women Physiologists, p107.

9 Bedford College, University of London. Report of the Council 1984–1985.

10.Achievements of Physiology Department, in Secretary's Office of Bedford College (found 1977).

All correspondence relating to the preparation of this article is housed in the Bedford College Archives at Royal Holloway.

Chapter 16

Psychology

Elizabeth R Valentine

Psychology was taught at Bedford College from shortly after its foundation, although a separate department was not formed until after World War II. It was taught both in the Department of Philosophy and in the Training Department. The development of Psychology as an experimental subject was relatively late in Britain in comparison with Germany and America, but Bedford College was one of the first places to establish a psychological laboratory. This was largely due to Beatrice Edgell, appointed Lecturer in Philosophy in 1897, who became the first woman Professor of Psychology in Britain in 1927.

Early days, 1849–1897

When the College opened in 1849, the Department of Mental and Moral Science, out of which Psychology subsequently developed, was headed by Frank Newman, the eccentric younger brother of the future cardinal, John Henry. One of Mrs Reid's early supporters, he also headed Political Economy and Ancient History. The Department of Moral Philosophy was headed by the Rev A J Scott, who was also responsible for English Literature. Both men were popular lecturers. However, the first lectures in Psychology were given by Alexander Bain, who succeeded Scott as Head of the Department of Moral Philosophy in 1851. Although he spent most of his life in Aberdeen, he was at that time living in London and working on *The Senses and the Intellect*, published in 1855, which became the established textbook in Psychology for the next half century. A transitional figure, he anticipated many seminal ideas[1] and would be better known if he had written in as accessible a style as his contemporary, William James. One of his several legacies was the journal *Mind*, less chastely philosophical then than it is now, which he established in 1876 and supported financially for its first sixteen years.

An account of Bain's dealings with Bedford College and the parallel progress on his book is given in his autobiography:

> "In the end of September [1851] I returned to London; having previously made an engagement to give lectures in the college for ladies in Bedford Square. I undertook two courses...physical and political geography...I was also expected to give a course of moral philosophy–that is to say, psychology; but the course was not accepted that year.[2] It was at the end of 1851 that I resolved upon the final draft of the *Psychology*, which was put in two parts as ultimately arranged...All the days that I had no lecturing, from the beginning of 1852 onwards, I devoted to composition.[3] In the Winter Session of 1852–3 I resumed the geography course at Bedford College, and also, for the first time, conducted a class in psychology, making use of my MS, so far as it went.[4] By the end of this year [1853] the *Intellect* was nearly finished. At the close of that term [Summer, 1854], I resigned the connexion with Bedford College, going in the recess to Scotland."[5]

So we know that Bain lectured in Psychology at the College and also have some idea of the content of those lectures. It is of interest that the writing of his book coincides so closely with the Bedford period.

In 1874 Bedford College moved to 8–9 York Place, Baker Street. York Place was the upper part of Baker Street between Dorset Street and the Marylebone Road. The University of London opened its degrees to women in 1878, being the first British university to do so. By the early 1880s Bedford students were gaining London University BA, BSc and Masters degrees. The first BA Honours degree in Mental and Moral Science (Third Class), awarded to a Bedford College student, was achieved in 1884 by Maria E Findlay (who however managed Second Class Honours in German).

The first edition of the Bedford College Calendar, of 1888, advertised courses taught by Miss Frances A Mason (Head of the Department of Mental and Moral Science from 1886–88) on logic, psychology and ethics; and a class in mental and moral science for the BA examination. Indeed, the College timetable for 1903–4 shows lectures on mental and moral science on Tuesdays and Fridays at 11.05, and lectures on psychology in the Training Department on Tuesdays at 2 and Thursdays at 12.30.[6]

The Training Department, one of the first three centres in England for training women secondary school teachers, had been founded in 1891, the year prior to John Muirhead's appointment as Head of the Department of Mental and Moral Science. The Report of Council for 1894–95 records, as a development in the Training Course during that session, that each student "has made a psychological study of one pupil in a practising school".[7] Certainly by 1895–96 (and probably before) Professor Muirhead was lecturing on psychology, logic and ethics in the Training Department.

1897 was an extremely important year for Psychology. In Cambridge Dr W H R Rivers was appointed University Lecturer in Experimental Psychology and the Physiology of the Special Senses and set up, within the physiological laboratory, a small psychological laboratory. He subsequently became famous for his part in the pioneering anthropological expedition to the Torres Straits, his research on the physiology of the senses–notably vision–for which he was awarded a Fellowship of the Royal Society in 1908, and his humane treatment of World War I shell-shock victims, notably Siegfried Sassoon (an episode brought back to public attention by Pat Barker's *The Regeneration Trilogy*, 1991). But in London, too, psychological laboratories were being set up. University College founded one that session, Rivers being one of the people who was hired to teach. At Bedford College John Muirhead resigned his Professorship in Mental and Moral Science and the post was advertised. At the first attempt no appointment was made; it was resolved to postpone the decision and admit a late application from Miss Beatrice Edgell, a recent graduate, who subsequently became the successful candidate.[8]

In 1897 a second Bedford College student, Nancy M Catty, had been awarded a Third Class degree in Mental and Moral Science; but things were about to change. Nine of the next sixteen degrees awarded to students from the Department up to the end of World War I (and 70% of those awarded up to 1912, including the first one in Psychology) were First Class. Thus the anecdote reported in the Bedford College Old Students' Association Magazine is justified: '"What did Miss X…get?", an old Bedford student once asked in my hearing. "Get?", was the indignant reply, "why a first of course. Miss Edgell's students always do."'[9] Beatrice Edgell took up her appointment as Lecturer in Philosophy and Head of the Department of Mental and Moral Science in January 1898. Thus began the special development of Psychology under Miss Edgell, to which Dame Margaret Tuke refers in her history of the College.[10] This involved the building up of a laboratory, developing the teaching and status of the subject in the College and the University, as well as substantial contributions to research.[11]

Beatrice Edgell, 1898-1933

In her first session, Beatrice Edgell stepped into Professor Muirhead's shoes and was lecturing in psychology, logic and ethics in the Training Department. The 1899 Calendar advertises an Elementary course on Psychology in the Training Department, given by Miss B Edgell, for which the recommended textbook was William James's *Textbook*; together with a more advanced course in Psychology given to final year students only, for which the syllabus was as follows: Elements and development of mind; the senses–perception, imagery, thinking; feeling and its expression; attention; volition. The recommended books were James Sully's *Outline of Psychology*, William James's *Textbook* and James Ward's article on psychology in *Encyclopaedia Brittanica.*

The following year Beatrice Edgell was away in Würzburg, pursuing her PhD under Külpe. On her return she set about building up a laboratory.

> "In 1900, when I returned from Bavaria, when I was anxious to start experimental psychology at Bedford College, little was known about it. But the College authorities gave me every facility, and a grant for equipment [£5]. True, I had not much accommodation; all one's equipment had to be stowed away into a cupboard after demonstrations. But it was a start."[12]

Margaret McFarlane relates that

> "under primitive conditions a laboratory came into being in a top back room in the Baker Street building. Here with a minimum of apparatus and much improvisation we learned the method of devising experiments and evaluating their results. Many a time an irreverent reference to the dark room as the 'bathroom' brought a smiling protest from her!"[13]

Beatrice Edgell herself referred to this era as "the days of makeshift and poverty", remarking that they were by no means the least happy.

The British Psychological Society was founded in 1901 and the *British Journal of Psychology* first published in 1904. It was not long before members of the Bedford Department were contributing papers to meetings of the Society, and publishing their work in the journal. Beatrice Edgell, who was later to become the first woman President of the Society (in 1929), presented a paper on time judgment to the fifth meeting, in 1903, and two to a meeting in 1905. The first, entitled 'Experiments on association', was published in *Child Study* in 1913, where it jostles with advertisements for baby foods (Benger's, Horlicks and Bournville cocoa) and gas fires ("a boon to mothers"); and formed the basis of a lecture given to the British Academy Education Section in Norwich in 1935, reported in *The Queen*. The second paper, with

W Legge Symes (who taught Physiology to medical students at St Mary's Hospital and subsequently became Professor of Physiology at the Royal Veterinary College) on 'The Wheatstone-Hipp chronoscope. Its adjustments, accuracy and control' was published in the *British Journal of Psychology* the following year (1906) and was still being cited thirty years later. This piece of equipment is, amongst others, now on loan to the Science Museum. Other research was being conducted by Gladys Martyn (a physical training instructor as well as psychologist) on mental fatigue. Several of the publications which arose from this work give the authors' affiliation as the Physiological Laboratory of the University of London. This "island of academic research amidst a sea of administrators"[14] was a central facility located in the Imperial Institute at South Kensington, which housed the central administration of the University. It consisted of a suite of five rooms, including two devoted to the physiology of the special senses (inclusive of physiological psychology).

In 1906 the Department of Mental and Moral Science was renamed the Department of Philosophy and Psychology, one step along the path from arts to science and the protracted separation of Psychology from Philosophy. The College Calendar for 1910 lists two main courses for BSc Psychology.

1. Psychology, for which the syllabus was: Scope and methods of psychology; relation of psychology to other sciences and to philosophy; analysis of consciousness; fundamental processes; detailed treatment of the phenomena of cognition, feeling and will.
2. Laboratory course, for which the syllabus was: Qualitative analysis of sensation; determination of psychical standards and units; psychophysical law and methods; conditions of normal perception and illusion; time relations and mental state, including reaction, memory and time consciousness; physiological correlates of feeling and action; construction and use of psychological apparatus.

In 1912 the first BA Honours degree in *Psychology* (First Class) was gained by a Bedford College student, Blanche A Lunniss. Another sign of the increasing recognition of Psychology as a scientific discipline was the award by the London County Council of a grant for the development of intercollegiate work in a science subject, which the College allocated to a course on Experimental Psychology taught by Beatrice Edgell. A report of some of the work carried out was published.[15] It included not only introspective studies in the tradition of the Würzburg psychologists but also experiments on mice learning mazes (which were scrubbed regularly with carbolic soap to prevent scent cues) and rats solving puzzle boxes.

On 4th July 1913, the Regent's Park buildings were opened by Queen Mary Psychology was among the departments for which a laboratory was provided. "The Department of Psychology, where research on rats was in progress, was especially interesting to Her Majesty."[16] "When the new college opened in Regent's Park in 1913 psychology had become such an important branch of study that it had its own department under the direction of Miss Edgell, and so popular had the subject become, mainly through the attraction of Miss Edgell's lectures, that the psychology lecture room was crowded to capacity."[17] "Since the move to Regent's Park in 1913, however, Professor Edgell has been installed in a laboratory which is the equal to any in London."[18]

In 1914 Victoria Hazlitt, who had graduated in 1910 with a first class BA in Philosophy, with Experimental Psychology as a special subject, was appointed Assistant in Experimental Psychology. She was to play an important role in the teaching of Psychology in the College and the University. During World War I, she courageously undertook the teaching of practical classes at King's College, during William Brown's absence on active service, and at Chelsea College, at a time when evening meetings in city centres were a virtual impossibility.[19] In the Bedford Department, she introduced new courses on psychological doctrines involved in mental tests, and colour vision.

In 1916 Olive A Wheeler was awarded a DSc in Psychology (equivalent to a PhD: PhDs weren't introduced until 1921). The title of her thesis was 'Anthropomorphism and science: a study of the development of ejective cognition in the individual and the race. The basis of comparative psychology'. She was later created a Dame in recognition of her services to education. Victoria Hazlitt was awarded her MA for a study of the acquisition of motor habits in 1917.

1920 is the first year in which Psychology courses are listed under Science as well as Arts in the College Calendar and the first BSc degrees in Psychology were awarded to Bedford College students. Psychology was represented, in the person of C S Myers, on the Board of Management of the new journal *Discovery* which dealt with recent advances in scientific knowledge–another sign of the increasing recognition of Psychology as a scientific discipline. In 1921 Psychology was established as an independent section of the British Association; several Heads of the Bedford Department served as its President.

Beatrice Edgell was granted a year's leave of absence for the session 1921–22. There is a charming letter from her to the Council: "I find it difficult to offer any very adequate reason for making the request–I am not in failing health and I have no great enterprise on foot, nonetheless I feel that a year free from lecturing would be very welcome and should mean greater freshness in my work afterward, and thus ultimately benefit the department…it would be good to recruit after twenty years fairly strenuous lecturing…I hope the Council will not think the request unreasonable. If for any reason it is an untimely one, I will gladly withdraw it."[20] Her teaching was carried out by three temporary visiting lecturers: Lucy Fildes, a graduate of the Department, who taught a course on the Psychology of mentally defective children; Frederic Bartlett, who lectured on Psychology and primitive culture;[21] and G E Moore, who lectured on Fundamental conceptions of psychology with special reference to Ward's *Psychological Principles*.

In 1924 Victoria Hazlitt was granted leave of absence because she "desired leisure to complete an important piece of research work". This was undoubtedly her book on *Ability*, which includes an account of her pioneering experiments on the selection of university students, published in 1926 and for which she was awarded a DLit.

Beatrice Edgell notes that by 1922 a divergence of interest between philosophers and psychologists was becoming apparent by the one-sided attendance at sessions of the British Psychological Society. "Some of the older members with a background in philosophy felt that some of the papers read lacked breadth of outlook and were trivial in character, even though they purported to have some immediate practical relevance."[22] In June 1926 she raised the issue of the separation of the department into two separate Departments of Philosophy and Psychology, at the Academic Board. There was some discussion but the Board felt unable to come to any decision without more time to consider the matter, which was deferred to the next meeting. The issue was in fact not satisfactorily resolved for almost another twenty years.

There was also an on-going saga concerning the roof of the North Science Block, in which Psychology was housed. Three Departments were contenders for the space. Botany had erected an experimental greenhouse on it, to the annoyance of Psychology, who wanted to develop an animal house there (partly because the closure of the Training Department demanded some redirection of activities). Zoology wanted it to keep pigeons and rabbits. Arguments were presented by Psychology for the removal of the greenhouse. The real reason was that it thwarted Departmental development, but others were adduced in addition: it caused frequent interruption to the work of the attendant attached to the Department of Psychology and rendered ineffectual the room for 'quiet study', whose only windows looked on to the roof. For the meantime, Psychology had to make do with the conversion of a cellar into a dark room, as testified by a number of memoranda: "The cellar is now cleared of all material objects, except dirt";[23] "I have asked a man from the Electric Production Co to call next Tuesday between 11 and 12 o'clock with regard to the possibility of a speaking tube from your department to the cellar. May I know some time before this exactly what it is you require?"[24]

It is clear from another memo of about the same period that laboratory equipment was being ordered from France. Beatrice Edgell to Miss Monkhouse: "What does your financial mind say to this?... He is the man who makes apparatus for Professor Piéron (Sorbonne)". A document dating from 1927 may be relevant, which lists apparatus to measure the subject's ability to discriminate active from passive touch; difference in temperature; position of body; colour; a large tuning fork to measure the lowest note that is audible; and an O K 300 Galton whistle. There were some problems in ascertaining whether or not the items were likely to attract customs duty. Victoria Hazlitt wrote the following memo to Miss Monkhouse: "The Customs Officer at Great Portland Street advised our saying 'To the best of our knowledge they are not dutiable'. It is quite impossible to tell for certain from the lists so we have the right to benefit of the doubt. In haste. VH." Miss Monkhouse replied sharply, in a note written at the bottom of the page, "Are they or are they not?"[25]

In 1927 the title of Professor of Psychology was conferred on Beatrice Edgell. A woman professor was a newsworthy item: she was certainly one of the earliest woman professors of Psychology and the first in Britain. Announcements of her appointment appeared in the *Morning Post, Sphere, Daily Chronicle, Times, Evening Standard, Yorkshire Post, Glasgow Herald, Westminster Gazette, Times Educational Supplement, Nature* and *The Lady*.

> "A career of patient and persistent endeavour underlies the appointment of Miss Beatrice Edgell, which was announced in yesterday's *Westminster Gazette*. When Miss Edgell went to Bedford College 30 years ago as lecturer in psychology she was pioneering on entirely new academic ground...From that small beginning has grown the comprehensive psychology department, with its splendidly equipped laboratories and lecture rooms, under Professor Edgell's control. Red cross nurses from the most remote states of central and eastern Europe go to Miss Edgell for a finishing course in conjunction with social science."[26]

At the end of 1929 the Department moved into the new Tuke building. The buildings were opened in June 1931 by Queen Mary; Victoria Hazlitt was amongst those presented to her. At the Department of Psychology there were exhibits to illustrate:

> (1) The study of learning (a) by sheer repetition: records showing improvement in writing with the left hand; (b) by practical trial with effort to gain control through understanding, illustrated by work on an old-fashioned snuff-box puzzle, and a complication box. (2) The study of child psychology: (a) Tests for children between eighteen months and five years. As a result of studies at the Merrill-Palmer Nursery School (Detroit) a carefully graded series of the activities normal for children of different ages between eighteen months and six years had been selected. The material on view was used in connection with this series. Some of the children at the Foundling Site Nursery School had worked with this material and their results suggested that nursery school life increases manipulative control and practical ability. (b) Tests for Older Children. A selection of non-verbal tests of intelligence and of practical ability were on view.[27]

Then disaster struck. On 19th April, 1932 Victoria Hazlitt was found burned to death in a passageway by the side of her house on North Hill, Highgate. The following announcement appeared in the *Evening News*:

> "A remarkable story of a woman who was seen burning like a 'human bonfire' in her garden was told at a Hornsey inquest to-day on Dr Victoria Henrietta Hazlett [sic], a lecturer in psychology at London University and Bedford Women's College, Regent's Park. A verdict of death from burns due to ignition of her clothing was returned. It was stated that Dr Hazlett was in the habit of cleaning clothing with petrol in the garden. Mr Harry Martin Terry, a stockbroker of Wembley Park, Middlesex, said he climbed over the wall of Dr Hazlett's garden and found her charred body in a small passageway. Joseph Leonard Collins, a gardener at the house adjoining that of Dr Hazlett, said they saw smoke and flames coming from Dr Hazlett's garden, but attached no importance to it, as they thought rubbish was being burned in

a bonfire. The coroner remarked that a mystery in the case was how the petrol was being used by Dr Hazlett at the time it became ignited. He said it had been known for sparks to come from artificial silk stockings when rubbed. Dr Pritchard said that he had tried experiments by dropping a china bowl on concrete, but no sparks resulted. It was stated that Dr Hazlett was cleaning a green dress of pure silk at the time. The nearest fire was in the house. She smoked cigarettes only when in company."[28] There was the usual fatuous comment from a psychologist, reported in the *Daily Mail*: "She might have thought, when the flames leaped about her, that she would conserve her energy for putting out the fire rather than scream for help. A strong-willed and highly trained psychologist might think that."[29]

Victoria Hazlitt's death robbed London psychology of a scholar with a keen interest in fundamental psychological problems, at the height of her career, and also seriously depleted the ranks of its teachers.

Three weeks later Beatrice Edgell asked permission to relinquish her post. A meeting was held to consider the arrangements for the Department following her retirement. The issue was whether or not it should be divided into separate Departments of Philosophy and Psychology. A factor which favoured such a division was the difference in scope of the two subjects but as usual the bottom line was cost. The committee concluded that "the department could not be separated without extra expenditure which might prevent the Council from doing what they thought essential in other departments." Thus, it was "agreed that though for academic reasons the committee were as a whole in favour of dividing the department, it would be better to keep the present arrangement of one department until at least the end of the present quinquennium".[30]

Susan Stebbing, Alec Mace and World War II, 1933–1943

Susan Stebbing, the eminent philosopher and logician, was appointed Professor of Philosophy and Head of Department in 1933, a post which she held until her premature death in 1943. Alec Mace was appointed Reader in Psychology, coming from St Andrews where he had set up a laboratory. He was assisted first by Annie Jenkin and later by Madeleine Folley (née Kerr); between them they taught all the Psychology courses. Mace's interests ranged widely from research on incentives undertaken for the Industrial Health Research Board, to lectures on character and temperament, and aesthetics. He also lectured on the history of Psychology and wrote a book on *The Psychology of Study* published by Penguin. Annie Jenkin's research interest was imagery and learning, the topic of her MA and PhD. Madeleine Kerr's PhD was on 'Emotional fluctuations in women'; in addition she published articles on temperamental tests applied to twins, children's drawings, and the validity of the mosaic test.

With the outbreak of war in 1939, Bedford College was evacuated to Newnham College, Cambridge. Sylvia Shimmin relates that it took her about a fortnight to find Alec Mace in order to register when she went up in 1943, since the Department was 'of no fixed abode'. The Regent's Park buildings were occupied by all manner of people. In May 1941 the College received damage by enemy action, as a result of which the North Science Block was "estimated a total loss". It was just as well for Psychology that it had moved out of it (albeit more than a decade before)!

On 28th January 1944 Council finally agreed to the division of the Department into two separate Departments of Philosophy and Psychology. H B Acton was appointed to the Chair of Philosophy. October 1st saw the institution of an independent Department of Psychology, with Mace as Head but not Professor. On 27th October Council received a letter from him informing them that he had been offered the Chair of Psychology at Birkbeck College, which he intended to accept, subject to satisfactory arrangements being made for the management of the Bedford Department. He agreed to hold the fort in the interim, working in both places simultaneously: Council was reminded that he had been doing so for the previous two years anyway! On 15th December, Council finally agreed to the Academic Board's recommendation that a Chair should replace the Readership in Psychology "on the grounds of the anticipated growth in the Department and the unusual scope offered for such development by the existence in one College of Departments of Sociology, Physiology and Philosophy". Finance Committee did not oppose this but warned Council "that it is with the greatest hesitation that they support the recommendation for any new commitments at a time when the College is faced with so heavy a deficit on the year's working". It was agreed to apply to the University for a Chair in Psychology to take effect from 21st October 1945.

Denys Harding, 1945-68

Thus it was that Denys Harding was appointed Professor and Head of the Department of Psychology in 1945. Although the author of two books on Psychology, he was better known for his work in literary criticism, and particularly for his association with Leavis's *Scrutiny*, of which he was an early co-editor and in which he published several early articles.

Initially he and Madeleine Folley taught the whole syllabus between them, students additionally attending inter-collegiate lectures. It is hardly surprising to find a letter of 1946[31] asking for a full-time Assistant in Psychology. In 1947 there was a request from Psychology for help with service teaching for the Social Studies Certificate: the staff could cope with the lectures but not the written work which Mrs Wootton (subsequently Dame Barbara) wished the students to do. During this period many staff appointments were made, the staff increasing from 2 in 1945 to 9 in 1968, the graduates from 1 to 17.

Following the war period, the quadrangle was filled with building materials. War-damaged internal walls in the Psychology Department were rebuilt and window frames in the Tuke building readjusted. Further repairs necessitated by war damage were carried out in 1948 and redecoration following the BBC's tenancy of the Tuke building. A celebration to mark completion of the reconstruction of war-damaged buildings was held in October 1952.

In July 1946 the Department requested that the former slaughter house in the grounds of The Holme be used as a play room for child observation for final year students. The proposal was rejected by the architect on the grounds of difficulties in drainage and heating. The Report of Council for 1952–53 drew attention to the needs of the Department of Psychology: "The development of promising lines of research of a precise kind which balance the work in social psychology already well established under Professor Harding's guidance, requires laboratory space which is not available in the Department. It would be a grave error to limit this research, and as a temporary alleviation makeshift arrangements in a converted basement room at The Holme have had to be planned for next session."[32]

On 2nd March 1960 the Queen Mother opened the new extensions to the Tuke Building. Her Majesty visited the new laboratories in the Departments of Physics, Psychology, Biochemistry and Chemistry and watched a number of experiments in progress, talking with staff and students in each department. (She also opened the Reid Hall extension, the Students' Union, and had tea in Herringham Hall.)

Brian Foss, 1968–85

Brian Foss succeeded to the Chair and Headship of the Department of Psychology in 1968. He was president of the British Psychological Society from 1972–74 and of the Psychology Section of the British Association for the Advancement of Science. He served as General Psychology Editor for Penguin for ten years, his own particular interests being imitation (the subject of his inaugural lecture) and infant development (he edited four volumes on the *Determinants of Infant Behaviour*). The personal interest which he took in students created a very happy atmosphere in the Department.[33]

During this period student numbers doubled with virtually no increase in staff numbers. Since then both have doubled. Staff appointments reflected a broadening of interests to include the psychology of politics, the media, psychophysiology and computing. A distinctive feature was the connection with medical education. The Todd report (1968) had recommended the linking of Medical Schools with Universities, and Bedford College became associated with St Mary's Hospital, Paddington. This led to several joint appointments and the teaching of intercalated medical students. In 1975 a postgraduate course in Clinical Psychology was recorded as a priority, if resources become available. This was finally achieved twenty-two years later with the launching of a clinical doctorate degree programme in 1997.

Funded research projects during this period included studies of neonatal behaviour undertaken at the perinatal research unit at St Mary's, Paddington; the effects of noise on information storage; optimal cage size for laboratory rodents; individual differences in the 'post-lunch dip' in efficiency; determinants of sleep depth in humans; and communication in the deaf.

In 1969 the Department was described to an intending visitor as "crammed in with a shoehorn". A Development Appeal was launched in 1978, and in 1982 the Department expanded into the Wolfson laboratory. However, with increasing financial stringencies, the argument for reorganisation of the University–the amalgamation of smaller colleges into larger units–became increasingly powerful. After several false starts and protracted negotiations, the merger of Bedford College with Royal Holloway College finally took place in 1985. It is to Brian Foss's credit that the move to Egham, Surrey, was accomplished in good spirit. Now, in its new location, and under the headship of Michael Eysenck, the Department continues to strive to combine research success with student care.

Acknowledgements

I should like to thank especially Sophie Badham, the College Archivist, and Dr Linna Bentley, for their help, guidance, interest and enthusiasm. I am grateful to Susan May for expert assistance with the reproduction of photographic materials and to the British Psychological Society for permission to reproduce from the *British Journal of Psychology*, 23 (1933).

References

1 E Valentine, 'Alexander Bain', in N Sheehy, A J Chapman & W Conroy, eds, *Biographical Dictionary of Psychology* (London: Routledge, 1997), pp34–36.

2 Alexander Bain, *Autobiography* (London: Longmans, Green, & Co, 1904), p229.

3 *Ibid*, p223.

4 *Ibid*, p234.

5 *Ibid*, p240.

6 See Linna Bentley, *Educating Women. A Pictorial History of Bedford College University of London 1849–1985* (Surrey: Alma Publishers in conjunction with Royal Holloway & Bedford New College, 1991), p27.

7 *Bedford College, London. Report of the Council*, 1894–95 (Bedford College Archives, RHBNC, GB113/1), p14.

8 Minutes of Council, Vol V, 1893–98, p304 (Bedford College Archives, RHBNC, GB110/1/5).

9 *Bedford College Old Students' Association*, Report No 20, July 1933 (Bedford College Archives, RHBNC, AS903/1), p9.

10 Margaret Tuke, *A History of Bedford College for Women 1849–1937* (Oxford: Oxford University Press, 1939), p252.

11 One of the people to contact me after the publication of my earlier, illustrated *Psychology at Bedford College London, 1849–1985* (Royal Holloway, University of London, 1997), was Jennifer Sherwood (neé Allard), who read History at Bedford College 1955-58. Her great great grandfather, Joseph Higginson, was Beatrice Edgell's great uncle.

12 *Westminster Gazette*, 11th February, 1927.

13 *Bedford College Old Students' Association*, 1948–49, (Bedford College Archives, RHBNC, AS903/2), p6.

14 N Harte, *The University of London, 1836–1986* (London: The Athlone Press Ltd, 1986), p178.

15 B. Edgell (Ed) *Psychological studies from the Psychological Laboratory, Bedford College for Women, University of London*. (London: University of London Press, 1915).

16 Margaret Tuke, *A History of Bedford College for Women 1849–1937* (Oxford: Oxford University Press, 1939), p216.

17 *Bedford College Old Students' Association*, report no 20, July 1933 (Bedford College Archives, RHBNC, AS903/1), p9.

18 *Sphere*, 26th February, 1927.

19 Beatrice Edgell, 'The British Psychological Society', *British Journal of Psychology*, 37 (1947), p128.

20 Personal file for Beatrice Edgell (Bedford College Archives, RHBNC, AR150/D263).

21 This series of lectures was later published: F C Bartlett, *Psychology and primitive culture* (Cambridge: Cambridge University Press, 1923).

22 Beatrice Edgell, 'The British Psychological Society', *British Journal of Psychology*, 37 (1947), p122.

23 Beatrice Edgell, Memorandum, 1922, Philosophy Department: Correspondence and Papers 1900–84 (Bedford College Archives, RHBNC, AR332/6/1-4).

24 Memorandum from Olive Monkhouse, College Secretary, to Beatrice Edgell, 1926 (Bedford College Archives, RHBNC, AR332/6/1–4).

25 The documents referred to in this section are all in the Departmental Papers (Bedford College Archives, RHBNC, AR332/6/1–4).

26 *Westminster Gazette*, 11th February, 1927.

27 *Annual Report of Council*, 1930-31 (Bedford College Archives, RHBNC, GB113/1).

28 *Evening News*, 23rd April, 1932.

29 *Daily Mail*, 21st April, 1932.

30 Minutes of Council, Vol XXIII (Bedford College Archives, RHBNC, GB110/1/23), p213–214.

31 Psychology Department papers 1923–77 (Bedford College Archives, RHBNC, AR334/10/1–5).

32 *Bedford College for Women. Report of the Council*, 1952–53 (Bedford College Archives, RHBNC, GB113/2), p27.

33 Brian Foss died on December 23rd 1997. Appropriately, a fund to support deserving students in financial need has been established in his memory.

Physics

26. Oliver Lodge on his honeymoon in 1877 in Heidelberg.

27. Frederick Womack: long-serving Head of the Physics Department. The spectrometer setting is curious.

28. The new Physics laboratory in Baker Street opened by Empress Frederick in 1891.

29. William Wilson: intellectual giant.

30. Kathleen Lonsdale: brilliant postgraduate.

31. William Wilson lecturing at Cambridge.

32. H T Flint: profound thinker.

33. Harold Richardson : ardent nuclear physicist.

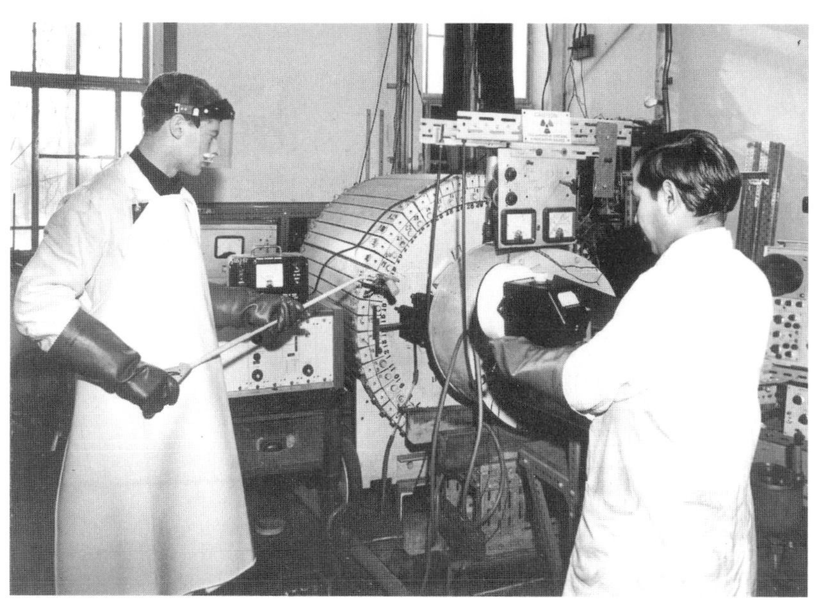

34. Richardson's beta ray spectrometer.

35. Laboratory scene, 1970.

36. *Physics staff and final year undergraduates in 1973. Standing, from left, 2nd Noel Stewart, 3rd Stuart Owen-Jones, 4th Michael Hoare, 5th Tom Taylor, 19th Robin Thomas. Sitting, from left, 2nd Nora Hill, 4th Dick Mansfield, 6th Harold Richardson, 7th Leo Pincherle.*

37. A student snapshot of Peter Rice-Evans in the Physics theatre in Acland.

38. Roland Dobbs with Her Majesty Queen Elizabeth The Queen Mother, Regent's Park 1984.

Psychology

39. Beatrice Edgell, 1871–1948.

40. Victoria Hazlitt, 1887–1932. Courtesy of British Psychological Association

A New Beginning

41. *Signing the partnership agreement with Royal Holloway College, 1982. From left, Dr Roy Miller, Principal of Royal Holloway College 1982-85, Sir Owen Saunders, Chairman of the Royal Holloway College Council, Professor Dorothy Wedderburn, Principal of Bedford College 1981-85 and of RHBNC 1985-90, and Sir Cyril Clarke, Chairman of the Bedford College Council.*

42. *The Fawcett Lecture on 17 February 1999. Professor Dorothy Wedderburn, Principal BC 1981–85, RHBNC 1985–90; Baroness Warnock, College Visitor 1997–2000, and Professor Norman Gowar, Principal RHBNC 1990–99.*

43. *Honorary Fellows Awards Ceremony on 5 May 1999. From left: Miss Patricia Brown, Member of Bedford and RHBNC Councils; Professor Janet Finch CBE, Vice-Chancellor of Keele University, and Mrs Sarah Tyacke CB, Keeper of Public Records and Chief Executive, Public Record Office.*

44. *Honorary Degrees Awards Ceremony on 15 July 1999. Professor Alec Smith, Honorary Fellow and former Head of Geology Department is being presented to HRH The Princess Royal.*

45. *Winifred Procter (née Nash), who graduated in 1933, was the oldest attendee at the 'Down Memory Lane Reunion'. There are multiple family connections with Bedford College: Winifred's sister Mattie worked in the Secretary's Office, her niece Helen Clay worked in the Library, and Helen's daughter Hazel was an Organ Scholar at RHBNC. However, Winifred could not know at the time of this photograph that her other niece Vivian Bone's husband, Drummond, would become the new Principal of the College in 2000.*

46(a)

46(b)

46(c)

46(d)

46 (a)–(d). 'Down Memory Lane' Reunion at Regent's Park on 23 May 1999. A good time was had by all.

47. 'Women and Brainpower' Conference 4–6 July 1999. Front row from left: Dr Lyndal Roper, History Department, RHBNC; Dr Amanda Vickery, History Department RHBNC; Professor Penelope Corfield (Conference Organiser), History Department, BC and RHBNC; Dr Yasodka Shanmugasundaram, Vice-Chancellor, Mother Theresa Women's University, India, and Professor Dorothy Wedderburn, Principal BC 1981–85, RHBNC 1985–90.

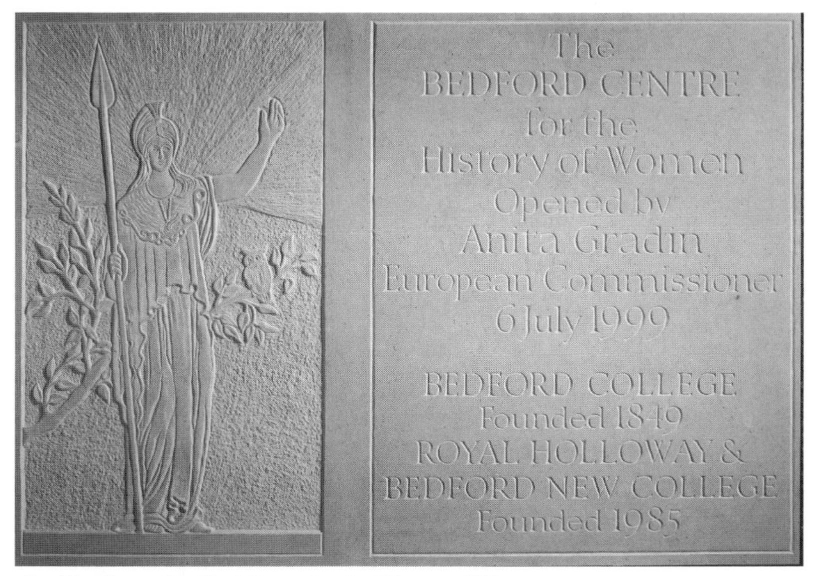

48. *The plaque. Bedford Centre for the History of Women.*

49. *Opening of the Bedford Centre for the History of Women on 6 July 1999. Baroness Helena Kennedy QC (left) who delivered the Public Lecture 'Women & Brainpower' with Dr Amanda Vickery, History Department, RHBNC.*

50. Honorary Degrees Awards Ceremony on 15 July 1999. Honorary Graduates seated with HRH The Princess Royal, left to right: Dame Pauline Neville-Jones DCMG, businesswoman and civil servant; The Hon Dame Mary Arden DBE, first woman Chair of the Law Commission of England and Wales; Professor Susan Greenfield CBE, first woman Director of The Royal Institution of Great Britain, and Professor Patricia Easterling, first woman Regius Professor of Greek at Cambridge University.

51(a)

51(b)

51.(a)–(b)'Down Memory Lane 2' Reunion at Regent's Park on 18 September 1999. Another memorable day.

52. Bedford Gala Dinner on 1 October 1999. Former Presidents of the Bedford Students' Union with Elizabeth Kirk, Reid Student (first from left) and Josh Davis, President of the Students' Union, RHBNC 1999/2000 (second from right).

53. Bedford Gala Dinner on 1 October 1999. Mrs Marta Baker, Alumni Relations and Events Officer receives a bouquet from Dr Caroline Barron for masterminding the Sesquicentenary Celebrations.

Chapter 17

Social Studies and Social Science

Gavin Drewry and Jenny Brock

The title of this chapter reflects the fact that its authors have from the outset been faced with some tricky problems of nomenclature and boundary drawing. One reason for this is that the social sciences are a broad church–occupied by the enthusiastic devotees of many different, and sometimes competing, sects, and our pre-emptive claim to the title might well be contested by the Bedford College psychologists and philosophers, not to mention some of the geographers and historians. At the time of the merger with Royal Holloway in 1985, and for thirteen years thereafter, the Department was Social Policy and Social Science. A generation before that it was the Department of Sociology–which was an abridgement of its former title, 'Sociology, Social Studies and Economics'. At the time of writing it has recently become, as part of Royal Holloway and Bedford New College, the Department of Social and Political Science.

The title of the chapter also indicates one of its recurrent themes–the perennial problem of reconciling the mainly vocational orientation of *social studies* with the rigorous scholarly requirements of an academic *social science* department.

The Department's origins, very much rooted in a vocational

mission, can be traced back to a 19th century Hygiene Department based in the original Bedford Square premises. But although it has sailed under a variety of different flags–and sometimes through waters stirred into turbulence by internal and external academic jealousies–the Department's core activities have remained surprisingly constant.

The variations in departmental titles over time have for the most part manifested a healthy responsiveness to changing demands, fashions and circumstances. In particular the changing nomenclature has reflected the shifting disciplinary boundaries of the social sciences and the ebb and flow of market forces particularly with regard to student recruitment.

Prehistory: The Bedford College Hygiene Course[1]

The opening, in October 1895, of "a special department for scientific instruction in hygiene, including lectures and practical work in hygiene, chemistry, physics, physiology and bacteriology",[2] may seem at first sight, to have little relevance to the subsequent teaching of social science in Bedford College. However, the Department of Social Studies which was established in 1918, a year before the Hygiene Department was finally wound up, was indisputably its direct heir, with elements of the curriculum, and some of the staff, transferring from the latter to the former. In addition, its natural science orientation notwithstanding, the Hygiene Course had certain key characteristics shared by its social studies/science successors.

There was, first, the explicit function of the Course in preparing its students for public service. It was, according to the 1899 College Calendar, "designed to furnish women with the necessary training for such posts as are now open to them–as Sanitary Inspectors, Factory Inspectors, or as teachers of Hygiene".[3] It was, perhaps also with an eye to women who had no urgent need to earn a living, also presented as "a most useful grounding for those who may serve on any Boards or Vestries, or engage in any philanthropic schemes".[4]

Much of the credit for establishing the Hygiene Course must go to Dr Louis Parkes, Medical Officer of Health for Chelsea and Lecturer in

Hygiene at St George's Hospital, who put the idea of Public Health training courses for women to the College Council and was, during its first year, Head of Department, delivering the lectures in practical and scientific hygiene.[5]

The launch of the new Course reflected a growing concern for the British population's health and hygiene which led in the 1890s and 1900s to a marked increase in state and voluntary sector intervention to secure and improve the health and hygiene of, primarily, the urban working classes. One aspect of this was the gradual formalisation and extension of a tradition of middle-class female philanthropy, and personal mission to the 'unfortunate', into occupational niches for women qualified to instruct and exercise surveillance over women and children's health and welfare in both public and private settings. This included opportunities for employment as female sanitary inspectors (later increasingly redefined as health visitors), as factory inspectors responsible for women workers and as teachers of hygiene in schools and training colleges. The women's colleges such as Bedford were keen to play their part in this mission, although, for the most part, wishing to do so without sacrificing their hard-fought for educational standards. The tension between educational standards, as traditionally defined by universities, and vocational requirements was to figure prominently in the history of the Department of Hygiene–and indeed it echoed on through much of the twentieth century.

Hygiene course lectures were complemented by visits to places of interest. Sociology students in later decades will remember the similar device of 'visits of observation' though, in the 1960s at least, these included tours of urban developments, car and shoe factories, Holloway prison and the Royal Courts of Justice rather than the "Dairies and Cowsheds, Infant Milk Depots, Slaughter-houses, Disinfectors, Dust Destructors and Sewage Disposal Works" enjoyed by the Hygiene students.

Distinguished alumni of the Hygiene course included Miss Hilda Bidelux, appointed as Head of Hygiene at Battersea Polytechnic in 1913, Miss Maud Hartland, appointed one of the first women inspectors under the National Health Insurance Act in 1913; Miss Irene Whitworth (later Mrs Drury), who became Assistant Director of the Health and Welfare Department of the Ministry of Munitions from 1916. The Course also set a precedent for the subsequent Department of Social Studies by attracting overseas students–including Miss Kirstin Hesselgren, the first woman Factory Inspector in Sweden(1912) and first woman member of the Senate of the Riksdag (1921) and Miss Sumi Miyakawa, head of the School of Domestic Economy, Tokyo.[6]

Perhaps the best known of all was the formidable Miss Hilda Martindale (who had originally studied at Royal Holloway with her elder sister, Louisa who later became a distinguished surgeon). Hilda Martindale passed the Certificate in Hygiene in 1898, being the only candidate for the 1897–98 session. Appointed to a temporary position as a Factory Inspector in 1901, and later serving in the Potteries and in Ireland, she went on to become a Deputy Chief Inspector of Factories in 1925 and, in 1933, was appointed to a new position in the Treasury as director of women's establishments.[7]

According to Margaret Tuke,

> "The Bedford College Hygiene Course, though it did not attract a large inflow of students, added to the prestige of the College by taking an early part in a new and important movement and in sending out women thoroughly equipped for work in which they were to a great extent pioneers. The students, too,...were somewhat older than the majority of students of the period and, being thoughtful and often highly educated, were able to co-operate with the more serious-minded of the undergraduates in stimulating the intellectual life of the College.[8]

Valuable though the Course had been to the College and to the part played by women in the sphere of public health when first instituted, it appeared not, however, to have shared in the general advance of the College. The numbers of entries for the Course never exceeded twelve. In the session 1916–17 the intake dwindled to four. The next year there was only one entry.

It was designed as an intellectually rigorous course at the insistence of the Bedford College staff. But from the start, it attracted criticism as being too demanding, and perhaps of producing women over-qualified for the relatively mundane tasks open to them. Thus, in 1896 a letter from Dr Thorne Thorne of the Local Government Board was received by Dr Russell, Professor of Chemistry in the College, in which the Certificate programme was described as "much more theoretical" than that needed for Sanitary Inspectors,

> "who, please remember, are but Inspectors of Nuisances[9] under a new name. We do not wish them to know anything about the classification of micro-organisms, pathogenesis, animal metabolism, predisposition, immunity or anything of a like nature, otherwise we should be creating a body which would prove utterly unfit to perform ordinary inspection of nuisance. I fear your course would be held to be largely foreign to the purpose…"[10]

Such criticism illustrates a long-standing debate in universities–particularly though not exclusively in the social sciences–about the boundaries between traditional academic scholarship and vocational training, and what part the university system should play in the latter. This debate has been particularly significant in relation to social work education and training–a core activity of the Department throughout its history.

The Department of Social Studies

When, in 1919, the Hygiene Course finally closed, some of the work for which it had been designed was being carried on already in the College under different auspices. This new development had begun in 1916 when the Charity Organisation Society approached the College seeking the introduction of lecture courses in Social Economics and Social Ethics as part of the preparation for the Charity Organisation Society Certificate for Social Workers. A joint Social Studies Committee was formed by the Society and the College and the desired lectures duly arranged.[11] The COS had earlier played a similar role in the establishment in 1912 of the Department of Social Science at LSE.[12]

Contemporary thinking about the nature and rationale of social studies in universities can be found in an illuminating report by the Joint University Council for Social Studies,[13] a body set up in the aftermath of a conference convened by the Home Office in July 1917 to consider the training of Welfare Supervisors–ie social workers. The Council–on which Bedford College was represented–was chaired by Sir William Ashley. The Report noted that "in the wide etymological sense" social study has a long tradition in universities, under the rubrics of philosophy, law, history and economics, while more recently "the side of social activity which is concerned with the form and functions of the State and its organs" has been studied in courses usually called political science and public administration. But, it went on, "Social Study", as the term is now coming to be used, differs from all these in spirit, in method, and in purpose:

> "In spirit, because it is distinctly and continuously conscious of the close interconnexion of all the several sides of human life in society. In method, because the formal instruction is closely associated with 'practical work', by which is meant the acquiring of a first-hand knowledge of existing social conditions and of personal experience of the working of social institutions. In purpose, because it invites students, who have a definite intention to devote themselves to what–with equal indefiniteness, but equal intelligibility–is known as 'social work', whether as paid officials of public bodies or organisations, as members of local authorities, or as public spirited citizens, and who in their future work will be brought into personal touch with people of different classes and with the varied civic agencies of a modern town."[14]

The Bedford College Course of Training in Social Work, which covered two years, was, according to the Calendar 1920–21:

> "so arranged as to include lectures on General Economics, Social Administration and Social Psychology for all students, and allows

for alternative courses either in Social and Industrial History and the Development of Political Thought or in Physiology and Hygiene. It is therefore suitable for women preparing for social work as members of Public Bodies or Voluntary Associations; as Welfare supervisors, Health Visitors, Care Committee Organisers, Club Leaders etc."[15]

Social work 'placements' were a key part of the course:

"By the kindness of various organisations engaged in social work, Mrs [Helena] Reid is enabled to arrange for students to have varied practical work in different parts of London, and thus to study social conditions for themselves under experienced supervisors."[16]

Much of the academic syllabus–Modern Social Institutions; Social Administration; Social Economics; Development of Political Thought and Social Psychology–would have been familiar to many later generations of students and teachers in the Department. The inter-collegiate links enjoyed by subsequent students were also established, with Modern Social History provided by R H Tawney at the London School of Economics. However, one or two of the other subjects on offer–Physiology; Health of the Individual; and the, continuing, Hygiene–played a transient and essentially supporting role in the subsequent history of the social sciences at Bedford College.

The success of the Charity Organisation Society lectures in attracting "women preparing for various branches of social work" had encouraged the College to establish, in 1918, a Department of Social Studies, with Mrs Eva Hubback as temporary Director.[17] Students who successfully completed the training course were awarded a Certificate in Social Studies. From 1920–21 the Department also provided courses of training for the Board of Education Health Visitors' Certificate.

A permanent appointment to the Directorship of the Department was made in January 1919 in the person of Mrs Helena M Reid, "under whose wise and sympathetic guidance the department proved progressively useful".[18]

In the session 1921–22, again following an external initiative–this time from the League of Red Cross Societies–an experimental new course was introduced. This was a special Public Health course for nurses holding scholarships from the League and was designed to equip trained nurses from all parts of the world for posts in public health nursing in their own countries. Lectures were provided both by members of the College staff and by specialists, both practical and professional, from outside. Thus 'public health'–albeit no longer in the guise of 'hygiene'–continued, and so did the tradition of visits, with excursions for the students to clinics and institutions devoted to the care of health in London and other parts of England.

The course had an interestingly cosmopolitan intake. Its first twelve students came Austria, Bulgaria, Canada, Czechoslovakia, Estonia, Finland, Great Britain, Hungary, Japan, Latvia, Mexico, New Zealand. Each year the course attracted a fresh group of 'Internationals' (as the nurse students came to be called), and by 1937 forty-two different countries had been represented amongst its entrants.[19]

During its first six years the course was organised directly by the League of Red Cross but in 1927–28 the College assumed responsibility for organisation of the course. The League, however, continued to play an important role, providing a substantial yearly subsidy for the payment of teachers and other expenses, and advising and assisting the College in a variety of ways, including the selection of students.

The new course Organisation Committee included alongside College members, representatives not only of the League but also of the College of Nursing. "Co-operation with the latter body [was] throughout an essential feature [of] the scheme and this became still more necessary when in 1925–6 a second course was added, intended for Nurse Administrators and Teachers in Schools of Nursing. In this new course representatives of the leading London Hospitals took an important place."[20]

Here then was an early forerunner of the successful association with the Middlesex Hospital School of Nursing that began in the 1960s, as described below.

The Department of Social Studies and Economics

In June 1924 the departmental title was extended to include Economics.[21] It does not seem unreasonable to infer some association between this revision and the appearance in the Department in 1919 of Gertrude (later Lady) Williams (1897–1983) as lecturer in Modern Industrial Conditions and Elementary Economics, followed in 1924, by Barbara (later Baroness) Wootton (1897–1980) as lecturer in Social Economics. Both of these formidable women went on to become Heads of the Department. In 1925 the Department's remit was extended so as to include preparation for the London University Intermediate and BA Pass Examinations in Economics.

In the same year there was a further development when the Department undertook to prepare students for the University's BA Honours degree in Sociology and in the following year the Department's first, albeit part-time, Lecturer in Sociology, Miss C H Wedgewood, appeared in the College Calendar.

The new University degree courses did not, however, replace the existing certificate and diploma courses and for some time to come the latter were certainly numerically more important, justifying perhaps Margaret Tuke's description of the Department of Social Studies and Economics as one which had "not a purely academic character".[22]

The Department of Sociology, Social Studies and Economics

The establishment of Sociology as a distinct subject area (if perhaps not yet quite a fully-fledged discipline) within the Department was publicly acknowledged in 1931–32 when the Departmental title was changed yet again to Social Studies, Sociology and Economics. Only a few years later it was further modified–probably in recognition of the shifting balance of esteem between the vocational traditions of 'social studies' and the academic social sciences–becoming now the Department of Sociology, Social Studies and Economics. It is debatable, however, whether this last amendment represented a significant shift either in the power base within the department at that time or in the relative popularity of the constituent subjects. Certainly during the

1930s there do not appear to have been many students proceeding to a Sociology Honours degree, and very few students took higher degrees in Sociology at this time. Between 1920 and 1937, out of a total of 131 Masters degrees and 60 Doctorates awarded at Bedford, just two students gained postgraduate degrees in Sociology, both of them at Masters level.[23]

Nevertheless the importance of Sociology within the Department continued to grow and, in the period leading up to Mrs Reid's retirement in 1935 there was evidently some concern–a concern that has regularly resurfaced throughout the Department's history–about how to reconcile the growing 'academic' demands of social science research and teaching with the 'practical' requirements of social work training. A Report by Academic Board to Council concluded that:

> "whilst…it is desirable that the Head of the Department should carry the title of University Reader, yet they anticipate that there may be difficulty in finding anyone who has both sufficient published wok to qualify for a University title, and also qualifications for directing the practical side of the Social Studies work. Should this prove to be impossible, the Committee are of the opinion that qualifications for directing the practical work should take precedence of those required for a University title."[24]

Happily, the circle was squared, and in 1935 Mrs Reid was succeeded as Director by Henry Mess (1884–1944) who was at the same time appointed to the newly instituted Readership in Sociology.[25]

The Postwar Era

Increasingly, particularly in the post-war period, the Department's name may be seen as a fair representation of its activities; of its teaching concerns with the broad based London University Degrees in Sociology, with the certificates and diplomas in Social Studies, intended mainly for those seeking employment in the post-Beveridge welfare state, and with Economics as a subsidiary subject for students both inside and outside the Department.

Thus the vocational flavour of the pre-war department remained crucial to its mission. In her memoirs, Barbara (later Baroness) Wootton, who had worked for a while as a Lecturer in the Department in the 1920s,[26] and who was appointed as Head of Department in 1944 in succession to Henry Mess, recalls that most of the students at the time "were working for a Certificate in Social Studies with a view to qualifying as hospital almoners, probation officers, child care workers youth leaders or in other branches of social work".[27] Although familiar with the role of some of these professions through her work as a magistrate, she found some of the attitudes that then prevailed in the world of professional social work "decidedly disquieting". She was, as a committed socialist, particularly offended by the "casework" ethos surrounding the treatment of the "underprivileged" classes. She went on to observe that the students admitted immediately after the war "were largely drawn from the Services or from various types of full-time employment, and [had] seen too much of life to be willing to swallow a lot of nonsense"; the maturity of these students "added greatly to the rewards of teaching".

She also noticed some changes in academic life since her first spell of service in the department in the 1920s:

> "Students were then expected to wear both stockings and hats in the vicinity of the College. Before the middle of the century hats had completely disappeared and stockings were worn or discarded according to individual preference. More fundamental changes had occurred also. In one week two students asked for leave of absence–one in order to see about her divorce, the other because she wished to ride her motor cycle in a Tourist Trophy race."[28]

By the time she was awarded her personal chair, in 1948, an increasing number of students were reading for Sociology degrees, and the department was beginning to attract a small intake of postgraduate students and to recruit a new generation of academic staff.

One of Barbara Wootton's established colleagues–and a personal friend–was the economist, Gertrude Williams (née Rosenblum), who was later to become Professor Lady Williams,[29] and Wootton's successor as Head of Department. Another future Head, the social historian, O R McGregor–who was also destined to enter the Lords as a life peer–joined the Department in 1947.

The Wootton era coincided with a growing recognition by government (encouraged by social scientists in the universities themselves) of the importance of social science research. In 1946 the Attlee Government set up a committee, chaired by Sir John Clapham to consider "whether additional provision is necessary for research into social and economic questions". The Clapham Report's main conclusion,[30] that existing funding provision was wholly inadequate, was accepted by the University Grants Committee, which made available to all universities an earmarked grant for the provision of chairs and other teaching posts, research staff and equipment, and library facilities, in the social sciences.[31] Barbara Wootton herself was particularly keen to use this opportunity to develop research initiatives in her Department, so she used the new allocation to set up a small research unit, headed by Margot Jefferys–who came to Sociology via an original background in economics and later became a key figure in establishing the Department's international reputation in the field of medical sociology.

The results of the unit's research, into mobility in the labour market, were eventually published,[32] but the story did not have a happy ending. In her memoirs, Wootton recalls how the research unit was, after a bitter struggle, disbanded in the face of what she saw as "the hostility, jealousy and ignorance of our academic colleagues" from other departments. She declared herself:

> "deeply dismayed–and no less astonished–to find that, even when funds were especially earmarked as a matter of public policy to promote the growth of the newer disciplines, there were those amongst our colleagues who so deeply grudged to our department money which was in no case available for their own that they would prefer that the college should forego these funds altogether rather than that we should have them."[33]

She attributes part of the hostility to the tendency, in some quarters, including some academic ones, to assume "that any word that begins with 'soci' must end in 'alism'". Whether or not this kind of prejudice lay behind the episode just described remains a matter for conjecture, but it is certainly the case that the social sciences have long faced suspicion and even outright hostility for the linked academic sins of being, in the eyes of antagonists, both ideologically tainted and lacking the credentials of a 'real science'. Probably Sir Keith (later Lord) Joseph had both these charges in mind when, as Secretary of State for Education in the early 1980s, he changed the name of the Social Science Research Council to the Economic and Social Research Council.

Meanwhile, in 1952, disenchanted by this experience (and irked by the administrative burdens that, even half a century ago, afflicted heads of department), Barbara Wootton handed over the reins to her old friend and colleague, the economist, Gertrude Williams. Wootton herself retained her links with Bedford College for a further five years, as a Nuffield Research Fellow, investigating the value of research in criminology and allied subjects, though she was not allowed to retain the title of professor that had been conferred on her in 1948: "the University was not...willing that this Fellowship, though it carried a professorial salary, should rank as a Research Professorship, and my title therefore lapsed".[34]

The Department of Sociology

In 1964, when Professor O R McGregor (1921–97) took over the Headship from Professor Lady Williams, the departmental title was abbreviated to Sociology. On the eve of this change of title and of leadership, the College sent a submission to the Heyworth Committee on Social Studies[35] which includes useful information about–among other things–undergraduate numbers at the time, underlining the substantial growth that had taken place in the 1950s. In the session 1962–63 there were 95 students reading for the University's BA and BSc degrees in Sociology[36]–compared with just 41 such students ten years previously.

In addition the department had 12 students reading for a Diploma in Social Studies–a one year conversion course, introduced in 1956 (replacing a Social Studies Certificate course) to enable graduates in other disciplines to go on to vocational training in social work. The latter course was subsequently replaced by a professionally validated Diploma in Applied Social Studies,[37] that offered a full qualification for social work practice, and the latter was eventually upgraded to a Masters programme–as described below.

It was during the 1960s too that the department began to enhance its research profile with the establishment of two externally funded research units. First, Margot Jefferys–who, since her early involvement with the Department in the Wootton era, had been employed at the London School of Hygiene and Tropical Medicine–was persuaded by McGregor to rejoin the Department, and she obtained funds from a variety of sources, including the then DHSS, to set up a new Social Research Unit. This developed several important research projects, and launched the successful MSc in Medical Sociology, supported by both the Medical Research Council and the Social Science Research Council. The Unit was strengthened by the appointment in 1966 of Professor George Brown, who subsequently developed his own very successful research initiatives, funded mainly by the Medical Research Council. In due course the University Grants Committee, recognising its success, provided permanent funding for the Unit, enabling the College to take over responsibility for some of the posts funded in the first instance by the research foundations.

The Social Research Unit also made an important contribution to general undergraduate teaching in social administration and medical sociology and to the supervision of research students. However, full integration between, on the one hand the Social Research Unit and the Masters Degree in Medical Sociology with which it had close links and, on the other, the main Sociology Department was always problematic, given the Unit's location in various off-campus locations–successively in Peto Place, 51 Harley Street, Fraser's Lodge (in Regent's Park) and Bedford Square–at inconvenient distances from the main Regent's Park site.

The other major research development in the Department in the early 1960s was the establishment of a Legal Research Unit by the then Head of Department, Professor McGregor, with support from the Rowntree Foundation. The barrister and criminologist, Louis Blom-Cooper[38] became joint-director of the Unit, which undertook several substantial research projects, notably in the fields of family law, the operation of appellate courts, and homicide. The work of the Unit continued in the 1970s but its development was stunted by the inability, and apparent reluctance, of the College to find space to house the SSRC's new Socio-Legal Centre (a much larger enterprise than the Legal Research Unit), which was thereupon established in Oxford–with Professor McGregor seconded to become its first Director (1972–75). Bedford College's Legal Research Unit continued to operate for a few years on a limited basis in the Department at Regent's Park.

For most of the forty years following the establishment of the post-Hygiene Social Studies and Economics Department in the mid-1920s, the academic staff complement had hovered around seven or eight–which was a fairly typical size for Bedford departments during this period. But–partly because of the expanding portfolio of research activities, and the recruitment of new research staff–by the mid-1960s, the Department of Sociology quite suddenly found itself to be, by a wide margin, the largest academic department in the College.

The 1966–68 College Calendar shows a list of no fewer than 20 established staff, comprising three Professors, one Reader, the Joint Director of the Legal Research Unit, two Senior Lecturers, nine Lecturers, two social work Tutors, and two Assistant Lecturers. In addition, there were ten research staff, a Director and two social workers associated with the British Adoption Project–and Dame Nancy Parkinson, former Controller of the Home Division of the British Council (and a graduate of the Bedford College Geology Department), who was attached to the Department as a Leverhulme Research Fellow. The next largest departments in the College–Chemistry and Mathematics–both had established staff complements of 12.

The Department of Social Policy and Social Science

The Head of Department, Professor McGregor, had in the meantime, become increasingly absorbed with the management of the Oxford Centre and increasingly involved in various aspects of public life: he was, among other things, a member of the Finer Committee on One-Parent Families (1969–74) and then became a member, and later the Chairman, of the Royal Commission on the Press (1975–77). When McGregor went to Oxford, the military and administrative historian, Dr Ivor Burton stood in for him, as acting Head of Department. Ivor Burton had transferred into Sociology from the History Department in 1962 to teach courses in politics and public administration, and he became Head of Department in his own right in 1977, after it became clear that Professor McGregor would not be in a position to resume his full time duties at Bedford.

Meanwhile, important changes had taken place in the undergraduate degree programmes. For many years the Department's main undergraduate degrees had been the University of London's intercollegiate programmes in Social Science and Administration and in Sociology–successors to the University Branch I and Branch III Sociology degrees offered in the 1950s and 1960s. The degrees had been taught and examined jointly with the LSE and with Goldsmiths and in the early 1970s the Department at Bedford decided to move towards greater self-sufficiency by substituting College-based course unit degrees. The last intake for the old SSA and Sociology degrees was in 1976, and the first students for the new degrees–in Sociology, Social Policy, Sociology and Social Policy, and Economics and Public Administration–entered the Department the following year.

However, further and highly controversial changes lay ahead. As for everyone at Bedford, the early 1980s proved to be a time of great turbulence in the Sociology Department. A recommendation by a University Subject Area Review Committee (SARC) that, on resource grounds, the Single Honours Degree in Sociology should no longer be offered at Bedford,[39] provoked bitter criticism from most of the rank and file staff[40]–exacerbated by the fact that the former Head of Department,

Lord McGregor (as he now was), had been a leading member of the SARC and strongly backed its recommendation, as did the other professors and Dr Burton. But this departmental crisis was soon engulfed by the encircling gloom about the financial plight of Bedford College as a whole, and the frenzy of speculation about possible mergers.

In the University of London Court letter in the summer of 1981, which had given the critical news about the 15 percent cut in the College's budget, Social Administration had been identified as a protected area, and this–reinforced by the SARC recommendations–played a significant part in the subsequent decision to reposition the department, and to rename it. The new name chosen was Social Policy and Social Science; and an established Chair in Sociology (unfilled since 1945) was retitled a Chair in Social Policy. It was filled by an internal appointment, by Dr Burton, in 1983. The disappearance of the Sociology degree meant that Social Policy was the only single honours programme offered by the department–and it remained so until the year 2000.[41]

During the 1980s the department's long tradition of social work training was enhanced by the establishment of a high quality professional course at Master's Degree level (incorporating the Diploma, validated by the Central Council for Education and Training in Social Work, required for professional recognition). The course initially admitted twenty students a year for a two year programme, just under half of them by secondment from local authorities, hospitals and private agencies. The first Masters students on this course graduated in 1982.

This upgrading of the status of the department's social work programme reflected the growing academic quality and research-orientation of what had, in the past, been largely a vocational training activity, taught by social work 'tutors' with practitioner backgrounds rather than 'lecturers' with strong academic records in research and publication.–We have noted the past tensions–particularly evident in the context of Helena Reid's retirement in the 1930s–between the practical and the academic missions of the department. The establishment of a Masters programme that so successfully combined academic excellence with professional recognition, reinforced by the academically very strong appointment of Brian Sheldon–later to be awarded a personal chair–as Director of Applied Social Studies, on the eve of the Royal Holloway merger, in March 1984, went a long way towards resolving those tensions.

Meanwhile, the department's increasing involvement with the medical world had been reflected in the introduction in the 1960s of an innovative, combined course, run in conjunction with the Middlesex Hospital School of Nursing consisting of a degree in social administration and a special shortened postgraduate State Registered Nursing course. This may be seen, in a sense, as a reincarnation of the original nursing connection established in the 1920s via the League of Red Cross Society courses for nurse administrators.

It proved to be a successful and popular course, though the intake had to be limited to six students a year because of the limited funding that was available from the General Nursing Council. The department, with encouragement from both the GNC and the Middlesex Nursing School, was keen to develop the course into an integrated degree in Nursing Studies, and it secured a special grant from the University Court to pursue this initiative. In 1980, Marion Ferguson–who had a somewhat unusual combination of nursing and political science qualifications–was appointed Director of Nursing Studies, and given the task of launching the new, four year, programme. But her appointment more or less coincided with the developing financial crisis that was to overtake the College, and the distance between the new merged College location and the Middlesex Hospital made the course unsustainable. The possibility of developing acceptable alternative links with hospitals in the Egham area was explored, but without success, and the last cohort of nursing students graduated in 1986. Thus, with the merger, this historical link with the nursing profession was severed.

Following the retirement of Margot Jefferys in 1982, and in the light of the department's prospective move to Egham, it was decided to establish the Medical Sociology Section, for a five year period, from July 1984, in the London base in Bedford Square established by the newly merged College. It would thus operate alongside, and with the strong support of, Professor George Brown's MRC Research Unit. George Brown's own post was transferred to the MRC payroll, while he retained his professorship as an honorary University title. Mike Bury, who had been appointed to a lectureship in 1979, succeeded Margot Jefferys as Director of the Section.

The department's last year in Regent's Park, in 1984–85, was a strange experience, not least because practically everyone else from Bedford College had decamped to Egham, and the department operated on rather a makeshift basis in unfamiliar rooms, scattered around the Regent's Park site. It was an even stranger experience for those in the Social Work Section, who remained in solitary splendour at Regent's Park for a further year before joining their colleagues at Egham.

One notable event of this period was an academic review of the department, undertaken by a College panel with two distinguished external representatives–Professor Maurice Kogan (Brunel University, in the Chair) and Professor Raymond Illesley (University of Hull). The main recommendation of this review was that there should be a consolidation of the department's main strengths, in Social Policy and Administration and in Medical Sociology, by establishing a second Chair, in Health Policy.

With this message ringing in its ears, the department departed to take its place (as an 'unmatched' department) in the merged College at Royal Holloway. The new Chair in Health Policy was duly advertised–but it was never filled.[42]

So the department's history has been characterised by bewildering complexity, a complexity that reflects in large measure the ever-shifting content and boundaries of comparatively young social science disciplines. But some common threads are discernible. In particular, the strong and in many respects pioneering vocational origins of the department have survived, but these aspects of the department's work have been increasingly complemented by–and have themselves absorbed–the ethos of a research orientated academic department. We would like to think that the founders of the department, back in the era of hygiene and social studies, would–albeit with reservations about the sometimes ambitious claims of modern social science–approve of the achievements of their successors.

References

1 The authors are grateful to Dr Mary Ann Elston for allowing them to use material derived from her own research into the origins of the Hygiene Department.

2 *Calendar of Bedford College 1899*, p21.

3 *Ibid*, p351.

4 *Ibid*, p21.

5 Margaret Tuke, *A History of Bedford College for Women*, Oxford University Press, 1939, p158.

6 *Ibid*, p159.

7 M D McFeely, *Lady Inspectors: The Campaign for a Better Workplace 1893–1921*, Blackwell, 1988, p166–7.

8 Tuke, p159.

9 This archaic terminology can be traced back to the 19th century legislation, beginning with the Nuisance Removal Acts of 1846 and 1855, empowering local authorities (in the first instance, the Poor Law Boards of Guardians) to combat public health 'nuisances' by the deployment of inspectors.

10 Bedford College Archive: AL/334/1. Dr Thorne Thorne to Dr Russell 24 April 1896. However, he did indicate that the College might apply for recognition when a new Sanitary Inspection examining board was constituted.

11 See AR/330/1 and AR/330/2.

12 Richard M Titmuss, *Commitment to Welfare*, Allen and Unwin, 1968, p48; Ralph Dahrendorf, *A History of the London School of Economics and Political Science 1895–1995*, Oxford University Press, 1995, p125.

13 *Social Study and Training at the Universities: A Report Drawn up by The Joint University Council for Social Studies*, P S King and Son, 1918. A descendent of the original JUC remains active to this day, and the Department has regularly been active in its work and that of its constituent committees.

14 *Ibid*, para 2.

15 *Calendar of Bedford College 1920–21*, p62.

16 *Calendar of Bedford College 1916–17*, p61.

17 Tuke, p261. See also Bedford College Archives, AR/330/6. The latter file contains a letter dated 18 September 1918 from Margaret Tuke to Major Darwin of the COS, observing, with a touch of wartime xenophobia, that "As [Mrs Hubback's] maiden name [Spielman] indicates, her father is of German origin but is quite sound".

18 Tuke, p261. See also AR/330/7–9.

19 Tuke, p261–3.

20 *Ibid*, p262.

21 Bedford College Archives, AR/330/5, letter from Secretary of Council to Mrs Reid, 23 June 1924.

22 Tuke, p260.

23 Tuke, p347 .

24 Bedford College Archives, AR/330/10.

25 A Christian sociologist, with experience on Tyneside, Mess had been trained at Birkbeck, King's and LSE (*Who Was Who*, iv).

26 Barbara Wootton, *In a World I Never Made*, Allen and Unwin, 1967, p62. See also *Who Was Who*, viii and the essay on Wootton by A H Halsey in *The DNB, 1986–1990*, Oxford University Press, 1996, pp491–3. Barbara Wootton entered the House of Lords in 1958, as Baroness Wootton of Abinger–one of the first batch of the new life peers instituted by the Life Peerage Act of that year, and one of the first women to enter the House. She was Professor of Social Studies from 1948 to 1952, then Nuffield Research Fellow, 1952–57.

27 *Ibid*, p100.

28 Ibid, p101.

29 Not through conferment of a peerage but by virtue of her marriage, to Sir William Emrys Williams, Chairman of the Arts Council. She was Professor of Social Economics from 1955 to 1964. See *Who Was Who*, viii.

30 Cmd 6868 of 1946.

31 The grant rose from £102K in 1947-48 to £400K in 1951-52, when it was merged with the UGC's quinquennial grant to the universities.

32 Margot Jefferys, *Mobility in the Labour Market*, Routledge and Kegan Paul, 1954.

33 Wootton, *In a World I Never Made*, p103.

34 *Ibid*, p104.

35 Bedford College Archives, AR330/20/1.

36 For many years, the term 'sociology' as applied to University of London degree titles was an umbrella term for social science programmes generally, rather than having the disciplinary exclusivity that it was to acquire in the 1970s and thereafter. The present authors, who began their own academic careers in the McGregor era, can remember many occasions when senior members of the Sociology Department–themselves trained in subjects like history or economics–expressed scorn at the jargon and intellectual pretentiousness of new-fangled 'sociology'.

37 AR330/20/22.

38 Sir Louis Blom-Cooper QC is now an Honorary Fellow of Royal Holloway.

39 The last intake for this degree, of 15 students, was in October 1981.

40 For example at an extraordinary general meeting of the Departmental Board held on 20 January 1982.

41 Macgregor had been Professor of Social Institutions, 1964–85; Head of the Department of Sociology 1964–77; and joint Director, Rowntree Legal Research Unit, 1966–84 (*Who Was Who*, x). The Department of Social and Political Science at Royal Holloway has recently reinstated Sociology as a single honours programme, along with the established programme in Social Policy and a new single honours degree in Politics. Since the merger, the former Economics component of the Department has passed to a separate Department of Economics, established in 1995.

42 Though a personal chair, with this title, was later conferred on Nicholas Bosanquet, who occupied it on specially negotiated contract basis from 1989 to 1994.

Chapter 18

Zoology

Rodney Dales

The enthusiasm of Mrs Reid in founding Bedford College in 1849 and her well developed powers of pursuasion lead to many friends giving their services in teaching the first students to get the new college off the ground. Amongst these was Professor William Carpenter FRS, "an unwearied investigator in the sciences of Zoology, Botany and Mental Phylosophy".[1] At that time he had lately been the Fullerian Professor of Physiology at the Royal Institution and was Professor of Forensic Medicine at University College. It was a good start for Biology. We have no details of what Professor Carpenter taught but he most likely provided classes in both animal and plant biology since 'Natural Science' was what was listed in the first Prospectus published in 1849.[1]

The first Biology Department at York Place, 1879

Teaching of biological subjects appears to have been sporadic in these early years in Bedford Square, partly, it would seem, because of the very few students who wished to study Biology. There was a gap of twelve years from 1856–68 without any recorded teaching in animal biology, although a Botany Department was established in 1872 with the appointment of Dr A E Bennett. There was evidently no teaching then of animal biology and probably few students wanting to study Botany either at that time. Eventually, in 1879, five years after the College had moved to York Place, a Biology Department was formed and Dr A T Parker was appointed Head of the new Department. As Botany teaching had continued over this period it seems likely that the Biology Department had been formed to provide teaching in animal biology and physiology. Dr Parker stayed for only a year. Dr Charles Stewart, a lecturer at St Thomas's Hospital, was then appointed, becoming Professor of Biology at Bedford in 1880 and of Physiology in 1882. The title of Professor was a courtesy title at that time. He was followed by Dr A G Bourne in 1884. There was at first no structured course and lectures were arranged as required.

During the 1880s, following the decision by the College to prepare students for the BA and BSc degree examinations, there was an increasing demand for advanced lectures. This commitment led to the need for properly equipped laboratories. A sub-committee of the College Council reported in 1886 that laboratories for Biology, Chemistry and Physics should be provided. Following acquisition of the York Place premises, the Shaen Wing was built to accommodate the laboratories which were completed in 1890.

Meanwhile, in 1885 Dr W Blaxland Benham, an internationally known zoologist, had been appointed as Head of Department. He was granted £20 to convert the old Council Room into a temporary laboratory for Zoology. This was probably the first laboratory which did not have to be shared with other sciences. Sadly, it seems that the new laboratory specifically planned in the Shaen wing for Zoology was never occupied by the Zoology Department, largely as a result of the contention of the redoubtable Miss Bostock, one of the first Trustees of the College, that Mr Shaen would not have approved. Miss Bostack was not alone in confusing vivisection with the need to dissect dead animals in order to understand their anatomy. She was also against "filling young minds with the facts and theories…now understood by Darwinism", going on to suggest that "a room, stable or outhouse should be hired in a cheap neighbouring street in which to carry on biological operations".[2] The resourceful Dr Benham nevertheless suggested that the old Physics laboratory in the basement at York Place could be adapted for Biology. This was later enhanced by the addition "of a screen with rope and pulleys fixed at one side of the laboratory required for hanging the diagrams". These diagrams were still in use in the 1950s. A photograph[3] of this laboratory shows also many of the specimens and wax models of embryos familiar to Bedford students of that period and used at that time by Miss Ince.

Dr Benham remained until 1898 when he left to take up the Chair of Zoology at the University of Otago in New Zealand. He had greatly improved the provision for teaching and resources for Zoology during his thirteen years at Bedford College. The syllabuses and examination papers which he set in animal biology remained largely unchanged for half a century.[4]

The turn of the century

On Professor Benham's departure, Bedford College decided to advertise for a Professor of Zoology. Dr H Marett Tims was appointed as Head of Department and he remained for twenty-four years (1898–1922) spanning the First World War. On his appointment Marrett Tims immediately sought permission to hold a BSc class in Zoology at the request of three students. He suggested that the course should be of two years duration and would consist of two lectures a week with two half-days of practical work. The syllabus changed little from that developed by Blaxland Benham but there was greater emphasis on vertebrate morphology. Miss Helen Pixell joined as Junior Demonstrator in 1904–05 and was clearly an asset to the Department both as a teacher and for her enthusiasm for research. She published work on the digitiform appendix of elasmobranchs and received a Reid Fellowship to travel to Nanaimo on Vancouver Island to investigate the marine fauna of the Straits of Georgia. She collected specimens for the Department and for the British Museum and published papers on the sabellids and serpulids. Forty year later she sent me reprints of these papers when I too stayed at Nanaimo. Helen Pixell must have been one of the earliest visitors to the newly established research station there.

The Zoology Department was clearly active in research at that time, Marett Tims publishing papers on foetal seals, lecturing to the Royal Veterinary College and delivering University Lectures on mammalian teeth and their development. The growing reputation of the Department attracted gifts both to the library and to the departmental museum. Miss Clayton came from Girton, Cambridge, for a time to extend her research on tooth genesis in phocids. Helen Pixell left in 1912 on the award of a Beit Memorial Fellowship in medical research and in 1913 married Dr E S Goodrich, the comparative vertebrate morphologist at Oxford. Miss M L Hett took her place and Dr R Ruggles Gates also joined the department in 1912–13.

The move to Regent's Park, 1913

It was in 1913 that the move was made from York Place to the new North Science Block in Regent's Park. Two new University Intercollegiate Courses were then offered, one by Marett Tims on vertebrate muscular systems, the other on cytology by Ruggles Gates. Dr Ruggles Gates left for Canada in 1914. That same year Dr J T Cunningham gave the special University Lectures, on 'Adaptation and Genetics', at Bedford College.

The war years, 1914–1918

With the outbreak of war in 1914 Marett Tims left to join the RAMC at Bermondsey Military Hospital. The Department was put into the temporary charge of Dr Philippa Esdaile. Miss Crump and Miss Jarvis were appointed part-time demonstrators in 1915. Miss Jarvis was an entomologist carrying on research at Imperial College. She became a full-time demonstrator when Miss Crump left in 1917–18 to accept an appointment at Rothamsted. Miss Jarvis left in 1919.

Philippa Esdaile held the Department together during these difficult years until Marett Tims was able to return, and the appreciation of her efforts and industry were recorded in the Council Reports.

Philippa Esdaile graduated from the University of Manchester and then went to University College, Reading. She published papers on the life of the salmon. Her notable paper on the development of the skull of the bandicoot led to conferment of a DSc degree by the University of Manchester. At the end of the war she went to Birkbeck College and then to King's College of Household and Social Science (later Queen Elizabeth College) becoming Reader and then Head of the Biology Department from 1925 until she retired in 1951. A remarkable teacher and organiser, one time Vice President of the Linnean Society, she was the only woman to serve on the Makere Commission on Higher Education in East Africa in 1936. She went to St Helena at the request of the Colonial Office and was an active member of the Council of the Girls' Public Day School Trust and was Chairman of its Sites and Buildings Committee for many years. She published *Economic Biology* in 1927. She died at the age of 101 in 1989.

After the First World War

Marett Tims rejoined the Department in 1920 and then two posts were advertised: a new demonstratorship, which was filled by a former student Miss H E Bargmann, and an Assistant Demonstratorship which was filled by Dr Doris Crofts. Marett Tims retired in 1922. The reputation of the Department must have been, in no small measure, due to his industry and also to the quality of the teachers he attracted, all of whom were active in research.

The establishment of a Chair of Zoology at Bedford, 1923

The University established a Chair of Zoology at Bedford College in 1923. Heads of Department had been given the courtesy title of Professor by the College, but it was Dr C L Boulanger who was the first to be appointed to the University of London Chair tenable at Bedford College. Miss Bargmann left in 1923–24 on the return of Miss Hett from war service. Doris Crofts stayed until 1926 when she went to the King's College for Household and Social Science, joining Miss Esdaile who was by then Head of the Biology Department, although later moving to the University of Reading. She was replaced by Miss G H Faulkner who remained until 1929.

Professor C L Boulanger was the son of G A Boulanger, who worked at the British Museum and is remembered, amongst other contributions, for his Royal Society Monograph on *The Tailless Batrachians of Europe.* Professor Boulanger's brother, another zoologist, was the first Curator of Reptiles and Director of the Aquarium at the London Zoo in Regent's Park. Professor C L Boulanger was a scholar from King's College, Cambridge. He went to the Stazione Zoologica in Naples in 1906–07 to study medusae, subsequently making excursions to parts of Africa and the middle east to further this research. Following his return to Cambridge, he went to the University of Birmingham where he did some work on *Myzostornum.* He subsequently developed an interest in helminthology. During the First World War he served with the RAMC in India and in Mesopotamia, where he contracted amoebic dysentery. From 1920 until his appointment to Bedford College he worked in Lahore on strongyloid parasites of camels and horses.

After 1923 there was a steady increase in student numbers and the Department became one of the largest in the College. It included students registered at Westfield College for whom there was no teaching in Zoology at that time. Luckily, the move of the Psychology Department into the newly completed Tuke Building in 1929 left more space in the North Science Block for Zoology. More staff were provided by the appointment of Miss Ince in the same year. Later, Miss E M Gaffney and E L Seyd were appointed in 1933. Dr P D F Murray joined in 1937–38 as Demonstrator and Dr A E Needham replaced E L Seyd who left in 1938-39. Dr Murray also left in 1939 but Dr Needham remained until 1941.

Continuing to give his energies to the College, Professor Boulanger battled against ill health, subsequently dying at the early age of fifty-five. This left Miss lnce as Acting Head of Department when the College was evacuated to Cambridge in time for the session starting in October 1939. The Bedford Department and the Zoology Department of Queen Mary College joined the Cambridge Department in Downing

Street. The museum material remained at Regent's Park and was moved down to the basement of the North Science Block. Much was lost when the building was bombed in 1941. The valuable microscope slide collection had, however, been taken to Cambridge and survived. The handwriting of earlier Heads of Department and of all four University Professors can be identified on some of these slides. The collection still forms a valuable scientific archive which contains slides of superb quality and historical interest.

The Sussex Lodge years, 1944–1952

Evacuation to Cambridge had indeed had its benefits. Bedford College students had lectures from Professor A J Gray and Dr Carl Pantin as well as from Professor A J Grove and others from Queen Mary College, London who were also evacuated to the Zoology Department in Downing Street. It was at this time that Grove and Newell wrote their *Animal Biology* which became the standard A-level text for the next twenty years. Dr A E Needham and Miss M A Tazellaar assisted Miss F Ince who was Acting Head of the Bedford Zoology Department until Professor H Munro Fox was appointed to the vacant chair in 1941. Miss B M Walshe came with him from the Zoology Department of the University of Birmingham and H P Moon was added to the Bedford staff from Cambridge. In the following year Dr A Stock helped as temporary demonstrator until he went to South Africa. Miss E J Hanson, a Bedford graduate, was then appointed. Both Jean Hanson and Betty Walshe remained in the department when it moved to Sussex Lodge in Regent's Park for eight years before the war-damaged North Science Block on the main site in Regent's Park was rebuilt. Jean Hanson left in 1948 to join the MRC Biophysics Research Unit at King's College, London and was later elected a Fellow of the Royal Society for her distinguished work on the ultrastructure and functioning of muscle. Sadly, she died in 1973 at an early age.

By 1948–49 the staff were Professor Munro Fox, Miss Ince, now Senior Lecturer, Betty Walshe, Assistant Lecturer and two demonstrators, Miss E M M Alden and Miss M K Black. In 1949–50

Miss Alden and Miss Black were replaced by Barbara Gilchrist and Wendy Hosking. Barbara Gilchrist had been with the Department in its Cambridge days and worked with J B S Haldane during the war on mosquitos. Wendy Hosking had graduated from Queen Mary College. Jim Green, also from Queen Mary College, joined as another demonstrator in 1951 when Betty Walshe left. Barbara Gilchrist was then appointed Lecturer and Wendy Hosking Assistant Lecturer. Wendy left the following year and was replaced by Gwyneth Parry in 1952.

Professor Munro Fox had already been elected a Fellow of the Royal Society while at the University of Birmingham. He was a pioneer in the study of invertebrate respiratory pigment function, research which was continued with other members of the department in Cambridge and on return to London. Despite the makeshift conditions of Sussex Lodge, these years were productive. It was in Sussex Lodge that the earlier work on *Daphnia* and other freshwater invertebrates was carried out with various collaborators including Elizabeth Dresel, Elizabeth Phear, Sheila Hardcastle, Barbara Gilchrist, Desmond Johnson, who went later to the University in Singapore, and Jim Green, who joined in 1951. It was also in Sussex Lodge that Dr Averil Lysaght translated Caullery's *Symbiosis and Parasitism.* As a consequence of the loss of much of the museum material due to enemy action, Mr E Purvis was employed from 1944–1951 to procure and mount skeletal and other material.

Fortunately, some skeletons did survive the war, including those of the aardvark, giant anteater and *Sphenodon* which will be familiar to most students today. The wall charts and wax models of embryos, which were bought fifty years earlier during Professor Benham's regime for use in the laboratory at York Place were also saved. Harry Wadleigh was then appointed Technician in 1951 and he was joined by Donald Field as Laboratory Assistant. Don Field retired in 1998 after a record number of years service and was by then responsible for the technical staff of all seven former departments that had come together as the School of Biological Sciences at Royal Holloway and Bedford New College.

The move to the new Darwin Building, 1952–1954

The laboratories for the new Darwin Building, which replaced the North Science Block, maintained the former allocation of space with the Zoology Department on the top floor, Botany on the first floor and Geology on the ground floor. The Darwin building was occupied in 1952. Professor Munro Fox with Miss Ince designed an 'open plan' arrangement of the main laboratory with 'general' students on one side and room for a dozen 'special' students on the other with museum specimens seen around the laboratory and along the corridor. This arrangement suited changing needs for many years to come. The departmental library was entered both from the main laboratory and from the corridor which led to all the staff rooms and to the research laboratory. The room for the Head of Department was on the south-east corner of the building and, at second floor level, commanded a beautiful view of the park towards Queen Mary's Rose Garden.

The departmental library was also impressive, thanks not only to generous donations but also to the personal interest taken by successive Heads of Department and staff who ensured that significant publications were acquired with both teaching and research in mind. Not only were there all the standard texts and manuals for identification, but also some older books of historical value, which could but enhance demonstrations for students and introduce them to the long endeavour to understand animal anatomy, function and evolution. These volumes all now form part of the new 'Bedford Library' on the Egham campus. Some readers may remember, for example, the superb copies of Swammerdam, Trembley and Stubbs. Our copy of Hooke's *Micrographia* was loaned to the Royal Society in 1965 on the occasion of the 300th anniversary of its publication, as it appeared to be the best available copy in the country.

The departmental library at Bedford remained for many years a meeting place for staff. Coffee and tea were taken there and through the 1950s and 1960s students always gave the staff a large box of biscuits at Christmas. When a member of staff published a major paper, the author provided a cake for tea. It was a venue for parties and for celebrations.

After the war departmental secretaries were at first shared with Geology and Botany at Regent's Park, but from 1953 the Heads of Department of Zoology were supported by quite outstanding personal and departmental secretaries, Anne Bins (1953–1958), Margaret Rayment (1959–1966) and Barbara Jago (1967–1984). Barbara Jago became ill in 1984 and died of cancer in 1986.

During Professor Munro Fox's tenure a tradition of research and teaching in Limnology was established. In 1946–47 the Prospectus noted simply that "as a Special Subject students study the ecology of inland waters, with lectures on Saturday mornings from 10 to 12.30". Many Limnology students attended field courses at the Freshwater Biological Station at Windermere. Bedford was the first and, for many years, the only London College to present this Special Subject for the degree course. At the same time Miss Ince continued to offer Embryology as another Special Subject.

When Professor Munro Fox retired in 1954 Miss Ince was once again left in charge of the Department. The staff then included Barbara Gilchrist, Jim Green and Gwyneth Parry. Professor Fox continued his research at Queen Mary College after his retirement.

Munro Fox's command of foreign languages was remarkable and included Russian, Arabic and Serbo-Croatian. He taught for some time at the University of Alexandria. After the war he often worked during the summer on Lago Maggiore. He was honoured by many institutions in this country and abroad, was Fullerian Profesor of Physiology at the Royal Institution from 1953–56 and became a President d'Honneur of the Zoological Society of France. His many scientific medals were presented to the College after his death. Professor Munro Fox died suddenly while out riding in Rotten Row in Hyde Park in 1967.

The Darwin Building and Peto Place, 1955–1969

Professor Norman Millott who had been Head of the Zoology Department in the University College of the West Indies was appointed to the Chair at Bedford in 1955. I joined at the same time as Assistant Lecturer. Gwyneth Parry left in 1956 to join the Ministry of Agriculture

Fisheries and Food Water Pollution Research Laboratory at Stevenage, later working for the NERC. I was appointed to the vacant Lectureship while two new Assistant Lecturers, Dr June Mahon and Dr Brenda Manley joined the department in the same year. June Mahon was a parasitologist, while Brenda Manley's interests were in vertebrate anatomy and physiology.

Professor Norman Millott graduated from the University of Sheffield. In 1936 he went to Trinity College, Cambridge, working initially with annelids and was appointed Lecturer in the Department of Zoology, University of Manchester, in 1938. He returned to Manchester in 1945 after war service with the RAF VR Technical Branch and in 1947 was offered the Chair of Zoology at the newly formed University College of the West Indies in Jamaica. He built up the department at Mora and established the marine station at Port Royal. It was there that he started work on the light sensitivity of *Diadema antillarum*, the long-spined urchin. This work was continued at Bedford. The echinoids for his research were maintained in the aquarium of the London Zoo. Dr Gwynne Vevers, Curator of the Aquarium, had also worked on echinoderms as a member of the staff of the Marine Biological Associations laboratory at Plymouth. He became an honorary research associate in the department. In 1957-58 Dr Masao Yoshida joined Professor Millott as research assistant. When Dr Yoshida returned to Japan, Dr Teiichi Takahashi joined Professor Millott to continue the neurophysiological work on echinoids. Professor Takahashi continued in this research field on his return to Tokyo and has had a distinguished career as Chairman of the Zoology Department in that University.

To strengthen the research and teaching in comparative physiology, Dr E G Healey was appointed to the newly established Readership in 1956. Dr Healey had worked in Munich before the war and subequently at the University of Wales at Aberystwyth on chromatophore control in fish. This research was continued at Bedford.

Comparative Physiology was built up during the 1960s and because of lack of space a laboratory was equipped in a building in Peto Place which was at that time leased by the College for several expanding departments. Marine Biology was also added as another Special Subject. Most students undertook an elementary field course at Port Erin or Cullercoats. With the introduction of Marine Biology as a Special Subject, students undertook more advanced field work in Gower based in the Zoology Department of the University of Wales, Swansea.

June Mahon left in 1959 to join the Zoology Department at Imperial College. Brenda Manley left at the same time to take up an appointment at the University of Birmingham. They were replaced by Dr John Pontin, from the University of Oxford, an entomologist particularly interested in ant biology, and Miss Rosalind Oldroyd, a former student and limnologist with a special interest in rotifers. They left as Dr and Mrs Pontin on John's appointment to the Zoology Department at Royal Holloway College in 1963. They were replaced by Dr Derek Wakelin, a parasitologist whose initial research was carried out at King's College, London, and Dr Elizabeth Andrews, whose interests in the anatomy and biology of gastropods had been inspired at the University of Reading. Derek Wakelin reinstated the Special Subject of Parasitology within the curriculum, and developed his research on the immunological relationships of gut parasites. In 1964 Jim Green went to Westfield College, London, on his appointment to a newly established Readership. Later appointed Professor, he continued the freshwater tradition at that College and devoted much of his later research to the fauna of crater lakes throughout the world. Also in 1966, Dr J T Y Chou joined the staff to enhance the growing need for a cytologist. He left the following year on appointment to a research position in Germany. He was replaced by Dr Ray Coleman in 1967.

It was in the session of 1966–67 that the new BSc degree based on course units came into operation. This led to profound changes in organisation and timetable. However, the transition was relatively easy for us since the expansion of staff and collaboration with other science departments in the College made it possible for students to be offered a range of sensible options for their degrees.

Miss Ince retired in 1968 after nearly forty years service to the College. On two occasions she had assumed the role of Acting Head of

Department and had taken responsibility for moving the Department to Cambridge in 1939. Her wise counsel and meticulous attention to detail played a significant role in the growth and expansion of the department in the 1950s and 1960s.

Dr Clive Catchpole joined the staff from the University of Nottingham in 1968 bringing a much needed interest in animal behaviour to the Department. His work on bird behaviour which he had initiated in Norfolk concentrated on sexual selection and evolution, especially in wetland birds. Clive was one of the pioneers in the use of electronic analysis of bird song. Field studies were carried out both in this country and abroad and included collaboration with colleagues at the Max Planck Institute Laboratories at Radolfzell, Germany, and as far afield as the Seychelles. More recently in collaboration with other workers in the United States, work has been carried out on the song centres of the brain in the two sexes. Clive has published several books on this subject. Later he was appointed Reader and then Professor at Royal Holloway and Bedford New College in recognition of his researches in this field. In the academic year 1968–69 there were then eight members of academic staff with a reasonable balance of interests in vertebrate and invertebrate zoology, but there was an urgent need for more research space.

In 1969 the Scottish Marine Biological Association's laboratory at Millport was bought jointly by the Universities of London and Glasgow to establish a University Marine Station. Professor Millott was appointed as its first Director. His experience gained in Port Royal and his talents and enthusiasm did much to establish the Station as a valuable University resource for both undergraduates and for research. He retired in 1976 and continued to live in Millport where he died in 1990.

The last fifteen years in Regent's Park, 1970–1985

Following Professor Millott's move to Millport I was appointed to the Chair of Zoology in 1970 after a period as Acting Head of Department. I had graduated from Queen Mary College in 1948 and after initial research on polychaetes with Dr G E Newell I was awarded Postdoctoral and Senior Fulbright Fellowships to work at the Scipps Institution of Oceanography in California in 1950. I returned in 1951 on appointment to the staff of Sir John Cass College, London. I established there the course approved for the University of London Special degree in Zoology before joining Bedford College in 1955. This enabled me to extend my research on the biology of polychaetes under Professor Millott and I was appointed Reader in 1964. At that time my research concentrated on the identification and function of the pigments in polychaete worms. Much of this work was carried out at the Plymouth laboratory, and at the Stazione Zoologica at Naples. This lead to work on the haem pigments, their synthesis and breakdown and their role in respiration in worms living in hypoxic and intertidal environments accompanied by field observations. Later I became more interested in the function of the free cells in the blood and in body fluids of invertebrates, and used tissue transplantation and bacterial infection to elucidate their internal defence mechanisms. Work on the taxonomy of the pelagic polychaetes was also continued whenever material was available. I published a book on annelids in a series edited by Professor Munro Fox, and later, with other collaborators, published a textbook on Invertebrate Zoology for undergraduate use.

I served as External Examiner for many Universities in the UK and abroad, served for several years as the Secretary of the University Board of Studies in Zoology, subsequently becoming Chairman. One of the most rewarding specialist committees on which I sat was that of the Committee of Management of the Marine Station at Millport. I also sat on the selection committee for Senior Fulbright Scholars for many years. I was Dean of the Faculty of Science of Bedford College 1974–76, and was appointed the first Dean of the Faculty of Science in Royal Holloway and Bedford New College.

Two important developments occurred in 1970

The first was the agreement of the University Board of Studies in Zoology to site the University Stereoscan Unit at Bedford College. This was at first accommodated in the bothy of The Holme alongside the EM6B transmission microscope which had been provided by the Science Research Council jointly to Professor Millott and Professor Audus, Head of the Botany Department. Better accommodation was found later in the basement of The Holme. Professor Spanner of the Botany Department acted as Director until his retirement. Dr Andrews was then appointed as Director of the Unit. The Unit was greatly enlarged under Dr Andrews' directorship with acquisition of further instruments and became a valuable facility for both Departments. Indeed, the first permanent building to be erected in 1983 on the Royal Holloway site after the merger, was built to accommodate the EMU.

Elizabeth Andrews continued her studies of the functional morphology of certain organ-systems in prosobranch gastropods. She published, over this period, many elegant papers on the ultrastructure of the heart and the organs involved in excretion, and their evolution in the *Gastropoda*. Many research students made good use of the excellent electron microscope facilities of the enhanced Unit.

The second important development was the building of the three-floor block in the quadrangle between the Darwin and Tuke buildings. This gave much needed extra accommodation for the Department by extending the top floor and most of the basement. The top floor provided an additional laboratory for classes in comparative physiology since the building of the infill coincided with relinquishing the accommodation in Peto Place. There was also more space for technicians, storage of equipment and preparation for classes. The basement was made into a large research laboratory with ancillary facilities: a radioactive tracer laboratory, an animal house and an aquarium with both circulating freshwater and seawater systems to house material for both teaching and research. The seawater system was modelled on that at the London Zoo, in consultation with Dr Vevers. It was built by Mr S White of the Science Workshop and ably maintained by Zygmund Podorhorodecki who had joined the technical staff in 1962. The Science Workshop, with Sid White as Head Technician, was a valuable resource for Zoology and the other science departments, building equipment for use both in the laboratory and in the field. Space and facilities of the infill building enabled expansion of research by staff, postgraduates and research assistants. Zygmund was able to develop the photographic and graphic facilities available for the growing research needs of both staff and students. Tom Butler, who joined the technical staff in 1972, assisted with the development of electronics in relation to the needs of neurophysiology.

The enthusiasm for research of all the staff attracted many postgraduate students and research assistants in the 1970s and early 1980s. They pursued their research with good support from the University, the College and the Research Councils. Many of those who worked in the Department at that time have contributed distinguished research and have since been honoured with Professorships and other academic awards. Of these the contributions of the late Professor Charlotte Mangum of The University of William and Mary in Williamsburg, and of Professor Rufus Wells FRS (NZ) of the University of Auckland, New Zealand, are outstanding. This was a time too when class sizes enabled advanced teaching to be effective, particularly in practical training, and when tutorial teaching could be properly maintained. There was still a 'family atmosphere' congenial for learning, both in the Department and in the College, tangibly recorded by the annual departmental photographs, the originals of which are now in the College Archives. There have been many 'glittering alumni' who started their careers in the Department.

In 1971 Barbara Gilchrist was awarded a personal Readership and extended her research on the biochemistry of the carotenoids and carotenoproteins, partly in collaboration with Dr Zagalsky in the Biochemistry Department. Her final gift to the Zoology Department after her retirement was to make a comprehensive inventory of all our museum material.

The 1970s were certainly productive years. Peter Credland, with interests in insect biology and freshwater biology, joined the Department in 1970 from the University of Nottingham. He developed work on species of the grain weevil, *Callosobruchus*, an important pest of stored grain and of special importance to third-world countries. He was able to maintain strains collected from all over the world in the laboratory and to study their biology and behaviour. Some collaborative work was later pursued with other workers in the University of Tours, France, and co-ordinated with field work undertaken by various organisatons worldwide.

Dr Alistair McVean was appointed in 1971 to increase the strength in comparative physiology. A graduate of the University of Edinburgh, his research into invertebrate neurophysiology was initiated in the University of Wales, and he extended his work on the neurophysiology of a number of invertebrates at Bedford. During sabbatical leave he worked in the University of Auckland, New Zealand, on the weta and, during a visit to the Ross Base laboratory in Antarctica, he studied the neurophysiology of muscle and temperature compensation in fish adapted to life in ice-cold water. On returning to Bedford College he also made studies of eye-muscle control in pigeons and has since made extensive studies of the neurophysiology of the leech.

Ray Coleman left in 1973 to take up an appointment at Haifa University in Israel, and Derek Wakelin moved to the University of Glasgow to develop further his immunological research. He was later appointed to a Chair at the University of Nottingham. Dr M Thorndyke was appointed in 1974 to maintain the teaching in cell biology and develop research in cell structure and function following the departure of Ray Coleman.

Mike Thorndyke has considerably advanced our understanding of the evolution of neurohormonal peptides, peptide production and function in both lower vertebrates and in protochordates. These interests had stemmed from his early work on thyroid-like hormone production in the protochordate endostyle. During the 1970s he made several visits to the Kristineberg Laboratory, on the Swedish Baltic coast, where cyclostomes could readily be obtained. Later work on peptides was extended to advanced invertebrates such as the echinoderms as well as to protochordates. Many of the animals for these studies were obtained from the Plymouth Laboratory and maintained in the departmental aquarium. He has been actively involved with the Society for Experimental Biology and has also served as a member of the Council of the Marine Biological Association. He was later awarded a Professorship in recognition of his research on peptide hormone function.

Dr Tim Healey retired in 1978. Dr Sky Alibhai then joined the department to develop the teaching in mammal biology, statistics and numerical methods. His was the last academic appointment to be made to the department. He had graduated from the University of Uganda. His research interest was the biology of small mammal populations. Sky was able to continue his research on small mammal populations including work on African species in Zimbabwe. He then became interested in the biology of the black rhino, and developed new methods for identifying and tracking individuals to further our understanding of the biology of this endangered species. He left the Department in order to be able to devote his time to this work in Zimbabwe in 1989.

The merger and the new department

From the mid-1970s it became clear that the smaller Colleges of the University of London faced an uncertain financial future. Mergers were an obvious solution reducing the nine science sites to five. Once the decision had been made to merge Bedford College with Royal Holloway College, Professor Chaloner, Head of the Botany Department at Bedford College, and I agreed that it was best for new Bedford students to start their courses at Egham, while enabling students who had already embarked on courses at Regent's Park to complete their degrees there. This meant a great deal of extra work and travelling for staff to service practical classes and to teach on two sites from 1982. Most research came to a halt for two years. The Bedford Department continued to function on two sites until the transfer was completed. By 1985 all the academic staff had moved, together with the remaining technical staff, Don Field, Zygmund Podhorodecki, Tom Butler and Ian Benjamin, to the Egham campus to join the staff of the Royal Holloway

College Zoology Department to form a combined Zoology Department of Royal Holloway and Bedford New College

The Physiology Department, which had no counterpart at Royal Holloway College, also joined the new Zoology Department. Subsequently, by combination with the merged former Botany departments, a Biology Department was formed in 1987. Together with the combined Biochemistry Departments of the two former Colleges, a School of Life Sciences was then formed, composed of no less than seven former departments. Later, this became a more closely integrated School of Biological Sciences in the Bourne Building on the main site at Egham.

Looking back we can review with some pride an excellent record of achievement during our first 150 years. Numbers of students rose steadily and the number of academic and technical staff was also increased to maintain ratios for effective teaching and opportunities for research. The course unit system adopted in the 1960s enabled all staff to have periods free from undergraduate teaching when they could most effectively pursue experimental and field research. By 1980 there were more technicians than academic staff. The foundations of a good Department had been well laid over a hundred years before and its reputation for both teaching and research significantly increased. All the academic staff in the 1970s were not only active in research and teaching, but undertook College and University appointments and were active in scientific societies in their chosen fields.

Acknowledgements

The staff of the College Archives (Bedford Centre for the History of Women).

Mr L Turnbull, Registrar, and staff of the Registry when in Regent's Park for allowing me access to Miss McNaulty's copies of the College Prospectuses and Council Reports.

Mr and Mrs Richard Ince for lending me Miss F Ince's last Passport and allowing me to copy her photograph from it.

The Hocken Library, University of Otago, Dunedin, new Zealand, for their help in searching for photographs of Professor W Blaxland Benham. I also wish to thank Dr Ken Miller for the colour prints of the oil painting of Professor Benham which adorns the Benham Lecture theatre in the Zoology Department there. These, and other original prints, have been deposited in the College Archives at Egham.

Authors of other chapters, especially Professor Leslie Audus and Professor Maureen Young, for exchange of our draft chapters and for discussion.

Margaret Dales for her constructive criticism of this chapter and, not least, the Editor for his suggestions and patience.

References

1 M J Tuke *A History of Bedford College for Women 1849-1937* Oxford University Press (1939), p302, p320.

2 College Council Reports (various).

3 Dales and Gilchrist. *A History of the Zoology Department Bedford College 1849–1985.* (1987) RHBNC.

4 College Prospectuses (1849–1985) see also Dales and Gilchrist (loc cit)

Chapter 19

A New Beginning

The Merger of Bedford with Royal Holloway College, 1981–85*

Dorothy Wedderburn

In 1982, at a meeting of the Court of London University, Lord Scarman, then its distinguished chairman, declared Bedford College to be the jewel in the Crown of the University. Admittedly this statement was delivered in the middle of a highly charged discussion, but it shows the importance attached to the future of Bedford, not just because of its unique historical contribution to the development of higher education for women, but because of its long standing contribution to the intellectual strength of London University. As it became clear, however, neither history nor reputation could protect Bedford from the winds of change. Over the next few years not only London University, but the whole of the British system of higher education, were to be transformed.

The process of merger between Bedford College for Women and Royal Holloway College, between 1981 and 1985, cannot be understood without first considering the wider context of the Universities from the sixties onwards. Here, four changes stand out. The first was the expanding number of students in higher education which followed the acceptance by the Government of the Robbins report in 1963; the second was the fundamental change in the financial environment of the Universities during the seventies and eighties; the third was the continuing change in the organisation of scholarship and research which became more marked from the fifties onwards; and finally, there was the change occurring in the governance of London University itself, culminating in the University of London Act of 1978, and the accompanying new Statutes, which began to take effect in 1981.

The Robbins report began the process of transforming higher education in Britain from a highly selective elite system (in 1962 there were only 216,000 students in total) into the mass system of today. By 1980 the number of students had already more than doubled. The initial post-Robbins expansion was met by the funding of several new universities on green field sites. But as capital resources came under pressure more and more of the increase was expected to come from existing institutions, not only the Universities, but also what came to be called the polytechnics (after 1992 they too became absorbed into the University sector). Bedford responded to the mood of expansion by planning to increase its 1962 numbers (which were just under 1,000) by 20 per cent over the next three years and to double them by the next quinquennium. The admission of men to Bedford in 1965 helped, but the College struggled to reach these targets. The limitation imposed by the size of the Regent's Park site, the very real difficulties in obtaining planning permission for developments, and the limited finance available to the College, all combined to block expansion. A slow increase had taken the student numbers to 1,800 but then the UGC intervened and imposed a limit of 1,640 students. It is not surprising, therefore, to find Bedford in the group of 'small' institutions over whose future Lord Murray, in his report on the future of London University, published in 1972, placed a large question mark.[1] The future for Bedford, Westfield, Queen Elizabeth and Royal Holloway Colleges, he suggested, lay in merger in order to achieve economies of scale and a sounder academic base. He also drew attention to the case for further exploitation of the 100 acre site which Royal Holloway occupied at Egham, which lay beyond the expensive and congested centre of the metropolis. The germ of the idea of London University expansion westward was thus planted.

But by this time finance had emerged as a major limiting factor on the nature of developments in the late seventies. As the government responded to growing economic problems finance for the Universities was held on tight rein. Rapid inflation was eroding the real value of the money available. In the middle of the decade the long standing quinquennial system of grant allocation broke down and the UGC commented: "The year under review (1975–6) marked a decisive down turn in a process of growth of resources which had continued for twenty years and it is unlikely soon to be renewed".[2]

Bedford College recorded deficits on its revenue accounts in each of the years 1974–75 and 1975–76, and although the next two years saw income and expenditure balanced, from 1978 onwards the annual deficit soared.

The third element of change affecting Bedford was academic in origin. The growth of knowledge which resulted in increased specialisation within subject areas for teaching, and increased organised research activity which, particularly in science required investment in expensive infrastructure, posed great problems for small institutions. The Science and Technology Act 1965 established four government-funded Research Councils (to which a fifth was soon added for the Social Sciences) and laid the foundation for what came to be known as 'the dual support system'. The principle of this was that the UGC grant was to cover the cost of the research infrastructure–libraries, laboratories, a proportion of the time of tenured staff to be devoted to research–while specific grants for particular projects were to be allocated on the basis of 'timeliness and promise'. Marigold Pakenham-Walsh shows in Chapter 2 how research activity financed in this way increased in Bedford College, but compared with some other London colleges, such as Imperial, University College, King's College and LSE, it remained on a small scale. The requirements of covering the ever increasing scope of the London University degree syllabus meant that the research interests of the staff were fragmented when the trend was towards more and more team work. Initially the full impact of these changes could be moderated by greater use of the federal system of teaching within London University and by the proximity of the College to larger research centres like University College. But as everyone felt the pressure of growing financial stringencies other colleges struggled to become more and more self contained and the federal system itself came under strain.

This leads us to the fourth element in the context of change, change in London University itself. The federal system had been described as "of Byzantine Complexity", and throughout the sixties and seventies efforts had been made to simplify the constitution and governance, and to find effective ways of reconciling the often conflicting interests of the University as a whole, those of individual schools and institutes, and even the aspiration of individual subject areas. A major investigation of some of these issues led to the Murray Report of 1972. The constitutional recommendations of that report were debated long and hard and only came to be implemented in 1981.[3] The bicameral nature of the system of governance was retained. The size of the Court was reduced to 24 members. It was responsible for the allocation of UGC grant to the individual schools and for the financial implications of academic policy. The latter was decided by a Senate with 120 members, drawn from the schools, faculties, convocation and students. It was of some advantage to Bedford that when I became Principal in 1981 I was immediately elected to the Court, as a result of some astute political thinking on the part of a few members of the Bedford academic staff. As a consequence I was close to the centre of University decision making through all the difficult years that were to follow, when the University itself was adjusting to change.

By the time that Royal Holloway and Bedford New College was established at Englefield Green in 1985 none of the 'small' colleges had survived unchanged and ultimately all have merged with larger institutions. Many of the specialist institutes of the University, such as the Institute of Archaeology, have also been absorbed into other bodies. The powers of the Central University have been eroded over the last ten years. HEFCE (formerly UGC) grants now go directly to the schools; decisions about appointments to chairs and readerships have been devolved; and even degree ceremonies are held in individual schools. The experience of Bedford can then be seen as a quite small step when viewed against the background of the upheaval that subsequently took place. But it assumed far more significance than this might suggest, because it had the distinction of being the first of the institutional mergers. It was a pioneer. Moreover for the members of Bedford, who were justifiably proud of the achievements of their College, it was a period of immense trauma. It is to the recording and analysis of that process that we now turn.

The academic year 1981–82 began inauspiciously. When the UGC grant to London University was announced in July it had appeared it was to be cut by 15% with further deductions of similar magnitude in each of the following two years. Everyone had expected some reduction, but this was worse than had been imagined, and most of the individual schools were shocked to learn their allocation for 1981–82, none more so than Bedford. Chapter 1 shows how slow the College had been to respond to the growing crisis, and the signs of the magnitude of the change that might be necessary. Eyes were still on growth. A public appeal had been launched in 1979 to raise funds to provide more accommodation on the Regent's Park site, with a view to increasing the number of students. In the first instance it was to provide more space for the successful Psychology Department. This was achieved, largely as a result of the generosity of the Wolfson Foundation, but in total the appeal had not reached its target in 1981. In all fairness, it has to be noted that the UGC itself did not send out alarm signals. Following its last quinquennial visitation in November 1978 it refused to assist the appeal, but it recorded its view that the policy of maintaining a wide range of disciplines "by exploiting the flexibilities of the course unit system and by developing joint degrees and subsidiary subjects", was the right one for Bedford to be following. It declared itself impressed by the College's efforts to make the most of University facilities. It did not underline the uncertainty of the general financial future. Thus any efforts of the Principal, Dr John Black, to persuade the College to evaluate options for merger including, incidentally, joining with Royal

Holloway on the Egham site, fell mostly on stony ground. The Academic Board did not believe that the threats were real. Those familiar with the history of the College from its foundation could comfort themselves with the thought that other crises had been survived in the past.[4] It took the cuts of 1981 to galvanise the College into action. By then the accumulated deficit stood at £120,000 after four consecutive years of failing to balance income and expenditure. All resources were exhausted, including those intended for repair and maintenance. After I had been appointed to take up office on 1 October 1981, the then Hon Treasurer sought to reassure me that this financial situation was manageable by telling me that he had negotiated an overdraft facility with the bank of £1m. The total College income from all sources in 1981–82 was estimated to be £6.4m, with anticipated expenditure of £7.5m.[5] Before the 1980s many university institutions had no professional financial management capacity, other than of an accountancy kind. Nor did academic staff themselves have either the ability or inclination to understand the financial aspects of their institutions.

Fortunately the Council of Bedford–the governing body–had finally grasped the gravity of the situation. In the spring term of 1981 it set up a working party "to draw up as quickly as possible a contingency plan which will enable the College to remain a viable and respected institution of teaching and research...where its grant/fee income is reduced by up to 15 per cent...". After meeting throughout the summer term its final report to Council made grim reading. It concluded that six Departments would have to close, three in the Faculty of Arts and three in Sciences (without grasping the nettle of naming which these should be). But it also recommended that an alternative solution should be considered by exploring the formation of an association with other school(s) in the University "with a view to forming, on one or more sites, an open consortium of 2,500 to 3,000 students". This report served, among other things, to reactivate talks with Westfield College, which had been established in the early seventies as a half-hearted response to the Murray report. Very preliminary contact was also made with King's College, another college becoming somewhat anxious about its future viability.

By this time, however, yet another university report had appeared. Professor Sir Peter Swinnerton-Dyer had been invited by the University to address the structural changes needed in the non-medical part of the University (the medical re-organisation, following the Flowers' Report of 1980 already being under way, albeit with reluctance in many quarters).[6] As well as advocating the rationalisation of subject teaching across the University in order to eliminate duplication and excessively small departments, the report once again called for the merger of small schools. The University itself then became more proactive. Lord Annan was about to retire at the end of the 1980–81 academic year and was to be succeeded by Professor (subsequently Lord) Randolph Quirk as the first *de jure* full-time salaried Vice Chancellor. The two men visited Bedford in June 1981. They attempted to persuade the Search Committee, which had been appointed to identify a successor to Dr Black (who had intimated his desire to leave the College to take up an appointment with the Wolfson Foundation), that they should look favourably upon the then Principal of Westfield. It seemed to indicate that the University was contemplating the possibility of a Bedford/Westfield merger. But Bedford did not warm to this suggestion. I was approached and eventually offered the position. After careful thought I accepted and in view of the critical developments about to occur I made arrangements to take up the post at the beginning of 1981–82 academic year.

With hindsight it is interesting to recall that in my discussions with friends and colleagues (including the then Vice Chancellor) about this course of action, most took the view that Bedford had no future and that I would be foolish to leave Imperial College to be Principal of Bedford. But even though it was clear that Bedford could not continue as it was, I felt that an institution with such academic assets could not simply slip into an association with another college without a very careful assessment of the options realistically available and of their various advantages and disadvantages. A prime consideration was that the great strength of Bedford should be preserved and if possible enhanced, albeit in a changed setting. During the weeks remaining of the summer vacation I briefed myself on the financial position of the College; on the range of opinions of members of the College including, of course, the members of the College working party and on the situation in those schools of the University with whom an association appeared possible. From that examination certain principles emerged which I felt should guide our future strategy. First there was the important academic objective of preserving Bedford College's academic strengths and, if possible, enhancing them. Second, was to overcome the weakness of small departments, relatively low research activity, and, particularly in the science departments, inadequate infrastructure. Third was, through association or merger, to achieve a significant reduction in unit costs. Finally to so distribute activities in a multi-site association that the advantages of the Regent's Park site could be retained and fully exploited whilst still achieving the much needed financial economies. With these goals in mind it appeared that a merger with King's College would be the most promising. I found that this view was shared by a number of key participants in the Council working party nor was it dismissed out of hand by influential figures in the University. Most academic staff at Bedford were supportive. Many could see the advantages of becoming associated with a college with the reputation of King's. At the very least the Regent's Park site would remain in use. But whoever we were to be associated with, speed of decision was of the essence.

King's was one of the larger schools of the University, being third, in terms of total income, after Imperial and University College. It may appear surprising that such an institution felt sufficiently threatened to be interested in associations or mergers. It was a proud establishment, founded in the early nineteenth century as a rival to the "godless foundation" in Gower Street, ie University College. Not only did its pedigree contrast sharply with that of Bedford, but it also had a tradition of appointing distinguished military men as Principals. At this time the post was held by Sir Neil, later Lord Cameron, former Chief of the Defence Staff. It contained a wide range of faculties, including law and engineering.[7] But the anxiety it felt about its future security was a reflection of the general apprehension felt in higher education in the light of the changed national financial situation. Moreover, the premises it occupied in the Strand were exceedingly cramped and would severely limit any possibility of further growth. A few days after my arrival in Regent's Park, the Principal of King's contacted me, and we agreed to explore the prospects of merger. It appeared that with Lord Cameron's military background, speedy and crisp decisions were the order of the day.

On 6 October 1981 the Council of Bedford College announced its intention "immediately to engage with the Council of King's College in detailed planning for the establishment of a close formal association leading to a single multi faculty school of the University of London which would not exclude the later accession of other interested parties". The Council of King's College followed with a parallel resolution. The Vice Chancellor of the University noted these declarations with interest. Feverish joint planning activities followed. Relationships at the level of Principals and Chairmen of Council were good. But gradually the Bedford negotiating team became aware of a marked lack of enthusiasm for the project at grass roots level in King's, particularly in some of the science departments. Apparently it was felt that the absorption of the relatively few staff from Bedford would seriously weaken the combined research standing. The ostensible point of difficulty was, however, reaching agreement on which departments should occupy Regent's Park and which The Strand. Just as the Bedford negotiating team had concluded that it should be ready to make concessions to King's, and armed with authority from Council to do just that, the Principal of King's announced at a meeting on 18 December 1981, that he would have to withdraw his college from the talks. It was a terrible blow not only to the *amour propre* of Bedford, but also because a whole term had been wasted.

We shall never know what, if any, informal part the University authorities played in this particular outcome. Over the next few years restructuring in the University was achieved by means of a complex mix of negotiation, arm twisting, guidance from bodies like the UGC and the government, and formal decision taking by bodies with authority, including the governing bodies of individual schools and the Senate and Court of the University. Constitutionally each school was an independent institution with its own Royal Charter or Act of Parliament. But control of finance was the ultimate sanction. Most schools were dependent, to a greater or lesser degree, upon the flow of grants from central government to the UGC, from the UGC to the Court of London University and from the Court to the schools. This control did not have to be spelled out very often because there was little desire on the part of any of the participants in the system to do so. If the University authorities still clung to their preference for a merger of Bedford with Westfield, or the move of Bedford to Egham it was not publicly articulated at this point, and the College was left to formulate an alternative strategy to merger with King's against the backcloth of further university-wide developments.

The implementation of the reorganisation of subject areas in the University following the Swinnerton-Dyer report of 1981 was being placed in the hands of specialist 'subject area committees' consisting of representatives of the schools but chaired by distinguished academics, external to the University. The view was also fast gaining ground that so strong were the arguments in favour of the concentration of resources for science subjects that these activities should be restricted to five sites only, compared with the existing nine; Imperial, University College, King's and Queen Mary Colleges were obvious front runners to be four of those five sites. Where the fifth site was to be located became of burning interest to the remainder, including both Bedford and also Royal Holloway which had the space on its 100 acre site for further development.

The beginning of 1982 was not a cheerful time in Regent's Park. Many informal discussions were held between myself and other heads of schools to explore possibilities of association. At the same time a planning group in the College set to work to produce a 'stand alone' plan revisiting many of the issues already explored in the summer of 1981, but with greater emphasis on the practical steps that would have to be taken following a decision to implement any reconfiguration that was decided upon. Foremost among these was the question of whether the Council of the College had power to declare redundancies of academic staff. It was widely believed in the university world that once academic staff had been granted 'tenure' after satisfactorily serving a period of probation, they could only be removed from post for misconduct or inability to perform their duties. The Conservative Government of 1979 had very early indicated its intention to challenge, indeed to remove, this principle of tenure from academic contracts. In fact on investigation something which had been assumed to apply across the university system, and indeed on the basis of custom and practice, had applied, was found to be legally quite complicated. For example, as a result of the closure of the Department of Hygiene in 1919, Bedford had enshrined in its statutes the power of Council to terminate academic staff contracts, with two year's notice or one year's notice and one year's salary as compensation. But national legislation was now in place to govern redundancy situations. How would this affect any decision which Council might wish to take to reduce the number of academic staff? The future looked so bleak that it was felt prudent to explore the legal position with the government Advisory Conciliation and Arbitration Service.

Meanwhile the college working group published its 'stand alone' plan. It involved the closure of five departments–Chemistry, Biochemistry, Physiology, Classics and Philosophy. The reasons for this particular selection were mixed. In the case of Physiology and Biochemistry it was clear that they were too small even to provide a reasonable range of teaching. Classics had difficulty in recruiting students and was grossly over-staffed in relation to its current student load. Philosophy was only able to function effectively as part of a pan-London consortium and it was highly likely that the relevant subject area committee would recommend its transfer to another school.[8] As for Chemistry, the cost per student was high, and it was below the optimal size for a chemistry department which concentrated on teaching, let alone one which could provide a critical mass for research. The outcry within the College, the University, nationally and internationally, was enormous. The Classics Department enlisted the support of the Royal Patron, petitions of protest abounded and there were many letters to the press. With hindsight it is difficult to believe that anyone could have taken the 'stand alone' plan seriously. It was born of desperation, and would have proved totally impracticable had there been any attempt to implement it. For, as we have seen, the arguments were all running against small departments and small institutions. Its main function was to alert members of the College to the necessity of deciding on a merger and implementing it as quickly as possible. There remained the possibility of approaching Royal Holloway College.

Royal Holloway had its own anxieties.[9] Although its financial position was not quite as dire as that of Bedford, it had fewer students and was vulnerable on grounds of size. Joining with nearby Brunel University had been explored but had foundered on the insistence, by RHC, that it must remain part of London University and the equally strong insistence, by Brunel, that it could not tolerate joining the byzantine structure of London. It is important to appreciate that the reluctance felt in Regent's Park to engage in talks with RHC stemmed not from any intrinsic opposition to the academic consequences of such an association or merger. Indeed, the academic profiles of the two Colleges were remarkably close fitting. They each contained departments not matched in the other, so that the range of subjects would be enhanced by joining together. And even where there were matching departments, specialities within them were complementary. In addition RHC was located on a site at Egham which had immense natural beauty. The Founder's Building was a famous architectural attraction. The real objection was that to open discussions implied the acceptance of a physical move of Bedford College and its staff to Surrey as a necessity, and hence the abandonment of central London as a location. However, as the enormities of the upheaval in the higher education system became more and more apparent, the hope that

Bedford could in any case continue in the Regent's Park site with or without merger with another central London college became more and more unlikely. A dispassionate assessment revealed a lease of the main site from the Crown Estate Commission with only 29 years to run. Even were it possible to renew the lease it was clear that the policy of the Commission was to secure market rents, leading inevitably to a big increase in the rent to be paid. The buildings on the site were badly in need of major refurbishment for which there were no reserves. Finally if growth was the name of the game for long term survival, there was little room to accommodate more students or more research activity.

By February 1982 what had seemed unthinkable began to appear possible and for some people inevitable. Talks between the two Principals were held, and the University then began to play a more active part. The Vice Chancellor visited both institutions extolling the advantages of merger and offering the prospect of a powerful new institution being established at Egham, with plenty of room for expansion. Still many academic staff members, particularly of the Arts Faculty at Bedford, remained unconvinced and sought to reopen talks with Westfield. The Principal of Westfield, angry at the hasty withdrawal of Bedford from talks in October, was prepared to give only qualified approval to renewed contact and there was no support forthcoming from the planning committee at Bedford. On 18 March 1982 the Council of Bedford College was asked to consider joining with its opposite number in RHC in declaring an intent "to seek a union of the two colleges as rapidly as proves practicable". It was crucial that this declaration be made available to the Court of the University for its meeting on 31 March when the location of the fifth science site was to be announced. The general advice to Council from Academic Board was in favour of this declaration, but the arguments against were sufficiently powerful for Council to adopt the declaration only in principle. Council resolved to review the situation at a special meeting on 30 March when the outcome of a decision, to be made by Academic Board on that day as to whether they wanted a merger with Westfield College to be further pursued, would be available. The days that followed were cliff hangers. There was a clear rift between the majority in the two Faculties, Arts and Science. A nightmare scenario emerged of the College being totally fractured, with some departments going one way and some the other. But by 30 March the official opposition to a merger with RHC had collapsed, and the Bedford College Council resolved to "seek a union between the two colleges".

All was not plain sailing however. It was at this point that the Bedford College Governors entered the decision making process. Chapter 1 describes their composition and power as guardians of the Constitution under the Royal Charter of 1909 which authorised Bedford to teach only in the counties of London and Middlesex. RHC was, of course, at Egham in Surrey. The 'Save Bedford Campaign' which had been gathering momentum with lobbying and demonstrations over the last few weeks, seized the opportunity, and focused its attention upon the Governors' meeting called to amend the Charter. With demonstrations outside, and cogent argument inside, both for and against change, the motion to seek an alteration of the Charter was carried but without the necessary two-thirds majority of those present and voting.

A second meeting, six weeks later, produced the necessary majority, after a strong steer from Council that to delay further would be disastrous as options were being closed off and financial deficits were accumulating. This opened the way for a petition to the Queen in Council, supported by a resolution from the Senate of London University for the Charter to be amended. On 26 July 1982 the Chairmen of the two college Councils "signed a partnership agreement to cooperate as closely as possible in the teaching of students registered in each college and to share the use of existing Royal Holloway buildings and facilities at Egham Hill; the intention of the Councils of the two colleges being to seek a union of the colleges, resulting in the formation of a new single institution incorporated by Act of Parliament". It took three more years for that incorporation to be achieved. But the July agreement was framed in such a way that, even though there was no legal union, the availability of spare capacity in the

Bourne Building enabled the Chemistry Department to be the first to move from Bedford to Egham in the summer of 1982.

The ten months from October 1981 to July 1982 had been fraught with anxieties and frictions of many kinds, but in retrospect the momentous decision to merge Bedford with RHC can be seen to have been taken relatively smoothly and rapidly. Many other university institutions experienced sharp confrontation between their Vice Chancellor and Academic Board which, in some cases delayed or even prevented much needed change, and left much bitterness. The two Colleges can be justifiably proud of their achievement. Moreover, their willingness to change served to restore some of the reputation of London University. After years of committees and reports advocating change, the first steps to reconfiguration on the non-medical side of the University had been taken.

In the months that followed the taking of the key decision by the two governing bodies the Government both directly, and indirectly through the University Grants Committee, began to play a more central role in developments. The whole process had been precipitated by the decision of the Thatcher government to cut funding for higher education. But the three years of planning involved in the implementation of the Bedford and Royal Holloway merger were played out against the elaboration of a national policy for higher education generally by the then Secretary of State for Education, Sir Keith Joseph. The principles underlying that policy were codified and clearly stated in the document produced in May 1985, the 'Development of Higher Education into the 1990s'.[10] The demographic projections on which the policy was to be based suggested that demand for university places would remain constant for the next five years and then would fall for five years after that. The Robbins' principle that "courses of higher education should be available for all those who are qualified by ability and attainment to pursue them" was rewritten to confine that provision to situations where the "benefit to the individual" was "sufficient to justify the cost". Emphasis was placed upon reducing reliance for funding upon central government "although reliance on public finance is to a great extent unavoidable, the Government wishes to see it reduced; because of the expected decline in student numbers in the 90s it is not improbable that some institutions of higher education will need to be closed or merged"; and because the prime value of higher education was seen to be its contribution to economic performance "the proportion of arts places in higher education as a whole can be expected to shrink".

Since the major part of the assets of Bedford College had been supplied over the years by public bodies, government permission to use them to finance building at Egham had to be obtained and because additional capital was going to be needed to supplement the proceeds from disposal of the Regents Park site, a business case had to be prepared. The approach was dictated by Treasury rules which required that the anticipated savings of recurrent expenditure in the new institution should be calculated as a rate of return on capital invested and judged against Treasury criteria. The plan was prepared on the assumption that we would build for 3,000 students. But because of the pessimistic forecasts of future student numbers prevailing at this time, permission was finally only granted for a student target of 2,750. The new College had been 'pre-shrunk'. It is impossible to refrain from commenting on the short sightedness of this approach. The view that student numbers in higher education would fall did not survive the departure of Sir Keith from the Department of Education, and there has been a steady expansion in the numbers of students ever since. Royal Holloway and Bedford New College has approximately doubled in size in the fifteen years since its founding.

The Government was also able to influence the governance and conditions of academic tenure of the new college because Privy Council approval for new statutes and regulations was required. The 'strong tenure' written into the Royal Holloway and Bedford New College Act 1985 was to be short lived. The Education Act 1988 made provision for its abolition in all universities. However positive assistance for restructuring was forthcoming from the government in the form of an agreement to finance, for a limited period, a relatively generous early retirement and resettlement scheme for staff who were displaced as well as contributions to removal expenses of individuals. As for capital development at Egham, grants were forthcoming via the UGC and the University, which together with sale proceeds enabled building to proceed. Government support for the merger was essential and foreshadowed what has been a continuous trend in the last twenty years, namely of greater government direct intervention in higher education and abandonment by the UGC of any pretence that it could exercise major influence over the running of the universities.

The sale of the Regent's Park site presented great problems. The Crown Estate Commissioners who owned the leases would only allow them to be disposed of to educational institutions and the shortness of the remaining years on the lease of the main site did not make it very attractive. With the help of extremely good estate agents we began negotiations with a North American College which wished to acquire premises in London for its year abroad programmes. In the end the obstacles were only surmounted by the device of the College surrendering its lease to the Crown Estate for a consideration. In turn they negotiated a new lease with Rockford College in the name of its UK registered company Regent's College. The arrangement with Rockford was important in other ways. It made it easier for Bedford to phase the transfer of activities to Egham and to share control with Rockford as it moved into Regent's Park as Bedford left. It was also particularly helpful in ensuring that many of the manual and support staff of Bedford who could not contemplate moving to Surrey, were able to continue their employment with Rockford.

All institutional restructuring has hidden costs and the human cost is all too often omitted from the equation. It is difficult to place a monetary value upon it. The threat to employment has been touched on above. But even those staff who moved to Egham frequently had to face longer and less convenient journeys. Research work faced major disruption as equipment had to be dismantled and reassembled. But perhaps the greatest burden of all was borne by the students. Students who had expected to complete their studies in central London suddenly found themselves at Egham, a fifteen minute walk to the station and a 36 minute train journey into Waterloo. Physical conditions on the RHC site rapidly deteriorated as the building work got under way. Pressure on student residential accommodation at times became almost unbearable. Part of the library was housed in prefabricated huts previously used as temporary terminal buildings at Heathrow. Mud and noise were everywhere. Those students who remained in central London had to move location two or three times as space was handed over to the new occupants. Recreational facilities were gradually disappearing. It is not surprising that there was a good-tempered demonstration when the Queen Mother, as Patron, paid her last visit to Regent's Park. What is surprising in retrospect was that there had been no occupation of buildings in protest at the hardship being imposed on students. One remarkable achievement was that degree results showed no sign of having been adversely affected and the student representatives made invaluable contributions to all the planning committees.

Finally, how far did a genuinely 'new' College with its own ethos emerge from this process? On the face of it the two Colleges were very similar. They had similar origins in extending higher education opportunities to women. They were both part of London University, both small and, as we saw above, possessed matching academic configurations. Yet as the process of merger proceeded differences of culture emerged. Different histories had left their mark. RHC had been founded and generously endowed by a wealthy philanthropist with no particular relationship to women's education. He had provided a magnificent building, modelled on the Chateau of Chambord in the Loire Valley, had secured a priceless collection of Victorian art for the edification of the 'young ladies' and had left a further capital sum to meet recurrent expenditure (sadly exhausted by the time of the merger). As Chapter 1 shows, the origins of Bedford were very different. Mrs Elizabeth Jesser Reid was a women of modest means who shared a vision of the importance of education for women with a number of middle class liberal reformers, none of whom was very wealthy. RHC was located on the very edge of London, and of the University. Bedford was at the hub of the city and within walking distance of the University Senate House. These differences appeared to be reflected in the approach of the two colleges to the planning and execution of the many facets of the merger process. RHC was cautious and wanted to proceed only after due consideration of all aspects of a problem. Bedford was in a hurry, even if it meant taking risks. The merger was on the RHC site so that the weight of tradition was loaded in its favour. Former Bedford College staff sometimes felt like exiles, while RHC staff felt that they were being invaded. Many academic staff in both places felt insecure about the effect of merger upon prospects of promotion and upon headships of departments. Administrative staff were burdened by the existence of two of everything, and although many took the opportunity of early retirement others had the discomfort of having to compete for their 'own' jobs. These rivalries and emotions could be said to have reached their nadir in the debate about the name for the new College. In the summer of 1985 the bill to effect the union was ready to be laid before Parliament. But it still had no title. New College had been canvassed without much support. There was a quite strong desire to retain the Royal connection on both sides, and so Queen's College was suggested. It was rapidly dropped in the face of strong protests from Queen's College in Harley Street. The 'Royal' we were informed could not be separated from Holloway if it was to be retained. So at the eleventh hour Royal Holloway and Bedford New College emerged and became, and remains, the legal title. When professional image makers became involved in the 'marketing' of the College in the early nineties, it was decided that it was too cumbersome, and usage reverted to Royal Holloway. This decision appears to have aroused little opposition among the staff and students which seems to indicate that among the contemporary members of the College the merger had been completed. It was a move, at least in the short term, which forfeited much support among Bedford College alumni.

Has the vision which Lord Quirk offered the two Colleges in 1982 been realised? There can be little doubt that the answer is 'yes'. The academic reputation of Royal Holloway and Bedford New College is high; it has shown an increasingly rapid rise in research success; it is popular with students and it has shown great strength in innovation. There has been a genuine merger which encapsulated the best of both traditions, and which has enabled success to be achieved in the totally different environment of higher education of today compared with twenty years ago. John Carswell[11] published in 1985 an interesting history of the relationship between government and universities between 1960 and 1980. He rightly viewed 1980 as a watershed. But he also commented "The notion that universities are somehow apart from the workaday world...has been nourished by literature and has a foundation in the professional detachment and mutual esteem of university people. Just the same it is an illusion. Far from being separated from the currents of ordinary life universities are almost always excessively sensitive to them and reflect them in a thousand ways". The final years of Bedford College amply support this view.

Acknowledgement

*I am deeply indebted to Marigold Pakenham-Walsh for allowing me access to her own work in the Archives and her personal dramatic account of the merger.

References

1 Final Report of the Committee of Enquiry into the Governance of the University of London HMS0, 1972.

2 Quoted in John Carswell, *Government and the Universities in Britain*, CUP, 1985, p158.

3 For an account of the battles between the parties see Negley Harte, T*he University of London 1936–1986*, The Athlone Press 1986, pp265ff.

4 Margaret J Tuke, *A History of Bedford College for Women 1849–1937*, Oxford University Press, 1939. Had Miss Tuke been providing a title for the present chapter she would, I think, have called it "The Storm Clouds Gather Again".

5 The UGC would not tolerate such a position today.

6 London Medical Education–A New Framework; Report of a Working Party on Medical and Dental Teaching Resources, London University 1980.

7 At this time King's had still not been rejoined with the medical school at Denmark Hill.

8 This was, in fact, the result and Bedford lost its highly distinguished Philosophy Department. The outcome of the subject area review committee deliberations are discussed in the individual chapters of this volume. The process was not without conflict between the interests of the individual schools (in retaining an attractive and balanced range of subjects); the interest of the subjects (to achieve a critical mass and a balance of research interests within the department) and the interests of the individual members of staff.

9 Royal Holloway College will now be referred to as RHC.

10 The Development of Higher Education into the 1990s. Cmnd 9524 London HMSO, May 1985.

11 John Carswell op cit p167.

Chapter 20

Postscript

Sesquicentenary Celebrations Year 1999

Marta Baker

The College celebrated the 150th Anniversary of the Founding of Bedford College on 1 October 1849. Announcing the Programme of Celebrations, the Principal, Professor Norman Gowar said: 'We are extremely proud to be part of the great tradition begun by Bedford's founder Elizabeth Jesser Reid. This Anniversary is a fine opportunity to trumpet both the achievements of women and the extraordinary progress in higher education over the last 150 years, and to inspire us to yet greater things in the next century.'

In her introduction to the Bedford Celebratory Brochure, Her Royal Highness The Princess Royal, Chancellor of the University of London said: 'In commending to you the Celebrations of the 150th Anniversary of the Founding of Bedford College, I ask you to regard this year as one of celebration not only of the achievements of Bedford College but also of the achievements of women in general'.

The Bedford Sesquicentenary Celebrations Committee under the Chairmanship of Professor Francis Robinson, Vice-Principal, was set up to plan, design and oversee the programme of events, to be held in London and at RHBNC, to commemorate this significant anniversary. Members of the Committee included Air Commodore Ruth Montague,

Dr Caroline Barron, Dr David Hilling, Mrs Enid Light, Miss Marigold Pakenham-Walsh, Ms Sophie Badham and Mrs Marta Baker (Secretary and Events Organiser).

The celebrations got off to a wonderful start with the 1999 Fawcett Lecture, given by The Baroness Warnock of Weeke, College Visitor at Senate House on 17 February. The lecture,'150 Years of Enlightenment', attended by 350 guests, touched on some of the high spots and turning points in the development of the higher education of women. In her talk, Lady Warnock looked back with admiration to the men and women responsible for liberating women from ignorance and idleness, and opening up for them the pleasures and excitement of the pursuit of knowledge.The Fawcett Lecture was endowed in 1929 by Miss Teresa Gosse, a student of Bedford College in the late 1890's, in memory of Dame Millicent Fawcett to deal with the 'change in the position of women since 1839.' The Reunion of the Department of Social and Political Science immediately preceding the Fawcett Lecture was attended by some 100 Alumni from the late 40's onwards. Every decade was represented and many friendships were re-established as much discussion ensued about friends, lecturers and professors from the past, as well as ways in which the subject matter of Sociology had evolved over the years.

The Stevenson Lecture on 'Biology and Human Freedom' in February was given by Professor Steven Rose, Professor of Biology and Director of the Brain and Behaviour Research Group at the Open University. The Stevenson Lecture was inaugurated in memory of Miss M M Stevenson, Councillor of Bedford College, who died in 1922 and left a legacy to the College.

The 1999 Hayes Robinson Lecture was given by Professor Olwen Hufton on 2 March. A world-acclaimed historian of early Modern European History and an alumna of the Royal Holloway College, Professor Hufton enthralled a packed audience on the theme 'Whatever Happened to the History of the Nun?'. The Hayes Robinson Memorial Fund was established in 1931 by past and present members of the Royal Holloway College to endow a lecture in memory of Miss Hayes

Robinson, a founder of the honours school of History in the College.

On 20 March, over 100 came to Egham to the Geology Gathering. In Queen's Building they found an exhibition of archival material covering the department's history from 1885 to 1955. Dr Grace Page gave a talk on the first 70 years of the department. Dinner in the Picture Gallery, followed by a ceilidh in the Crossland, was enjoyed by old Bedfordians and recent Hollowegians alike.

On 24 March, The Lord Plant of Highfield, Master of St Catherine's College, Oxford gave the Lakeman Lecture on 'Electoral Reform Now'. The Lakeman Lecture was endowed in 1981 by the Electoral Reform Society in memory of Miss Enid Lakeman, to cover the field of electoral systems and democratic processes, embracing political, sociological and technological aspects of representation at all levels. Enid Lakeman, a student at Bedford College kept close links with the College until her death in 1995 at the age of 92.

On 5 May, two distinguished Bedfordians, Professor Janet Finch CBE and Mrs Sarah Tyacke CB received Honorary Fellowships in recognition of their achievements in academic and public life. Janet Finch, Vice-Chancellor of Keele University, graduated in 1967 with a 1st class Honours degree in Sociology and subsequently specialised in family relationships and family policy, gender issues, education policy and research methods. Sarah Tyacke was appointed the first woman Keeper of Public Records for the UK Government and Chief Executive of the Public Record Office of England and Wales. She was responsible for the strategic approach to records management and digital records in government, for completing the New Public Record Office at Kew and for the Family Records Centre in Central London, opened in 1997. At the same ceremony, Patricia Brown, a long-standing member of both Bedford and RHBNC Councils, also became an Honorary Fellow, to honour her signal service to both Colleges.

The highlight of the Celebratory Year was undoubtedly the 'Down Memory Lane' Reunion at Regent's Park on Sunday 23 May attended by over a thousand Bedfordians including students and staff from as long ago as the early 30's. Helen Clay (BC62/63) summed up the feeling of many when she wrote: 'We had a splendid time: good food, good company, and a lovely chance to revisit old buildings, and revive many pleasant memories.' Stella Baker (nee Harrison) added: 'It was truly wonderful to simply be back in the building, remembering things that have been tucked away in the mind for so many years.' Geographers held their own ' Reunion within the Reunion'on the same day in Tuke Hall. Sue Kitching wrote: 'What a wonderful stroll 'Down Memory Lane' you provided for us all. I'm sure I speak for all alumni who were lucky enough to be able to revisit the former home of Bedford College for such a happy reunion. The Geographers had a very good time and we felt especially privileged to have our reunion there. I feel it was most generous of Regent's College to allow us to wander so freely and they are to be congratulated on the care they have taken with the buildings and beautiful grounds. I would like to congratulate you on a splendid feat of organisation.' The most magical moment of the day came when a crowd of over 600 packed into Herringham Hall to hear David Hilling, John Prebble and Dorothy Wedderburn share their 'Memories of Bedford'. In response to a huge demand, a second Reunion at Regent's Park, 'Down Memory Lane 2' was held in September.

The Garden Party in June was attended by over 1200 people of all ages. It attracted 100 alumni who joined in the family fun and also had an event of their own–cream tea in the Dining Hall. The day ended with the Thanksgiving Service when Bedford Alumna, the Revd Professor Frances Young, Pro-Vice Chancellor, Birmingham University, preached on 'Wisdom and Womanhood'.

The 'Women and Brainpower' Conference in July brought together top academics from England and the USA to explore the contribution of women to intellectual life–asking what the advent of women into the world of learning has meant for the community's stock of brainpower. The Conference launched the Bedford Centre for the History of Women, a new research and archive centre. The Centre not only houses the College archives and deposited collections of the papers of distinguished women, but also has search and seminar rooms and a library. It aims to attract scholars from the UK and abroad to use its resources and contribute to the study of the roles played by women in the present and past. The Bedford Centre plays a key role in the teaching and support of the MA in Women's History: Gender and Society in Britain and Europe 1500-1980. The Official Opening, which followed a Public Lecture by Baroness Helena Kennedy QC, was performed by Anita Gradin, a member of the European Commission.

On 15 July Her Royal Highness The Princess Royal awarded Honorary Degrees of the University of London to four distinguished women:

> The Hon Dame Mary Arden DBE, first woman Chair of the Law Commission of England and Wales, received the Degree of Doctor of Laws.
>
> Professor Patricia Easterling, first woman Regius Professor of Greek at Cambridge University, received the Degree of Doctor of Literature.
>
> Professor Susan Greenfield CBE, first woman Director of The Royal Institution of Great Britain, received the Degree of Doctor of Science.
>
> Dame Pauline Neville-Jones DCMG, businesswoman and civil servant, received the Degree of Doctor of Science (Econ).

The Bedford Gala Dinner on 1 October was attended by over 100 guests including former Governors, staff and students of Bedford College as well as current staff, Council Members and Honorary Fellows and Associates of RHBNC.

The final event of the Year of Celebrations was the History Department Reunion on 6 November, attended by some 200 alumni, staff and friends. Since the Beveridge Hall was closed for refurbishment they were unable to relive the experience of the Monday morning Senate House Lecture Hall lectures. Instead, they sat in the comfortable SOAS Lecture Hall and listened to Professor Joe Mordaunt Crook's witty and polished account of the mavericks, eccentrics and scholars who had served as Professors in the Bedford History Department. Professor Tony Stockwell, Head of RHBNC History Department paid tribute to the rich Bedford tradition which contributed so much to the style and scholarship of the present department. The evening finished with a buffet supper and much laughter, rekindling of old friendships and the making of new ones.

The Sesquicentenary Exhibition, open throughout the year, explored three themes: the early history of Bedford College, in particular the role of Elizabeth Jesser Reid and the Reid trustees in promoting women's education; Bedford women staff and students and the University of London; and the history of the Fawcett Lecture.

May Bedford traditions and memories long continue!

Index of Names

(numbers in italics refer to illustrations)

Abercrombie, Lascelles, 101, 102
Acland, Rt Hon Sir Arthur Dyke, Bt, 3, 26
Acton, H B, 255–6
Acton, Henry Dalberg, 1st Baron, 208
Adrian, 1st Baron, 280
Agar, Delia (née Simpson), 87
Ahmed, Shaki, 91
Albino, Felix, 228
Alexandra, H M Queen, 27
Alibhai, Sky, 352
Allen, J W, 214, 216, 220, ***13***
Andrews, Elizabeth, 346
Annan, Noel (later Baron), 164, 171, 361
Aquilecchia, Giovanni, 237
Arber, Agnes (née Robertson), 64
Arden, Hon Dame Mary, 381, ***50***
Armarego, W L F, 91
Armour, Peter, 238
Arnold, Matthew, 207
Arnstein, Henry, 59
Ashley, Sir William, 318
Ashton, Jonas, 245
Athlone, HRH Princess Alice of, 37
Athlone, HRH The Duke of, 37
Atiyah, Sir Michael, 251
Audus, Leslie J, 71, 72, 73, 75, 76, 78
Ayrton, Maxwell, 31, 36
Bacon, Sir Francis, 216
Badar, Yasmeen, 91
Baddeley, Sue, 74
Bagehot, Walter, 205
Bailey, Wilfred Norman, 247
Bain, Alexander, 256, 295
Bain, Arthur, 131
Baird, Alastair, 167
Baker, G F, 289, 290
Baker, J N L, 134
Baker, Marta, 378, ***53***
Bakshi, S P, 91
Balestrieri, –, 239
Baly, E C C, 69
Banham, Peter H, 162, 165, 174
Barcroft, Sir Joseph, 280
Barrer, R M, 92
Barron, Caroline (née Hogarth), 214, ***15***, ***53***
Bartlett, F C, 254
Barton, Anne, 106
Baxendale, Lily, 91
Baynes, Thomas Spencer, 96, 206
Beecham, Sir Joseph, 28
Bellamy, David, 75
Benest, G E, 138
Benham, W Blaxland, 336-7, ***23***

Bennet-Clark, Thomas G, 75
Bennett, A E, 335
Bennett, Alfred William, 63
Bennett, Arnold, 121, 122
Bennett, G M, 84, 86
Bennett, H S, 103
Bennett, Joan, 103
Bentley, Linna E, 72, 73, 75, 77, 79
Bereton, Isobel, 93
Bergson, Henri, 122-3
Besant, Annie, 85
Bevan, Rt Hon Aneurin, 214
Beyts, E M (née Davidson), 89
Biaggi, –, 239
Bidelux, Hilda, 315
Bins, Anne, 344
Bishop, W W (Bill), 162-3
Black, John, 43, 359
Blackburn, K B, 68
Blackburne, Thomas, 96
Blanc, Louis, 203
Bloch, Jean, 109, 127
Blom-Cooper, Sir Louis, 327
Blundell, Derek, 172-3
Bocquet, –, 110
Bodichon, Barbara, 20
Bolton, Roger, 92, 94
Booth, Rev James, 131, 244
Bosanquet, Nicholas, 334
Bostock, Eliza, 18, 27, 336
Boulanger, C L, 339-40, ***16***
Boulanger, G A, 340
Bourne, A G, 336
Bragg, W H, 266
Bratton, Jacqueline, 105, 106
Bremer, Frederika, 181
Brett, Donald, 76, 77, 78
Brewer, Douglas, 272
Brewer, Rev John Sherrer, 204–5
Britton, Geoffrey, 105, 106
Broad, C D, 254
Brooke, C F Tucker, 100
Brooks, Gladys, 93
Brown, Robert, 70
Brown, George, 326, 331
Brown, Patricia, 379, ***43***
Brown, Robert, 147
Browning, Robert, 97
Brüningh, Baroness von, 203
Bryant, Sophie, 25, 86, 254
Bryce-Smith, Derek, 92
Buckley, Cecilia, 141
Buisson, B, 112
Bull, Karen ***15***
Bull, Alan, 71, 76
Burcheim, Charles Adolphus, 182
Burton, Ivor, 328, 329
Bury, Mike, 331
Busk, Henrietta, 14
Butler, George, 75
Butler, Kathleen, 234
Butt, John, 102, 103
Byrne, Muriel St Clare, 104
Byron, Lord, 96
Cameron, Sir Neil (later Baron), 173
Campbell, Ishbel G M, 87
Canon, Mike, 60
Cargill, H C, 156
Carlile, Sir Hildred, 6, 29, 32
Carlile, Maria Louisa, 99

Carlyle, Thomas, 97, 205, 215
Carnap, Rudolph, 254
Carpenter, Edward, 213
Carpenter, William B, 63, 335
Carré, M H, 68
Carswell, John, 374
Cary, Francis, 227
Cary, Max, ***10b***
Casement, Roger, 214
Cassal, Charles, 110, 128
Cassirer, Ernest, 254
Catchpole, Clive, 347
Cave, Richard, 105, 106
Cazalet, Peter, 143
Chaloner, William G, 78, 79
Champneys, Basil, 27, 31
Chapman, Greg, 163
Cheek, Barbara, 285
Cheesman, Dudley F, 48, 50, 51, 54, 55, 56, 60, 61, 282, ***1***
Chiapelli, Fredi, 235
Chilver, Mrs E M (Sally), 41, 43, 164
Chisholm, Michael, 141
Chomsky, Noam, 254
Clapham, Sir John, 324
Clark, Gordon L, 249
Clark, Jean, 141
Clarke, Sir Cyril ***41***
Clarke, John, 57
Clarke, Louis, 136
Cobban, Alfred, 216
Cohen, Averil, 129
Cohen, J B, 85
Cohn, P M, 249, 251
Coldstream, J N, 12
Cole, Grenville A J, 150, 154
Cole, Monica, 138, 141-2, 144, 272
Coleman, Ray, 351
Conolly, Ann, 71
Cooke, Ann (née Mellor), 92
Cooke, Ron, 144
Cooke, Rev William, 245, 261
Cooper, J P, 217
Cope, B C, 156
Corfield, Penelope J, 220, ***47***
Coscia, C F, 239
Covernton, A V, 97
Cowan, Brian, 267, 273
Craggs, Beatrice, 87
Crawford, Ilse, ***15***
Creasy, M A, 73
Credland, Peter, 350
Creighton, Mrs Louise, 4
Crespi, Angelo, 234
Crofts, Doris, 339
Crompton, Holland, 81, 82, 84
Cromwell, Valerie (later Lady Kingman), 218
Cromwell, Oliver, 208
Crook, J Mordaunt, 2, 214, 217-8, 221–2, 381, ***15***
Cunard, Lady (née Maude Burke, known as Emerald), 27
Cunningham, J T, 338
Curie, Madame, 261
Dales, Rodney, 337, 344, 347, 352, ***19***
Darbishire, Helen, 100
Darlington, R R, 218, 220
Darlow, George, 288, 290
Darwin, Erasmus, 19

Darwin, Major Leonard, 36
Darwin, Lady Maud, 136
Davey, A J, 65
Davey, A S, 64, 66
Davis, Josh, ***52***
Davy, Humphrey, 260
Deansley, Margaret, 218
Debenham, Frank, 136-7
Decio, –, 234
Degani, E, 239
Dego, Giuliano, 238
De la Mare, P B D, 92
De la Mare, Walter, 100
De Morgan, Augustus, 244, 254
De Tivoli, Cesare, 239
De Tivoli, Vital, 239
Devonshire, L M, 152
Dickens, A G, 223
Dickens, Catherine, 96
Dicks, W, 251
Dionisotti, Carlo, 235-6
Dirac, Paul, 266
Dix, Emily, 156, 158-9
Dixon, W T, 93
Dobbs, Roland, 271–2, ***38***
Dobelli, Emma Bice, 229, 231
Dodd, Barbara, 284
Dowden, Richard, 222
Dowman, Ian, 144
Drabble, Margaret, 121, 122
Dretske, Fred, 255
Drew, John, 261
Du Boulay, F R H, 214, 218, 222
Duckworth, Colin, 125
Duncan, Eric, 71, 73
Dunlop, Grace M, 162
Dusouqui, Osman, 91
Dworkin, Ronald, 257
Easterling, Patricia, 381, ***50***
Eccles, Francis Yvon, 119, 120
Eddington, Arthur, 254
Eden, Michael, 143
Edgell, Beatrice, 155, 295, 298–300, 302, 304, 306, 311, ***39***
Edkins, John S, 48, 277, ***20***
Edkins, Nora (née Tweedy), 279
Edwards, Sir Sam, 273
Eggleston, H Gordon, 248
Eggleton, Grace, 284
Eliot, George (née Mary Ann Evans), 96, 228
Elizabeth, H M the Queen Mother, 27, 44, 218, 309, 372, ***38***
Elliott, Rev William, 205
Ellis-Fermor, Una, 100, 102, 104, 105, 107
Elton, Sir Oliver, 100
Embleton, Clifford, 141
Esclangan, A, 113
Esdale, Philippa, 338-9, ***22***
Evans, W D, 156
Ewbank, Inga-Stina, 106
Eysenck, Michael, 310
Faithfull, Glynn, 238, 241
Faraday, Michael, 260
Farago, M E (née Baldwin), 92
Faulkner, Barry, 71
Faulkner, G H, 340
Fawcett, Dame Millicent, 378
Feldberg, W, 280

Fensom, D S, 76
Fernau, J C, 251
Ferguson, Marion, 330
Ferry, Brian, 71, 74, 76, 79
Field, Don, ***24***
Field, Rosalind, 106
Finch, Janet, 379, ***43***
Findlater, Andrew, 96
Fisher, Geoffrey, 144-5
Fisher, H A L, 7
Flint, H T, 266, ***32***
Flood, John, 188-9
Folley, Madeleine, 308
Foot, Michael, 214
Ford, Tom, 78
Forsling, Mary, 287
Forster, E M, 214
Forster, Mary, 150
Forster, Norvella (née Jones), 91
Foss, Brian, 309, 312
Foster, Carey, 262
Foster, Sir Gregory, 5, 97
Fox, H Munro, 56, 341-4, ***17***
Frankerd, T L, 65, 66
Gardam, Jane, 107
Gardiner, Samuel Rawson, 208–10, 214, 222, ***11***
Gardner, Alice, 211
Gardner, Edmund, 230
Gardner, Elizabeth, 127, 130
Gardner, E W, 156
Garratt, F W M, 157
Garrod, William, 100, 101
Garside, S, 68, 69
Gasne, Augustin, 114
Gates, R Ruggles, 338
Geikie, Archibald, 152
Gibbs, Alan D, 165
Gibson, Ian L, 165, 169
Gilbert, E W, 134
Gilchrist, Barbara, 342, 350
Gladstone, Rt Hon W E, 115
Glock, Gertrude, 57, 284
Goldberg, Valerie, 89
Goodyear, F R D, 12
Gosiette, Clare, 254
Gosse, Teresa, 378
Gowar, Norman, 377, ***42***
Grace, W G, 214
Gradon, Pamela, 104, 105
Grant, A J, 217
Gray, A J, 341
Grayson, Cecil, 236
Greaves, R W, 218-9
Green, Christopher, 143
Green, Jim, 342, 344, 346
Greenfield, Susan, 381, ***50***
Grierson, Herbert, 100
Griffith, John S, 248
Griffiths, Hywel, 142
Grigg, Monty, 142
Grove, A J, 341
Grundy, Joan, 104
Guercico, F M, 234
Guildersleeves, –, 284
Guppy, E M, 156-7
Gupta, Anil, 255
Gutkind, Curt Sigmar, 35, 231–3, 240
Haldane, Richard, 1st Viscount, 3, 5, 11

Hales, John Wesley, 97
Hales, Stephen, 75
Halket, Ann C, 64, 65, 67, 69, 70
Hall, Muriel (later Hargreaves), 89, 90
Hanson, Jean, 286, 341
Hardiman, N Jessie, 249, 251
Harding, Denys, 308
Harding, Percy John, 246, ***20***
Hardisty, Jack, 145
Harington, Sir Charles, 281
Harris, Margaret, 141
Harrison-Church, Dorothy, 70, 71
Hart, J V, 65
Hartland, Maud, 315
Hawkes, Ted, 53
Hawkes, Leonard, 149, 155-6, 158-9
Hazlitt, Victoria, 301-2, 305, ***40***
Haywood, Audrey, 167
Healey, E G, 345, 352
Heath, Henry Frank, 97
Heath, M, 133
Heimann, Adolph, 182
Henrici, Olaus M F E, 245
Herringham, Sir Wilmot, 36
Hesselgren, Kirstin, 316
Hetherington, A P, 157
Hett, M L, 338
Hicks, Mary Easterbrook, 64
Hill, J E Christopher, 209, 217
Hill, Norah, 267, 270, ***36***
Hilling, David, 143, 145, 380, ***9***
Hilton, Beth, 288, 290
Hilton, Harold (later Simpson), 247
Hoare, Michael, 268-9, ***36***
Hoblyn, R D, 96
Hodges, Wilfred A, 248, 251, 256
Hodgson, Phyllis, 104, 105, 106
Holland, Charles H, 159, 162
Holland, Michael, 140
Holmes, Arthur, 153
Hooper, Max, 75
Hope, Margot (later Butt), 102
Hopkins, Sir Frederick Gowland, 49
Hose, Rev Henry J, 245
Hosgood, Blanche, 133–4, 137, 139
Hosking, Wendy, 342
Hospers, John, 254
Howlett, K E, 92
Hubback, Eva (née Spielman), 319, 333
Hufton, Olwen, 378
Hughes, Norman, 159
Hughes, Vivian, 214
Hughes, William, 132
Hunt, John Dixon, 106, 107
Hurlblatt, Ethel, 24, 25, 26, ***20***
Hussey, Joan, 218
Hutton, Richard Holt, 245
Hyndman, H M, 213
Illesley, Raymond, 331
Ince, F, 341, 344, 346–7, ***21***
Incoronati, –, 228
Ireton, Henry, 208
Irons, Nancy, 82
Irving, Rev Edward, 208
Isoz, Claire, 127, 130
Jacobs, Eva, 125, 130
Jacobs, Warwick, 146
Jago, Barbara, 344
James, Arthur, 93

James, Prue, 238
James, William, 296
Jameson, Anna, 181, 227
Jebb, Geraldine E M, 32, 33, 34, 38, 88, 232
Jeffery, Violet May (later Saunders), 229, 231, 234
Jefferys, Margot, 324, 326, 330
Jenkin, Annie, 307
Jephson, John, 96
Johnson, Fanny Cecilia, 116, 118
Joliffe, Ivan, 143
Jones, E, 159
Jones, Norman Sinclair, 163
Jones, Raynor, 74
Jones, William Neilson, 65, 67, 68, 71
Joseph, Sir Keith (later Baron Joseph of Portsoken), 325, 369
Judd, J W, 150, 154
Juniper, Barry, 75
Keith, Jack, 161
Keltie, J Scott, 133
Kennedy, Helena (later Baroness), 381, ***49***
Kenworthy, Joan, 141
Kerr, Madeleine, 307
King, Basil, 149, 159–60, 163–6
King, B C, 156
Kinkel, Johann Gottfried, 203
Kinkel, Johanna, 197
Kinton, J Lewis, 97
Kirk, Elizabeth, ***52***
Knaggs, I E, 156
Kneebone, Geoffrey T, 248, 251
Koenigsberger, Renate, 91
Kogan, Maurice, 331
Kolnai, Aurel, 255
Kropotkin, P A, 213
Lacey, Alan, 255
Lacey, Norman, 104
Lagnado, John, 53, 55, 56, 61
Landau, L J, 251
Lange, Helene, 184
Lake, Peter, 222
Lakeman, Enid, 379
Latham, Agnes, 103, 105, 106, 107
Lawrence, C H, 214, 218, 220–21
Laycock, Blanche, 124
Lea, Michael, 271–2
Leakey, Felix, 126–7, 130
Le Breton, Eileen, 124–5, 127
Ledeboer, J A, 156–7
Legouis, Emile, 100, 117
Legros, René, 119, 121, 122
Lesslie, Mary, 82, 84, 85, 90
Levisohn, Isa, 69, 71
Lewald, Fanny, 181
Lewis, Dalene, 284
Limentani, Uberto, 240
Ling, Cheung King, 91
Lippold, Olof C J, 290–91
Little, Victor, 267, 269, 270
Lloyd George of Dwyfor, 1st Earl, 214
Lodge, Sir Oliver, 81, 261, ***26***
Lonsdale, Dame Kathleen (née Yardley), 86, 265–6, ***30***
Love, Alex, 264, 273
Lowe, I H, 153
Lyons, Faith, 125, 127
Lysaght, Averil, 342

Macaulay, Thomas Babington, 1st and last Baron, 216
McCance, R A, 280
McCarthy, P J, 251
McDonald, A I, 156
MacDonald, George, 96
Macdonald, Margaret, 255–6
McDonaugh, Malcolm, 72
Mace, Alec, 306–7
McFarlane, Margaret, 299
McGregor, Duncan, 143–4
McGregor, O R (later Baron McGregor of Durris), 324–5, 328, 329, 334
McKenzie, Alexander, 85
Mackie, J D, 216–7
McLynn, Pauline, 125, 130
McNair, P M J, 238
McNaulty, Norah, 45
MacNeice, Louis, 87, 102
McQueen, Jane, 167
McWilliam, G H, 238
Mahboob, Sardar, 91
Mahon, June, 345
Manley, Brenda, 345
Manley, Gordon, 139-40, ***7***, ***8***
Mansfield, Richard, 266–7, ***36***
Marler, E E J, 87
Martindale, Hilda, 316
Martindale, Louisa, 316
Martineau, Jane, 18
Martyn, Gladys, 300
Marx, Karl, 203
Mary, H M Queen, 27, 28, 32, 37
Masefield, Sir John, 212
Mason, Caroline (née Pearce), 91
Mason, Frances A, 297
Massey, Yolande, 71
Matthews, A H, 137
Maurice, F D, 204
Maxted, William, 142
Maxwell, Sir Alexander, 233
Maxwell, James Clerk, 4, 261
Mayer, Claude Adrien, 125
Mazengo, Richard, 91
Meager, Ruby, 255–6
Mellanby, Sir Edward, 47, 280–81
Menzies, Barbara, 71, 73
Menzies, Martin A, 170
Mess, Henry, 322–3
Midgely, Graham, 105
Miller, Roy, ***41***
Millot, Norman, 289, 344–5, ***18***
Minhaj, Fatima, 91
Mitchell, Ron, 93
Mitchell, Rev Walter, 245, 261
Miyakawa, Sumi, 316
Moodie, A E F, 138
Mole, Jessie, 87
Moravia, Alberto, 267
Morgan, Margery, 104
Morris, S H, 152, 161
Morissey, Sheila, 73
Morton, Alan G, 69
Moss, A J, 159
Mountjoy, Alan B, 139, ***7***
Muir-Wood, Helen Marguerite, 153
Muirhead, John, 297
Mullinger, J Bass, 210
Murthy, David, 93

Murray, Jessie, 124
Murray, Margaret M, 47, 48, 50, 281–4
Murray, P D F, 340
Murray of Newhaven, Baron, 43
Myers, C S, 302
Needham, A E, 340
Neville-Jones, Pauline, 381, ***50***
Nevinson, C R W, 212
Nevinson, Henry Woodd, 212–14, ***12***
Newman, Francis William, 96, 244, 295
Nichols, Dinah, 222
Nicholson, Robin, 159
Nicolau, K C, 94
Nicolay, Rev C G, 13
Norden, Daphne, 50, 52
Notcutt, Rachel, 31
Nutt, Marjorie, 285
Oger, Victor, 114, 117
Ogston, A G, 49
Oliver, Louise (née d'Este Courtenay), 248
Oliver, Hon Richard, 28
Olmo, V S del, 91
O'Shaughnessy, Brian, 256
Owen-Jones, Stuart, 268, 272–3, ***36***
Page, Grace, 379
Pakenham-Walsh, Marigold, 357
Pantin, Carl, 341
Parker, A T, 336
Parkes, Louis, 314
Parkinson, Dame Nancy, 157, 327
Parry, Gwyneth, 344
Patel, P K, 91
Pater, Walter, 206
Paterson, Agnes J, 35
Paterson, John, 141
Patman, Colin, 143
Paton, Jean (née Comyn), 71
Patterson, John, ***7***
Pattison, Mark, 19
Pauling, Linus, 84
Peacock, Ronald, 193-4
Penrose, Dame Emily, 22, 23, 25, 114
Penson, Dame Lillian, 1, 191, 217–9, 221, 222, ***14***
Penston, Norah L, 38, 41, 72, 76
Perutz, Max, 89
Peters, Sir Rudolph, 49
Pettoello, Decio, 234
Pick, Marianne, 191
Pick, Robert, 191
Pickering, S U, 81
Pickford, Mary, 278
Pilbeam, Pamela (née Cartlidge), 214
Pilcher, Giles Theodore, 31, 67
Pilet, Paul-Emile, 76
Pincherle, Leo, 267, 270, 273, ***36***
Pitt-Rivers, Rosalind (née Henley), 86, 281
Pixell, Helen (later Goodrich), 337–8
Plant, C T H (later Baron), 379
Pollard, A F, 216, 222
Pollard, A W, 97
Pontin, John, 346
Pontin, Rosalind (née Oldroyd), 346
Pope, Sir William, 84
Porter, Helen (née Archbold), 68
Potter, Rob, 144-5, 174
Powell, Derek, 162

Powell, F York, 209
Prakobsantasukh, Birawan, 91
Prebble, John, 53, 56, 60, 74, 380
Prichard, F E, 92
Pridham, Jack, 59
Priebsch, Robert, 185, 187
Procter, Winifred (née Nash), ***45***
Purdie, Edna, 189-91, 193
Quarmby, Rhoda, 57
Quirk, Sir Randolph (later Baron), 7, 173, 274, 361, 367
Rae, H C, 251
Ragon, Adolphe, 110, 128
Raisin, Catherine A, 63, 64, 133, 149, 150-52, 154-5
Raleigh, Sir Walter, 5
Ramsay, Sir William, 5
Ravenstein, E G, 132
Rayleigh, 4th Baron, 69
Rayment, Margaret, 344
Rayner, Mabel Chevely, 67, 69, 71
Reed, Richard, 167
Reich, Dorothy (née Knight), 192, 196
Reid, Elizabeth Jesser (née Sturch), 14, 15, 16, 17, 22, 95, 109, 128, 182, 227, 243–5, 335, 372
Reid, Helena M, 319, 329
Reynolds, Barbara, 234
Reynolds, Doris Livesey (later Holmes), 153, 157, 166
Reynolds, Samuel Harvey, 206–7
Rice-Evans, Peter, 259, 268–9, 272, ***37***
Richardson, Ethel (later Robertson), aka Henry Handel Richardson, 188–9
Richardson, Harold, 259, 268, 271, ***33***, ***36***
Richardson, O W, 263, 270
Rickett, Mary, 111
Ridley, M R, 104
Rippmann, Walter, 183
Rivers, W H R, 297
Rivett, M S, 68
Robbins, Lionel (later Baron), 39
Roberts, Alan, 169
Robertson, John George, 116, 185-8
Robinson, Francis, 377
Robinson, Fred, 93
Rogers, Nick, 167
Roper, Lyndal, ***47***
Roscoe, W C, 205
Rose, Edward P F, 162
Rose, Francis, 71, 73, 74
Rose, Hilary (née Griffiths), 75
Rose, Stephen, 378
Rosebery, Archibald Primrose, 5th Earl of, 209
Roulier, A, 110
Routh, H V, 100
Royal, HRH Princess, 377, ***44***, ***50***
Rucker, Sir Arthur, 185
Rudler, Gustave, 118, 119
Ruskin, John, 97, 213
Russell, Bertrand, 3rd Earl, 255, 265
Russell, Conrad, 5th Earl, 218, 220, 222
Russell, William, 261
Rutland, Frances E, 238
Sainsbury, Mark, 256
Saintsbury, George, 207

Salmon, Vivien, 105
Saltmarsh, Maud, 264
Samuel, Ida, 183
Sandall, John, 93
Sanders, Lloyd, 211-12
Sanford, J Langton, 205
Sargant, Alice Caroline, 31, 66
Sargant, Ethel, 64, 66
Sargant, Lord Justice, 68
Sassoon, Siegfried, 297
Saunders, Andrew D, 169
Saunders, John, 272
Saunders, Sir Owen, ***41***
Savazzi, –, 239
Savile, Anthony, 256
Saw, R L, 255
Scarman, Leslie (later Baron), 355
Schüddekopf, A W, 184
Scott, Rev A J, 95, 253, 295
Scott, Andrew, 168
Scott, Pearl, 286
Scott, Sir Walter, 183, 215
Scott Holland, Rev Henry, 213
Seeley, L B, 207–8
Seeley, S R, 207
Semmens, E S, 69
Shaen, William, 21
Shanmugasundaram, Y, ***47***
Sharman, Bernard, 71, 76, 77
Shaw, Elizabeth, 141
Sheldon, Brian, 330
Sherwell, May, 93
Sherwood, Jennifer (née Allard), 311
Shine, Henry, 91
Siegel, Herb, 91
Singh, Shyam, 91
Sitwell, Dame Edith, 121
Small, James, 67, 68
Smart, Leopold, 96
Smee, Dora, 134–5, 137, ***7***
Smith, Alec J, 149, 168–9, 170–75, ***44***
Smith, Julia, 182
Smith, Eleanor Elizabeth, 18
Smith, J W, 92
Smith, Malcolm, 127, 130
Smith, Stanley, 155
Smith, Sydney, 28
Sommerfield, Arnold, 263
Soons, Jane, 141
Soulié, Marguerite, 121
Spanner, Douglas G, 73, 74, 76
Spate, O H K, 138
Spearing, E M, 98
Spears, Kathleen, 45
Spence, Nicole, 125, 127
Spencer, J F, 82, 84, 86, 90
Spink, John Stephenson, 124–6
Spurgeon, Caroline, 98, 99, 100, 101, 107
Stead, Anthony D, 78
Stebbing, L Susan, 103, 255, 306–7
Stephenson, E M, 86
Stephenson, W, 251
Stevenson, M M, 378
Stewart, Charles, 336
Stewart, Noel, 268-9, ***36***
Stewart, Rev W C, 254
Stockwell, Tony, 382
Stone, Lawrence, 217
Stopes, Marie, 64

Storey, Doris (née Greaves), 93
Storrie, Margaret, 141
Streater, Raymond F, 249, 251
Sturt, Brian, 159, 162, 165
Summer, Mrs Morton, 151
Sutherland, Diana, 166
Sutherland, G B B M, 88
Sutherland, Nicola M, 220, ***15***
Swanwick, Anna, 181
Swinnerton-Dyer, Sir Peter, 7, 44, 273, 361, 364
Symes, W Legge, 300
Symonds, Kathleen, 72
Takahashi, Teiichi, 345
Tamblin, J L, 141
Tarski, Alfred, 254
Tarrant, Dorothy, ***10a***
Tate, Amy, Lady, 28
Tate, Sir Henry, 28
Tawney, R H, 319
Taylor, Sheelagh, 220
Taylor, Tom, 268, ***36***
Temperley, Eileen, 50, 53
Temperley, H W V, 217
Temple, J T, 159
Tennyson, Alfred, 1st Baron, 1, 96, 97
Tennyson, Sir Charles, 40
Thirlwall, Matthew F, 170
Thoday, D, 65
Thomas, David Lloyd, 256
Thomas, Ethel N M, 64, 65, 66, 67, 68, 79, ***3***
Thomas, Percy Goronwy, 98, 104
Thomas, Robin, 268-70, 273, ***36***
Thompson, Don, 145
Thompson, F M L, 219-20, 222
Thomson, Alex, 287
Thorndyke, M, 351
Thorne, E H (née Bigg-Wither), 234, 238
Thorne, Thorne, 317
Thornes, John, 144-5
Thurley, Simon, 222
Tichner, –, 134
Tillett, John, 93
Tillotson, Kathleen (née Constable), 102, 103, 104, 105, 106, 107
Tillyard, E M W, 103
Timberlake, Eunice M, 135, 138, 144, ***7***
Tims, H Marett, 337, 339, ***20***
Todtleben, Teresa (née Poole), 91
Tooley, Marion, 218
Toscani, Giovanni, 239
Townsend, Meredith, 205
Travers, Newenham, 206
Treves, Paolo, 240
Treves, Piero, 233
Trevor-Roper, H R (later Baron Dacre), 217
Trew, V C G, 83, 85, 86, 90
Truckle, Peter, 163
Tuke, Dame Margaret, 3, 27, 32, 95, 97, 100, 156-7, 185, 188, 228, 244, 260, 316, 321
Tulloch, Doreen, 255
Turquet, Gladys (née Milnes), 122, 123
Turle, Robert J, 27
Turnbull, Leslie P, 73, 75, 77
Turner, Brenda, 141

Turner, E E, 82, 84, 90, 92, 93
Tweedy, May (later Lady Mellanby), 79–80, 281
Tyacke, Sarah (née Jeacock), 222, 379, ***43***
Unwin, Tim, 145
Valetta, Ignazio, 228
Véricour, Raymond de, 109, 128
Vickery, Amanda, 222, ***47***, ***49***
Vollans, Eleanor, 141, 144, 5, ***7***, ***8***
Waddell, Helen, 100
Wakelin, Derek, 346, 351
Walshe, Betty, 341-2
Walshe, Maurice O'Connell, 196
Warburg, E F, 71
Wareing, Philip F, 71
Warnock, Baroness, 378, ***42***
Waters, Stephen, 78
Watts-Liquorish, George, 93
Wedderburn, Dorothy, 44, 173, 355 *et seq*, 380, ***15***, ***41***, ***42***, ***47***
Wedgewood, C H, 321
West, M L, 12
Wheeler, Dame Olive, 301
Whitehead, Ann, 61
Whitworth, Irene (later Mrs Drury), 316
Whitfield, J H, 234
Widdas, Wilfred, 51, 53, 282, 288–9
Widdowson, Elsie, 280
Wiggins, David, 255-6
Wilde, I F, 251
Wilden-Hart, Margaret (née Oblitas), 91
Wilkinson, Dave, 222
Wilkinson, Elizabeth M, 191
Williams, Alwyn, 173
Williams, Bernard, 255
Williams, Gertrude, Lady (née Rosenblum), 321, 323, 325, 333
Williams, G H, 92, 93
Williams, Sir William, 333
Williams, William T, 71
Williamson, E Margerie, 267
Wilson, A A, 159
Wilson, Frank Percy, 102, 103, 104, 107
Wilson, John Dover, 100
Wilson, Rev Thomas, 96, 131, 244
Wilson, William, 263-4, 266, ***29***, ***31***
Wing, Wong Ka, 91
Womack, Frederick, 262, ***27***
Woodward, R B, 94
Wootton, Barbara (later Baroness Wootton of Abinger), 308, 321, 323, 325
Worrall, George, 143
Worth, Katherine (née Lorimer), 104, 106
Wright, G, 288, 290
Wroe, Ann (née Bristow), 222
Yarburg, E F, 69
Yoshida, Masao, 345
Young, Rev Frances, 380
Young, Maureen, 285
Yuill, William E, 193–6
Zagalsky, Peter, 53, 56, 61